WORTHY FIGHTS

WORTHY FIGHTS

A MEMOIR OF LEADERSHIP IN WAR AND PEACE

LEON PANETTA

WITH JIM NEWTON

PENGUIN PRESS

NEW YORK

2014

PENGUIN PRESS
Published by the Penguin Group
Penguin Group (USA) LLC
375 Hudson Street
New York, New York 10014

USA · Canada · UK · Ireland · Australia
New Zealand · India · South Africa · China

penguin.com
A Penguin Random House Company

First published by Penguin Press, a member of Penguin Group (USA) LLC, 2014

Photograph credits appear on pages 497–498.

ISBN 978-1-59420-596-5

Printed in the United States of America
1 3 5 7 9 10 8 6 4 2

Designed by Amanda Dewey

*To my wife, Sylvia; my boys, Chris, Carmelo,
and Jimmy; and to the memory of my parents,
Carmelo and Carmelina—their love, support,
and sacrifice gave me the opportunity to live
the American Dream of a better life*

Contents

WORTHY FIGHTS

Prologue

I said good-bye to a fallen CIA colleague, a personable, driven young woman named Elizabeth Hanson, on a warm May morning in Washington in 2010. She was laid to rest at Arlington National Cemetery, in the shade of a stately line of willow oaks, amid thousands of American heroes and in the company of hundreds of friends, family, and coworkers from the Central Intelligence Agency. I was at the time the director of the CIA. Elizabeth Hanson had worked for me.

It was a graveside service, modest and brief; she was buried in Area 60, beside many veterans of the wars in Afghanistan and Iraq, just over a small rise from the Pentagon. Hanson and six other members of our agency were killed on December 30, 2009, at a remote CIA base in the Khost province of eastern Afghanistan. Liz Hanson and her colleagues were there that day to meet a potential agent, a jihadist who said he wanted to work for the CIA and steer us to the leadership of Al Qaeda. Instead, when he arrived at the meeting he detonated a diabolically powerful suicide vest, killing seven of our best and injuring a dozen more. That explosion was a signal tragedy for the CIA—one of the largest losses of life in the agency's history.

The attack shook the CIA, and I had spent much of that winter and spring consoling our employees and traveling around America to share the grief of the families of those men and women. Hanson's funeral was the last of seven such services I had attended. They included small private services and a large Catholic mass. Some were packed with dignitaries, others limited to friends and family. I met with mourners in Fredericksburg, Maryland; Virginia Beach; Clinton, Massachusetts; Akron, Ohio; and central Illinois. And this was my third trip to Arlington. After the funeral mass in Clinton, boys and girls stood in the snow outside the church, some quietly waving flags or signs that read, THANKS FOR KEEPING US SAFE. In Akron, the widow of one of our fallen, Scott Roberson, was carrying his child, a girl. One eulogist imagined the day when their daughter would come to visit the CIA and touch the star etched into the marble of our Memorial Wall, marking her father's sacrifice, her heart full of pride for a man she never had the luck to know.

Two realizations connected all of those ceremonies: Nothing could return those young men and women to their families, and I could only offer them a promise. America would do everything in its power to bring those behind the murders to justice. They hit us; America would hit back.

By 2010, nearly a decade after the events of September 11, 2001, the sustained response by America and its allies had significantly degraded Al Qaeda, but it remained a fighting force, still under the spell of Osama bin Laden and directed by him and his close lieutenants. Now, with the burial of Elizabeth Hanson still fresh in my mind, American analysts reported that they had found one of those deputies—in fact, one of those directly responsible for the attack at Khost. He was down for the night, deep in a terrorist compound.

That was a significant piece of news. This terrorist was a shrewd and methodical operative who had risen within Al Qaeda in recent years while repeatedly eluding our attempts to take him off the battlefield. Khost was only the latest of his crimes. So finding him represented a victory in and of itself.

There was, however, a catch: He was not alone. Al Qaeda leaders knew that American policy was to avoid civilian casualties wherever possible, and they had adapted their habits to that realization. By 2010, the organization's top terrorists would often stay close to family members or other noncombatants, theorizing that those shields would dissuade the United States from conducting operations against them. Some leaders who had long traveled by themselves now brought along children, exploiting our humanity while debasing their own. Now with our target in the house half a world away were a wife and at least two children. The reports suggested that others might be in the house as well. Any operation against him might kill others too.

That was not a prospect I took lightly. I was raised Catholic. I was an altar boy. Since my earliest years, I've attended mass on Sundays and holy days. I carry a rosary and believe that life is sacred. Moreover, I'm a husband and the father of three sons. But I also deeply believe in duty to country. I have spent the majority of my life in the service of the United States—I was in the army, I was a Senate aide and later director of the Office for Civil Rights at the Department of Health, Education, and Welfare, aide to the mayor of New York City, congressman for the Central Coast of California, Office of Management and Budget director, and chief of staff to President Bill Clinton. I've had the honor of being elected by the people of my hometown and endured the stress of being fired by President Nixon. In 2010, at the helm of the CIA, this time placed in a position of responsibility by President Obama, I was once again mindful of my duty. In each of those jobs, I've tried to focus on the obligations that they entail. I've fought to desegregate schools, to protect the California coastline, to balance the federal budget. I've done so out of a sense of duty, and also of obligation, of repaying a debt that my family owes this nation.

That's because this nation made my family's dreams possible. I'm the son of Italian immigrants who came to this country to give their children a better life. That was their dream of country and family, and I am acutely conscious of fulfilling that dream, of recognizing the opportunities that the United States offered. This country has given me much, and I take seriously my obligations to serve and protect it.

So in this situation the moral dilemma was this: If one of those responsible for Elizabeth Hanson's murder was allowed to escape, he might kill others, including more Americans. But to eliminate the threat on that night might require taking the lives of innocents. In such a situation, how does one balance duty to country and respect for life?

From a small room at the National Security Agency, which I happened to be visiting, I spoke to White House officials to review the matter. They sounded a note of caution. Avoiding collateral damage had been a hallmark of President Obama's approach to these operations. All of us knew that any operation that killed civilians was to be authorized only under extraordinary circumstances. Did these qualify? We all understood that if our target was spared in order to protect his family, he would strike at us again, and without the compunctions that we had regarding the deaths of civilians.

After a few searching moments, I made up my own mind. The professionals working on this mission needed to keep looking for a way to isolate him, to minimize any risk to anyone else. But all of us working on national security matters for the United States had an overriding obligation: He could not be allowed to get away.

Hours later, he was dead. A grave threat to America had been eliminated. His wife, with whom this country had no quarrel, died in the same operation.

The challenges of protecting this nation, safeguarding its economy, providing opportunity to its citizens, and preserving its treasures have been mainstays of my life. Those challenges are rarely easy, and they sometimes demand deep searching of one's soul, the fingering of a rosary, the whispered Hail Mary. In considering those questions, I have been blessed with gifted mentors and, especially, loving parents whose devotion to the United States was forged in their appreciation for the opportunities it offered. It is with my parents that my story begins.

PART I

POLITICS AND PROGRESS

ONE

"A Better Life"

M y father arrived in the United States in the fashion of so many who came before and so many who would follow: He came in search of opportunity, and found it after passing through the sober and hopeful halls of Ellis Island. He was one of eighteen hundred third-class passengers aboard the *Providence,* which landed on October 25, 1921. He declared his profession as "peasant" and his total assets as twenty-five dollars. He was en route to join his older brother Bruno, then in Sheridan, Wyoming. My father was the youngest of thirteen siblings. His name was Carmelo Panetta, and he was twenty-three years old.

He first left home during World War I, when he was drafted into the Italian army. He was wounded in 1918 during the Battle of the Piave River, an important Italian victory. He rarely talked about that experience, for my father was a quiet man, resolute and hardworking, devoted to values that some might find quaint: family, duty, faith. He did not lecture on those ideas, but he lived them. He also was a very good cook.

After working briefly in New York and Wyoming, he joined the sibling to whom he was closest, his rambunctious brother Tony, in California, and found a job as a cook. Like so many immigrants before and since, he took jobs wherever he could. He worked in Huntington Beach, south of Los Angeles, and Marin County, north of San Francisco, making a decent living but finding himself lonely in his adopted country. He was past his thirtieth birthday, and his vision of himself as a husband and father was missing a few pieces. Though my father had been in the United States for nearly a decade by then, his search for a bride turned him toward home. He knew where to look for a nice Italian girl. In 1932, he sailed for Italy.

He found my mother in church. Family lore is a little murky on the details but clear on the basics: Having returned to Calabria, at the toe of the boot of Italy, my father ventured down the mountains from his native Gerace to the slightly more prosperous coastal village of Siderno. There, he stood at the back of a church one Sunday and spotted a tall, dark-haired, attractive young woman. He made inquiries and discovered that the lovely eighteen-year-old Carmelina who had caught his eye was the daughter of Giuseppe Prochilo, a local member of the merchant marine. Inquiries were made and at least one obstacle was overcome: My Nona initially objected to the union, preferring instead that my father be betrothed to Carmelina's older sister, who wasn't getting any younger. Nona also objected to my father's plans to bring his new bride to America and thus away from her family. But my father persisted. He wanted the girl he had seen in church. Eventually, and with the help of my Nono, he prevailed. Perseverance was one of his strongest traits.

Now wed, Carmelo returned to the United States with his young bride and retraced his steps. They arrived in New York, where Carmelo had bought a small piece of property, but elected to move on, heading again for Wyoming and his brother Bruno. Bruno was a hard worker and had a big family; his three sons proudly served in World

War II and later ran a successful food wholesale business. It was there, in Sheridan in 1933, that my mother gave birth to my brother, Joe. But both the harsh winters and the tough economic times were hard on my parents. They did not stay long. Seeking better weather and opportunity, they pushed forward to California, where they rejoined Tony. This time the young couple with their infant son eventually landed in Monterey.

It's easy to see what appealed to them. Monterey in those days—and even today—has an Italian feel. It's nestled in a beautiful bay, and the deep water of the Pacific Coast offered a bountiful fishing ground. Much of the city was devoted to fishing—many men fished and many women worked in the processing factories made famous by John Steinbeck's *Cannery Row,* which was published just a few years after the Panetta family made Monterey our home. Steinbeck's great novel captured the spirit of Monterey—raucous, tender, a little threadbare, but very tightly knit. In Steinbeck's words, Monterey was "a poem, a stink, a grating noise, a quality of light, a tone, a habit, a nostalgia, a dream. Cannery Row is the gathered and scattered, tin and iron and rust and splintered wood, chipped pavement and weedy lots and junk heaps, sardine canneries of corrugated iron, honky tonks, restaurants and whore houses, and little crowded groceries, and laboratories and flophouses."

It was there that I was born in 1938. We lived in an apartment building on Van Buren Street, in a largely Italian-American community, naturally known as "Spaghetti Hill." Many of our neighbors were fishermen, and nets were hung through the alleys and backyards in the afternoons to dry. I can remember playing among them and once getting so trapped in the webbing that my brother had to come and untangle me.

My father had been working at a restaurant called Biff's up until about the time I was born. It was then that he and a fellow Calabrese, Dominic Luscri, decided to go into business together, with Dominic opening a bar and my father launching a restaurant of his own. The two establishments abutted each other, and a swinging door between them allowed patrons to take their drinks from Dominic's place to my father's. The new restaurant was located at the intersection of Alvarado and Del Monte in the heart of old downtown Monterey. It was called Carmelo's Café, and it became the center of our lives.

Modeled on a restaurant called New Joe's in San Francisco, the café served casual Italian fare, along with steaks and chops, hamburgers and salads. Some guests sat at the counter, others in booths. The tabletops were plain wood, no tablecloths. Carmelo's Café was open six days a week, closed on Tuesdays. Both my parents worked there, my dad as the chef, my mother anchoring the cash register. Joe and I also helped out sometimes, washing dishes, peeling potatoes, or doing other chores. The café was part of a lively downtown, surrounded by bars and pool halls. Customers included the colorful mix of men and women who made up Monterey in those days: fishermen, shop owners, business-people, and servicemen from nearby Fort Ord, which was a huge train-ing post at the time. Thousands of young men from across the nation came to the post to train for the battlefields of World War II, so Mon-terey was their last stop before war, a last chance for a drink or a plate of spaghetti.

There was a button beneath the cash register that my mother used to summon the military police from the base when soldiers got too frisky with her, which was fairly often. One particularly moony soldier begged her to "leave that Greek," a mistaken reference to my father, "and run away with me." My mother hit the button.

Not long after I was born, my mother's father, my Nono, Giuseppe, came to pay us a visit. He was used to traveling—his time in the mer-chant marine had taken him around the world several times in the old sailing and steam ships—but he never could persuade my grandmother to travel far from home. As a result, he arrived by himself, thinking it would be for a brief visit, a chance to meet his youngest grandson, me.

Instead, war broke out in Europe. Nono, as I always called him, was an alien and could not return. He was stuck with us. It was my good fortune.

Through my early childhood, Nono and I were together almost constantly. He was a big, garrulous man, with hands like catchers' mitts, a mop of thick white hair, and a lyrical Italian accent. He loved life, good food, and a glass of wine that he would pour from a gallon jug of Gallo that rested on the floor near his chair. He'd carry me around on his shoulders, and take me down to the local Italian market, Genovese's, or the wharf. He fished a bit, and the fishermen would always be happy to see him. They gathered there or in a little plaza at the end of Alvarado Street, where they smoked Toscanellis and talked about the war and Mussolini and Hitler as I strained to hear and understand. My Nono, after all, was only in the United States by chance, and he warned that the war might not be as easy as some Americans thought. "Watch out," he once told my father. "Mussolini and Hitler could win." My father didn't buy it: "Papa, that's not going to happen."

Although we spoke both English and Italian at home, Nono knew only bits and pieces of English. My father told the story of one of his dishwashers who had to have a serious operation. When he returned from his stay in the hospital, Nono asked him where he had been. Jack, the dishwasher, said he'd been hospitalized with a very serious illness.

"Thatsa good, Jack . . . Thatsa good," my Nono said.

My father quickly explained to a shaken Jack that it was Nono's way of hoping all went well.

For me to take full advantage of my grandfather's generosity, it was critical for me to learn Italian. He spoiled me, as grandparents do, and I sat on his shoulders calling out things I wanted from the market. One day I begged for a cantaloupe, and he heard that as "lupe." Arriving at the market, Nono was perplexed but determined to give me what I wanted. In Italian, he asked the owners, "Ma dove trovo un lupe?"— "But where am I going to find a wolf?" People in Monterey still tell that story.

It was an Italian market, of course, and the grandson of the owners was Joe Genovese. Joe and I were boys together. We played almost every day. He would come around the apartment complex on Van Buren and stand outside yelling "Leee-on, Leee-on, come out and play." We roamed the neighborhood together, fashioning slingshots and rubber-band guns. We struggled to keep up with my brother and his friends, who played at another level, building tree forts and playing with axes. One of those axes cost my brother half of his right thumb— neighbors still talk about the screams of my mother when Joe came running home, half his thumb dangling from his hand.

On weekends, Joe Genovese and I would walk to the Monterey Theater, where we'd see the serials for twenty-five cents. They played the Phantom, Roy Rogers, Gene Autry, Batman, Superman—all our favorites. After the movies, we'd go by the restaurant and have a hamburger before heading home. Those were the days when two kids, six years old, could walk all around Monterey by themselves; families looked out for one another.

Joe and I loved to play make-believe, but I made him play by my rules: I always got to play the lead, and he was forced to be my sidekick. We tied my mother's dishrags at the corners and made them into capes. Properly outfitted, we then challenged and vanquished enemies of every stripe—not exactly a precursor of my years at the CIA or the Defense Department, but perhaps a glimmer.

I attended Catholic schools as a young boy, and worked to be a good student. I walked to school—about ten blocks through downtown Monterey—and got there early. Too early for the Franciscan nuns, who were bothered by my loitering around campus before school opened. They made me write "I will not get to school early" a thousand times on the blackboard. That, plus the occasional whack of a ruler across my hands, taught me a lot about discipline. Other than the occasional mark-down for "deportment," I generally received good grades—history and English were my strongest subjects; math was fine up until I reached Algebra 2, at which point I hit the wall and began to say Hail Marys. And my Catholic education extended beyond the classroom. Although my parents worked hard and did not make every mass, they were Catholic in their souls, and there was no question but that I would be raised Catholic. I attended mass often during the week and every Sunday. I was an altar boy and received First Communion and the other sacraments in the church as well. And my make-believe life bled into my religious observance. There was a vacant shed not far from our house, and I would occasionally sneak inside and deliver stirring sermons to the empty rooms. To this day, I carry a rosary and attend mass on Sunday. And I steady myself with Hail Marys, especially during these most tense recent phases of my life, when it was my responsibility to order young people into harm's way.

My parents were a loving and supportive presence throughout my childhood. They came to America because they believed they could give their children a better life. And they did, but they also worked hard to make that happen. The restaurant was often open until 2 a.m. and then again for breakfast, so they barely had time for a nap before they needed to return to work. Even Tuesdays, when the restaurant was closed, were filled with restocking, paying bills, buying and replacing supplies. That made me all the happier to have my Nono, as he stood in for my hardworking mother and father.

During the early years of the war in Europe, events on that continent were of intense interest but still seemed remote. That changed after Pearl Harbor. Suddenly, many Americans, especially on the West Coast, feared invasion, and that fear was stoked by the unfounded suspicion that the December 7, 1941, attack had been aided by Japanese spies. Those inside the United States with ties to the Axis powers came under grave and increasingly shrill suspicion. It was ludicrous to think that my grandfather posed any such threat—he was a retired sailor with no loyalties to Mussolini, and there was not so much as an allegation against him—but he was among those Italians living in America who were forcibly removed from their homes, in his case because he was living in the coastal zone.

In early 1942, some ten thousand Italians living on the West Coast were targeted for removal because they lived in areas that were designated as prohibited.[1] The order did not apply to American citizens and was in many cases waived even for first-generation immigrants, especially those with American children. Presumably, that is why my parents were spared. My grandfather, by contrast, had not immigrated to the United States but rather was an Italian citizen in this country merely for a vacation. That was enough to render him a threat, and, to my shock and dismay, he was ordered to leave Monterey.

My parents helped him find an apartment in San Jose in a boardinghouse run by an Italian family. When it came time to leave, we drove Nono to San Jose. That car ride was one I will never forget. Through my tears, I struggled to understand why my Nono was being forced to move away. I'm sure it was painful for my parents to say good-bye to my grandfather, but they did not let on to me, and they certainly did not allow themselves to become embittered against the United States. "To be free," my father used to say, "we must also be secure." Did he apply that sentiment to the removal of my Nono? Neither my mother nor my father said a word; there were only tears.

My grandfather's case was one of thousands involving relocation or internment of Italians and Italian Americans during the war, a shameful example of segregating out a portion of the public solely on the basis of background. As a civil rights issue, it paled next to the treatment of the Japanese and Japanese Americans, 110,000 of whom were interned for most of the war; nearly two-thirds of those were American citizens, forced to spend years behind barbed wire in camps throughout the West, extending as far east as Arkansas. Though most American-born Italian Americans, myself included, escaped that fate, the entire episode stands as a bracing reminder that even those most committed to civil liberties can lose sight of their responsibilities when confronted by a threat to security. It was a lesson I would later have the opportunity to reflect upon.

In the meantime, the war was in one sense good for my family. Fort Ord kept growing as a major hub of training activity for American soldiers bound for the war. Monterey was jumping with off-duty soldiers and sailors—and the restaurant was too. Business boomed through those years, and my father proved to be a street-smart investor. He bought a couple of rental properties and supplemented his income from the café with rent payments. Then, just as the war ended, he sold the restaurant at the height of the market, and was done with his days behind the counter.

He and my mother took the money from the sale of the café and bought twelve acres in the Carmel Valley. They planted walnut trees so that the land would produce some income, as well as some peach trees that would begin producing while the walnuts matured. In 1946, they began work on a house, and by 1948 it was complete. We moved from Monterey to the valley. I would spend the rest of my youth in that home. Indeed, I have spent much of my life there. My sons grew up in that house, and my wife, Sylvia, and I live there today.

The orchard required plenty of work. I helped with irrigating the trees three times a year, picked the fruit, and often manned a fruit stand out on the road. But the property was more than a chore—it was a wondrous retreat, vast and limitless, for a boy with an imagination. I crawled over the hills, pretending to be characters from Tom Mix to Zapata. I built an imaginary city out of wooden blocks close to the house, constructing roads and dams and waterways. And though the crop never did make much money—I suspect it just about kept pace with the taxes—it connected my mother and father to the land, and grounded me in the real work of farming. Today, when I see the vegetable garden that one of my sons nurtures in his backyard, I remember my young days in Carmel Valley and happily note that my parents' gift to me continues to yield fruit.

I enjoyed sports as a boy, particularly baseball and basketball, but I showed my greatest potential as a pianist. My parents arranged for Joe and me to take lessons. Joe soon moved on to sports and friends in high school, but I stuck with it for a while because of the encouragement of my mother and the kindness of a local piano teacher, David Alberto. He would pick me up at school, buy cookies, and off we would go to my lessons on his old Steinway in his Carmel home. I loved the music, and my skills improved. I gave some recitals and even attracted a little notice.

When I was about ten years old, I gave a performance at a home in Carmel that the local newspaper covered. "This boy," the reviewer wrote of me, "possesses a phenomenal musical talent. He played with a depth of feeling and understanding far beyond his years." Of my interpretive ability, this generous reviewer marked that it was "nothing short of genius." Unfortunately, practicing the piano meant not playing sports or studying. I stuck with it for several years and even gave a formal concert at the Sunset Center in Carmel, but eventually my interests turned elsewhere. And though I still play often, I abandoned thoughts of a musical career before I finished high school. It was not just the hours of practice required for a pianist; it was the realization that I liked being with people, not performing for them.

After eight years of Catholic grammar school, the horizons of my life suddenly expanded when I enrolled at Monterey High School, my first experience with public education. After a rocky start—I came home in tears the first day, overwhelmed by the size of my classes and worried about making friends with boys and girls who already had been together for years—I got my bearings and discovered a knack for politics. I joined all kinds of clubs—Key Club, Latin Club, and the like—and I ran for student council and was elected, first as student body vice president and later as president. One of my projects was to create a student union—a place for students to play cards or listen to records. I proposed the idea, and the administration signed off on it. I then solicited contributions of used furniture, including a big unit of a record player that sat in the corner, and a couple Ping-Pong tables. It was an instant hit. My commitment to constituent services was born.

As a young person, I hadn't given a lot of thought to a career. Piano had come and gone, and my father periodically floated the idea that he thought being a dentist would be smart—good money, regular hours, and Wednesdays off seemed ideal to him. But the thought of spending my life looking in other people's mouths didn't do much for me. Joe, meanwhile, headed off to Santa Clara University—the first member of our family ever to go to college—determined to head from there to law school. I had tailed him for years, following him and his friends through the streets of Monterey. This too seemed like a path worth following. My parents approved, and I matriculated in the fall of 1956. My father paid my tuition in regular cash installments, and I chipped in by extending my ROTC service at Santa Clara—ROTC was required for all students the first two years in those days—for two more years and getting my army commission.

ROTC was my first real service to my country, and I enjoyed it, both for the sense that I was contributing to my education and because I liked the specifics of my experience—the military history, the schooling in weaponry and tactics. When I graduated from Santa Clara, I received my bachelor of science degree at the podium, then all of us who had completed ROTC stripped off our graduation robes to reveal our uniforms underneath. I circled back up to the podium a second time, this time to receive my commission. It was a like a scene from an old Doris Day–Gordon MacRae movie.

In retrospect, the combination of law and student government may look as if I was building toward a career in politics even then. If so, it wasn't conscious.

I was drawn to the idea of service—my parents' gratitude to this country for the opportunities it gave them profoundly affected me, and my ROTC training reinforced that. But I was never a particularly ideological young person, and my political role models in those days made their impressions as much through character as philosophy. I remember Eisenhower visiting Carmel during his presidency—he liked to golf at Pebble Beach—and I was captivated by his presence. I had rooted for him during the 1952 Republican convention in Chicago; I didn't think of him in terms of political philosophy so much as I admired his style of sturdy, comforting leadership.

In California, Earl Warren was elected governor in 1942, when I was still a young boy, and went on to be twice reelected (he is the only governor in California history to win three consecutive elections), so he was the governor for my whole youth, and he too captured my interest and support. Like Eisenhower, he was a big, forceful presence, as well as a commanding and bipartisan leader. And, like Eisenhower, he was a Republican.

So when it came time for me to align with a party, I joined the GOP of Ike and Warren, and considered myself part of the socially liberal, fiscally conservative Republican Party that those two leaders helped create and nurture through the 1950s. My first presidential vote was for Richard Nixon in 1960; I supported him because of his association with Eisenhower and in the belief that he represented moderate social policies in areas such as civil rights. The party would change a great deal in later years, and I would eventually leave it, but I believe I remain faithful to those progressive ideals that once grounded Eisenhower Republicans.

College and law school were formative in many ways, but no moment was more meaningful than a mixer in the fall of 1958. I was a student body officer at Santa Clara—commissioner of social activities or some such thing—and since it was an all-men's school, we hosted regular get-togethers with our sister Catholic schools in the Bay Area. Buses brought in the young women, and we greeted them with corsages. That day, as they disembarked, I exchanged looks with one dark-haired beauty from Dominican. We didn't connect at first—she was surrounded by other girls, and I couldn't get to her. But later that evening, after I considered skipping the dance, I was encouraged by my friends, particularly Butch Erbst, to see what the possibilities might be at the mixer. We walked out of the dorm, and there was a group of women passing by.

Sylvia was part of that group; our eyes met again. We struck up a conversation at dinner. We ended up spending the evening, the first of many, chatting away. Soon I met her family, and we too hit it off. Her parents, like mine, were Italian, hardworking, and dedicated to the success of their children—her dad was a partner in a garbage company that held a franchise with the city of Petaluma, just north of San Francisco.

After a long courtship, I proposed to Sylvia, and then, in the fashion expected of Italian men of my generation, I sought her father's approval. He happily gave it. We were engaged on June 20, 1961. I gave Sylvia a ring, and she gave me a watch. It was a self-winding Movado. More than fifty years later, I still wear it. And it's always been set to California time, so that no matter where I am in the world, I am reminded of home.

A year later, on July 14, 1962, Sylvia and I were married at her family's parish. Our first son, Chris, was born on Mother's Day of the following year, and our family began to take shape. For our part, Sylvia and I are still having that talk that we began in 1958.

Although I voted for Nixon in 1960, I admired Kennedy as well, and as a Catholic, my heart was with him. I attended a Kennedy rally in San Jose during the campaign, and I had the chance to shake his hand as he passed in an open car. Even that passing moment left a feeling of connection, and when he won the election I joined with the rest of the country in anticipating his presidency.

His charisma and charm, his sense of style and panache, his young wife and attractive children—all struck a hopeful chord in the country as the first American president born in the twentieth century took command. It was his inaugural message that struck me most strongly, however. His call to service—"Ask not what your country can do for you, ask what you can do for your country"—powerfully expressed the lessons of my father and my experiences in the army. I felt that sense of duty; Kennedy's appeal to patriotism resonated deeply with me and many of those close to me.

The final words of that speech are often overlooked in favor of the famous "ask not" passage, but they are among the most stirring appeals to service ever uttered by an American president, and they fused country and faith in a way that spoke directly to me: "With a good conscience our only sure reward, with history the final judge of our deeds, let us go forth to lead the land we love, asking His blessing and His help, but knowing that here on earth God's work must truly be our own."

By the middle of 1963, I had a wife, a son, and a law degree. And I owed the first of many debts to my country. I had received a military deferment while in law school, but now my time was up, and we shipped out. Our first stop was Fort Benning, Georgia, where we were greeted by a blast of humidity and an unpleasant introduction to the military's family housing barracks. Happily, the end of basic training brought a transfer to the U.S. Army Intelligence School outside of Baltimore, where our second son, Carmelo—named after my father—was born in 1964 at Mercy Hospital.

I was next scheduled to move to Washington to work in defense intelligence, but as we were preparing to go, we received word that my mother had been diagnosed with colon cancer. I requested and received a compassionate reassignment and headed home. Soon my mother had recuperated, and I took up duties at Ford Ord, just a few miles from where I grew up, working as an intelligence officer and assigned to brief young men on their way to Vietnam even as Joan Baez and other protesters demonstrated against the war just a few miles away. Those were hard briefings, many to soldiers who didn't want to be there and didn't understand why they were being asked to fight. One consequence was that we had a major problem with soldiers going AWOL. We'd round them up, and then, of course, they shipped out. A lot of those kids never made it back. In 2014, I presided over a commemoration of the Vietnam War as secretary of defense and spent a few minutes perusing the wall of names at the starkly beautiful memorial in Washington. I spotted a few familiar ones, young men who gave their lives to a war that neither they nor their leaders fully understood.

But there were rewards to my posting as well. As an intelligence officer, I was responsible for operations and plans for security in the event of crisis—good training for the future. I also had the support and friendship of some great fellow officers and enlisted men and women. In particular, my commanding officer, Colonel Harry Fair, was a tough but compassionate officer who taught me about leadership and did me the honor of awarding me the Army Commendation Medal for my service.

As a lawyer, I also was asked to represent servicemen in courts-martial, and found I enjoyed the life of a defense lawyer. I defended lots of AWOL cases, but also some more serious charges—assaults and the occasional rape. I got good enough and was called on so frequently that Sylvia joked my name must be up on a stockade wall someplace. In fact, one commanding general warned me that if I kept it up, I'd find myself reassigned to Fort Irwin, a post in the California desert. Thanks to Colonel Fair, I was able to stay at Ford Ord as long as I promised to spend my remaining time as an intelligence officer. I gave up my legal work a little reluctantly—I must admit that I enjoyed the chance to challenge authority in military courts, where most defendants were more likely to be presumed guilty until proven innocent.

When I was preparing to muster out of the military in 1966, I faced the future that had been awaiting me ever since I finished law school but that had been delayed by the fulfillment of my service obligation. I was intrigued by the idea of working in Washington—Kennedy's speech still rang in my ears—but I had no contacts there or any real insight into the place. On a lark, I tossed off a letter to Joseph Califano, then working as a lawyer in the White House (later that year he was named general counsel of the army), and already a formidable Washington insider. We were both lawyers, and he'd worked in the army too, but my appeal to him was a little more basic. I wrote him because he was Italian, and I asked if he would lend a hand to another. Amazingly, he did, calling me a few days later and offering to make some introductions around Washington.

In those days, servicemen flew on major airlines for half-price if they were in uniform, so I donned mine and headed for the capital. Califano had made appointments for me at Defense and Justice and the Office of Personnel Management, among others, and I dutifully made my way around town. But it was a chance trip to the Senate office buildings that landed me my first civilian job since college.

I was an admirer of Senator Tom Kuchel, who had been appointed to his post by Governor Warren when Richard Nixon vacated it to become Ike's vice president. Kuchel was another of those centrist, forward-looking Republicans who dominated California at the middle of the century. Warren had moved to the Supreme Court by 1963, but Kuchel had won reelection and was still holding down that tradition in the Senate.

I didn't know Kuchel any better than I knew Califano, but I figured there was no harm in asking, so I went to Capitol Hill, presented myself to his secretary, and asked if there were any openings. As it turned out, one of the senator's two top aides—in those days, he had a principal aide for foreign policy and another for domestic policy—had recently left, so there was in fact a vacancy. And there I was, armed with a law degree, a native of California and in a U.S. Army uniform. Kuchel wasn't in, but his administrative assistant, Ewing Hass, an old pal of Kuchel's throughout his political years, looked me over and figured it might be worth a chance. He arranged for me to meet with

Kuchel back in California a few weeks later, and I did, chatting at the Fairmont Hotel in San Francisco. He offered me a spot on his staff and a salary of $10,000 a year. I accepted it right there.

A few days later, I broke the news to my parents, who had hoped I would stay in Monterey. I assured them it was a great opportunity and predicted I'd be back in a couple years after picking up some useful experience. Sylvia and I then packed up our blue VW bug, strapped a luggage rack to the roof, and put the boys, still in diapers, in the back. Our first stop was Disneyland, which had just opened a few years earlier. Then it was across the country—Las Vegas, the Grand Canyon, St. Louis—one Holiday Inn at a time. We arrived in Washington on a cold April day, and soon found a house for rent in Northwest D.C. We had made it across the country to the nation's capital. Our Washington life began that spring.

I was twenty-seven years old, four years older than my father was when he came to America. He had arrived in the East, gone west, and reaped the rewards of a generous nation; I had begun where he ended up and now was back east, determined to return the favor.

TWO

"Look at Yourself in the Mirror"

W̶e are not always able to pick our mentors, and some of those who take on those roles later disappoint. Not so with Tom Kuchel. He was a good, principled, moderate man, unafraid of being attacked, unwilling to give up on what was right in order to adapt to what was popular. His career was studded with accomplishment and riddled by base and false accusations. It was my great luck to work with him early in my career, when his lessons could leave lasting imprints.

His father was a crusading California journalist who had helped expose and oust the Ku Klux Klan from elected positions in Anaheim early in the twentieth century. Kuchel inherited a taste for combat, a love of stories, and appreciation for a punch line. His friend Ewing Hass collected jokes, and as the two of them walked side by side from the Old Senate Office Building to the Capitol whip office, Hass would share the latest, and Kuchel's laugh would boom through the underground train tunnels.

Kuchel radiated strength. His will matched his voice, and he even strode with purpose. He was not very tall, but was one of those men whom others remember as taller than they were, perhaps because he met friends and adversaries eye to eye. He would seal deals over a bourbon, and he deeply believed that in politics, your word was your bond. He expected the same from others. For him, politics was not trivial or cynical, but rather a commitment to public service.

Kuchel's rise through California politics was largely the work of Earl Warren. First elected to the California State Assembly in 1936 and then the State Senate in 1940, Kuchel was called to active duty in the Naval Reserve, where he served until 1945. When he returned, Warren saw a young senator with similar beliefs, experience in Sacramento, and a war record; ever canny, Warren appointed him state controller in 1946, a move that reflected well on both of them. And of course it was Warren a few years later who put Kuchel in the U.S. Senate.

Barely had I begun to comprehend my duties when I received my first lesson from Kuchel. We met in his Capitol office, a space just off the Senate chambers reserved for the minority whip. Kuchel could be warm and welcoming, but in this session he was stern.

"Look," he said, "you're going to be tempted in this town. There are going to be a lot of people who will want to take you to lunch. They'll try to give you gifts. They'll try to use you to get to me on issues. And I just want you to remember that our job here is to serve the public interest and the people of California. That's number one."

He spoke with such conviction that I'm sure I swallowed hard at that. But he wasn't done.

"And number two, remember: When you get up in the morning, you have to look at yourself in the mirror."

Some may regard those sentiments as corny or old-fashioned, out of kilter with the wry cynicism that pervades so much of Washington today. I received those words differently. They spoke to my sense of obligation and even to the self-importance that I felt as a young aide suddenly thrust into the fast currents of national policy. They meant something genuine, and they came from a man worthy of admiration. I have never forgotten them, and I have always tried to live up to them.

As I came to know Kuchel better, I grew to appreciate what an uncommon character he was—principled without being particularly ideological, forceful without being doctrinaire. He was supportive of the president on foreign affairs, which meant that in 1966, when I arrived, he was a determined backer of President Johnson on Vietnam, as he had been of Eisenhower's foreign and military policy. He greatly admired Senator Richard Russell on national defense questions, and consistently voted to increase defense spending. He subscribed to the notion that politics stopped at the water's edge.

On budget matters, he was reliably conservative, again in the Eisenhower tradition. He believed the nation should balance its budget, and he carefully scrutinized spending for hints of waste or misuse.

In those senses, he could be considered a modern conservative, but he also felt deeply about causes that would be associated with today's liberals. He was a committed environmentalist who devoted much of his work on the Interior Committee to protecting California redwoods. When he introduced a bill to create a redwood preserve in Northern California, he did it with typical aplomb. He wanted the legislation passed, Kuchel said, "because God's magnificent, awe-inspiring northern California virgin redwood giants ought to be preserved for humanity, rather than be chopped down from mountainsides to be made into 2 by 4's."[1] Kuchel described the passage of that bill, in 1968, as "a most satisfying note on which to close my Senate career."[2]

Kuchel supported federal aid to education and the Atomic Test Ban Treaty, and he voted for Medicare, which he cited as an example of "governing for the many."[3]

Perhaps most important, he was a leading advocate for civil rights: Working closely with Senator Hubert Humphrey, Kuchel delivered Republican votes for the Civil Rights Act of 1964 and the Voting Rights Act of 1965—landmark bills in President Johnson's legacy that could not be won on party-line votes because southern Democrats, led by Russell, bolted from the president's coalition. Kuchel, joined by such Republican moderates as Jacob Javits of New York, Clifford Case of New Jersey, Hugh Scott of Pennsylvania, and George Aiken of Vermont, made possible the passage of those bills.

For Kuchel, politics was personal, and he both worked the relationships that made progress possible and appreciated others who did it well. One year, Lyndon Johnson called Kuchel's mother on her birthday. Kuchel was delighted, and Johnson knew he'd sealed a friendship.

Kuchel also understood enemies, and he had his share. Just before I went to work for him, a Los Angeles police officer and a New Jersey publisher determined to smear him had conspired to fabricate a police affidavit alleging that he was homosexual. Needless to say, those were different times, when the mere accusation that a politician was gay carried strong negative consequences. The senator, who was married and had a daughter, was shocked. He flew to California and met with the Los Angeles district attorney and chief of police, who promised an investigation. It concluded that the allegations were false, and the LAPD officer was fired. Kuchel sued for libel and the defendants pleaded no contest. Nevertheless, the damage was done, and suspicion would long hover around him.

Among my first responsibilities as Kuchel's assistant was to coordinate our office's efforts on federal housing legislation to strike at racially discriminatory practices in that field. Housing was a contentious issue at the time, particularly in California. In 1964, California voters overwhelmingly approved Proposition 14, which overturned a fair housing law passed by the legislature. The proposition specifically permitted all property owners the right to refuse to sell or rent to anyone based on his or her race or religion. It was one of my home state's periodic populist convulsions, and like some of the others, it raised the specter of leading other states to follow.

In Washington, the civil rights leadership in and out of Congress concluded that the best way to head off a state-by-state stampede for such measures was to enact federal legislation that would preempt any such state action. That meant that Congress's civil rights attention moved from public accommodations and voting to housing. Kuchel, having played an influential role in those other debates, was naturally well suited to help lead this one as well, this time with me as his legislative aide.

We established a legislative team to work for passage of the bill, the Fair Housing Act of 1968. The key players were legislative aides from the offices of senators Phil Hart of Michigan, Robert Kennedy of New York, Jacob Javits, and Hugh Scott, among others. We were working on revisions of the bill to attract more votes when Senator Everett Dirksen of Illinois, the minority leader, made the decision to support it because "the time had come." His support was critical to passing the bill because he brought along other conservative Republicans.

Kuchel was up for reelection in 1968, the year that the center seemed to collapse in American politics. Consumed by the war in Vietnam, Lyndon Johnson stunned the country on March 31 when he concluded a national address by announcing that he intended to devote the remaining months of his term to the war and that, consequently, "I shall not seek, and will not accept, the nomination of my party for another term as your president." Less than a week later, Martin Luther King Jr. was assassinated, and city after city, including Washington, dissolved into riots.

It was early evening in Washington when word of King's death swept the city. Kuchel was meeting in a Capitol office with a group of Hollywood CEOs. I was in the Senate Office Building. I could see police officers putting sandbags in place, as if expecting an assault on the Capitol. Worried that we might be about to be trapped, I rushed over to pull Kuchel from his meeting.

"Senator, these riots are getting out of control," I told him. "We probably ought to let these people go."

He went to the window and took in the dismaying sight of smoke curling from distant fires and nervous guardsmen taking positions. "You'd better get moving," he announced to all of us. Everyone left, the CEOs to their hotels and planes, and the staff scattering to our homes.

As I drove home that night, it felt as though the efforts of the past two years had come to nothing. We had passed important bills to give the government new power to enforce and extend civil rights. School districts that discriminated on the basis of race now stood to lose federal funding. State efforts to enforce all-white neighborhoods now violated federal law. And yet King's assassination peeled back the frustration and anger of those who felt those efforts to be far too little. Detroit burned. Washington burned. Baltimore and Chicago erupted. Other cities, large and small, North and South, trembled with violence and apprehension.

It was difficult to believe that the Capitol of the United States was under siege and that the work of civil rights was going up in all too literal smoke. Was everything we had tried to achieve lost? The American promise of equality was truly being put to the test, and so were all of those, like Kuchel, who had embraced that promise.

What's more, Kuchel still had a reelection to win. His support for civil rights and antidiscrimination legislation solidified support from the left, but the phony allegations about his sexual orientation and his general disdain for the right wing of the Republican Party—Kuchel had refused to endorse Richard Nixon for governor in 1962, Barry Goldwater for president in 1964, or Ronald Reagan for governor in 1966—made him vulnerable to an attack from the right. In 1968, he got it from Max Rafferty. Rafferty may not warrant more than a footnote in most histories, but in 1968 he played a decisive and tragic role.

Rafferty was the California superintendent of public instruction, best known for educational writing that advocated a rejection of modern teaching methods and a return to "basics." Under normal circumstances, that wouldn't have been much of a résumé to challenge a sitting U.S. senator who occupied a leadership position in his party in Washington, but the personal allegations against Kuchel found purchase in the right-wing crannies of the California party, and the John Birch Society saw its opportunity to tear down a senator who had long aggravated its leadership.

The Birch Society's charge against Kuchel seems almost absurd to mention today. The group had alleged that a group of Chinese communists were training in Mexico in preparation for an invasion of California. Society members wrote to Kuchel to demand that he take action. He investigated, concluded that the scenario was ridiculous, and sent back form letters to his correspondents dismissing the entire idea. For this, he was accused of "treason." Kuchel, who had fought for his country in wartime and devoted his life to service on its behalf, was flabbergasted and furious.

Admittedly, he could come off as high-handed in his fencing with the right. After Reagan won the Republican primary in 1966, for instance, Kuchel barely could stomach a congratulatory remark, and the state's party chairman, Gaylord Parkinson, warned the senator that he expected his support in the fall. Failing to give it would "be a disappointment to me and all loyal Republicans," Parkinson warned.

I'll never forget Kuchel's reply: "Who the hell is Parkinson?"

That was a fair question, but it didn't help patch things up with California conservatives. By 1968, Kuchel was fairly alienated from his own party, and that made Rafferty unexpectedly viable. Still, those of us working for Kuchel assumed he would pull off a victory in the primary, and we busily fed position papers to his political consultants to make sure that his record was accurately portrayed and that the absurd questions about his patriotism were put to rest.

We thought we'd made the case, and on election night we gathered in Los Angeles for the returns. At first the news was good. Precincts throughout Northern California showed him with a commanding lead in that part of the state, in those days its more liberal half. But as returns came in from the south, Kuchel's lead shrank. Orange County, where he was from, went solidly for Rafferty; Los Angeles was closer but broke in Rafferty's favor. The crusher was San Diego, where Kuchel had hoped to hold his own. Instead, it went heavily for Rafferty. In the end, with more than two million votes cast, Rafferty won by sixty-nine thousand.

We glumly absorbed that news—my recollection is that Kuchel took it better than the rest of us—only to be shocked from our sulking by a report from across town. Bobby Kennedy, who had just won California's Democratic primary for president, had been shot at the Ambassador Hotel and was gravely wounded. Kennedy lived through the night and the following day before being pronounced dead at 1:44 a.m. on June 6, a little more than twenty-four hours after the shooting in the hotel pantry. In a sense, the shock has never faded.

It's sometimes said that you don't really understand politics until you've lost. If so, 1968 was my real immersion in politics. We had won what I considered important victories in the Senate and produced bills of lasting consequence to protect the environment and remedy discrimination. But it wasn't enough. Progress on civil rights wasn't enough to allow the nation to peacefully absorb the death of King, and legislative progress wasn't enough to protect Kuchel against political retaliation. As usual, he handled it better than I. His farewell to his colleagues captured his essential philosophy of government:

> Some of the votes I have cast I know have been very costly to me
> politically. I think, however, if there is one measure of satisfaction
> in the life of a legislator, it comes at the time he tallies the votes
> which he believed in his own mind were right, just and appropri-
> ate, even if he knew that the balance of public opinion was against
> him, and, sometimes, violently against him. . . . I think it is not
> only permissible but, indeed, vital that the Senate of the United

States lead public opinion instead of following it. That is the difficult path but the only one to tread if our republic is to remain.[4]

At a time of growing turmoil in politics, Kuchel remained true to himself. Integrity mattered more to him than survival. It was a lesson I would not forget.

THREE

"You Did What Was Right"

I was out of a job. It was tempting to ditch politics altogether. Kuchel offered me a position in the law firm he was joining, and there was always the option of returning to Monterey and practicing law there. I considered both, but it's in moments such as those that the lessons of youth matter. In this case, I reflected on the perseverance of my parents—their steady commitment to the restaurant and their children, their abiding gratitude to the country that had made that possible. With those notions kicking around my head and with Sylvia's support, I decided I'd try to stick around Washington a little longer.

I had a couple of options, including an appealing invitation to join the Senate staff of Ed Brooke of Massachusetts. Brooke's politics were reminiscent of Kuchel's, and Massachusetts seemed less likely to rise up behind the Birch Society than California had. And I'd gotten to know Brooke a bit during my time in the Capitol. Still, it felt a bit like a continuation of my work for Kuchel rather than a new challenge, so I hesitated before accepting.

In the meantime, Nixon won the general election in November, and began building his cabinet. One promising selection was Bob Finch, a California politician and longtime Nixon supporter who had been serving as lieutenant governor of California. Finch, whose plainspoken style and steely blue eyes made him a media favorite, fit squarely within the moderate Republican tradition that I considered myself a part of, and I was encouraged to hear that he was the leading contender to head the Department of Health, Education, and Welfare.

Finch was a successful political figure—in 1966, he actually received more votes for lieutenant governor than Reagan did on that same ballot for governor. And his ties to Nixon were long and deep, since he had first worked with him in 1948, when Nixon was up for reelection to Congress. Finch helped persuade Nixon to vote for the Marshall Plan and put together a pamphlet for the young candidate entitled "The Amazing Richard Nixon."[1] Their friendship was sealed from that point on.

So in the fall of 1968, when I got a call from John Veneman—a former California state legislator and friend of Finch's—asking if I'd be interested in helping organize a transition team for Finch's HEW, I accepted. Veneman promised to create an "action team" that would put HEW at the forefront of the Nixon cabinet. On December 13, 1968, I found myself in the lobby of the agency's headquarters, a bit awed by the black-and-white photographs of HEW employees around the country delivering medical services, helping children in school, working in labs. I was impressed.

Which is not the same as saying that I accepted the position without at least some reservations. Like many close political observers in 1968, I was unsure where Richard Nixon stood on some of the preeminent social issues of the day, especially in the area of civil rights. As vice president under Eisenhower, he was associated with some of that administration's solid, if underappreciated, work on racial discrimination—eliminating segregation in the District of Columbia and on federal military bases, as well as support for the Civil Rights

Act of 1957 and the appointment of a number of judges and justices committed to the cause of ending segregation in schools and other public facilities. At the same time, however, Nixon had actively courted the support of leading segregationists, including South Carolina senator Strom Thurmond, during the presidential campaign and had consequently run well in the South. That was the much-discussed "Southern strategy," and it naturally raised the question of what commitments Nixon had made in return for that support. So while I was optimistic about Finch and his priorities, I was torn over what to think about Nixon and where he might lead HEW.

Although nominated, Finch still had to be confirmed. There didn't seem much doubt that he'd be approved—he was popular in Congress and with the media and a favorite of the president—but his comments would be closely watched for evidence of the administration's resolve on school desegregation. Finch traveled to the Hill to testify before the Senate Finance Committee on January 14, and at first it seemed to go well. His transition team had prepared a meticulous binder of briefing papers, and Finch had studied well. "We must keep the pressure up," he said of the school integration efforts, "and it must be constant pressure."

So far, so good. But then Finch improvised a bit. "Each community is a different slice of America," he noted. "Each area has a chemistry all of its own. You don't just come in with a meat-axe and bludgeon somebody into compliance." That was the sort of equivocation with which I was soon to become painfully familiar.

With his nomination secure, Finch then asked me to join him at HEW as a special assistant. I accepted, though again with some hesitation about how much latitude the department would have to pursue its mission. Key to that question was the role that HEW had when it came to enforcing school desegregation. Essentially, the lever that Congress gave HEW was school funding. In order to receive their share of federal education money, districts were required to submit desegregation plans to the department for approval. HEW's Civil Rights Office would review those plans and determine whether the federal money should continue or be cut off. That gave school districts—most, but not all, in the South—a powerful reason to comply and to end the long stalling game many had entered into in the 1950s and 1960s.

Underlying HEW's role was the Supreme Court's landmark rulings in *Brown v. Board of Education*. The first *Brown* decision, handed down by the young Warren Court in 1954, less than a year after Earl Warren became chief justice, concluded that separating students by race in public schools violated the Fourteenth Amendment's guarantee of equal protection. It famously held that "in the field of public education the doctrine of 'separate but equal' has no place. Separate educational facilities are inherently unequal."[2]

The Court declined in that first ruling to issue a specific order to guide school districts, but returned to the issue the following term. Then, in what became known as *"Brown II,"* the Court directed that desegregation proceed with "all deliberate speed," an unfortunately vague formulation that led, as scholars have noted, to much deliberation and not much speed. Indeed, the decade or so following *Brown* saw monumental efforts to avoid desegregation—the best known being the Little Rock Crisis of 1957, when Arkansas governor Orval Faubus cynically obstructed integration of Little Rock's Central High School until Eisenhower responded by sending in the 101st Airborne. Notably little progress was made.

The Civil Rights Act of 1957 was the first federal law since Reconstruction to place the federal government in defense of the rights of ordinary black Americans. Though that act accomplished relatively little, it did allow the Justice Department to enforce voting and other rights. Then, in 1964, President Johnson picked up the civil rights efforts that Kennedy had pursued halfheartedly and ham-handedly and secured passage of a much more far-reaching bill. The act he signed that year was meant to eliminate segregation in public accommodations, and it also included language under Title IV and Title VI that affected schools—in the former case, through the use of a carrot; in the latter, a stick. Title IV allowed HEW, through its Education Office, to lend assistance to school districts in their desegregation efforts; that was hardly controversial. Title VI, however, forbade the federal government from spending money on any activity that discriminated on the basis of race, color, or national origin. In practice, that meant the federal government, again through HEW, was obligated to cut off funds from any school district that segregated its students.

Still, there was no overstating the tenacity and creativity of segregationists. They fought in the courts, in Congress, and in school boards across the South, bitterly contesting any effort to allow black and white children to sit beside one another in classrooms. By 1969, there still were far too many communities with a pair of high schools—one named for Booker T. Washington, the other for Robert E. Lee.

The job of evaluating school district desegregation plans fell to HEW's Office for Civil Rights, which was headed in early 1969 by Ruby Martin, a strong black woman who was rightly admired within the department. In my role as special assistant, I worked closely with Martin, and we were confronted right away with challenges from southern officials who believed that Nixon would grant them more time and latitude when it came to the integration they so virulently opposed.

In the closing days of the Johnson administration, the departing head of HEW, Wilbur Cohen, had notified Congress that five South Carolina school districts were about to lose their federal funding because their desegregation plans were inadequate. The money was scheduled to run out on January 29, nine days after Nixon took the oath of office. The timing and location of the districts ensured that their fate would send an early signal of the new administration's approach to these questions: South Carolina was the home of Senator Thurmond; no man was more instrumental in persuading southern segregationists to trust Nixon, and no set of school districts mattered more to him. It was, as Veneman put it, "cashing-in time for the southerners."

Finch could have met this threat with resolve. He could have let the money simply run out and forced the districts back to the table with a new plan. In fairness, cutoffs did hurt innocent people—some children lost programs and teachers, and sometimes it was black schools that were hurt the worst. So there were good reasons not to go that route cavalierly. But we all knew that if we didn't fight now, we would only have to fight harder later, because any indication that these terms were negotiable would invite more negotiation. Unfortunately, Finch vacillated.

Stories in the press began to suggest that the cutoff was up for debate, and various congressional aides and others said a deal was in the works to postpone the cutoff while the districts prepared new plans. Finch's response was to order the rest of us not to comment. The department's official position was only that the matter was under discussion.

The problem with that was that it suggested there was something worthy of discussion. These districts' plans had been rejected by the secretary of HEW, Cohen. They had been warned of the consequences, and now they had to face them, or the agency would appear to be driven by politics rather than the law or the principles it was required to uphold.

I suggested an alternative to postponement: Cut off the funds as scheduled, but also dispatch negotiating teams to South Carolina in an attempt to reach a quick agreement, and then restart the funds once the terms were accepted. Ruby Martin received that idea warily, and Veneman captured the mood of the staff when he broke it to her: "Ruby," he said, "we've decided not to sell out completely." When she heard the proposal, she was relieved, but still worried that we'd cave in the end.

What followed were days of grinding diplomacy—with Thurmond leaning on the White House in one direction, the Civil Rights Office and Finch's deputies pulling in the other, and Finch desperately searching for a center. In the end, my proposal held. It was exhausting and largely successful, but it hardly reassured me about Finch's core principles. Jim Batten, a reporter for the *Charlotte Observer,* who followed the debate quite closely, summarized it best: "If the lively jousting of the past few days is any indication, more behind-the-scene struggles can be expected inside and outside the Administration before Nixon's own policy becomes clear-cut. . . . The end of the confusion is not in sight."[3]

Finch's reflection: "Christ, I hope we don't have to do this every time."

Well, it didn't happen every time, but one consequence of that early deal was that segregationists figured it wouldn't hurt to fight—and to call in their chits with members of Congress and the administration. Ruby Martin wearied of it quickly and left in March of that year. On March 28, Finch asked me to replace her. I'd been at the agency for just three months, and the offer carried immense responsibility as well as considerable prestige for a thirty-year-old lawyer who less than a year earlier had been a fairly anonymous Senate aide. Sylvia urged me to take it, and my friends warned of the inherent difficulties of representing the Nixon administration in this charged and conflicted area.

After sleeping on it, I told Veneman I'd give it a stab, but asked him if I could be sure of the secretary. Rather than speak for him, Jack put me through to Finch at home, where the secretary was recovering from the flu.

We exchanged a few clipped pleasantries—he was rasping and wheezy—and then I got to the point. "As you know," I said, "there's been a hell of a lot of pressure on this issue and I'm pretty committed to seeing the law enforced strongly. I hope I have your commitment for that kind of enforcement and wanted to make mine clear."

Finch may have been sick, but he was clear: "Hell yes, it's a tough area and we'll have to walk some thin lines, but there'll be no relaxation of enforcement."

With that, I took the job.

Tom Kuchel had cast one of the proudest votes of his life for the Civil Rights Act of 1964. He'd gone to the Senate with a blanket and a pillow to ride out any filibuster of the bill. He'd prevailed. It was now my job to make his vote matter. For the first time in my life, I held a position of executive responsibility. I had a staff of 278 lawyers and others, most in Washington, the rest in regional offices around the country.

Before I could settle in to my new duties, Sylvia's mother arrived for a visit and had news I had long dreaded. My mother, whose cancer had first been detected years earlier but had then gone into remission, was now gravely ill. Those years between were a godsend. They allowed her to return home and to get to know her older grandchildren. She cooked and immersed herself in her family, enjoying a respite from a lifetime of hard work amid the shade of walnut and peach trees in the Carmel Valley. As her health deteriorated, my father set up a bed for her downstairs in their home so that she could lie peacefully with her family nearby. They had no health insurance, but my father used savings to bring in nurses and to make sure she was comfortable—what we today would describe as hospice. But my mother could not hold off cancer forever. Hearing that she was failing, I booked a flight home. As I prepared to leave, my father called to tell me my mother had died. It was May 8, 1969. The obituary in the *Monterey Peninsula Herald* noted that she would be "remembered by her many friends as a lady of great beauty and gentle dignity."[4] Although I was too late to say good-bye—something I have always regretted—I flew home to comfort my father and bury my mother. I stayed a few days, and then returned to Washington.

Over the next nine months, the pattern of the first South Carolina debate was replayed time and again—the Civil Rights Office, now under my leadership, pushed hard to enforce the law in Louisiana, Georgia, Mississippi, South Carolina, even a few northern school districts. Local representatives pushed back and put pressure on the White House, which invariably tried to reassure us that it was committed to the law while winking at our opponents and hinting that they could get time or substantive relief and suggesting that the office—and I—were out of step with the administration.

Occasionally the mask would fall away and the politics of the situation would stare at us directly. That happened during a visit from a group of Mississippi politicians who came to complain that we were pushing too hard. I explained our determination and responsibility to enforce the law, and the head of the delegation, a man named Charlie Reed, responded, "Look, we had a commitment from Nixon that he was going to back off. We expect you to follow through on that."

I replied the only way I could: "I have a responsibility to enforce the law, and I'm sworn to do that."

The work was tense and frantic and sometimes frightening. When my staff and I visited particularly hostile communities in the Deep South, we would put Scotch tape on the hoods of our cars before leaving them; when we returned, we'd check to see that the tape was still there to make sure they hadn't been tampered with. Bombs were on our minds.

I was called periodically to testify before or otherwise communicate with members of Congress, and no less an ardent racist than Senator James Eastland, the immensely powerful head of the Senate Judiciary Committee, once chomped on his cigar, looked me in the eye, and coolly informed me of what I was up against: "Let me tell you something. It is never going to happen. You are never going to integrate schools in the South." I guess it goes without saying that he said that without a hint of apology or admission that his determination defied the law of his country and his oath to uphold it. Such were the tensions of those days.

As the pressure mounted through 1969, I tried a couple of times to reach out to the White House, hoping for support or, failing that, at least clarity. John Ehrlichman agreed to meet with me. We had lunch at the White House mess in June. Ehrlichman didn't show much that day, asking more questions and playing with me like a prosecutor grilling a witness. He asked me about the law and the room for flexibility. At one point he pressed on the issue of "free choice," districts that purported to be integrating by allowing students to choose their schools; in practice, very few blacks chose predominantly white schools, and virtually no white students volunteered for historically black schools, so "choice" really was a mask for continued segregation. I explained that. He nodded without comment, nibbling on his hamburger and cottage cheese, which was already known to be President Nixon's favorite meal.

I left the meeting feeling I had not accomplished much but that at least I had helped make clear that the law offered no options other than desegregation, even if the administration preferred options for political purposes. A few days later, however, Finch confronted me in his office and told me that my conversation with Ehrlichman had confirmed his impression of me as a "bloodthirsty integrationist." I could tell that Finch was growing impatient with me and with the pressure that this issue was putting upon him and his relations with Nixon.

As the pressure mounted, Sylvia gave birth to our third son, Jimmy, on October 1, 1969, at Sibley Hospital in Washington. Both he and a new collie pup—we named her Lassie, of course—joined our family at about the same time and gave us great comfort during those difficult days.

Work, however, was growing more and more difficult. In desperation, I drafted a letter of resignation to demonstrate how serious I was about doing my job or leaving it if I was not allowed to. I worried about that. I wanted to prevail in these debates, not run from them. Besides, I was a young father with three sons, so I was hardly in a position to simply walk off a job. After a few stressful days, Finch checked with the White House and reported back to me that my offer to resign had been rejected. I breathed a little easier and kept on with the work, though mindful that I had few friends at the top levels of the Nixon administration and thus could hardly count my position as secure.

One morning, that became abundantly clear, in uniquely Washington fashion. I woke up early on February 17, 1970, and opened the *Washington Daily News* (this was back in the days when Washington had several morning papers) to discover a story that caught my eye. NIXON SEEKS TO FIRE HEW'S RIGHTS CHIEF FOR LIBERAL VIEWS, it announced. I didn't need to be told who that was about. It was attributed to "Congressional sources," and indicated that I was all but finished.

Partly puzzled and plenty worried, I raced to Finch's office to make sure he hadn't heard anything. "No, no," he said, "continue to deny it." He promised to call the White House and inquire about how to respond to this false report.

The first response was an ominous silence. The next was a staggering falsehood: Asked about the report at an afternoon news conference, Press Secretary Ron Ziegler responded, "It is my understanding that Mr. Panetta has submitted his resignation to Secretary Finch. . . . I think it has been accepted, and HEW, as I understand it, will have an announcement on that sometime today." At that point it didn't seem like there was much reason to fight on, so I offered to spare the secretary any further embarrassment by writing out a resignation letter and submitting it to him.

He was chagrined and apologetic—and mindful, I'm sure, that this was a pretty stark demonstration of the White House's disregard for him as well. "I'm sorry that this happened," he said to me. I believed that.

I was allowed to meet briefly with the press, and that was a tricky affair. I tried not to inflame the issue and did my best not to add to Finch's embarrassment, but reporters understood that this wasn't my idea, and correctly concluded that I'd been the victim of pressure from Nixon's political team, which wanted slower progress on desegregation in order to shore up Nixon's southern support. The coverage was respectful of me and skeptical of the White House, a precursor of the power struggles—and public response—that would eventually sink Nixon. It goes without saying that I was one of the least surprised people in the country when details of the Watergate scandal began emerging a few years later.

But that was still in the future. For now, I was out of work and chiefly consumed with how to support my family. Thankfully, Sylvia never wavered. As the walls were closing in on that fateful day of Ziegler's press conference, I confided my fears to her. "I'm worried about you and the kids and our future. What's it mean to us?" She was calmer than I was. "Don't be worried—we've always managed before," she said. "You did what was right."

I learned some lessons from my first firing. I'd been naïve not to cultivate a better relationship with the White House and instead to rely on Finch to run interference for me. And I'd made the rookie mistake of assuming that because I believed so strongly in our mission others would come around. I filed those realizations away.

But I'd also been able to reinforce some old values. Helped by my wife and supportive colleagues, I tried to be clear on the difference between being personally accommodating and philosophically consistent. I've never set out to be deliberately antagonistic or to embarrass those with whom I disagree, but I also felt that there were lines I wouldn't cross. I would not refuse to enforce the law because of political calculations any more than Tom Kuchel would endorse Goldwater or Reagan when he thought they were ill-suited to the offices they sought. Those decisions had cost Kuchel his position permanently; for me, the setback was more temporary, though I had no way of knowing that as I left the HEW building a few days later with a cardboard box full of the contents of my desk, including pictures of Kuchel and Nixon—one who gave me my start in government, the other who kicked me out the door.

There was one other observation I made from my run-in with the Nixon White House, and it influenced my next career move. As I mentioned earlier, I supported Nixon in 1960 in part because I believed that he and I shared a common political heritage—the moderate Republican tradition that was so influential during my youth. But governing in that tradition was not compatible in 1969 with nurturing the Southern strategy, and it seemed clear to me that Nixon was being pulled to his right. Moreover, the demise of moderate Republicanism was afoot elsewhere too. In 1964, Goldwater had bragged that "extremism in the defense of liberty is no vice" and that "moderation in the pursuit of justice is no virtue."[5] Those boasts were deliberately intended as a repudiation of Eisenhower's moderation,* and even though Goldwater was trounced by Johnson in that election, the party had commenced a cleansing of its moderate elements, a self-immolation that eventually claimed the likes of Charles Goodell, Jacob Javits, and Edward Brooke, among so many others. Those Republicans who survived it were forced to change, and onetime moderates such as Reagan, who talked tough as California governor but also repeatedly raised taxes and cut deals with Democrats, reinvented themselves as heirs to Goldwater. It is striking to realize that Dwight Eisenhower, the commanding and immensely popular Republican president, would have a tough time winning his party's nomination today.

In 1970, the purge of moderates was under way but incomplete. And as I was looking for a place to land, there was still at least one promising Republican centrist with national ambitions and seemingly

---

*Eisenhower considered Goldwater a buffoon even before the 1964 convention. The speech sealed his enmity.

a chance to advance them. John Lindsay was mayor of New York. He was an attractive leader who rode a flashy, patrician image from his years in the House of Representatives to a successful mayoral run in 1965. He reminded many people of John Kennedy—he was witty and cultured; he enjoyed the company of celebrities yet also roamed the streets of New York in shirtsleeves picking up trash or scolding limo drivers for double-parking.[6]

Few people were immune to Lindsay's charms—interestingly, one who found them easy to resist was New York governor Nelson Rockefeller, who used to drive Lindsay crazy by calling him "Johnny." I certainly saw promise in Lindsay. At the same time, he saw an opportunity in me as well. Lindsay was positioning to run for president as a liberal alternative to Nixon's rightward drift, and I'd just been offed by Nixon after a struggle over the pace and direction of school integration. For me, Lindsay represented a job, which I was desperate for, and another opportunity to join a politician who espoused my values; for him, I was a potential aide with Washington experience and a reputation for fighting on behalf of the party's waning liberal values. He tendered a job, and I accepted.

I didn't go immediately. My minor celebrity over the Nixon flap generated a book offer, and I took it, working with Peter Gall, a friend and former colleague from HEW and Kuchel's office. We holed up in an office lent to us by Marian Wright Edelman at the Children's Defense Fund and pounded out an account of my brief, heated tenure at HEW. Titled *Bring Us Together*, it wasn't the great American novel, but it was well received and helped establish me in political terms as an early foe of Nixon, an investment that would pay off when the depth of Nixon's dishonesty and lawlessness was revealed to the public.

Once Peter and I had finished the manuscript, we shipped it off to Lippincott, our publisher, and then I headed for New York to begin work with Lindsay. Sylvia and I found an older home on the northern tip of Staten Island, not far from, of all things, Nixon Avenue. The home looked out toward the newly built World Trade Center towers at the southern end of Manhattan. I took the Staten Island Ferry to work—not a bad commute. I passed the Statue of Liberty every day on the way to city hall.

It wasn't long before I realized that I'd overestimated Lindsay a bit, and that his mastery of his office wasn't as impressive up close as it had seemed from a distance. That may have reflected his route through New York politics.

As a young lawyer and World War II veteran, Lindsay had impressed Herbert Brownell, a close adviser to Eisenhower and later his attorney general. Brownell had brought Lindsay to the administration, and he nurtured him as a potential candidate. In 1958, Lindsay saw his opportunity and ran for a congressional seat on Manhattan's East Side. He built a solid record there: He supported the Civil Rights Act of 1964, opposed the war in Vietnam, and refused to endorse Goldwater for president. In many ways, he resembled Kuchel.

After four terms, he was still only forty-three years old, but when Mayor Robert Wagner decided not to run for reelection in 1965, Lindsay took a chance and announced his candidacy, despite no real experience in urban politics. He won a very close race, threading the needle between Democrat Abe Beame and William F. Buckley's Conservative Party candidacy, and then faced the far more difficult challenge of governing the ungovernable city. It did not go especially well.

Yes, he had charm and charisma, but he often seemed overmatched by the rough politics of New York. By the time I came to work for him, he'd already bumped up against those politics, memorably during the snowstorm in the winter of 1969. The storm paralyzed much of Queens, where city plows could not get through. Stranded residents blamed Lindsay, and with some good reason, as his relations with the city unions were famously raucous.

My job was to coordinate his intergovernmental relations, and Lindsay kept me busy. His presidential campaign wasn't official at that point, but the people around him were pushing it, and he warmed to the national stage. He was often testifying in Congress or giving speeches, and looking for opportunities to offer big, creative ideas. He had me play around for a while, for instance, with a proposal for New York City to break off and become its own state. That didn't go far, but it was illustrative of Lindsay's leadership—grand, provocative, but not so great at the basics. When New York's garbagemen struck, Lindsay sent me out to talk with them on the theory that they might listen to an Italian. They didn't.

I only stayed with Lindsay for a year, but I did learn some things. Even in the chaotic, combative politics of New York, relationships matter. Lindsay thought he could lead by intellect and ideas, and he neglected the more basic work of making allies. It's impossible to imagine John Lindsay calling up the mother of a city council member and wishing her a happy birthday, the way Johnson did with Kuchel. I also came away with a deeper appreciation for the complexity of urban issues— the labor relations and service demands that lie at the core of municipal government. At a fundamental level, the work of local government really isn't political, ideological, or even particularly intellectual. It's about picking up trash and clearing streets of snow, and there really isn't a Republican or Democratic way of providing those services. In fact, local government can teach federal officials a great deal about what the public wants. At the local level, politics can be heated, but constituents have a way of grounding it. They'll get mad at any politician who puts them at risk or lets them down, and responsibility is far easier to fix than in Washington's more abstract debates.

Lindsay and I parted on good terms. He turned to his presidential campaign, which didn't go far, and I headed for home. Sylvia, Jimmy, and Lassie flew on one of the new 747s back to California. My father had located a home for us to rent on Valle Vista in Carmel Valley. Sylvia settled in and waited for the rest of the family to arrive, as the older boys and I set out on a cross-country car vacation. Christopher and

Carmelo joined me in our family station wagon—we still had the VW, and this time we towed it—for the drive west. Like my parents before me, we stopped in Sheridan, Wyoming, to visit our cousins. The morning after we arrived, there was twelve inches of new snow on the ground. After a pleasant visit, we set out again, but struggled. It took several tries on icy roads, but we finally made it out of Wyoming and back to California.

We were home in Monterey, this time for me to join my brother's law practice. He and I would work together for the next five years. But it would not be long before public life would call again.

FOUR

"No More Excuses"

After a rough couple years, it was a relief finally to be home. And after a lifetime of admiring my older brother, it was a treat to practice law with him. He already had a healthy practice and an office in one of the properties my father had bought with the money from the sale of the restaurant. Along with two other partners, we operated in a modest two-story building right across from city hall in Monterey (my brother's office is still there today).

As was true for many lawyers in those days, we did a bit of everything—criminal, civil, corporate, probate. Given my background with the Civil Rights Office at HEW, I was drawn to civil rights cases, and clients with discrimination grievances naturally sought me out. One group of prospective Latino students and employees sued the newly opened University of California at Santa Cruz, and we settled with the university after agreeing to hiring and admissions standards that would encourage ethnic diversity. I also took on the local NAACP as a client.

One thing about practicing small-town law is that it's a foolproof way of getting to know people and their issues. My brother was already well known in the area, and gradually I developed a reputation as well, as someone who understood politics and the community and who knew the law. It was professionally and personally satisfying and a welcome change of pace. Leading a normal life with my family in one of the most beautiful spots on earth was not bad. But politics still tugged at me. Indeed, it seems in retrospect as if it was just a matter of time until I was drawn back into politics, though I didn't intend it at the time.

I did some political soul-searching upon my return home. I remained committed to the ideals that initially animated my interest in public service—duty to country and a conviction that government could play a constructive role in the lives of its citizens. But some of the officials I most admired had passed from the scene: Eisenhower died in 1969, Warren retired from the Court the same year, Kuchel was back in Los Angeles practicing law. The party of Eisenhower and Warren had become that of Nixon and Agnew. Those tidal shifts—the ascension of the more conservative wing of the party and the evisceration of its liberal faction—convinced me that while my principles had not changed, the party to which I belonged no longer had room for me and people like me. The Democrats, by contrast, seemed to offer a bigger tent, with more room for disagreement among members united by broad principles. In 1972, I changed my registration to Democrat in time to vote for Hubert Humphrey in California's Democratic primary.

It was not long after I left the Republican Party that it began to unravel from the top. The first reports of what would become known as Watergate began to trickle in during the summer of 1972, when the *Washington Post* reported that one of five men arrested after a break-in at Democratic headquarters in the Watergate office and hotel complex was the security coordinator of the Nixon campaign. The scandal simmered for a while, but persistent reporting by the press, especially the *Post*'s famous team of Bob Woodward and Carl Bernstein, revealed a far-reaching and malevolent political operation run from the highest levels of the White House. The administration targeted "enemies" for tax audits, played dirty tricks on political opponents, conducted break-ins and wiretapping, paid hush money to discourage operatives from testifying, and deliberately impeded investigations into wrongdoing by top administration officials. On March 1, 1974, seven of those officials, including the same John Erlichman who had stymied me at HEW, were indicted by a grand jury. Nixon resigned on August 8.

I was hardly surprised. I'd seen the Nixon administration's willingness to bend principle to politics during my run at HEW. Nixon's political operation was profoundly corrupt and a manifestation of the president's insecurity and paranoia. It was only a matter of time before trouble caught up with it. And though I worried whether the presidency itself was damaged by the scandal, I was not sorry to see Nixon go and to have Gerald Ford, whom I used to see on the Hill when I worked for Kuchel, take his place.

By the mid-1970s, I'd been gone from Washington for five years, but I'd never left politics far behind. Much of my law practice had political overtones—fighting civil rights cases and representing the regional park district, for instance—and a number of clients and friends suggested that I consider a run for public office. One day in the spring of 1975, a good friend from the small town of Aptos, California, Leo Greenberg, and the local head of the California Teachers Association, Win Nelson, took me to lunch in Salinas. They urged me to make a run for public office—we discussed state as well as federal possibilities—and laid out their case for how I might win. I left with the idea firmly in mind.

As I considered it, I realized quickly that federal office had far greater appeal for me. I'd worked in Washington and liked the atmosphere. And I was much less fluent in the issues that legislators tackled in Sacramento. My background, interests, and orientation all pointed toward Washington. Standing in my way was Congressman Burt Talcott.

Talcott was an unusual character. A graduate of Stanford and decorated bomber pilot who had been held as a prisoner of war by the Nazis during World War II, he was smart and good-looking and seemingly well ensconced in his district, which had been represented by Republicans since the days of FDR. But Talcott was also a bit of an oddball. He was a teetotaler and self-conscious dresser who once addressed his colleagues from the floor of the House to scold them for wearing sport coats rather than suits. He frowned on cursing and was known to blurt comments like "to health with it" because he disliked using the word "hell." (My linguistic habits even then were, well, more colorful.)

He was also prone to the impolitic outburst, which occasionally revealed an unpleasant set of instincts. During the early 1970s, for instance, when the fall of South Vietnam led to a flood of refugees seeking the protection of the United States, Talcott publicly complained that California should not be asked to shoulder that burden for the perplexing reason that "we have too many Orientals already. If they all gravitate to California, the tax and welfare rolls will get overburdened, and we already have our share of illegal aliens."[1]

Aside from those flashes of intolerance, there was the matter of Talcott's record. He had first won office in 1962, but didn't have much to show for his long tenure. He'd won passage of only three bills during that time, and his attendance record on his committees was poor. Moreover, he had fallen into the occupational hazard of mentally relocating to Washington and spending little time in the district. The inland farm community that was an important part of the economy of the area—and whose political support was especially important for a Republican—was restive. And while Talcott was missing committee meetings back in Washington, the district, which ran along the California coast from Santa Cruz down to San Luis Obispo, was changing fast. Coastal towns that had been historically Republican, such as Santa Cruz, were absorbing the counterculture and transforming into centers of liberalism.

In 1972, Talcott won reelection to his congressional seat. But he prevailed by only about eight points over his Democratic challenger, Julian Camacho. The following election was even closer, with Talcott winning a rematch against Camacho but this time squeaking out only a two-point win—about 2,000 votes of more than 150,000 cast.

Camacho elected not to run a third time, and I had my opening. I announced in November 1975 and began the yearlong effort to unseat the incumbent. Campaigns in the 1970s were much less expensive than they are today, and I'd put away a little cash, but it still was a stretch; I had to use my savings and also forgo income since I was committed to campaigning almost full-time.

My advantages were the district's Democratic tilt, the disarray of Republicans in the wake of Nixon's resignation and his pardon by Gerald Ford—Ford was at the top of the Republican ticket that year, and did not seem likely to have long coattails—and the general dissatisfaction with Talcott. But Talcott had advantages too: He had almost universal name recognition, a long history of winning races in the district, and plenty of people he'd done favors for. And of course, there are always the issues that bubble beneath the surface: Would some voters resist supporting an Italian American? Would some regard me with suspicion for having switched parties or having fought for civil rights?

One thing I learned early: As someone who had been born and raised in the district, I enjoyed campaigning. Some politicians don't. They like governing or deal-making or hobnobbing, but they can't be bothered to hear a farmer's problems or a veteran's complaint or a family's immigration difficulties. Some like the glamour of Washington but find their districts dull or distracting. They resent having to provide basic services to constituents when they imagined writing laws and making history. In my experience, those tend to be the ones who end up losing touch and being tossed out. Luckily for me, perhaps because of the gratitude for this country that my parents felt so deeply, I genuinely liked the part of politics that was about listening and helping.

Good thing, too, because I did a lot of it in late 1975 and most of 1976. I visited every city in the district, met every mayor and council member. I marched in parades, worked the crowds at rodeos and fairs, spoke to Rotary clubs and Kiwanis clubs and every other gathering we could elbow a spot at. Sylvia and I did a bunch of these together, and while I would talk, she would distribute our literature. I had a challenger in the primary, a more liberal Democrat named John Bakalian, and that turned out to be a good thing, as it forced us to build up a campaign during the primary. I beat him fairly easily, and that positioned me well for the general election against Talcott, since I was now able to argue that I represented the center and that he was an out-of-touch conservative.

Tom Kuchel endorsed me, as did Representative Pete McCloskey, a moderate Republican representing the Bay Area. The national Democratic Party, seeing Talcott as vulnerable, provided support and resources, and environmental groups rallied behind me as well. The latter were especially important, as the group known as Environmental Action named Talcott to its "Dirty Dozen" list of members of Congress most unfriendly to the environment. Talcott responded by calling the organization "a small clique that has distorted the environmental record of the Congress for its own partisan reasons."[2] Meanwhile, Norm Mineta, a good friend going back to his days as mayor of San Jose, was a respected Japanese-American congressman who couldn't wait to campaign for me—he remembered all too well Talcott's remarks about Japanese Americans. The cumulative result was that I was able to point to support that stretched from the Republican center to the Democratic left—a broad base compared to Talcott's narrower hold on conservatives.

After winning the primary, we invested in a small poll and discovered that I was about five points behind. I realized I had a fight on my hands, and I was lucky to land an up-and-coming political consultant, John Franzén, to head my effort in the general election. John had done press for George McGovern and other candidates, but had never run a campaign himself. Then again, I'd never run for office before either. We met during the Democratic convention that year and hit it off immediately. We agreed to take a chance on each other.

John's advice took two forms. The first was substantive. Camacho had challenged Talcott mainly in ideological terms, arguing that Talcott was too conservative for an increasingly liberal district; he'd made headway but run up against the truth that much of the district, particularly inland, remained Republican and was reluctant to toss out a conservative for a liberal. John's advice: Challenge Talcott's effectiveness, not his politics. When it came to tactics, John's recommendation was even simpler: television.

First, though, we needed money. When John arrived, the campaign had $2,600 on hand and bills payable of $2,754. That meant we needed to move fast, and we did, appealing to national Democrats with the argument that this represented a serious opportunity for the party to pick up a seat. Representative Phil Burton, a San Francisco Democrat who was renowned for his political acumen, agreed, and arranged for Tip O'Neill, the legendary Speaker of the House, to visit the district and help us raise money. We were thrilled, and reached out to every supporter and potential supporter we could think of.

O'Neill arrived for the event as scheduled and found a healthy crowd awaiting him. He was in fine spirits, ebullient and welcoming as always, obviously pleased to be surrounded by like-minded Democrats. When it came time for him to tout me, though, he stressed that we were gathered to help "my good friend Leo." I winced, as did John, and that wasn't the end of it. O'Neill kept extolling my potential, urging the crowd to dig deep to help "Leo." When it was over, finally, my friends in the audience took it all in stride and donated generously. Fortunately, everyone, including myself, loved the big Irishman from Boston. He could say whatever he wanted if it got people to donate to our campaign.

We had a message, a strategy, and now money. With that fund-raiser and a few others, we built up a treasury of about $180,000 and went up with a string of television ads aiming at what we saw as Talcott's essential weakness. Boy, what a difference that made. It was my first introduction to the power of advertising that reaches inside the voter's home. Suddenly, I was in demand. Voters jostled to shake my hand, and we felt we had gained the momentum of the race.

Our slogan was "No more excuses," and it boxed Talcott in. He'd been arguing that it wasn't fair to judge his record because Democrats controlled Congress, and therefore it wasn't realistic to expect him to get bills passed. That put him in the awkward position of trying to run against Congress while seeking his eighth term as a member of that same Congress. A *Los Angeles Times* headline captured his predicament: GOP INCUMBENT LASHES OUT AT CONGRESS, the paper reported in October. "I'm not responsible for the Congress," the paper quoted Talcott saying. "The Democratic majority is responsible for the Congress. They vote me down every time."[3] That, of course, begged the question of why voters needed a congressman who couldn't deliver for them. And it sure sounded like an excuse. We kept hammering: "No more excuses."

Once we had established Talcott's habit of skipping committee meetings, we went up with what we called the "empty chair" ad. An offscreen voice ticked off the meetings Talcott had missed while the camera stayed steady on an empty chair. It raised the obvious question: Who, if anyone, really was representing this district in Washington? Another ad highlighted his place among the "Dirty Dozen," and that hurt on the Central Coast, where one thing Republicans and Democrats agreed on was the protection of the area's scenic beauty. And to keep Talcott further off balance, I played up my family farm background with images of me on our Carmel Valley ranch. One ad featured a picture of me throwing hay into the back of a pickup truck, my dad alongside me. Even the weather helped: It was a bad drought year, and Talcott hadn't been able to deliver on a water project that might have helped. Talcott's insistence that he couldn't be held responsible for problems because Democrats ran the show in Washington wasn't much comfort to a farmer who needed water. It just represented another "excuse," and thus played to our theme.

There was no doubt that the ads were having an impact. Suddenly, we had scores of people volunteering for the campaign and large crowds turning out for events and encouraging my candidacy. But when we conducted another small poll, we were astounded to discover that it didn't register any improvement. We had planned to use it to encourage donors, but when we saw the results we chose a different course: We buried it, told no one of the results, and pretended we'd never done a poll at all. That left us to trust our instincts rather than data, never an entirely comfortable approach, but we really didn't have a choice. As election day approached, we ran low on money, so I waged a last round of fund-raising, borrowed another $25,000, and kept our ads on the air.

On election night, we nervously gathered at a hotel on the beach in Seaside to await the returns. First came the absentee ballots, and Talcott was beating me handily; that wasn't encouraging, but not too worrisome either, since absentees tend to be more conservative. Then came Santa Cruz, and we split the vote there, though I was leading. I carried Monterey, my home turf, and a cheer went up for that. I lost San Benito, which hadn't voted for a Democrat since 1936, but I won big in San Luis Obispo. Finally, after twelve months of campaigning and a long evening of counting ballots, I was the newly elected congressman from California's 16th District. I ended up with 53.6 percent of the vote.

The next morning, I walked over to my dad's house and hugged him. He had come to the United States with twenty-five dollars and few skills other than the ability to cook a good Italian meal; indeed, he'd arrived with little more than the dream of what might be and the dream of giving his children a better life. That journey had brought him to Monterey, where he now comfortably grew walnuts and tended his piece of American soil. He had worked hard, devoted his life to Joe and me and to creating a secure place for his family. This country had taken him in, and he had given back. And now his son would serve in the U.S. Congress as the representative of the community where he still lived. He was rarely expressive, but he beamed that morning with joy, his own dreams and those of my mother finding fulfillment in the life they had built.

Running for Congress and serving in Congress are two different things, of course, and the first question that my election brought was how Sylvia and I would balance my new responsibilities with our job of raising our boys. That turned out to be an easy decision. We had moved enough in our lives, and we wanted our sons to grow up in California and to be near their grandfather. We decided that the best approach would be to keep our family in Carmel Valley. I would commute to Washington, and Sylvia, who had played such an important role in the campaign, would be my district administrative assistant, managing my five district offices without pay and being my eyes and ears at home.

Although not exactly orthodox, it was the perfect fit for the strong partnership that Sylvia and I had in our family and our work. She knew the district as well as anyone. And of course, she'd been around politics as long as I had. I was determined not to repeat Talcott's principal failing—his drift away from the district and its concerns. What better way to anchor me in the life of the Central Coast than for my wife to serve as my official representative? From my first day in Congress, constituents knew that when they spoke with Sylvia, they were speaking with me.

So Sylvia began the work of setting up our offices and hiring district staff while I flew back to Washington to learn the ropes of Congress. My first move, and maybe my best, was to ask John Franzén, who had managed my campaign, to run my Washington office. He agreed, and set out to build my staff there.

We arranged our offices, hired assistants, such as Diana Marino, who later became my administrative assistant, and in January 1977, as Jimmy Carter prepared to assume the presidency and Democrats were in full ascent, I became a member of the U.S. Congress.

FIVE

"Working for Us"

My time in Congress began with a brief but helpful set of orientation meetings in Washington, Williamsburg, Virginia, and Boston—helpful for refreshing my knowledge of parliamentary procedure and also for meeting incoming freshmen, both Democrats and Republicans. Once those were done, the challenges started quickly, and reality set in fast. Based on the orientations, I imagined that my first votes as a freshman might be on budget or foreign policy issues. Instead, I learned a basic lesson of Congress: Members are expected to take care of their own. My first challenge, then, was how to navigate a scheduled vote on a pay raise for Congress itself.

Needless to say, that's a vote that both the public and the members felt strongly about. Tip O'Neill pulled me aside early to lecture me on my responsibility to my colleagues. He assured me that no member had ever lost a seat over a pay raise and that it was my duty to my older colleagues to vote for the raise. We'd take the vote right at the beginning of the term so that plenty of time would have passed before any of us would have to run again. "It's not a big deal," Tip promised, and added, "We want you to do it."

I heard Tip out. "Look," I told him, "I come from a district that has been voting Republican since World War II. I just was able to get in, and I ran on economic issues. My constituents are still recovering from a recession. I cannot imagine coming back here and voting myself a pay raise as my first vote. I just can't."

He didn't like that answer and still thought I might come around, but as I thought the matter through, I was bothered not just by the politics of it but also by a matter of substance: It struck me as improper for members to approve a pay raise that would affect themselves, rather than making it prospective to the next Congress. I voted against it. And then, when it passed anyway, I refused to accept the increase. Instead, every time I received a paycheck, I'd return the raise by writing a check back to the U.S. Treasury. And I made the most of that. John had me photographed in the act of writing those checks and made the return of a pay raise a staple of my next campaign. To reinforce the point that my Central Coast constituents were more important to me than the politics of Washington, John made the theme of that campaign "Working for Us." It became the tagline for every one of my reelection efforts after that.

Most of my colleagues understood my predicament on the pay raise and eventually forgave me for it. Another early battle, however, earned me a lifelong enemy. I arrived in Washington with a big class of Watergate-era congressmen, as many of us were swept into office as part of the country's revulsion over the Nixon administration's malfeasance. Two ideas that strongly bound those new members, which included Dick Gephardt and Al Gore, among others, were a refusal to accept casual misconduct and an unwillingness to sanction leadership traditions that protected members from being held to account for those actions.

With that in mind, it seemed to me that we shouldn't tolerate the

continued service of any committee chairman who'd been found to
have committed misconduct. That led me to join a challenge to Representative Bob Sikes of Florida. Sikes was a tough customer. He was
nicknamed, believe it or not, "He-Coon," after a particularly wily rac-
coon native to north Florida, and he wielded considerable power in his
position as chairman of the Appropriations subcommittee on Military
Construction—a post that allowed him to decide where bases were
built and where they should be closed. Since that translated directly
into local jobs, he could make or break a member of Congress. It was
no coincidence that Sikes had fourteen military bases in his district.[1]

Just before I arrived in Washington, Sikes had been reprimanded
by the House Ethics Committee for money that he'd made—and not
disclosed—from his holdings in a Pensacola bank that he had helped
establish, and in Fairchild Industries, which profited by defense work.
He was also a bigot and a segregationist, though plenty of his southern
colleagues, even in 1976, fit that description at the time. It was the financial dealings that the House viewed as intolerable, and in July 1976
the members voted 381 to 3 to reprimand him.

It's hard to get 381 members of the House to agree on anything, so
that represented a fairly resounding attack on his integrity. Still, it did
not cost Sikes his chairmanship, which he clung to when I and my fellow freshmen arrived. We considered that a blemish on the House, and
raised a challenge. We circulated a letter demanding that he be removed.
Signed by fourteen freshmen members, including me, Gore, Gephardt,
Ed Markey of Massachusetts, Mary Rose Oakar of Ohio, and Anthony
Beilenson of California, it urged other members to oppose Sikes's re-
confirmation. "In our home districts," we wrote, "Congress as an institution stands in alarmingly low repute, largely as a result of recent
disclosures of questionable conduct by individual Members." Under
the circumstances, we added, "to return [Sikes] to that position now
would be the clearest kind of signal that we simply don't mean what we
say when it comes to policing ourselves."

Our argument prevailed. Sikes was defeated.

Sikes, who was once accurately remembered for "his tenacity at directing taxpayer dollars back home, concern for his constituents and vengeful attacks on his enemies," did not take it well.[2] He blamed "flaming liberals," and set out to get even. In my case, he took aim at the Naval Postgraduate School and sought to shut it down. The school is right in the center of Monterey, so closing it would have hurt my district badly. A colleague and member of the Defense Appropriations subcommittee, Bob Giaimo, warned me that Sikes was maneuvering for vengeance, and I confronted Sikes directly, urging that he not get even with me in a way that would harm the military. That seemed to defuse the matter, but I was relieved when he decided to retire in 1978. The postgraduate school survived.

Among the important events in the life of a freshman congressman is his committee assignments, and mine proved both helpful and illuminating. I was eager to serve on the Education Committee, but my instincts told me I'd be of greater service to my district if I angled for Agriculture. In general, members of that committee use their positions to look out for agricultural subsidies for the farmers in their districts, but in my case, few of my farmers qualified for subsidies, which tend to support grains, cotton, and other large crops. The farmers in my area grew mostly fruits and vegetables, which don't often qualify for such government help. Still, the committee regulated what are known as "marketing orders," which set parameters for the sale of those crops, and it also occasionally ventured into oversight of pesticides, another important issue for my district. Tip O'Neill must have at least partially forgiven my refusal to support the pay raise, because he agreed to let me join Agriculture and also understood when I asked him to reconsider his decision to put me on the D.C. Committee, which supervises the District of Columbia, because it could not help me out in any way back home.

Once on Agriculture, I moved up quickly because one of my subcommittees was Nutrition, which manages the Food Stamp Program. The chairman of that subcommittee was Fred Richmond of New York, and it wasn't long before he was swept up in a series of scandals that included financial misdeeds, possession of marijuana, and soliciting sex from a sixteen-year-old boy. That's enough to damage even the safest congressman, so he moved out, and I became chairman.

I also landed a spot on House Administration, a committee responsible for everything from election laws to parking spaces. It has never ceased to amaze me how much some members value their parking spot, so I acquired some early leverage.

Finally, at the urging of some of my colleagues, I pushed for a spot on the newly created Budget Committee. Like so much of what was going on in Congress in those years, the Budget Committee was an outgrowth of the deterioration of trust between Congress and the White House during Nixon's self-destruction. Before that, the House of Representatives, as required by the Constitution, originated all spending bills, but it had no real body to monitor the overall budget for spending and revenues. But when Nixon refused to spend money that Congress had appropriated, the House responded by creating the Budget Committee. It came into existence in 1974, so it was still brand-new when I arrived. I sensed that it could become an important entity in Congress and lobbied for a spot on it. Soon after I was reelected in 1978, I got it, and that was the beginning of what became the most important work I would do in Congress—developing and overseeing the federal budget.

First, however, there was the matter of settling in and representing my district. Sylvia got our offices running. After a few years of living alone in Washington, I joined a group of members in a house just a few blocks from the Cannon House Office Building, where my Washington office was located. George Miller of California was the landlord, and Chuck Schumer of New York, Marty Russo of Illinois, and I all shared the place. We'd often walk home after work, play a little basketball, have a drink, talk politics over dinner. I'd often return to the office in late evening and make calls to California, checking in first with Sylvia and then with constituents, trying to stay connected.

There was a genuine camaraderie to it, a welcome check on the arrogance that infects so much of Washington. We were conscious of being young and new—eager to change these institutions but also still a bit in awe of them. There were nights when I would get a glimpse of the Capitol, lit up against the dark sky, and catch my breath. I still can't approach the building without a sense of awe.

It was also fairly grueling. I'd work until Thursday or Friday afternoon when we were in session, and then head for Carmel Valley. I flew direct from Dulles to San Francisco, rented a car at the airport—Hertz didn't have many better customers in those days—and drove down the coast to Carmel Valley, usually not making it home until very late at night. Sylvia would greet me with any pending constituent issues that demanded my attention, and I'd usually have constituent hours on Fridays or Saturday mornings. Saturday afternoons were devoted to this event or that—there was always something to attend—and Sunday morning, after church, I'd try to drop by gatherings as well. We did try to hold Sunday afternoons open for the family, and I'd cook over the grill in our backyard under the grape arbor—the same grill and the same arbor that my father had built in 1948. Some Sundays he would join us.

There was a great sense of accomplishment and meaning as I circulated through the district, and those weekly trips guaranteed that I wouldn't fall out of touch—few things are more humbling for a member of Congress than to hear from constituents pleading for help. But there were hard moments. Many evenings I would put the boys to bed, straighten up after dinner, and then get in the car to head to the airport to return to Washington. As I drove away, I'd look in the rearview mirror and think, *What the hell am I doing?*

My district was a varied place. We didn't have any real urban areas or inner-city problems, but there were poor communities in Monterey and San Luis Obispo, and communities of staggering wealth in Pebble Beach and Carmel. The inland areas were mostly agricultural, while the coastal towns thrived mostly on fishing and tourism. Santa Cruz was changing rapidly as the University of California there opened and grew. But all those communities had one thing in common, and it was among the first issues that captured my attention as their new representative: They all enjoyed the remarkable beauty of our coastline.

The Monterey coast is dramatic, and its waters are clean and productive. There are broad beaches in Santa Cruz, Seaside, and San Luis Obispo; crashing waves on cliffs and rocks in Monterey, Big Sur, and Carmel. Pebble Beach's eighteenth hole is familiar to every golfer on the planet. That coastline supports fishing and tourism, mainstays of the California economy. Beneath the ocean floor, however, the shelf includes at least one other resource of value: oil. And that's where my concerns lay.

South of my district, Santa Barbara had experienced the effects of offshore oil exploration, and it had left an indelible impression. On the morning of January 28, 1969, a week after Richard Nixon was sworn in as president, a surge in pressure in an oil extraction pipe on a Union Oil platform a few miles off the coast caused a rupture. Workers on the platform tried to cap the problem, but the pipe casing failed, and a burst of natural gas cracked the seafloor surrounding the well. By noon that day, oil was gushing into the water off the Santa Barbara coast.[3] It would continue for eleven days, and during that time roughly three million gallons of oil poured from the cracks in the ocean floor into the water and onto thirty-five miles of some of the nation's most beautiful coastline, beaches, and harbors. Nixon himself was staggered by the damage, promising to send federal troops if needed to help the cleanup. Earth Day began the following year, and many still regard the Santa Barbara spill as the germinating moment of the modern environmental movement.

The Big Sur coastline—and my district—escaped damage in the Santa Barbara spill, but the disaster sent a shock through my constituents, as many considered the repercussions of oil fouling our fishing grounds or washing up at Pebble Beach. Soon after I took my seat, I began to look for ways to protect our coastline from the type of damage that Santa Barbara had endured. In my first term, I proposed creating a working group made up of federal and local representatives to study the coast. That effort didn't go far, as some of my more militant constituents worried about bringing the federal government into that study; I dropped the working group idea and instead backed an entirely local planning effort. In September 1978, I joined with Pete McCloskey and a group of county supervisors from counties along the coast in order to make our case to Cecil Andrus, the secretary of the interior, that the Big Sur coast should be off-limits to any oil exploration.

We came away from that meeting optimistic, but were soon disappointed. On October 10, Andrus announced that Interior was launching a study of 243 tracts off the California coast for possible oil and gas leases. Included in those were about 75 tracts that I had specifically asked Andrus to permanently exclude because of their extreme environmental sensitivity. I expressed my outrage and laid down my marker: "I intend to fight this decision down the line and to make sure that other congressmen join with me in preventing offshore drilling off this coastline."

That was just a month before my first reelection campaign came to a head, so before I could defend the coastline, I had to defend myself. Fortunately, the challenge came in the form of one Eric Seastrand, a stockbroker who lived in Salinas and worked in Monterey. It's generally true that members of Congress are most vulnerable to a challenge after their first term, and I was no exception. And if the Republicans had picked a moderate with a strong environmental streak, I might have had a hard run—I'd carried only 53 percent of the vote in my race against Talcott, and there still were wide swaths of the district that tilted Republican. Instead, however, they gave me Seastrand, an attractive and energetic campaigner but also a former member of the John Birch Society—he'd been a member until 1977, quitting just in time to run for Congress—who made the strange decision to attack me as fiscally irresponsible.

By this time, I'd already made hay out of my vote against the pay raise and my refusal to accept it once my colleagues approved it. In my first year, I returned $35,000 of my office budget to the Treasury, including $4,257 of unused raises, $5,000 in unused travel and office supplies, and about $25,000 in unused staff salary allowances. My refusal to accept the money I was allowed to spend hardly stamped me as irresponsible with money, so Seastrand's campaign came at my strengths, not my weaknesses. We had a debate or two, and I made sure that pictures of me signing checks to the Treasury were a mainstay of my campaign advertising. I got the endorsement of the newspapers in the district, including a much-appreciated one from the *Monterey Peninsula Herald*. The editors there described me as having "managed to represent faithfully the moderate and sensible judgment of the vast majority of voters in this district." The paper's recommendation for Seastrand: that he "be restored to the bosom of his medieval, right-wing fellowship in the John Birch Society, where he belongs."

On election day, I carried all four counties in my district, including the most conservative of the four, San Benito. It was the first time since 1936 that San Benito had voted for a Democrat for Congress. Overall, I got 61.4 percent of the vote. That really was the last time I felt much of a threat in a reelection campaign. In the coming years, I would never again take less than 70 percent.

Reelection plunged me back into the fight for the coast, and I sparred with the Carter administration through 1979 and 1980, eliminating some tracts but continuing to fight over others. The battle really escalated in 1981, however, when Ronald Reagan became president and appointed James Watt as his secretary of the interior. Andrus had been bad enough; this was a whole new level of problem.

Soon after Watt took over, a couple of us in Congress decided that we'd try to educate him on the special qualities of our coast. My partner in that effort was Don Clausen, a Republican who represented the Mendocino coast, his district covering the gorgeous country north of San Francisco and running up to the Oregon border. Don was a moderate, affable centrist holding office in an increasingly Democratic district, and one, like mine, where coastal protection was a unifying issue. So we invited Watt to come talk with us, figuring that a bipartisan appeal might reach him.

Watt arrived at Clausen's office right on time, and we ushered him inside. I spoke first. "Areas like Big Sur and the Mendocino coast are really national treasures," I began. "It's like Yosemite or Yellowstone." I conceded that there might be some areas that should be explored, but some were too valuable or too pristine to risk contamination.

In the conference room where we were meeting, Clausen had an arresting photo of the Mendocino coast, one of the nation's most picturesque. So behind me was this panoramic view of waves crashing at the base of cliffs, spray shining in the sun. I gave my pitch and turned to the photo. "This is the kind of coast we're talking about," I said.

Watt sat for a moment, then stood up and walked over to the picture. He pointed at it and said, "Not a bad place for an oil rig." I still remember the thought that shot through my head: *Holy shit.*

If nothing else, our meeting with Watt was clarifying. We obviously weren't going to be getting any help from the White House or Interior. That meant our only recourse was Congress. Happily, that's where we knew the ropes.

Clausen and I agreed that there wasn't any point in taking the issue head-on. Outside of California, there was no reason to believe that members would feel strongly about protecting the coasts in our districts. Moreover, some colleagues might resent the effort to curtail drilling in our areas while the country explored oil reserves in theirs. So rather than approaching the authorizing committees, we instead attacked the issue through Appropriations.

We drafted language that would withhold funds from the Interior Department for any work to authorize drilling off the California coast. The oil companies fought back hard, but we worked our votes. Norm Dicks, a Washington Democrat elected the same year as I was, supported us from the beginning, and was on the relevant subcommittee. Pennsylvania Democrat Jack Murtha couldn't have cared less about offshore drilling in California, but he recognized how important this issue was to us, and gave his full support, no doubt realizing that we'd owe him one (he was a consummate vote trader). Their backing got it through the subcommittee, and then other supporters began to line up.

The final House vote was 275 to 73. For good measure, the House also stripped $3.6 million from Watt's office, snidely instructing him that he should "set an example in times of fiscal restraint." And it barred him from using National Park Service facilities for political and social functions—a slap at Watt, who had used the Custis-Lee Mansion at Arlington National Cemetery for a couple of parties the year before. All in all, it was, as one commentator noted, a bill "clearly aimed at stopping a Cabinet secretary."[4]

Once we had it through the House, I quickly took the proposal to Senators Alan Cranston and Pete Wilson. Cranston, a Democrat who took over Kuchel's seat in 1969 (after Rafferty beat Kuchel in the Republican primary, Cranston clobbered Rafferty in the general election), was an easy sell, as he was already known for his strong support of environmental causes. I was less sure of Wilson, who was then a newly elected Republican and would go on to compile a more conservative record once he became governor a few years later. At the time, however, he was still regarded as a moderate, and coastal protection was so widely supported in California that whatever reservations he might have had, he didn't acknowledge them. He too signed on enthusiastically.

Their support was vital because that meant both houses of Congress approved identical language, meaning that no conference negotiation was possible. As a result, once the Senate acted, the moratorium was approved, and President Reagan, recognizing the bipartisan support behind it, signed the measure into law. Beginning in 1982, no federal funds could be used to advance oil exploration off the California coast. That ban was renewed year after year, and support for it grew as other parts of the country lobbied to be included.

Still, it was a fragile device. At any point, we could have lost our annual appropriations vote, and the blockade against drilling would have fallen. So even as the moratorium went into effect, I continued to look for a more permanent way to hold off drilling. It took another ten years, but in 1992, I introduced legislation to amend the Marine Protection, Research, and Sanctuaries Act of 1972 to designate the Monterey Bay National Marine Sanctuary. That designation protected the entire Central Coast of California, and continues to do so today. Even if Congress were to reauthorize offshore drilling in California, the beaches and cliffs where I grew up will never look out at an oil platform.

I think of that long effort every time I stroll the Monterey coast or enjoy a sunset over the Pacific. And here's an admission: If Watt had been more flexible—if he'd proposed, for instance, that we open some tracts to leasing while agreeing to protect some of the more sensitive areas—I might have gone for it. I'm proud of my role in protecting those beautiful areas, but they also owe a debt to the intransigence of the man I was fighting.

Protecting the coast was a natural undertaking for a member of Congress in my district, but other causes arose less predictably. Two of those touched me on level of basic humanity, and both resulted in changes that I believe rendered our country a more compassionate one. They involved the neediest Americans—those living in hunger and those dying in pain.

Early in 1982, I was meeting with a group of constituents in the district when they raised a humanitarian matter with me that struck me as so obvious that it warranted a new federal law. One of them, Jerome Rubin, was the founder and medical director of Hospice of the Monterey Peninsula, and he spoke compellingly of his mission and his patients.

Rubin and the others described terminally ill patients who were approaching the end of their lives. Those who were in hospitals were covered by Medicare, so they could afford treatments to ease their pain or provide other palliative relief. But for those who sought to end their lives at home, under hospice care, no such protection existed. They could turn to private insurance if they had it, and of course the very wealthy could pay for it themselves. So the only ones who were blocked from the relief offered by hospice were working people who had paid their taxes and helped support Medicare, only to be denied this important benefit at precisely the moment of maximum anguish.

It didn't take more than that for me to be convinced, so upon returning to Washington, I drafted a bill to extend Medicare coverage to hospice. Specifically, under the language of the bill, anyone diagnosed as having six months or less to live would be entitled to Medicare benefits for psychological or medical services provided by hospice. I estimated that the bill would save the Medicare program $15 million in the first year, and possibly as much as $130 million by the fifth year, since hospice services generally are less expensive than traditional care.

These being the days when some semblance of bipartisanship still existed, I took the idea first to Senator Bob Dole, the Kansas Republican, and asked if he would be a cosponsor. He agreed, and we reeled in support. Within a few days, we had 143 House members signed as cosponsors and more in the Senate. By the time of the bill's first hearing, that number was over 200, on its way to more than 300.

Not everyone was convinced. The Reagan administration, which already was annoyed with me over the Central Coast dispute, came out against the bill. The objection was entered by Paul Willging, deputy administrator of the Health Care Financing Administration, and it was sufficiently dubious that it was hard to know whether to take him seriously. The administration, he said, believed "we should proceed with extreme caution" in creating this new benefit before fully understanding its potential cost. He cited as an example the unanticipated rise in costs for coverage of end-stage kidney disease, which had ballooned from $229 million in 1974 to $1.6 billion in 1981.

In the case of hospice, however, we had solid evidence that it would save money, not cost more, so Willging's objection seemed more like reflexive opposition to something I was proposing than a serious reason not to proceed. The House shrugged him off, and with Dole's help, so did the Senate. Both approved the benefit, which was included as part of that year's Tax Equity and Fiscal Responsibility Act.

As a way of enlisting support from some wavering members in 1982, we agreed to study the effects of the benefit and allow it to expire in 1986 if it was not delivering the desired service and saving the government money. That study emphatically endorsed hospice, and rather than let the provision sunset, Congress made it permanent. Today, 100 percent of the costs of hospice are covered by Medicare. No terminally ill person need remain in a hospital nor in pain should they prefer this alternative.

My mother was able to die at home, where she was comfortable and at peace, because my father was able to pay for it. Now all Americans have that same right and ability.

My exposure to hunger came about differently, and bore almost no deep connection to my district. Though the Central Coast does have hungry families, and though some of our seniors benefit from programs such as Meals on Wheels, my enlightenment on the deprivations of starving Americans grew out of my assignment to the Agriculture Committee, notably its subcommittee on Nutrition. Among our responsibilities was oversight of the federal Food Stamp Program.

In the course of researching the program and assessing the need for it, our subcommittee traveled widely and to some of America's poorest communities. What I saw frankly shocked and saddened me. In areas as disparate as Appalachia and the slums of Chicago or New York, we saw parents who simply could not provide for their children. Too often we saw children who were wasting away.

Those meetings became more poignant and desperate during the 1980s, as Reagan's policies cut key food programs for many hungry Americans. In 1989, one survey concluded that requests for emergency food assistance in major American cities increased 96 percent that year. Roughly 60 percent of those requesting food were children or the parents of children. Poverty spread and deepened during the Reagan years; by the end of his time in office, there were more poor people and they were on average significantly poorer. What's more, most were working and still not able to afford the basics of life. Of the 32.5 million Americans living in poverty at the end of the 1980s, 18 million lived in households where at least one person had work. For many, food stamps were the difference between living and dying. I suppose I was naïve, but until seeing that for myself, I would not have believed that such desperation could coexist in this country with such bounty.

One of my principal guides through this discovery was Congressman Mickey Leland of Texas, a passionate and committed activist who dedicated his public service to eradicating hunger after visiting the Sudan in 1984 and seeing a starving girl literally die before his eyes.[5] Leland, who chaired the Congressional Black Caucus, impressed upon me the deep urgency of his cause, and we worked closely together, mostly on programs to alleviate hunger in the United States but also on supplying some aid to countries in famine. At his request, I joined his

Select Committee on Hunger in 1984, and remained a member during the rest of my years in Congress.

For a time, Congress accepted and appreciated the need for this most basic responsibility of government. A smart political coalition grew up around food stamps by including them in the same legislation that provided price supports for many agricultural products. Members of Congress from cotton, wheat, and corn states, for instance, would support the bill because it supplied their members with crucial supports, while urban members and those with very poor districts would sign on for the food stamp provisions. It wasn't a model of conscientious governance—it locked in expensive agricultural supports that in many cases went to agribusiness rather than the family farmers who were its more popular beneficiaries—but it was politically astute and enduringly effective. Year after year, we were able to secure passage of food stamp legislation that saved families. I have on my wall the various pens that presidents used to sign those bills. I can't look at them without thinking of the families who received that aid.

Among the many tragedies that have accompanied the collapse of leadership in Washington in recent years has been the breakdown of the consensus on food stamps. Tea Party conservatives, delighting in labeling President Obama the "food-stamp president," pointed to the dramatic rise in requests for emergency food as evidence of our slide into a welfare state or, more absurdly, socialism. It was not. It was the result of a bitter recession that commenced under President George W. Bush and that has gradually given way under President Obama. Nevertheless, food stamps remain a whipping boy. Members of Congress have demanded limits on the time that any recipient can qualify for food, and have demanded that recipients be cut off if they can't find work quickly.

Sensible people can disagree about the reach and effectiveness of welfare or any relief program. Food stamps are admittedly expensive, and there is undoubtedly waste to be addressed. Compassionate people, however, do not let children starve in order to make political points.

After my mother died, my father lived alone for a time at his home in the Carmel Valley. But solitude didn't suit him, and he became impatient for a companion. And when it came to matrimony, he knew what to do: He headed for Italy and back to Siderno. Amazingly, he struck gold again, meeting Teresa Ruggiero—we always called her Tita—and marrying her in the spring of 1970. The two of them lived in a guesthouse on the property while Sylvia and I and our sons enjoyed the main house—or at least I enjoyed it when I was home from Washington.

As the 1970s unfolded, my father's health faded. In February 1983, I was in Washington when Sylvia called to say he had died. I sat alone in my congressional office overlooking the Capitol and cried, my heart full with memories. He was buried next to my mother in the main cemetery in Monterey, inside a crypt he had picked out years before. He left me with an unshakable commitment to family and country, and a powerful sense of the responsibilities of a father. I loved him, admired him, and when he was gone missed him suddenly and deeply.

My stepmother stayed on at the house for another two decades, sharing the property with me and Sylvia and our children. Tita died in 2012.

One of the most complex and challenging tasks of my congressional tenure began with a failure.

The area in and around Monterey has been home to soldiers since even before California entered the Union, as it served as an army post during the Mexican-American War and the Gold Rush. In 1917, the army founded Camp Gigling in the area just north of Monterey, and that camp became first Camp Ord and later Fort Ord. At its peak, it was home to thousands of soldiers at any given time. Indeed, more than 1.5 million soldiers, including such diverse luminaries as actor Clint Eastwood and Jerry Garcia of the Grateful Dead, passed through the base between the beginning of World War II and the time I was elected to Congress. By the 1980s, it was the home of the army's 7th Infantry Division (Light). The American troops who participated in the invasion of Panama in 1989 were drawn largely from Fort Ord, and it played important roles in other U.S. actions as well.

It thus had seen its share of history, but more tangibly the fort was a major economic force in the Central Coast and my district. It had supplied jobs and economic benefit to the region for decades—the success of Carmelo's Café during the war, I well recalled, was largely fueled by the servicemen who came to appreciate my mother's friendly face and my father's homestyle cooking.

So as the United States began to consolidate its armed forces in the 1980s—in 1988, Congress approved the Defense Authorization and Base Closure and Realignment Act, which established a commission to identify and recommend base closures—I viewed it as my responsibility to my district to keep the base open. I began to work on Defense Department officials, pressing the case that the weather on the Central Coast was ideal, and very few if any bases enjoyed a longer training season. That also made it a useful staging area. When I first heard that Fort Ord was to be included on the list of bases slated for closure, I convened a group of retired officers in my district and we took our case directly to Colin Powell. The first list of recommended closures came out, and Fort Ord was not on it. We'd dodged a bullet.

But the process wasn't over, and the arguments for shutting down Fort Ord were formidable. For one thing, it lacked sufficient family housing, and finding affordable places to live outside the base was almost impossible in the expensive communities of Monterey and Carmel. Seaside, where the base was principally located, was a bit cheaper, but still out of reach of most army families. Recognizing that, I worked to develop affordable housing, but Powell worried, with some justification, that we'd never have enough. Moreover, Fort Ord lacked a major airfield, which complicated rapid deployments, as troops had to be moved to an airport before they could be sent on their missions. Finally, one criterion for base closures was how much the Department of Defense could get in return if it shut down facilities and sold them. Fort Ord sat on twenty-eight thousand acres of California coastland, including beaches and bluffs to rival those of Malibu. From the military's perspective, then, closing Fort Ord would save money, and selling it would bring in much more money. It was hard to argue with that logic.

When the next list of recommended closures appeared in 1991, Fort Ord was on it, and I recognized that our number was up. I came home one weekend with the bad news. "I think it's better if we accept this decision and move on," I told a group of community leaders who had been working on the issue for years. "We can't go on fighting this. . . . We have to replace Fort Ord in a way that will minimize damage to the area."

Those were hard words for many of my constituents to hear, and I have no doubt that many of them thought I'd let them down. But it moved the conversation forward, past a losing battle and into a constructive discussion about the future of that part of the Central Coast.

Making that shift was not easy. Before communities could work together on a plan, we had to confront the many rivalries and competing visions for the property. Seaside thought it should take the lead, since it was the community most directly adjacent to the base, but others had claims as well, since no town on that stretch of coastline had been unaffected by the presence of the army over so many generations. Anger over the decision also clouded easy debate over it. Many of my constituents believed the closure was done in retaliation for my vote on January 12, 1991, against the resolution authorizing President George H. W. Bush to take the United States to war in Iraq—a fear that I don't subscribe to, but mention here only because it demonstrates how high passions were running at the time.

In an effort to bring communities together, state senator Henry Mello—another great, pragmatic leader from the era—proposed the creation of an agency that would take the lead in implementing a re-use proposal. That became the Fort Ord Reuse Authority, which acted as the development agency for the property. Every city in the area was represented on the authority, and through the early 1990s a vision of the property began to take shape. Thankfully, early talk of locating a prison there faded away, and turned instead to the idea of building some sort of school on the land.

The University of California wasn't a good fit—for the sensible reasons that the Santa Cruz campus was just a few miles away and the university was committed to building its next campus in the state's Central Valley. That eventually became UC Merced, the newest state university campus. But the Cal State system was another option, and I happened to know that system's chancellor, Barry Munitz. I invited him to tour the property in the fall of 1991, and he immediately saw the potential. Not only was there a huge amount of land in a beautiful area, but there was also a gymnasium, roads, dormitories, water and sewer lines, electricity—infrastructure that would have cost millions of dollars to build from scratch. "You know," Barry said to me at the end of our tour, "this makes sense." Barry took the idea to the Cal State trustees, who approved, with the idea that the campus would initially be an adjunct of Cal State San Jose and eventually mature into a stand-alone school. The military, meanwhile, recognized that a high priority for former bases should be conversion for public purposes, so it agreed to donate a large swath of the property on the coastal edge to the new school.

Conversion began in the early 1990s, and my role in it changed in 1992, when President Bill Clinton named me as director of the Office of Management and Budget. One of my first calls upon accepting the assignment was to Barry. "You're going to read something about me in the paper tomorrow," I told him from Little Rock, where I'd gone for the announcement. "Don't worry about it. This could help." I assumed, rightly, that it wouldn't hurt our project for it to have the enthusiastic support of the president's budget director.

The school was dedicated on September 4, 1995, by President Clinton—who by then had been my boss twice, first during my time as budget director and then as the president's chief of staff. When the president agreed to attend, he asked for just two favors in return: He was planning on returning that weekend from Pearl Harbor, so he asked that he be able to fly from that ceremony to Monterey. And then he wanted to get in a round of golf at Pebble Beach on the morning of the dedication. We arranged for those, and the university's first class of incoming students was welcomed by the president of the United States.

Today, Cal State Monterey Bay is home to fifty-six hundred students, as well as the Panetta Institute for Public Policy. Other portions of the base are still being developed, and there's plenty of work yet to do, but already the reused base is generating more economic activity than Fort Ord did. And the future of the region is far less tied to a single entity, so the district today is better positioned to weather changes in the economy than it was when so much depended on the army's presence. It wasn't easy, but converting Ford Ord turned swords into plowshares and brought lasting benefit to my district.

The most far-reaching of my duties in Congress began in my second term and increasingly dominated my service through the 1980s and into the early 1990s. That was my work with the House Budget Committee, which I joined in 1979 and chaired from 1989 to 1994. At first the challenge was serious but more of management than conflict. That's because the Carter budgets were reasonable and fairly balanced, though stressed by the struggling economy. In my first term or so, my focus was on broadening some of his proposed budget cuts to include defense, which he had excluded for political reasons but where I was convinced we could find savings. I was also determined to look for waste in programs popular with my fellow Democrats, including Medicare and Medicaid and some areas involving veterans. In all, my goal was to find about $4 billion in so-called legislative savings, cuts from programs that were added to the president's budget by Congress and that I felt we needed to show greater discipline about.

As with the ethics questions I raised early in my first term, these weren't always popular, and some of my colleagues questioned why I was so determined to bring down the federal deficit. Then and now, I have two answers. The first is personal. My father was forcefully frugal. He never carried any debt, and once blew up at me when he discovered I was using a gas card. From as early as I can remember, he impressed on me and my brother the importance of paying our bills. Debt placed the debtor at risk, and saddled him with interest payments, both of which my father abhorred. With my father's voice thus ringing in my head, deficits struck me as irresponsible, especially in the context that the federal government accumulates them, effectively allowing one generation to borrow for its own prosperity while pushing off the repayment of that extravagance onto its children and grandchildren. My father was determined not to leave his children in debt; I saw no reason why my responsibility to the country should be any less.

Then there was the more policy-driven reality. Deficits over time create debt, and that debt has to be serviced. Every federal payment that goes toward debt service represents money taken out of today's economy. That is—or ought to be—as offensive to liberals as it is to conservatives, because money spent on debt service could otherwise be spent just as easily on education as on national defense, food stamps, missiles, or the post office. Debt service advances no policy or ambition. It is merely the price of having borrowed in the past.

As I learned the procedural niceties of Congress and the Budget

Committee, I also discovered a tool just waiting to be used in the service of reducing deficits. Known as "budget reconciliation," it allows the Budget Committee's subcommittee on Reconciliation to direct the authorizing committees to make cuts in order to bring their budgets into conformance with the overall budget resolution—"reconciling" the budget resolution with the individual spending authorizations, which can only be done by decreasing the proposed spending. That sounds technical, and it is, but it boils down to this: The chairman of the Reconciliation subcommittee can tell the chairs of the authorizing committees how much to cut, and if they refuse, that subcommittee chairman can effectively make the cuts himself by including them in a reconciliation bill for the entire House to consider. That strips the authorizing committees of their power and shifts enormous authority to the Reconciliation subcommittee chair. In 1981, as Ronald Reagan came to office, the authorizing committees of the House included some of its most veteran and venerable figures. The chairman of the Reconciliation subcommittee was me.

I spent much of that summer shadowing the work of House and Senate conference committees as they worked to hash out their differences and bring down the size of the budget deficit. I rarely spoke, but appeared often, sitting on the edge of the room and by my presence reminding the conferees that they'd better do the cutting or I'd do it for them. What's more, neither the budget resolution nor the reconciliation bill can be filibustered, so my power to oversee reconciliation wasn't subject to some of the more time-tested means of obstruction.

Nevertheless, it didn't go easily. As I told a reporter at the time, "Nothing in four and a half years compares to the time commitment and the totally consuming challenge" of implementing budget reconciliation that year. And much of my struggle was with fellow Democrats, who were fighting to preserve domestic programs while Reagan axed them to make room for his tax cut. I remember paying a visit to Billy Ford of Michigan. Ford had been in Congress since 1965—when

I was still in the army—and he chaired the Post Office Committee that year. I showed up one day with Ralph Regula of Ohio, my Republican Party counterpart on the Reconciliation subcommittee, and warned Ford that if he didn't make the necessary cuts to his budget, we'd make them for him.

"Are you kidding me?" Ford asked, incredulous. I assured him we meant it. He made the cuts. By the time we were done, we'd cut roughly $38 billion from the budget, and I'd used my authority to deliver on those reductions while wherever possible avoiding devastating cuts to the programs most vital to the poor, sick, and elderly, those most in need of the services of their government.

Soon the press was calling me the "chief enforcer" of federal budget cuts, and I began to be referred to as a "rising star" of the Democratic House.[6] Martin Tolchin of the *New York Times* in late 1981 included me as one of a "new generation of Democratic leaders" coming into our own in the Capitol. Tolchin generously said of me, "He is one of the best-liked men in Congress. He gained the esteem of his House colleagues whom he cajoled, wheedled and occasionally bullied last spring as chairman of a budget task force responsible for making House committees comply with budget cuts ordered by Congress."[7] The story was accompanied by a picture of me with an armful of documents and a big grin on my face.

I learned a couple of lessons in those months. First, the budget controls everything in Washington, and yet very few members of Congress really look carefully at it. Instead, members focus on their areas of interest and leave the big picture to others. By attending all those meetings, I genuinely knew the budget in a way few others did. That gave me the power of knowledge. In addition, I discovered the inherent power of reconciliation, and recognized it as a tool that could be used explicitly to override authorizing committees but implicitly to force others to act for fear that I would act for them. That gave me the power of position. In Congress, mastery of rules and information can trump position or tenure, though not many members understand that.

Finally, I realized that authority is best wielded with a smile. Rarely did I have to lecture or wag a finger in those months. I mostly listened and put my foot down only when I had to. I don't believe I ever used the power at my disposal to settle a score or get something solely for myself. For the most part, I had good relations not only with Democrats but also with Republicans. We were united in our conviction to get things done, and that actually did overcome our differences, at least most of the time.

When Reagan was elected in 1980, I braced for the worst politically. But President Reagan turned out to be less ideological and partisan than he appeared (and than he is remembered). A sort of residual bipartisanship persisted in those years. Despite the posturing and elbowing for advantage, eventually the leadership got to the deal, and the members generally fell in line.

I also soon realized that Reagan brought to the presidency something Carter had lacked—the ability to relate to the American people. When Carter spoke to the nation, the response was a yawn. When Reagan gave an Oval Office address urging support for one of his initiatives, our phones in Congress would ring off the hook with constituent calls.

As I noted earlier, he proposed a large tax cut and, with the support of conservative Democrats, got it. When he proposed a budget that cut some favorite Democratic programs, it passed over the opposition of many of my colleagues. With it came a requirement that put me, as chairman of the Reconciliation subcommittee, in a difficult position. Would I simply refuse to enforce the Reagan budget, or would I work with the leadership and the Republicans to implement reconciliation in the best way possible? I decided to be a chairman, not a partisan. It was a difficult challenge, working with Democratic chairmen who had to cut spending on programs many of them had authored. But I urged them to recognize that they, and they alone, could best minimize the damage from these cuts. Fortunately, Republicans in the Senate largely agreed with many of the priorities of Democrats in the House. The result was the largest reconciliation savings ever enacted by Congress. The effort held down deficits, though nothing could eliminate them in the face of Reagan's tax cuts and increased spending on defense. Always gifted with the personal touch, Reagan called me himself to thank me for my work on the budget, a courtesy Carter never showed me.

As time went on, Reagan and his staff developed working relationships with important Democrats, such as Tip O'Neill and Dan Rostenkowski. Together, those unlikely allies reformed Social Security, immigration, and the tax code. Reagan had his beliefs, but he was pragmatic enough to understand that bipartisan support would produce successful legislation. Yes, we had differences, but I recognized his gift for governing.

As the Reagan presidency wound down, Bush moved to succeed him, but Republicans were skeptical. Until his association with Reagan, Bush had represented the moderate faction of the party. He had supported abortion rights as a younger politician—his father was an early and vocal supporter of Planned Parenthood—and he had grown up as a privileged son of Washington, hardly the kind of outsider that Reagan had seemed to be. Tacking to reinvent himself, Bush announced his opposition to abortion. He also endorsed prayer in public schools and new federal death penalties. That positioned him correctly among social conservatives, but economic conservatives, the other demanding faction of the party with doubts about Bush, continued to view him as untrustworthy. Bush responded by trying to portray Bob Dole and later Democratic nominee Michael Dukakis as favoring tax increases. By contrast, Bush described his commitment to Reagan Republicanism with the most quoted and remembered line of his political life, his declamation on taxes: "My opponent now says he'll raise them as a last resort, or a third resort. But when a politician talks like that, you know that's one resort he'll be checking into. My opponent won't rule out raising taxes. But I will. And the Congress will push me to raise taxes, and I'll say no, and they'll push, and I'll say no, and they'll push again, and I'll say to them, 'Read my lips: no new taxes.'"

The delegates to the convention in New Orleans responded wildly to that promise, but Bush knew better—or at least he should have. Not long after his election, but before he was inaugurated, he invited me up to the vice president's house, and we talked about the budget challenges that he would face as president. I was candid with him. "If you're serious about dealing with this, ultimately you're going to have to move away from the whole 'Read my lips,'" I said. He answered, "Look, I know. I've taken that position, but my hope is that after a little time here, I may be able to adjust that position."

It wasn't that I was determined to raise taxes; rather, it was that I'd learned that serious attempts to balance the budget required that everything be on the table, including tax increases, cuts to discretionary spending, and reform of entitlement programs. We continued to talk it over, and I gave him my standard lecture on deficit reduction, one that appeals to leaders of both parties. "This is about resources," I said. "It's about whether you, as president of the United States, are going to have the resources you need to be able to invest in whatever your priorities are. Because if you allow these deficits to grow, they're going to rob you of your resources."

Bush stood firm for a while, but with the economy sluggish and deficits rising, he recognized that a responsible budget package needed more revenue. In May 1990, he convened a domestic budget summit at the White House, inviting twenty-one congressional leaders to join with his administration in trying to produce a budget that would stem rapidly growing deficits. Our goal was to cut the spending gap by $50 billion.

On June 26, 1990, Bush released a short statement on the status of the budget summit. Based on the talks, he said, "It is clear to me that both the size of the deficit problem and the need for a package that can be enacted require all of the following: entitlement and mandatory program reform, tax revenue increases, growth incentives, discretionary spending reductions, orderly reductions in defense expenditures, and budget process reform to assure that any bipartisan agreement is enforceable and that the deficit problem is brought under responsible control. The bipartisan leadership agree with me on these points."[8]

The reaction was immediate and withering. His next news conference was dominated by the breaking of his pledge—the first question he faced was whether his endorsement of new revenue represented a "betrayal."[9] To his credit, President Bush did the right thing for the country when he agreed to make tax increases part of that year's negotiations, and he defended his decision, at first, in just the way I would have argued it. "Good politics," he said, "is rooted in good government."

Bush's popularity plummeted in the months after he endorsed a tax increase, and Congress eventually passed a budget that did raise taxes on the wealthiest Americans. I thought then and still think that Bush could have ridden out the criticism from within his party, particularly because his numbers rebounded after the beginning of the Iraq war. But his reversal of his memorable pledge encouraged opponents to regard him as beatable, and he now faced an uprising on his right led by the unlikely candidacy of columnist Pat Buchanan. Bush defended the increases for a while, then got cold feet and began apologizing for them. It's glib to say that reneging on his promise cost Bush the 1992 election, but it certainly weakened him by reinforcing questions about his convictions and demoralizing the Republican base. Any group of voters willing to seriously consider Pat Buchanan for the presidency is, by definition, desperate. All of that created an opening for Bill Clinton, and he made the most of it.

Years later, I was a guest of President Bush at his library, and in a private moment I complimented him for having done the right thing on the budget that year. "It was," I told him, "one of the most important steps toward arriving at a balanced budget." I faulted him only for apologizing for it. "I know, I know," he said, "but I was concerned that I'd have a hard time at reelection if I didn't back off."

History has treated Bush's promise—and his reconsideration of it—harshly, but he demonstrated courage when he had to, and he put the country first. As the economy began to improve, and as Clinton took his own steps to bring down the deficit further, eventually the budget was balanced. Bush deserves his share of credit for that turnaround.

My years in government have given me many satisfactions. There have been opportunities to lead, to fashion policy, to see ideas translated into programs, to build and defend the country that my parents chose. And each of my assignments has been different—and with different rewards. I must say, though, that there are few jobs better than serving as a member of Congress. In those years I had a staff that made me proud, my wife was my partner in our work, I was allowed to roam the landscape in search of ways to make a difference, and I had no boss but my constituents, for whom I worked happily. I made my own schedule and reported to no one. I never thought I'd want to do anything else. Until one day I did.

SIX

"It's the Right Fight"

O n November 3, 1992, the voters of my district reelected me to my ninth term, this time with the support of more than 70 percent of those who cast ballots, more than three times as many votes as those of my closest opponent. In Washington, I chaired the Budget Committee and enjoyed good relations with my colleagues, and Bill Clinton's victory on that same election day meant that for the first time in twelve years, I would go about my work with the support of a Democrat in the White House. Safe in my district and well positioned in Congress, I looked forward to 1993 as an opportunity to make real progress on issues close to my heart.

By the time voters actually went to the polls, Clinton's election was not entirely unexpected, though no one would have predicted it eighteen months earlier. On March 3, 1991, Iraq had reluctantly accepted the terms of a cease-fire that brought the Gulf War, Operation Desert Storm, to a conclusion. It had not succeeded in what some regarded as its fundamental mission—the ouster of Saddam Hussein—but Iraq had been driven from Kuwait and bombarded into submission. As of that day, nearly nine out of ten Americans approved of George H. W. Bush's work as president.[1] Any pundit taking the measure of Bush's presidency at that point would have been laughed off the talk show circuit if he'd predicted that Bush would not be reelected. Leading Democrats took note, and many of those who aspired to the presidency put their plans on hold. New York governor Mario Cuomo flirted with a bid, but opted out, as did New Jersey senator Bill Bradley. House Speaker Dick Gephardt and Senator Al Gore, both of whom had run in 1988, took a pass as well. Along with many Democrats, I resigned myself to another four years of Republican rule in the White House.

But one lesson I had learned long ago was that public opinion is fickle, and a faltering economy quickly overtook the glow of wartime victory. Bush's popularity began a precipitous descent as the recession set in, and his invincibility collapsed. Between October 1991 and February 1992, he dropped twenty points in the polls, and he continued downward from there. By the middle of 1992, fewer than one in three Americans approved of his performance. Few presidents have ever squandered more goodwill more quickly.

Bill Clinton, meanwhile, doggedly marched on. Determined to present himself as a "New Democrat," Clinton ran as a southern moderate—liberal on many leading social issues but supportive of the death penalty and gun ownership, in favor of a tax cut, and willing, even eager, to depart from Democratic orthodoxy in areas such as welfare reform. He announced his candidacy on October 3, 1991, with a direct appeal to the middle class, much of which had drifted into the Republican column during Reagan's terms. Clinton's mission, he said, was "restoring the hopes of the forgotten middle class." I've never known a politician with a better instinct for the political center. Clinton grabbed it firmly.

That year's presidential election was both clarified and complicated by the third-party candidacy of Ross Perot, the personable if slightly eccentric Texas businessman who ran an idiosyncratic race that year.

Backed by homemade charts and homespun charm, Perot launched blunt attacks on Washington and especially the national debt that earned him a substantial legion of followers and made him difficult to ignore. He campaigned through a series of thirty-minute infomercials in which he colorfully took aim at President Bush and other political leaders responsible for job losses—the "giant sucking sound" of Mexico taking formerly American jobs was one of Perot's more memorable images—and for leading the nation to financial ruin by running up increasingly unsustainable deficits and debt. Somewhat to my surprise, after years of my arguing the significance of deficit reduction to often glassy-eyed audiences, Perot's pitch hit the mark. He appeared briefly to be a serious contender—at one point he actually finished first in a presidential poll—and forced the rest of the field to grapple with his issue. Since that also happened to be my issue, I was glad to see the field contend with it, even if deficit reduction's champion was the slightly goofy Perot.

Clinton always had a sensitive ear for the populace, and Perot's message began to influence him as well, though he had to fight through controversies to get there. Although he was substantively trying to make the case for a "New Covenant," his campaign careened from explaining his relationship with Gennifer Flowers to defending his avoidance of the draft to insisting that while he had tried marijuana he had not inhaled. He persevered, one of the qualities I would come most to admire in him. After finishing behind Massachusetts senator Paul Tsongas in New Hampshire, Clinton bounced back on Super Tuesday, when a sweep of southern states propelled him into the lead for the nomination. Tsongas dropped out, and Clinton was the last man standing.

On the Republican side, Bush was paying the price for inviting Americans to read his lips. Pat Buchanan seemed unlikely to convince a majority of voters, even of his own party, to support him, but he stirred conservative unease with Bush, and won nearly 40 percent of the New Hampshire primary vote. Like Clinton, Bush rebounded, but he was clearly wounded.

With the country slogging through a mild recession and Perot gnawing on the issue of the debt, it was natural that Republicans would debate the nation's fiscal strength. What surprised me was that Bush would do it so badly. He never seemed to find the right answer to questions about the economy. During one debate, a member of the audience asked each of the candidates how the national debt and recession had affected them personally, and Bush looked cross and confused as he fumbled around for an answer. His disavowal of the 1988 tax hike didn't bring conservatives back to him, and it denied him what I believe would have been his stronger argument—that the nation's needs were more important than any political promise. Bush had shown guts by doing what he believed was best for the country; instead, he appeared weak.

Clinton pounced on the divisions within the Republican Party and the nagging uncertainties about Perot's temperament. The Clinton campaign already was advancing the notion of a middle-class tax cut as part of an economic stimulus package, but Perot's emphasis on the debt—and Bush's reluctance to talk about that issue for fear of reminding people of his tax hike—led Clinton to embrace deficit reduction as well. His specific promise was to cut the deficit in half in four years. The result was a bit incoherent—the middle-class tax cut would increase the deficit, so the two proposals were at cross-purposes—but it nevertheless marked an important moment in my mind: For the first time in my political career, we were engaged in a serious national discussion of the deficit, with a Democratic presidential candidate endorsing the need to bring the budget into balance.

As the campaign progressed, Clinton's connection to the American people deepened. He defied conventional political wisdom at the convention and, rather than balancing his ticket geographically or ideologically, picked fellow southerner and fellow moderate Al Gore as his running mate. The two then decamped for a bus tour that crackled with energy. I'd known Al from my first days in Congress—we were freshmen together—and I could sense the enthusiasm he brought to the campaign and the friendship he shared with Clinton.

There was one particular moment when I realized the Clinton-Gore ticket had luck on its side. We were preparing to dedicate the Monterey Bay National Marine Sanctuary, and I invited President Bush to attend—he had been supportive, and I appreciated his work on behalf of that important issue for my district. By then, however, the Bush campaign had written off California, and the president declined. Instead, Al Gore made an appearance. As he strode to the lectern to address the crowd on a perfect, blindingly blue Central Coast day, a sailboat swept across the water behind him, providing a picturesque backdrop. *This*, I thought to myself, *is something special.*

Perot, having helped shape the race, abruptly dropped out as the Democrats were nominating Clinton, and then just as abruptly dropped back in. That reinforced questions about his judgment, as did his selection of Admiral James Stockdale, who memorably distinguished himself during the vice presidential debate with his opening question: "Who am I? Why am I here?" Still, while Perot didn't come close to winning, he drew almost 19 percent of that year's presidential vote, torpedoing any chance that Bush might have had at being reelected. Clinton did not win a majority of the popular vote (nor would he in 1996), but he prevailed over Bush and headed for the White House.

With Clinton elected president, Democrats in charge of both houses, and the deficit squarely on the national agenda, I had great hopes and was preparing for the coming term. It did not turn out as I imagined.

I was home for Thanksgiving and out on the ranch pruning apricot trees one afternoon when the phone rang. Sylvia answered it, and called for me. It was Warren Christopher, the universally respected Los Angeles lawyer and political operative whom I had known for years, going

back to when he served under President Carter—Christopher had been
a deputy attorney general under Lyndon Johnson and then a deputy
secretary of state under Carter, perhaps best remembered for negotiating the successful release of the American hostages in Iran. He returned
to Los Angeles during the Reagan and Bush years—he chaired the
commission that examined the Los Angeles Police Department after
the beating of Rodney King and that led to profound reforms of that
agency—but Clinton had summoned him back to help the president-
elect form his cabinet. That meant that a call from Christopher in November 1992 was something many leading Democrats were hoping to
get. I dropped my pruning shears and hustled inside.

Always discreet, Christopher did not spell out precisely what he
and Clinton had in mind for me, but he asked whether I would be willing to pay Clinton a visit in Little Rock. I was honored to be asked,
though a bit unsure about taking a spot in the administration. After
all, I had just been reelected, liked my work, and had an important job
in Congress. Nevertheless, the following morning I was en route to
Arkansas.

Truth be told, while I was flattered and a bit nervous about the
conversation I was headed into, I was not entirely surprised to get
the call. House majority leader Dick Gephardt, whom I had known
since he first arrived in Congress as my classmate in 1976, had already
made the trip to Little Rock, and when he returned he told me that he,
Speaker Tom Foley, and George Mitchell, the Democratic leader in the
Senate, had recommended me to Clinton as a possible budget director
in the new White House. Although Christopher hadn't mentioned that
possibility, I figured it was probably the reason I was heading to Little
Rock. Still, nothing had been offered, and Clinton and I barely knew
each other, so it was hardly certain that I'd get that position or any
other.

The national political press corps had relocated to Little Rock immediately after the election—the Holiday Inn and the Capital Hotel

both were teeming with reporters—and a number were staked out at the governor's mansion, a stately, fenced-off residence in a leafy neighborhood just a couple miles from downtown. When I arrived at the Little Rock airport, I was hurried into a waiting SUV with tinted windows and driven to a back entrance of the mansion so I could enter unobserved. I did, though I caught a glimpse of the reporters as my car slipped through the gate—my first brush with the cat-and-mouse game that the Clintons and the press would play with one another through the presidency. Once inside, the first person I encountered was Hillary Clinton, whom I had met only once, at an education event in Washington during the campaign.

Hillary was warm and welcoming. She extended a hand and spoke briskly. "I'm glad you're here and glad you'll be talking with Bill," she said. Though friendly, our conversation was notably professional, not social. She was there to vet candidates, not make them feel at ease. Before parting, she took me upstairs and introduced me to her husband.

Wearing a shirt and tie but no coat, Bill Clinton welcomed me into the library, both of us recalling that we had actually met one other time, before he became a presidential candidate. Our first meeting came about when Clinton, then still a governor, joined his gubernatorial colleagues for a discussion with the House leadership on increasing federal aid to education. On that occasion we spoke only briefly, but I recalled raising with him my concerns about the ramifications of increased spending on the federal deficit. As a result, though this was a get-acquainted session, it was also a return to familiar topics.

Clinton was serious and focused, ravenously intelligent, and eager to understand the federal budget process, which was very different from the system he'd worked in Arkansas. There, he pressed his proposals directly with the Arkansas legislature, even working the chamber in person, whereas the federal process—including the budget resolution, the potential for reconciliation, and the need for the two houses to resolve conflicts by conference committee—was all new to him. I took a few minutes to explain the budget process—it's byzantine enough that most members of Congress don't really understand it—and was impressed by how quickly he got it. Most important, he understood without any prompting from me the essential fact of any government spending plan: Budgets are not really about numbers; they are about priorities.

Clinton had been elected by an American people convinced that he was the best option for restoring the economic health of the country, and he knew that process would be centered on the ways the federal government raised and spent money. What would it invest in? How much compassion could the government extend to the poor without undermining the larger budget? How much of the tax burden could the rich afford to pay without stifling incentives to invest and grow? What actions could the government take to guide the private economy and encourage investors? Those decisions would shape Clinton's legacy and the nation's history, and he was grappling with them already, even before he had named his economic team or taken the oath of office.

Consummately political, Clinton also understood that even a perfect economic plan is useless if it remains a plan. He wanted to know what the deal might look like. Was bipartisan support possible? he asked.

Ah, I thought, *there's the $64,000 question.* The politics of Washington were quietly in flux just at that moment, and Clinton was stepping into a changing world. There were many contributors to the increasingly noxious environment that would soon engulf the Clinton administration, but the man I regard as most responsible was Newt Gingrich. The congressman from Georgia arrived in Washington in 1979, not long after I did, but really made his debut in 1984, when he spied a loophole in the House's rules for televising its proceedings. Those rules dictated that only the member speaking be shown on camera. Late on an evening when the chamber was almost empty and during the time reserved for special orders—an open period where members can speak on any subject—Gingrich launched a tirade against Democrats, accusing us of betraying the military by supporting cuts in defense spending, and daring us to respond. He knew, of course, that there was no one present to offer any such response, but he was playing to the camera and manipulating the rules—two characteristics that would come to define him. Tip O'Neill was incensed and made the decision to let the cameras pan back to show the empty chamber during special orders. Tip had called the bluff, but it only encouraged the Republicans allied with Gingrich to push harder.

Later that year, their ire turned on me. I was at that time still a member of the House Administration Committee, and our responsibilities included reviewing disputed elections to determine whom the House should seat. Frank McCloskey, a Democrat from Indiana running for reelection for the first time, finished neck-and-neck with his Republican challenger, Rick McIntyre, the beneficiary of Reagan's coattails. Indiana's secretary of state called it for McIntryre, but by less than fifty votes. That was close enough to warrant an investigation, and I headed it, joined by one Democrat, Bill Clay of Missouri, and one Republican, Bill Thomas of California. At first, things seemed to go pretty well. We agreed on rules for counting ballots, how to examine chads, how to discern a voter's intent. (All this would become a national obsession in 2000, when the race between Al Gore and George Bush hung on the same questions, but it was new for us in 1984 and 1985.) Having agreed on rules, we then proceeded to count. In the end, we determined that McCloskey had won by four votes. Although Thomas had agreed to the rules and process for the recount, he wasn't prepared to accept the result. He screamed of improprieties, but the General Services Administration certified it. As I said at the time, I wish it had been a hundred votes, but we were stuck with the result.

Gingrich smelled the political possibilities of Democrats helping another Democrat to reelection in such a close race. Disregarding our work and the validation of the GSA, he led a walkout. For weeks there were bitter feelings, but those Republicans with whom I had worked closely in the past quietly drifted back, acknowledging that the count was what it was and that Republicans would have done the same if one of theirs had won by four votes. McCloskey returned and two years later stood for reelection again. To my relief, that time he won by more than a thousand votes, so we didn't have to go through such a process again. In the meantime, Gingrich's divisive tactics had scored another publicity point.

There are two other incidents worth mentioning in chronicling Gingrich's rise at the expense of working relations in Washington. In 1987, he accused House Speaker Jim Wright of a list of low-rent ethics charges, and the House Ethics Committee assigned a special counsel to investigate. The case dragged on—special counsels have a way of eating up time and money—and Wright eventually quit. "I was worn out," he told journalist and author Joe Klein.[2] Who could blame him?

Finally, during the House banking scandal that broke in 1992, Gingrich insisted that the names of House members who had overdrawn their accounts be made public. He knew that once he demanded a vote on the matter, the rest of us would have to agree, and his stunt upended many relations in the chamber merely for the sake of attention and publicity. Incidentally, it turned out that my accounts were slightly askew—the bank had mistakenly charged my account twice for one withdrawal, so I was owed $2,500. Gingrich, by contrast, had overdrawn his account more than twenty times, including writing a bad check to the Internal Revenue Service.

To be fair, Republicans had been burned too. When they had endorsed cost containment for Social Security as part of their deficit reduction budget during the Bush presidency, Democrats turned the issue against them, charging that they were undermining security for the elderly, a reliable and easily spooked voting demographic. And going back further, when Reagan nominated Judge Robert Bork to the Supreme Court in 1987, Democrats, led by Senator Kennedy, waged a furious and highly ideological campaign against him. The politics of personal destruction may have been perfected by Gingrich, but both sides practiced it by the time Clinton became president. And with leaders on both sides feeling beaten up, they were not enthusiastic about exposing themselves again.

Nevertheless, as I told Clinton that afternoon, I did hold out some hope of bipartisan agreement on a budget, and I argued that any deal would be better if members of both parties joined it. The Senate had some Republicans—Bob Dole of Kansas and Pete Domenici of New Mexico were two I mentioned—who might be persuaded to support an overarching deal that included both revenue and cuts. On the House side, Gingrich and his aggressive partisans would be unreachable, but I had worked closely with Bill Frenzel, a moderate Republican from Minnesota, for many years. He retired in 1991, but there was a tradition of deal-making on the budget that might be resuscitated if Clinton's package included something for everyone. Moreover, Bob Michel was still minority leader, and he believed that both parties had a responsibility to govern.

Finally, Clinton asked about investments. Throughout the campaign, he had argued for federal investments in education, technology, and research—promises that were going to be hard to keep if deficit reduction was going to be his central goal. "You can't do everything," I responded, "but you can make some key investments." What would guide those decisions, I said, would be his vision for the country, what programs he chose to invest in, and where cuts could be made to accommodate those new investments. As I stressed to him then, "This is not just about who you're going to screw."

Clinton laughed at that, and though he took no notes, I could see him file away fact after fact mentally. We had been scheduled to talk for an hour, but more than three passed before I snuck out the back door and returned to the airport.

It seemed to me that the meeting had gone well. As we prepared to part, he asked if I might be interested in the budget director's job. I said I would be prepared to support his budget, either as chairman of the House Budget Committee or as his OMB director, if offered the job. I returned to California wondering what would happen next.

I appreciated Clinton's intuitive grasp of politics, his obvious intelligence and astonishing ability to sift through facts. What most impressed me then and later, though, was his empathy for average people. He read a budget document and saw intuitively the way that changes would ripple out into the world.

There were drawbacks to Clinton's gift: He could talk an issue into the ground as he searched for its real-life implications. There was, at least in those early days, no such thing as a short meeting with him. Still, we enjoyed each other. He later wrote that he was impressed by my "knowledge, energy, and down-to-earth manner," and that certainly was true of me with regard to him.

No word came immediately from Little Rock, so I returned to Washington in early December to prepare for the coming congressional session. One Sunday evening, I attended the Kennedy Center Honors and was sitting near the left aisle in an orchestra seat. I was dressed in my tuxedo and accompanied by Frank Vaca, a good friend and lobbyist for the dairy industry (his name, in both Spanish and Italian, means cow), when an usher quietly approached and asked if I was Congressman Panetta. After I assured him that I was, he told me I had a message in the lobby. It was from Warren Christopher, and when I called him back from a lobby pay phone, he asked if I would come to Little Rock that week to accompany the president-elect for an announcement.

A little unsure of the etiquette involved, I gingerly asked whether I was being offered "that position."

"The president-elect wants to ask you to accept that position," Christopher responded. He also asked if I had any objection to Alice Rivlin's being named my deputy. To the contrary, I was honored to have her on board, and told him so. Needless to say, I don't remember much about the rest of the Kennedy Center program that night.

I didn't mention the conversation to anyone but Sylvia, and the Clinton team insisted on keeping the announcement quiet until the president-elect could make it public, but nothing stays quiet for long in Washington. The next day, as I was making the rounds in the House, members sought me out to congratulate me. I played dumb. The newspapers were less constrained. Even before I had publicly been offered the job, they were soliciting reactions to my appointment.

On December 9, I flew to Little Rock and was taken to the Hilton, where a reservation had been made for me under the name L. P. Currie—chosen, I presume, because Betty Currie was Clinton's personal secretary. After briefings from Christopher, George Stephanopoulos, and Harold Ickes, Clinton introduced his economic team to the press.

The biggest name on that team was Senator Lloyd Bentsen, whom Clinton nominated to be his first secretary of the treasury. Tall, elegant, almost regal, Bentsen was perhaps best known for his withering dismissal of Dan Quayle during their 1988 vice presidential debate. Staring down at Quayle after Quayle compared himself to John F. Kennedy, Bentsen let him have it: "Senator, I served with Jack Kennedy. I knew Jack Kennedy. Jack Kennedy was a friend of mine. Senator, you are no Jack Kennedy." That remark defined Quayle's image for the campaign, but in a sense it was uncharacteristic of Bentsen, who was a moderate, fiscally conservative millionaire at ease with leaders of both parties. (He had once been the youngest member of the House, and when he won his Senate seat in 1970, he did it by beating Congressman George Bush, whom many Texas Republicans viewed as suspiciously liberal.)

Clinton also nominated Robert Rubin as chair of a new entity, the National Economic Council. Bob had experience on Wall Street at

Goldman Sachs, had advised the president-elect on economic issues during the campaign, and was also a strong advocate for controlling the deficit.

Taken together, then, Clinton's selections of Bentsen, Rubin, and me signaled that his approach to his presidency—at least in its approach to budgets and spending—was indeed going to be a departure from Democratic orthodoxy. In fact, some of the early reaction to our appointments was praise—from Republicans. Senator John Chafee of Rhode Island, a ranking Republican on the Banking and Finance committees, called Bentsen "thoughtful and sound" and said I was "someone who is concerned about the deficits and is willing to do something about them."[3] As those comments suggested, Bentsen, Rubin, and I were regarded as "deficit hawks," determined to cut spending and, if necessary, raise taxes in order to reduce or eliminate the deficits that were absorbing an increasing amount of government spending. In the battle that was about to ensue—one that would in many ways define the Clinton presidency—Bentsen and I were to occupy one camp.

The Clinton economic program began, in perfectly Clintonian fashion, with a large public seminar on the economy. On December 14, less than a week after Clinton had named his economic team, the president-elect hosted a two-day gathering in Little Rock that brought together policy makers, academics, and business leaders from around the country to discuss the state of the economy and proposals to get it back on track. That meant long discussions over arcane matters— exactly what Clinton loved most. He presided over the entire ten-hour discussion, swiveling in his chair at the head of the table and grilling participants with an array of questions. NPR and C-SPAN carried the event live, though it's hard to imagine any listener as attentive as the president-elect.

With those conversations still ringing in our ears, Clinton and the economic team convened for the first of a series of defining deliberations in early January. As we did, the Bush administration dealt us one last difficulty, announcing that the projected budget deficit for the coming year had leapt by 30 percent. We now faced a shortfall of $300 billion, with later years soaring even higher unless action were taken now. Those increased estimates added to the burden on Clinton, since his campaign promise was to cut the deficit in half in four years.

Within Clinton's team, there were distinct factions over how seriously to regard the deficit and how aggressively to attack it. Bob Reich, Clinton's old friend and his newly appointed secretary of labor, believed the emphasis of our program, at least at the outset, should be on stimulating the still-sluggish economy and investing in areas such as education and technology. Bob, whom I thought of as the administration's conscience, was a formidable advocate, and was joined by George Stephanopoulos, who had played an important role in the campaign and was preparing to become the administration's chief spokesperson. In addition, the campaign people—James Carville, Gene Sperling, and Paul Begala—questioned the political value of deficit reduction, since cuts invariably are painful and since their chief concern was reviving the economy quickly so the president could reap the electoral rewards of recovery. Finally, there was Laura Tyson, the newly named chair of the Council of Economic Advisers. Laura approached these questions not from the perspective of politics but rather from a deep conviction that government existed to help those most in need, and that protecting and expanding social programs was thus essential.

Those colleagues represented what you might consider the "left" of our team. They were not opposed to deficit reduction, but they argued that it should not trump social programs, economic stimulus, or investment.

On the other side of the debate were me and my deputy, Alice Rivlin, along with Bentsen; Rubin; Larry Summers, Rubin's deputy; and Roger Altman, the new deputy at Treasury. In addition, Vice President Al Gore believed in—and had voted in Congress for—deficit reduction.

His style was to discern the president's views on the issue and then help inform and guide them, but he did so against the backdrop of his own deeply held beliefs formed as a representative from Tennessee. As with those on the other side of these discussions, none of us were absolutists. We were Democrats too, and none of us argued for deficit reduction at the expense of a decent society. We too saw value in investment and the need to protect the elderly, the impoverished, and other vulnerable members of society. Our central argument, however, was that deficit reduction helped liberate the private economy and free the government, long-term, to achieve precisely those goals.

The debates between those camps, and later in Congress, was in my view one of the most consequential acts of government during my years of service.* It tested the values of both parties and the resolve of the president. And though the debate may seem remote from this point in history, it represents an example of government successfully identifying a need and accomplishing a task of great importance. It thus seems important to me to revisit it at some length in order to understand how in 1993 we embarked on a series of decisions that would, for the first time in nearly half a century, balance the federal budget.

The Clinton-team deficit debate began in earnest on January 7, even before Clinton had been sworn in as president. His economic team was summoned back to Little Rock, this time without the subterfuge of assumed names and SUVs with tinted windows. Clinton set aside five hours for the meeting, and Rubin organized the session, deciding not to argue on behalf of any policy position himself but rather to lead the conversation and move it between the various advisers.

We were scheduled to begin at nine that morning, but Clinton was

---

*A fascinating study by the Brookings Institution in 2000, based on a survey of 450 history and science professors, ranked reducing the federal budget deficit as one of the ten most important achievements of the federal government in the second half of the twentieth century, and found that it was exceeded in terms of difficulty only by reducing workplace discrimination. The study may be found at http://www.brookings.edu/research/papers/2000/12/11governance-light.

habitually late in those days, and this was no exception. While we awaited his arrival, the rest of us chatted and drank coffee around a large conference table that dominated the room. It was mostly small talk, but there was a powerful sense of significance to the day—all of us recognized that we were opening a debate that would determine the new presidency's place in history. Clinton finally arrived, and we all sat down at the conference table. He and the first lady and vice president sat to my right at one end of the table. Most of the economic team spread out to my left, and much of the campaign staff sat across from us.

Rubin made brief introductions and outlined the agenda, then turned to me to open the formal meeting. I dove immediately into what I regarded as the principal challenge confronting us: The deficit, I said, was large and growing and threatening to swallow up other priorities. Every dollar spent to service the national debt was a dollar that could not be used to lift up the poor or care for the sick, so deficit reduction would over time give us money to spend on those who needed it. Clinton had heard this before, in our meeting a few weeks earlier. As I made my pitch, he nodded but did not speak.

Others then filled in. Laura Tyson outlined the state of the economy and warned that without some change in approach, growth would be slow over the next few years, held back by skittish investors and high unemployment. Alan Blinder presented a series of charts explaining the relationship between federal spending, interest rates, and economic growth. His presentation suggested an appealing economic idea—bringing down the deficit would likely encourage Alan Greenspan and the Federal Reserve to lower interest rates, which would generate growth—but raised a daunting political cost. If the result was to delay an economic recovery, the benefits might not be realized for years and thus could cut short the Clinton presidency. It all depended on interest rates dropping and the bond market responding.

In Bob Woodward's account of this meeting, he recorded the

president-elect's response, and though I can't recall Clinton's exact words, Woodward's reporting mirrors my memory of Clinton at that moment. As Woodward wrote, "Clinton's face turned red with anger and disbelief. 'You mean to tell me that the success of the program and my reelection hinges on the Federal Reserve and a bunch of fucking bond traders?'"[4] There was unfortunately some truth to that.

When the discussion returned to me, I had my own stack of charts, and I riffled through a long list of potential places to cut spending—ideas that I'd accumulated through my time on the House Budget Committee. Defense, of course, was one, as were entitlement programs such as Medicare. In some cases we could reap significant savings not by cutting benefits dramatically but rather by limiting growth in the programs. Still, nothing is painless when it comes to deficit reduction. And the politics of this issue could be brutal on all sides—any Medicare savings could be attacked as robbing from the elderly, any fee or tax as stealing from working families, and any defense cut as weakening America.

One overarching uncertainty involved another aspect of Clinton's campaign and vision for the country. As a candidate, he had made a forceful pitch for reforming health care, and he was committed to pursuing some sort of revamp of that system in his first term. As we discussed the budget that January morning, however, none of us knew precisely what he had in mind, nor how much it might cost or save. Alice Rivlin suggested that for the purposes of the budget, we should consider health care a wash—in other words, it would neither add to the deficit nor subtract from it. Others thought it might tip one way or the other, and some later estimates suggested that it might require an additional $100 billion a year in federal spending to implement and enforce a mandate on all employers to provide health insurance and to extend Medicare to more of the unemployed. It was telling and portentous, though, that predictions varied wildly and that the proposals were vague.

On the other side of the budget discussion was revenue. There, Clinton was wrestling with his pledge to advance a middle-class tax cut against the arguments made by me and others that the first priority should be to cut the deficit. It was possible to do both, of course, but that would only deepen cuts or require other sources of revenue. Into that conversation suddenly charged Al Gore with a proposal to impose a tax on energy, known as the BTU tax (British thermal units are a common measure of energy). Gore liked to think big—he specifically urged Clinton that day to be bold—and the BTU tax certainly fit that bill. It could help close the deficit and encourage the development of alternative energy sources like solar and wind power by making them competitively more advantageous.

All of that sounded good, and it was the kind of idea that had often been raised in Washington think tanks. Like many proposed new taxes, it came with complicated questions. How would we collect it, for instance? Was it a tax on oil producers or refiners or gas stations? And what were the politics of the idea? I assumed it would cost us support in oil-producing states; Bentsen, from Texas, viewed the idea warily from the start. As chair of the Senate Finance Committee, he was very aware of the political pressures that could confront the BTU proposal; there is no more formidable lobby in Washington than the oil lobby, and in this case the tax's complexity would make it especially hard to defend. Bentsen instead favored raising taxes on top incomes and corporations, sin taxes, and possibly a gas tax.

Still, Gore's proposal survived that first meeting, and we began to build our budget with it in play. It also allowed Clinton to cling to the idea that he could still cut income taxes for the middle class and reduce the deficit by making up the losses taxing energy.

My focus remained on the deficit, and I presented the president-elect with three alternatives at that January meeting. The most ambitious would bring the deficit down to $195 billion over four years; the least would reduce it to $240 billion in that same period. I favored the lowest possible deficit, and liked the symbolism of getting it under $200 billion, which I thought would send the right message to the Fed and the markets. Alice Rivlin, along with most of the economic transition team, and Al Gore agreed. Tyson worried about cutting too much, too fast. Clinton kept his counsel.

Finally, there was the issue of economic stimulus. "It's the economy, stupid," was Clinton's well-known slogan during his campaign, and though the economy showed some signs of improving by early 1993, many of those at the table worried that without a jolt in the form of business tax credits or an injection of short-term federal spending, the recovery could falter. At our January meeting, Clinton seemed inclined to back some stimulus, though he did not settle on a figure or a precise way to allocate it.

As the conversation that day wound on, others at the table warned of the potential downsides of significant deficit reduction, especially if unaccompanied by a stimulus package. The Fed might not cooperate, leaving interest rates high and thwarting recovery; drawing $50 or $60 billion a year out of the economy in the form of reduced federal spending might throw the country back into a recession. And after the meeting, the president-elect's political advisers chimed in, reminding him of the obvious: Tax cuts are more popular than deficit reduction, and he was elected largely because the American people believed he was better equipped to help working men and women get back on their feet. Those were not small matters, and Clinton sized up the risks. At stake were nothing less than the health of the American economy and the future of his presidency, which he had yet to commence.

In his memoirs, Clinton said that at the conclusion of that day's long meeting, "I decided that the deficit hawks were right."[5] He did not, however, share that decision with the rest of us. I left feeling that while we had made our case, the president-elect still seemed undecided about what direction he would take.

Over the coming weeks, Clinton plunged into the minutiae of the budget. He loved details, and rather than let his advisers hash out the specific cuts and reserve himself for setting broad policy, he dove into the most minute matters. We proposed raising the fees assessed against state-chartered banks in order to cover the full costs of examining their books, a proposal that would raise $1.4 billion. Clinton worried that it might push some banks into insolvency and hurt us politically in North Carolina, a major banking center. We proposed having the government take over the student loan program rather than backing loans made by private banks, potentially saving $2.2 billion. Clinton liked the idea, a version of which he had floated during the campaign, but it required a short-term expenditure in order to set up the new program. We shelved it. We wanted to trim agricultural price subsidies, but each one of those subsidies had a devoted constituency, so cuts there threatened to come at a high political cost. We proceeded with caution. We considered ending below-cost timber sales, where the government allows loggers to fell trees on public land at less than the cost to taxpayers, but recognized that it might increase unemployment in certain areas of the Northwest. We even looked at fees for boaters who were rescued by the Coast Guard. That one tickled Clinton. "So, Harry's out there drowning," he mused, chuckling, "and before you can throw him a lifeline, you're going to make sure he can pay?"

On and on this went. Clinton spent hours going through those proposals one at a time, accepting some, tossing out others. Bentsen famously described Clinton as "the meetingest man I ever met," and that was evident in January 1993, as he prepared to assume the presidency of the United States by debating how much we could raise from charging boaters to be towed to a nearby dock when their craft ran out of gas.

One inviting target for cuts, though one with a particular political nuance, was transportation. There the budget included dozens of projects that had received appropriations but had not been authorized by the Senate's Transportation Committee. That made them easy to cut on a principled basis because they had no business being on the books without authorization. And since they amounted to more than $8 billion, eliminating those projects would buy a big chunk of deficit reduction. The trouble was that many of those projects were in the budget because Senator Robert Byrd, the wily West Virginia veteran of the Senate, had put them there, and as the chairman of the Appropriations Committee he was a dangerous man to antagonize. We went ahead and included those cuts in the proposed budget, but we knew we weren't done with that issue.

As a matter of fact, just before the budget was to go to press, Senator Byrd found out about the transportation cuts and called me. "Leon," he said, "your budget and appropriations process is going to be extremely important to this administration, and you're going to need me in your corner." If we insisted on balancing the budget by cutting those projects, the senator added, his rich accent coating his threat, "I'm not going to be with you." Nervously, I took that news to Clinton, who understood without prompting from me how difficult it would be to win passage of this budget without Byrd's help. Clinton folded. As he said, "We can't afford to lose Byrd." We restored the projects and scrambled for other cuts to make up the difference.

Our meetings were daily affairs, often lasting several hours, and eating up much of January and February. The president attended all of them, as did Gore, Bentsen, Rubin, Stephanopoulos, Commerce Secretary Ron Brown, Bob Reich, and I. The first lady attended some but not all, and other staff members came and went depending on that day's issue. It was exhausting and sometimes tedious, but by the time it was over, Clinton understood the range of activity of the federal government better than almost anyone else alive. As far as I know, no other modern president has ever taken the time to examine every line of the federal budget.

Over the course of those meetings, the specifics of our proposal gradually hardened. It would include one dollar of cuts for every dollar of new spending (we had started with the goal of two dollars of cuts per dollar of spending, but fell back when we simply felt we could not cut more and get a deal with Democrats or spend more and hope for Republican backing). It included Gore's BTU tax, a hike in the top income tax bracket from 31 percent to 39.6 percent (individuals earning more than $115,000 per year or couples earning more than $140,000 would pay a marginal tax rate of 36 percent, while single or married filers earning more than $250,000 would pay a 39.6 percent marginal rate; in 1993, that amounted to increases for about 1.2 percent of all taxpayers). It also included a $30 billion stimulus package and cuts to about 150 federal programs. We aimed to trim the federal workforce by one hundred thousand workers, starting with reductions already made in the White House staff itself.

It did not include a tax cut for the middle class, as Clinton had reluctantly concluded that he could not afford it. The budget also proposed an expansion of the earned income tax credit, allowing poor families to pay less in taxes or qualify for refunds.

After weeks of this feverish work, we prepared to unveil the proposed budget with two speeches by the president, one on February 15 from the Oval Office and the second on February 17 in a formal address to Congress. The first was intended to break the news that we were pushing for a tax increase—and dropping the tax cut—so we knew it would be a hard sell. Clinton's performance made it worse. He seemed nervous, and his message was confused. More than half of the talk looked backward, concluding that twelve years of Republican rule had favored the wealthy and exacerbated the deficit, and that opportunities for investment had been squandered. All that was true, but as Clinton spoke, he seemed to be stalling and making excuses. What's more, we were still hoping to court Republican support for the package, which after all did make sizable cuts in federal spending. Blaming them for the problem was hardly the best way to enlist their support for the solution.

Finally, Clinton came to the bad news: "I had hoped to invest in your future by creating jobs, expanding education, reforming health care, and reducing the debt without asking more of you. And I've worked harder than I've ever worked in my life to meet that goal. But I can't because the deficit has increased so much beyond my earlier estimates and beyond even the worst official government estimates from last year."

The stock market fell almost 100 points the next day, and press reaction was a combination of negative and perplexed, as analysts attempted to explain why the administration was simultaneously spending more to stimulate the economy and cutting programs to reduce the deficit. The *Los Angeles Times* analysis captured the mood well. "The initial reaction in many quarters," the *Times* reported, "was one of alarm."[6]

But they didn't call Clinton the "Comeback Kid" for nothing. With much of the staff still reeling from his first performance, he pivoted to his second. And this time he delivered.

As I sat with the cabinet on the House floor that evening, I was struck by how different this was from any previous time I had come to this chamber to listen to a president. For more than a decade, I had attended presidential addresses with interest and yet a certain detachment—my responsibility had been to consider and react to proposals. Now I was there as a member of a team not only with responsibility to develop a program but also with the job of making it happen.

Although the stakes were enormous and the speech was not complete until minutes before he delivered it, Clinton seemed at ease as he took his place before Congress. He opened with a self-deprecating joke, noting that he welcomed the opportunity to give another long speech, a reference to his much-mocked Democratic convention address in 1988.

He spoke that night with force, interrupted time and again by applause, which even Republicans joined. This speech was everything his Oval Office address had not been. The talk two nights before was negative and backward-looking. Now Clinton reminded Americans that "we have always been a people of youthful energy and daring spirit." The earlier speech blamed Presidents Reagan and Bush for the present economic difficulties. In the second talk, Clinton seemed almost to recant those statements: "There is plenty of blame to go around in both branches of the government and both parties. The time has come for the blame to end. I did not seek this office to place blame. I come here tonight to accept responsibility, and I want you to accept responsibility with me. And if we do right by this country, I do not care who gets the credit for it."

In considerable detail, and over the course of sixty-five minutes, Clinton brought forward his budget and economic plan and hinted at the efforts that would follow, health care and welfare reform and a crime bill. He announced a freeze of federal government salaries and explained that his budget—our budget—would cut $246 billion in federal spending. Even Clinton's acknowledgment that some would pay more under this plan was presented better this time—not as a gloomy repayment for past profligacy but rather as a common commitment to bold action with potentially profound ramifications. "This must be America's new direction," he concluded. "Let us summon the courage to seize it."

It was a triumph. Editorial boards applauded the president's clarity and willingness to address these serious problems without papering over the difficulties. Bill Schneider of CNN said that "for the first time since taking office, Clinton seemed completely in control."[7] Ross Perot proclaimed it an "excellent speech" and evidence that Washington had "stopped going through denial."[8] And most important of all was the reaction of Alan Greenspan, at whom so much of this was directed. He called the plan "serious" and "credible" and said it represented "a very positive force for the American economy."[9]

Not everyone was impressed. Gingrich, predictably, was haughty.

"It was a very good speech," he said, "and a very destructive program."[10] Dick Armey, a swaggering Texas congressman with whom we were soon to tangle, was even nastier. "It won't work," he said. "That's the bad news. The good news is that it will cost Clinton his presidency."[11] Though hindsight is always clear, I can't help but point out how wrong both Gingrich and Armey were—in Gingrich's case, half wrong. It *was* a very good speech.

For the moment, our job was to get the bill passed.

In my first meeting with Clinton, I had held out some hope that there could be bipartisan support for the right kind of budget bill. Perhaps naively, I thought this was a bill that moderates of both parties might be able to agree upon. Clinton had made the case that Democrats were recommending hard cuts, some to programs he and others in the administration favored. Given that, I hoped that at least some Republicans would meet us halfway on some of our tax proposals. Those hopes were soon dashed.

Just a few days after the president's speech, I went to the Hill to meet with Pete Domenici. I started by pointing out the depth of the cuts we were proposing. "The president really is going through a very difficult process of looking at everything," I told him. "We're looking at entitlements, we're looking at discretionary, and we're looking at revenues." Domenici was a good guy and genuinely committed to finding solutions, but this time, he told me, there just wasn't anything he could do. Republicans felt too burned by the Social Security debate and the Bush tax hike. Republicans, he told me, were going to sit this one out. If there was to be a political price to be paid for raising taxes, Democrats would pay it, and if there weren't enough votes on the Democratic side to get our budget through, well, that was our problem, not the responsibility of Republicans.

Democrats held solid majorities in both houses, so we could in theory pass this budget without any Republican support, but that meant keeping our own coalition united. That's never easy, especially for

Democrats, and already there were rumblings on the left, where members were concerned that we were holding down cost-of-living increases in Medicare and cutting other popular programs. If we were going to do this without Republicans, we needed to convince liberals in our party that those cuts were necessary to keep the programs—and the government—solvent, while also convincing the more conservative of our members that the tax package was both economically sound and politically survivable. Any concession to the left risked the loss of votes on the right, and vice versa.

At the same time, we also were trying to build support for the budget with the public, reaching out to influential reporters and making our case. For me that came naturally, as I enjoyed my relations with the press and was, I think, regarded as plainspoken and honest. That's usually a good thing, but my habits of candor were something of a mixed bag in this instance. The occasion was a Washington lunch with a small group of reporters. I was fine during the lunch, but afterward a few of them continued to gently grill me about the budget and other items on the Clinton agenda—economic stimulus, taxes, and the proposed North American Free Trade Agreement, among others. I told them that I thought Congress would ensure that the president had a tough road ahead, that the agenda needed refining, and that NAFTA in particular was in trouble. All true, by the way, but not exactly what the White House had in mind for our messaging.

I woke up the next morning to a headline in the *Washington Post* that no senior administration official ever wants to be responsible for: PANETTA: PRESIDENT IN TROUBLE ON HILL, AGENDA AT RISK, TRADE PACT "DEAD."[12] *Welcome to the White House*, I thought. My extremely able—and on this morning, pretty beleaguered—press aide, Barry Toiv, was on the phone seconds after I'd seen the paper, warning me that Dee Dee Myers of the White House Press Office was livid. For a moment, it seemed my job might even hang in the balance. I called Clinton personally and apologized; I hadn't meant to say that NAFTA was doomed, only that if a vote were held today we might not win it. He accepted my explanation and apology and chose to laugh the whole thing off. "Everybody gets a strike one," he said.

Publicly, he also let me off the hook. Asked whether he'd taken me to the woodshed, Clinton responded, "I don't need to take him to the woodshed. I needed for him to get his spirits up a little." And I did my part, acknowledging that my comments were "a little exaggerated" and making clear that I was expressing frustration with the Hill, not the president.[13]

That crisis blew over fairly quickly, and we were back to working the Hill day and night for weeks, operating from a war room headed by Roger Altman in the White House and reaching out to every Democrat in Congress. We made good progress at first, and our tally of support inched upward.

We had to make the numbers work, though, and we were still $3 to $4 billion short of our targets, the result mainly of having restored the transportation funding to keep Byrd on our side. That's when I indulged in a bit of manipulation. Our estimates on deficit reduction depended, of course, not just on hard numbers but on somewhat more debatable assumptions. Unemployment, for instance, contributes significantly to the state of the budget—when people are working, they collect income and pay income taxes; when they're out of work, they're not paying income taxes, and they're often drawing on welfare. So predictions of unemployment, particularly in years three and four, made a big difference as to whether we could credibly claim to be meeting our deficit targets. With that in mind, I went to our economists—in particular Joe Minarik, who had been my economic adviser on the Budget Committee. The economists were responsible for those predictions, and I asked them to consider whether it might be possible that unemployment could drop a bit faster than they had originally estimated if the economy improved. They looked it over and gave me a half-point improvement in the estimate. That was enough.

From June through August 1993, with Clinton's presidency still just six months old, we navigated a series of votes through the House and Senate that would define the balance of his time in office. Clinton had other issues on his plate at the time—his first tries at nominating an attorney general were rebuffed by the Senate; terrorists exploded a bomb at the World Trade Center in New York, killing six people; ATF agents stormed the Branch Davidian compound in Waco, Texas, inflaming America's domestic terrorist right wing; Bosnia descended into chaos; Hillary Clinton's father died in April; the press fulminated about sloppiness in the White House travel office and imagined it as a full-bore scandal; Byron White retired from the Supreme Court and Clinton named Ruth Bader Ginsburg to succeed him. In other words, another summer in the life of the American presidency. But we soldiered on with the budget, badly needing a win both to set the economy on the right track and to dispel the impression that Clinton's presidency was flailing.

The House and Senate each passed the budget on close votes in the early summer—the House by six votes and the Senate by an especially tight 50–49—but those were actually the easier round. As is usually the case, it was easier for members to support the resolution because they could still reserve the right to vote against the eventual legislative package implementing the budget. The next step was to enact a reconciliation bill that included both the spending cuts and the revenues. That vote, not the vote on the resolution as submitted, would decide the matter, and that's the one that members would have to defend to their constituents. The trouble that summer was that any concession in one chamber could cost votes in the other, and we had none to spare. As Clinton later wrote, "For the next six and a half weeks, the economic future of the country, not to mention the future of my presidency, hung in the balance."[14]

The most significant objections came from the Senate, especially Oklahoma senator David Boren, who voted for the resolution but told

My father, Carmelo Panetta, came to this country in 1921, arriving at Ellis Island with twenty-five dollars in his pocket and nothing else. He worked as a waiter, bought a restaurant, and invested wisely. In 1946 he purchased twelve acres in Carmel Valley. Here, he and I take a break from tending the walnut orchard he planted on that land.

As a boy, I was an accomplished pianist, even getting a pretty glowing review in the local paper when I was ten. Practicing wasn't my favorite way of spending time, though. Sports won the day.

I met Sylvia at a mixer at Santa Clara University, where I was a student, in 1958. We hit it off that evening and began dating regularly. We were married on July 14, 1962. I still wear the watch she gave me as an engagement present, and I've always left it set to California time.

I graduated from Santa Clara Law School in 1963, following in my older brother's footsteps. My parents joined me for the occasion. My brother and I were the first in our family to attend college.

Sylvia gave birth to our first son, Chris, on Mother's Day 1963; our second, Carmelo, after my father, was born in 1964, while I was still serving in the army. (Not pictured here, because he wasn't yet born, is our third, Jimmy.)

My first boss and one of my most important mentors was California senator Tom Kuchel, a moderate Republican and civil rights champion put in the Senate by California governor Earl Warren, who named him to the office when Richard Nixon vacated it to become Ike's vice president.

ABOVE In late 1975, I announced my candidacy for the U.S. Congress, challenging an incumbent Republican, Burt Talcott. This photo of me, my boys, and my dad at the ranch helped make the point that I understood the district while Talcott did not. I beat him by more than six percentage points. And I still own that truck.

OPPOSITE, ABOVE As a member of Congress, I returned home almost every weekend and regularly met with constituents. Here I'm talking with a group of seniors outside the house my dad built.

OPPOSITE, BELOW Some campaign mail from my early years.

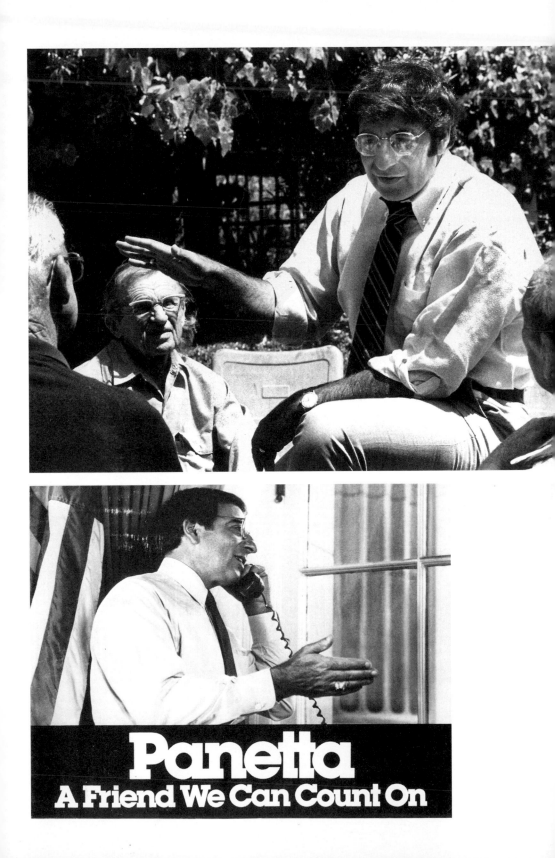

Panetta
A Friend We Can Count On

ABOVE One of my proudest accomplishments as a member of
Congress was to halt offshore oil drilling along the central California
coast and establish the Monterey Bay National Marine Sanctuary,
a struggle that took more than a decade but was deeply satisfying.
Imagine this same image dotted with oil platforms.

OPPOSITE, ABOVE In 1992, President-elect Bill Clinton asked me to
leave Congress and become his budget director. I accepted and
later served as his chief of staff. Here we are in the Oval Office,
joined by Press Secretary Mike McCurry, Secretary of State Warren
Christopher, who, as Clinton's transition team chairman, helped
recruit me to the administration, and National Security Adviser
Sandy Berger.

OPPOSITE, BELOW A lighter moment from the Clinton years. This was
his birthday in 1995, and we all rode horses around the White House
grounds. On the left is Harold Ickes, and on the right is Erskine
Bowles. None of us is much of a cowboy.

OPPOSITE, ABOVE In late 1995, House Speaker Newt Gingrich, reluctantly joined by Senator Bob Dole, forced a confrontation over the federal budget that resulted in a government shutdown. Polls showed that the public strongly blamed Republicans for the mess, helping Clinton to rebound the next year.

OPPOSITE, BELOW The government shuts down.

ABOVE After serving for two years as OMB director and helping win passage of an economic plan that ultimately balanced the federal budget, I moved over to become Clinton's chief of staff. Here we are on Air Force One.

OPPOSITE, ABOVE This is from late 1996, near the end of my time as chief of staff. Clinton and I are walking across the South Lawn of the White House to the waiting helicopter.

OPPOSITE, BELOW I got two opportunities to work closely with Rahm Emanuel. He worked in the White House when I was Clinton's chief of staff, and he was chief of staff to President Obama when I went to work at the CIA. Here the two of us celebrate Memorial Day in Chicago in 2013. By then he was mayor and I was home in California.

BELOW That's me on top of the budget.

ABOVE Senator Dianne Feinstein and I are old friends, but she initially was cool to my appointment as director of the CIA, in part because the Obama transition team had not consulted her about it even though she chaired the Senate Intelligence Committee. Still, she came around, supported my nomination, and worked closely with me on intelligence operations when I went to the agency.

OPPOSITE, ABOVE Taking the oath of office as the new CIA director, with Sylvia by my side.

OPPOSITE, BELOW Soon after taking office, President Obama approved the release of memos from the Bush era laying out the legal arguments surrounding "enhanced interrogation." I opposed the release, and worried about the implications for morale at the CIA. Recognizing the importance of the issue, Obama visited the agency on April 20, 2009. He got a rousing welcome.

ABOVE Mike Morell and I get the news that bin Laden is dead and our forces are safe. This was one of the proudest moments of my life.

OPPOSITE, ABOVE The *Washington Post* reports the news of bin Laden's death. Behind me is a flag that flew over the World Trade Center and that hung in my office throughout the months we tracked and ultimately located the man responsible for 9/11. The flag is now displayed in the CIA Museum.

OPPOSITE, BELOW This brick came from bin Laden's compound in Abbottabad, Pakistan. I was given it as a souvenir after the successful operation.

Within the administration, I argued against concluding our combat mission in Iraq without leaving some residual force to protect our interests and preserve stability. I lost that debate, and on December 15, 2011, presided over the casing of the colors in Baghdad.

us he would vote against the eventual deal because he objected to our proposals for increasing revenue. He attempted to scrap any energy tax and he offered an alternative to lower the burden on high-income tax-payers; his counter to our bill also would have eliminated the expansions of the earned income tax credit, which was the budget's biggest help to the poorest Americans. We fought back to tax the rich more and the poor less, but pressure grew against the BTU tax, with some members opposing it on substantive grounds—the difficulty of levying and collecting it—and others simply wary of creating a whole new federal tax. Gore was admirably unwavering, but we couldn't win without either Republicans or conservative Democrats. Over his objections, we dropped the BTU in favor of a simpler gas tax.

Bob Kerrey of Nebraska also worried us. He had run for president in 1992, and his loss to Clinton meant there were still some bruised feelings. He would not come out and say he opposed the bill, but he waffled and seemed unwilling to commit for it either. Clinton felt he'd be there in the end; I was less sure. On the other hand, Dennis DeConcini of Arizona, who had voted against the resolution, now was indicating he might come back to the fold, in part because of our efforts to protect Social Security.

In the House, conservative Democrats continued to hold out, using their leverage to try to muscle us for more cuts in social programs. But anything we could give them would almost certainly have cost us just as many votes among liberals as it gained among conservatives. I pleaded with Tim Penny of Minnesota, who seemed to speak for a number of conservatives, to back the president on this round and trust us to return to his issues once the budget was behind us. He still wouldn't budge, so I offered him the chance to propose more cuts that fall when the various committees debated appropriations. He agreed, and his half dozen followers went along.

Finally, it was time for the vote. I was in Speaker Foley's office when they began to call the roll, and I followed along with our chart showing where we thought the votes were. As the members began to weigh in, I believed we could win, but my tally didn't guarantee it. We were within a few votes of passage, but there were five to ten Democrats who still were uncommitted; if most broke against us, we would lose. Billy Tauzin of Louisiana voted against it, as did David Minge of Minnesota, and suddenly we were in trouble. That meant we desperately needed to hold on to another nervous freshman, Marjorie Margolies-Mezvinsky, from Pennsylvania. But as she hit her button, it registered a no. Stunned and genuinely concerned that we were about to go down, I turned to Gephardt and urged him to get to the floor and turn her around.

He rushed to the chamber, and as I watched on television, he and Foley came lumbering down the aisle and loomed over Mezvinsky, who had made the rookie mistake of sticking around after casting a vote against the leadership. They spoke with her, and then Gephardt broke off, practically running back to the office where I was waiting. He reported that Mezvinsky would switch to yes if Clinton would agree to come to her district to make a personal appearance and explain the importance of this vote to her constituents. I didn't even call the White House to check. I cut the deal. She changed her vote. We won. By one vote.*

The next day, it was over to the Senate. There too we had cut our deals. Abandoning the BTU tax got us Boren and a few of those around him. Putting back the transportation projects had cleared Byrd's potential opposition. But Sam Nunn of Georgia opposed any new taxes, and a few other Democrats also warned us not to count on them.

It was clear that the result was going to be perilously close. On the day of the vote, I scanned the chamber, looking for Bob Kerrey and

---

*Clinton did come to her district and did his best for her in 1994, but she was defeated by eight thousand votes. I'm sure that had she voted against us, she would have won, making her vote on the budget one of the bravest I have ever seen a member cast. One other note: Her son later married Chelsea Clinton.

hoping he might be with us if we needed him. I didn't see him any-where, so I asked one of our people to check with his staff and find out where he was and how he planned to vote. My jaw dropped when I heard the response: He was at a movie. I don't often lose my temper, but I did then. "Shit," I bellowed, "a movie? For God's sake, we're coming down to the final vote. What the hell's he doing at a movie?"

Nearly panicking now, I dispatched a couple of aides to scour nearby movie theaters and find him. Amazingly, one of them did—Kerrey had slipped out to see *What's Love Got to Do with It?*—and dragged Kerrey back to the Senate. He voted for the budget, making it a 50–50 tie. Vice President Gore broke it, and we won again. By one vote.

The president signed the budget legislation on the South Lawn on the foggy morning of August 10. It did not ignite an instant economic recovery, but it marked the beginning of the turn from deficits to a bal-anced budget. The $290 billion budget deficit of 1992 dropped to $107 billion by 1996. Four years after that, in 2000, it was a surplus of $236 billion.

Those numbers eventually spoke for themselves, but in the mean-time, sticking to fiscal discipline was an ongoing struggle in the White House. The political people never liked it, as it kept them from win-ning otherwise popular spending increases and investments. Through 1993 and 1994, before the fruits of deficit reduction had begun to pres-ent themselves, I would fight rearguard actions to protect what we'd done. I remember one particularly grueling meeting in the Solarium of the White House, where Begala, Carville, Stephanopoulos, and even Hillary Clinton all picked at our economic program, asking why there wasn't more room for health care reform or other initiatives within our plan. For some reason, Rubin and my other usual allies were absent, so I was left to the defend the program by myself. "Look," I said, "we've made this decision. We've taken this fight on. And it's the right fight."

Clinton silently nodded, but not everyone was convinced even then. Deficit reduction required short-term pain in return for long-term reward, and it demanded not just discipline but patience. "Pain," Begala muttered at that meeting, "is not good."

The pain slowly subsided, and we reaped the rewards for those decisions. When he left office, Clinton became the first president since Eisenhower to leave his successor with a surplus. Meantime, the American economy boomed. Unemployment was above 7 percent when Clinton became president; it was below 4 percent when he left. Poverty shrunk. Inflation barely budged, even though wages markedly increased. Even the rich, who paid higher income taxes as a result of that first budget, got richer in the 1990s, as investments and the markets skyrocketed. The Dow Jones Industrial Average closed at 3,242 on the day Clinton became president; when he left, it was above 10,000.

Clinton later wrote that the budget package of 1993 was the "most important domestic decision of my presidency." Certainly no other work of those years had more profound effect on the well-being of more Americans. And it all came down to one vote in the House and one in the Senate. Leadership matters.

SEVEN

"If the White House Is Falling Apart..."

Clinton's first year in office was a wild one. The White House was undisciplined, almost chaotic, and yet it would produce landmark victories. The same president who stumbled into a controversy over gays in the military and had to withdraw nominees for attorney general and assistant attorney general for civil rights also secured passage of a historic budget and the North American Free Trade Agreement.

His year was marked by personal travail as well. Whitewater haunted the administration, even though the land deal at the center of it was soon forgotten as Clinton's pursuers veered off in other directions; an investigation that began with a real estate deal in Arkansas concluded, six years later, with impeachment for lying about sex with an intern. There were many victims along the way, the first of whom was claimed in those early months. Vince Foster, the president's boyhood friend, who had been staggered by the vitriolic politics of Washington, committed suicide on July 20; a shredded piece of paper found later in his briefcase lamented a culture in Washington where "ruining people is considered sport."

Over that first year, my principal concern was the budget, and there we hewed a careful course, reducing the deficit and working closely with the congressional committees to steer our programs and cuts through the appropriations process. The politics were always delicate: Liberals were worried we'd cut too much. Republicans lay in wait for our tax increases to hurt us with the public. So we treaded lightly but tried to build on the principles that undergirded our first budget— bringing down the deficit, protecting the poorest Americans, investing in technology and education and other programs that would prepare the country for the future. We were remarkably successful. As Clinton later noted, those first two budgets were adopted on time and produced three consecutive years of deficit reduction, the first time that had happened since Truman was president. And we still found money for investments.

The steadiness of our economic program was in glaring contrast to the overall atmosphere of the early Clinton administration, which could charitably be described as informal. Meetings were endless, with aides coming and going as the president mulled this policy or that. Many of those sessions tailed into the early morning hours and often broke up without a decision, only to resume again a day or two later and again wind on for hours. One of my colleagues from those years described a meeting in the Clinton White House as a grammar school soccer game, where everyone always ran to the ball. That captures the feeling just right.

Speeches, meanwhile, were written and rewritten, often to the very last minute, exhausting aides who raced to make changes. Paradoxically, Clinton's schedule was exceptionally tight, booking him in fifteen-minute increments, a manifestly unwise way to try to corral him. Rather than keep to it, he would often go long on his first meeting of the day, and by evening would be so far behind that visitors would be kept waiting, their irritation growing and their tales of it reinforcing the image of the White House and the president as undisciplined. Those problems were made worse by a prevailing sense that staff could reach out to him directly; Clinton inadvertently encouraged that because he enjoyed the contact, so he rarely rebuffed a well-meaning overture. In early 1993, his scheduling staff sent out a brusque note telling aides to "cut it out," but it didn't have much effect.[1] Clinton earned his reputation for lacking self-control—it was an undeniable part of the larger personality that made up this brilliant and complicated man—but his staff was partly to blame as well.

In fact, Clinton had not given great thought to his White House staff during the transition from candidate to president. He'd labored greatly, with Warren Christopher's help, to build his cabinet, but the staff was put together more hastily and with less consultation. The result was that it had structural gaps and some obvious weak spots. The top job went to Mack McLarty, an accomplished businessman and childhood friend of Clinton's, though one with limited political experience in Washington—he'd served one term in the Arkansas legislature in his twenties. In some ways, McLarty was perfect for the job: He was conscientious and serious—"born 40 years old," as one friend described him.[2] He also was intensely loyal to Clinton, and he was smart, insightful, and decent. That last quality, however, is not always the most valued in a chief of staff, whose job requires him to say no, especially in the service of a president who liked to say yes to everything and everybody. McLarty's nickname, "Mack the Nice," was not a compliment.

Still, with disorganization came flashes of brilliance. Right on the heels of Congress's cliffhanger approval of our budget—without a single Republican vote on our side—Clinton turned to a more bipartisan undertaking. The North American Free Trade Agreement had been negotiated by President Bush, but Congress had not ratified it when he left office and Clinton became president. Clinton supported NAFTA, arguing that it would open up trade and create jobs, but the politics of the agreement were unusually complicated because NAFTA's benefits were likely to be diffuse—jobs here and there in varying industries—while its costs were localized and readily apparent: When a factory closed in California and that company opened a new one in Mexico, it would be easy to blame NAFTA. Our allies in the NAFTA debate included President Bush, whom Clinton had just defeated, as well as Republicans in Congress, who had just shunned us on the budget. Our opponents included the unlikely combination of organized labor, Ross Perot, and Jesse Jackson. In Congress, Speaker Tom Foley and his nemesis, Newt Gingrich, both supported the deal; most of our labor friends opposed it, some of them ferociously. In September, the *New York Times* took stock of the votes and pronounced us "well shy" of what we needed to prevail.[3]

As a Californian and as a congressman, I had been a strong supporter of free trade—California agriculture needed those markets. The California border with Mexico also meant that opening up greater trade opportunities might benefit both economies by stimulating growth on both sides. Moreover, the politics of NAFTA were as appealing as they were treacherous. Yes, we risked antagonizing some old allies in labor, but Clinton was still out to prove himself as a "New Democrat," and the bipartisan appeal of NAFTA reinforced that willingness to reconsider old politics.

Over the next few weeks we lobbied hard for the bill and cut a few deals in exchange for votes. Clinton agreed, for instance, to limit imports of orange juice, sugar, and wheat, among a few other commodities.[4] Each deal was enough to bring a few wobblers over to support NAFTA. The final House vote came on November 17, and NAFTA passed by 234 to 200. A majority of Democrats opposed it. The economics of NAFTA were debatable; the politics of it, by contrast, were dazzling. Less than six months after winning the most important domestic policy vote of his presidency without a single Republican supporter, Clinton had turned around and won a landmark victory with the GOP's backing and over the objections of his own party.

Clinton spent many hours considering and preparing what would constitute his first real State of the Union address, since the 1993 speech had been almost exclusively about the budget. Beginning that year, he used the State of the Union as an opportunity to set broad themes and goals for himself and his staff, so preparing for the speech was about more than simply drafting—it was an attempt to organize priorities and to persuade Congress and the American people to join in those ambitions. It was, in other words, both a policy and a communications exercise.

As the deadline approached for the 1994 address, Clinton wanted to list the administration's accomplishments, of course, but he also was searching for a bigger story, a narrative that would unify the efforts to date with the challenges ahead. We were trying to change a lot in those months—the budget had dramatically recalibrated spending and tax policy—and Clinton now was looking ahead to reforming health care and welfare and to passing a crime bill, which Congress so far had refused to do. He called it a "renewal agenda," and it bore all the earmarks that were so distinctively Clintonian: It blended conservative notions of personal responsibility with liberal commitment to social justice, and it was politically calculated to reposition the president—and the Democratic Party—as the representatives of the American mainstream.

Like so much of the work of those months, the speech reflected a whirlwind of internal debate and conversation, and the drafting went on right up until the moment the president was about to speak. In fact, Clinton was fiddling with the text on his way up to the Capitol, and when he arrived there was briefly some confusion about whether the right draft had made it to the chamber in time. Before beginning, Clinton fiddled with his pages for a moment and confessed, "I'm not at all sure what speech is in the teleprompter tonight, but I hope we can talk about the state of the union."

The achievements and ambitions of the Clinton presidency found near-perfect expression in that speech, with its quest for the political center, its deliberate populism, and its blend of threat and blandishment. He boasted of the gains we already were making on the budget and deficit reduction and shouted down Republicans who guffawed when he mentioned the tax increase. "Only the top 1.2 percent of Americans . . . will face higher income tax rates," he said to sustained applause from Democrats. "Only the wealthiest 1.2 percent of Americans will face higher incomes tax rates, and no one else will, and that is the truth."

That sounded a combative note, but, with one notable exception, the balance of the speech really was a call to common purpose on behalf of everyday people. Substantively, Clinton called for action in three areas—health care, welfare, and crime. The last two were naturals for bipartisan action. On crime, Clinton favored tough sentencing—he advocated a three-strikes policy for federal offenses similar to what California had recently enacted for state crimes—as well as a significantly expanded federal death penalty. And though his rhetoric on welfare reform emphasized the indignities of the present system, his solution was largely to limit recipients, another proposal tailored for Republican backing.

On health care, however, the alignment was different. There, opponents of reform were solidly Republican, and some GOP leaders already were questioning whether there was a crisis worth confronting. The president's tone shifted palpably when he confronted those objections in his speech. He told the story of a Nevada man, Richard Anderson, who "lost his job, and with it his health insurance." His wife then suffered a cerebral aneurysm and was hospitalized for twenty-one days. Anderson got another job, this one paying eight dollars an hour, but he and his wife faced more than $120,000 in medical bills.

"I know there are people here who say there's no health care crisis," Clinton said. "Tell it to Richard and Judy Anderson. Tell it to the fifty-eight million Americans who have no coverage at all for some time each year. Tell it to the eighty-one million Americans with those preexisting conditions." He went on for a bit, pressing and serious, then concluded, "So if any of you believe there is no crisis, you tell it to those people, because I can't."

Two other moments in the speech signaled that Clinton's approach to health care would be a departure from his general tendency to look for middle ground. Those working for a plan to reform the system, he said, deserve "our thanks and our action." As Democrats stood to applaud, he looked up at Hillary Clinton in the audience and mouthed the words, "I love you. I do." And a few minutes later, he warned Congress not to send him any bill that did not "guarantee every American private health insurance that can never be taken away." Should Congress offer up anything less, he vowed, reaching for a pen on the dais where he spoke, "you will force me to take this pen, veto the legislation, and we'll come right back here and start all over again." With that gesture, and by virtue of the decision to entrust this matter to the first lady, Clinton effectively wiped out any chance for a compromise that might have extended insurance to millions but not all. We were locked in.

Moreover, Hillary Clinton was growing understandably impatient. She had pushed for health care to be included in the president's budget proposal, and I, frankly, had pushed back. I was worried that we were trying to do too much with the budget, and that adding health care, particularly when the plan was still half-baked at that point, would give our opponents reason to tank the whole budget. Given the razor-thin margin by which we prevailed on the budget, I still think that was the right call, but as 1994 opened, the next question was whether to shelve health care yet again, this time to put it behind either crime or welfare. I thought we should move welfare first and take advantage of a Democratic Congress to produce meaningful but humane reform to that system. Hillary demanded that we bring something to the Hill and that we not relegate health care to the back burner again; with this State of the Union speech, the president made clear that he too was ready to go now.

But health care, as we all know now, is a devilishly difficult matter to reform legislatively. Congress rarely handles complexity well, and no attempt to restructure a system as complicated as health care can be undertaken without it. Detailed descriptions of the employer mandate or managed competition bump up against simple slogans in opposition—"socialized medicine," for example. The health care bill we ultimately sent to the Hill was more than thirteen hundred pages long. That gave opponents plenty to seize on.

The difficulty of selling complexity was further complicated by a health care team that was deeply knowledgeable about the health system but sometimes painfully naïve about politics. I thought of Ira Magaziner, who was Hillary Clinton's deputy on health care, as a sort of nuclear physicist—very smart and truly an expert in his field. But he had little sense for what could be accomplished legislatively and little feel for public reaction to his ideas. During one 1993 meeting, he warned that there would be short-term costs of implementing a new health care system. Knowing of my aversion to programs that would add substantially to the deficit, he proposed addressing that by having the president impose caps on all health care spending for a period of up to five years. "The move will anger much of the medical sector," he conceded. Talk about understatement. To assert such sweeping power over such a large segment of the economy would have invited charges that Clinton was a liberal dictator, and in my view severely weakened his presidency, perhaps cripplingly so.

And even with imposed controls, the estimates of the program's potential cost were astronomical and wildly divergent. In one presentation to the president and the economic team, the health care group distributed charts that detailed cost options for the program. They ranged from $66 billion to $146 billion—this at a time when all program cuts combined in our budget came to about $240 billion. All the work we had done to cut those programs would be swamped by this single reform. It seemed to me that we were risking too much.

I don't recall ever confronting Hillary Clinton directly with my concerns, but it was obvious that we were on opposite sides of the health care debate within the White House. And she vented her frustration about me and other members of the economic team who shared my views of the proposal. At one session, for instance, she complained to Chief of Staff Mack McLarty; Pat Griffin, the exceptionally able head of Legislative Affairs; and others that our economic program was too restrictive and was strangling the president's other initiatives. "You're screwing the president," she said, incensed. I ran into Pat as he was straggling out of that session. He looked like he'd been beat up.

Nevertheless, we sent up a health care bill in early 1994 as promised, and initially thought we might have some takers. Democrats in both houses were generally supportive, and Senator Bob Dole of Kansas was a longtime advocate for health care reform; he indicated a willingness to help forge a compromise that would achieve Clinton's goal of universal coverage. Dole's support did not last long. He soon redirected his political sights on the presidency, determining to vie for the Republican nomination in 1996. To do that, he needed the support of his own party's conservatives, including Gingrich's feisty caucus in the House. Any support for the president on health care would throttle Dole's presidential campaign, or at least he believed it would. Dole was a solid and admirable public servant who gave his country much, but his decision to walk away from health care reform was a disappointing capitulation to politics, and it sent a clear signal that the Republicans, as with the budget, would not give an inch on this issue.

Health care batted around for a few months, and opponents waged an expensive and deceptive campaign to frighten the American people over what the bill would do. Public support plummeted, dragging Clinton's approval ratings with it, just as Truman's attempt to reform health care had damaged him politically and as Barack Obama's would in 2009.

In fact, one interesting side note from those months would reveal itself when the issue of health care reform returned to the American agenda under President Obama. In 1993 and 1994, one of the leading opponents of Clinton's employer-based model was the Heritage Foundation. The foundation, a leading conservative think tank, argued against Clinton's approach, which it said would place undue burdens on employers, hiding costs, discouraging hiring, and "eliminating economic opportunity for many lower paid Americans without significantly increasing the health care services available to them."[5] The foundation's rejection of Clinton's program helped galvanize conservatives, including Gingrich, who predictably took to deriding the administration's package as "Hillarycare."

The Heritage Foundation's alternative to employer-based mandates was to advocate for a requirement that all individuals or households be required to purchase health insurance in the same way that many states already required automobile drivers to purchase car insurance. "Under the Heritage plan, there would be such a requirement," the foundation concluded. "Health care protection is a responsibility of individuals, not businesses. Thus to the extent that anybody should be required to provide coverage to a family, the household mandate assumes that it is the family that carries the first responsibility." And yet when President Obama introduced his health care proposal, based precisely on that reasoning, Heritage and other leading conservative groups, again including Gingrich, opposed it. The only consistency across those two debates was that unprincipled ideologues will go to great lengths to rationalize their intransigence, even if it means rejecting their own ideas.[6]

Health care reform sputtered along in the spring and summer of 1994, but the momentum was palpably slipping away. At the same time, the administration's efforts to revive it made us seem weak and flailing.

The president's approval rating, which had reached nearly 60 percent shortly after his well-received State of the Union speech, tumbled during those months, cratering to 39 percent by August. With the midterm congressional elections approaching and the rest of the president's legislative agenda in peril, Clinton was looking to make changes. Specifically, he wanted to reorganize his staff.

In June 1994, President Clinton made his second trip to Europe, this time with two main objectives: meeting Pope John Paul II and commemorating the fiftieth anniversary of D-Day. His first stop was Rome, and he kindly invited Sylvia and me to join him as part of the delegation. We were seated on Air Force One en route to Italy when the president asked me to come forward and join him for a private conversation. It was my first visit to the working quarters of the plane, and I made my way forward with a tinge of nervous curiosity.

Clinton gestured for me to take a spot on a small couch in a seating area near the front of the plane, and he sat down next to me.

"Leon," he began, "what do you think needs to be done to improve the operations of the White House?"

I took a deep breath. I liked Mack McLarty, and didn't want to undercut him with his friend and president. On the other hand, I did think the operation was struggling and doing a disservice to Clinton, whom I was there after all to serve. So I answered candidly. I told the president that the staff needed to be more focused and disciplined, that meetings needed to be structured in order to produce a clear decision, and that once decisions were made they needed to be acted upon, and the office then needed to turn quickly to the next issue. Dawdling and endless debates, I emphasized, were a hindrance to an effective White House. Clinton listened carefully, asked a few more questions, and thanked me for my thoughts. I returned to the back of the plane not knowing whether I had helped or offended him.

Making my way back to my seat, I ran into George Stephanopoulos and told him of the conversation I'd just had with the president.

George, who was on the outs with Clinton at that moment—the president and first lady both believed he was responsible for leaking inside information to reporters, notably Bob Woodward of the *Washington Post*—was heartened to hear that Clinton was raising questions about the effectiveness of his staff leadership. George happened to be reading a book about the Nixon White House, and he shared a passage with me in which Nixon made clear that H. R. Haldeman, his chief of staff, needed broad power to be effective. I took note.

In Rome, Sylvia and I joined the president and first lady for a memorable event, one of the highlights of my time with Clinton. The occasion was largely ceremonial, as the mayor of Rome had arranged to welcome the president to the city by presenting him with an emblem of it. The setting was what made it so special. Rome's city hall, formally known as the Palazzo Senatorio, sits within sight of the Forum and atop the chambers that once housed the archives of ancient Rome, so Clinton would be receiving this honor in one of the founding sites of Western civilization. The steps from which he would address the crowd were designed by Michelangelo. It is one of the world's most majestic and historic locations.

The event was to be held in Italian, of course, and Clinton asked me if I would translate his remarks to the mayor and the expected crowd. He thought it would be fun, and though I worried at first that my Italian might not be up to it, I warmed to the idea. With some justification, the U.S. ambassador to Italy didn't like the idea. He was nervous that I'd screw it up, and he argued for a professional interpreter. We compromised, agreeing that I'd translate the president's opening remarks and welcome, and the interpreter would take over from there.

On that bright summer morning, with thousands of people spread before him, Clinton accepted the emblem graciously, slowly delivering his remarks in English and pausing every few moments to let me translate. The crowd cheered both of us. After a few sentences, I moved to step aside, but the crowd wouldn't have it. They began chanting, "Panetta, Panetta," until I resumed my translation. For an Italian to be cheered by Italians made this a special moment for me. Clinton was delighted too.

Later, Clinton recalled that at one point during the ceremony he turned to the mayor and asked what the people nearest to us were saying in Italian.

"Do you really want to know?" the mayor asked.

"Yes," Clinton answered.

"They're saying, 'Who's that guy up there with Leon Panetta?'"[7]

Sylvia and I broke off from the trip a couple days later and returned to Washington. Back at work the following week, I was walking across the street that separated the White House from the Old Executive Office Building when Al Gore spotted me and asked me to stop for a moment. "Look," Al said, "the president's seriously thinking of asking you to be chief of staff."

That took me by surprise, and my first response was to push back. It was my feeling that Clinton should have a chief of staff whom he'd known very well for a very long time, someone in whom he had long-standing trust. We'd worked together in my sixteen months as his budget director, and I was proud of that work, but we didn't have the kind of relationship I thought would be valuable for a president and his chief of staff to share. Gore and I talked it over for a few more minutes that afternoon, and he ended with some advice. "I'll tell you," he said, "the president is thinking about it, so you'd better give it some thought."

I had shared with Sylvia my conversation with the president on Air Force One. When I now told her of this exchange with the vice president, she saw better than I did what was coming. Any reservations she might have had, however, were buried beneath the advice she always offered in situations such as this: Above all else, do what's important to help the president.

A week or so later, on a Saturday morning, Al approached me again, this time to tell me the president wanted me to join him at Camp

David. When? I asked. Now, he answered. This time, I knew what was coming.

I went to the vice president's residence, where a helicopter was waiting. Tipper Gore was already on board, and as the doors closed and we took off, the two of them let me know I was about to be offered the job. I told them how much I appreciated that, but that I'd been thinking it over and my intention was to turn it down and ask to remain where I was. They did not respond.

It's a short flight from Washington to Camp David, near Gettysburg, by helicopter, so we were there before I knew it. On the ground, we proceeded directly to the president's cabin. Al and Tipper Gore took seats on one of the sofas, and Hillary Clinton sat down on another. Bill Clinton took an armchair. All four faced me.

The president spoke first and got right to the point: "All of us really feel that we would like you to be chief of staff."

"Mr. President," I responded, "we just did your economic plan. We were able to get that put in place. We got reconciliation passed. We've been doing the appropriations bills. We've gotten all your programs funded. I really think this is a major centerpiece of your administration."

But, I continued, the fights over budgets were annual affairs, and we needed to continue to work for our priorities or risk losing ground on them. Budgets were my specialty, and I felt I was the best person in the administration to continue leading that phase of our work. I told Clinton I thought I could best serve him and his administration by staying where I was.

Clinton thought it over for a moment while the others stayed silent. When he spoke, it was clear I hadn't budged him in the slightest. "Leon, you can be the greatest OMB director in the history of the country," he said, "but if the White House is falling apart, nobody is going to remember you."

I knew I was done at that point. "Look, I have deep respect for you as president," I told Clinton. "If you ask me to do this, I'm willing to do it."

With that, the conversation moved from whether I would take the job to how I would be allowed to operate it. I told the Gores and Clintons that I'd want to review the staff and perhaps move some people around. I'd feel the need to impose stronger discipline and assign some staff members clearer roles—George Stephanopoulos and David Gergen were just two of a number of senior staff whose positions were ill defined. I said that I would insist on controlling access to the president more closely. To do that, I needed the support of the president and vice president, I told them.

Clinton answered first. "I will support you," he said. "Whatever you want to get done, you can be assured of my support and Hillary's support." The Gores agreed, and we had a deal.

It did not take long for me to realize how much work there was to do. McLarty had done some good things. There were capable people in most positions, and I was immediately grateful to inherit Deputy Chief of Staff Harold Ickes, a tough and shrewd operator who oversaw issues and politics in the chief of staff's office and who agreed to stay on and work for me. The offices bustled with young people too, many of them talented and utterly devoted to the work of the White House.

But Mack's instinctive gentleness had come at a cost. He hadn't built strong organizational systems—it wasn't always clear who reported to whom—and he'd allowed Clinton to indulge his freewheeling style rather than imposing some structure around it. As he prepared to go, and was graciously helping me to settle in, I asked Mack for a copy of the organization chart for the White House staff. He looked puzzled. "I don't believe I have one of those," he conceded. *Man, I thought to myself, I really am in deep shit now!*

When I had moved from Congress to OMB, a number of my top staff had come with me. John Angell, Jennifer Palmieri, Barry Toiv, Jodie Torkelson, and Martha Foley all had become indispensable to me, some over many years, and now I asked them to move again. They agreed, and thankfully my core team continued to surround me. I warned them that we had some tough challenges. On our first day, I put my hands on John Angell's shoulders and looked him in the eye. "John," I said, "this is going to be tough." He laughed but never hesitated. None of them did. So quickly did they scatter around the White House and plunge into their new duties that other staff members called them "the mice."

I also wanted a second deputy chief of staff, for while Harold handled politics and issues, I wanted someone else to take over the president's schedule and personnel. Clinton agreed and asked me to consider Erskine Bowles. I did, and never regretted it.

Meanwhile, Sylvia and I once again had to rearrange our lives. As chief of staff, there was no way I could regularly leave Washington on weekends to return to the Carmel Valley, and our boys were now grown and leading their own lives. So Sylvia agreed to join me in Washington. She wanted to work in some capacity, though. Luckily, the vice president was willing to offer her a staff job on his Crime Prevention Council, a job for which Sylvia's work as the director of my district offices for more than a decade had well prepared her; a few months after I started my new job, Sylvia settled into hers. The commission offices were not far from the White House, and we settled in to the busy life of a Washington couple, often even commuting together to work. It is fair to say that I could never have done my job without her support and partnership in yet another demanding task.

For me, the model chief of staff—and the one whom I most consciously emulated—was James Baker, who had done the job for Reagan. I called him just before taking over, and one point he emphasized was that the chief of staff needed to be the conduit for anyone trying to reach the president. I got it: If anyone can get to the president without going through the chief of staff, then the president will be deluged and the chief of staff incapable of organizing decision making. What's more, the chief of staff then won't know what the hell is going on. By contrast, a streamlined information system keeps decisions on track and the president focused on what's most important. I'd seen that first-hand during the Reagan years. I admired the efficiency of that White House, and I knew that much the same was said regarding the effectiveness of the Eisenhower administration, under the surly leadership of Sherman Adams, the first person to impose what was effectively a chief of staff system in the White House.

So on Baker's advice, from the moment I became chief of staff I directed that all communications to the president pass through me. I braced myself for what I feared would be pushback from aides who were accustomed to being able to drop in on Clinton and make their pitch for this idea or that. Instead, I mostly sensed relief, as the new system restored some sanity to the operation by letting everyone know how decisions were being made and when we could move to the next issue. Most important, it kept Clinton focused, and it kept me informed.

I also was concerned that Clinton himself might bolt the program, that he would resent being pulled away from his late-night bull sessions over pizza and soda, or that he would feel confined by his more modest schedule. To the contrary, he too seemed to like it. Erskine made it a point to build in time during most days—two hours for lunch, say— when Clinton could think or read or make calls to members of Congress simply as a courtesy. I remembered the lasting impacts of Lyndon Johnson's personal touch, and tried to create a White House where there was time for such overtures.

One other thing Baker impressed upon me was to remember my place and frame advice to the president with that place in mind. "You're the chief of staff," he told me firmly. "You're not the president." I urged anyone who was briefing the president to bring him options, not to force him into preselected decisions. It was our responsibility to bring him background and explain what appeared to be realistic alternatives.

But the people of the United States had elected him, not us, to make decisions. Our job was not to back him into corners. It was to provide him with choices and then implement the choices he made.

Clinton himself, though accustomed to a looser-limbed organizational style, actually made our transition to this new system considerably easier. That's because he was a master at sifting through complex material and asking pertinent, probing questions. He was, as they say in Washington, an "easy brief."

In place of the crisis-response atmosphere that pervaded in the administration's first eighteen months, I tried to impose a regular structure to the day so that the various pieces of our operation— congressional liaison, scheduling, communications, foreign affairs, national security, economics—all would understand what was expected of them and the others. I started every day with a 7 a.m. meeting of a dozen or so top officials from those areas. I soon added a representative of the White House Counsel's office, which became increasingly important as various scandals—most of them petty but distracting— forced their way into our planning.

I would open that meeting typically by calling on Mike McCurry, the new White House press secretary, to report on what the press was asking about. Then I would turn to Erskine to tell us what to expect in the president's day. Was he in the White House or traveling? With whom was he meeting? What issues would he be discussing publicly?

Then we moved to economic matters, then legislative issues, international events, and, usually last, any updates from the general counsel—the latest on Whitewater or what have you. I led the meeting, ticking off items from the yellow legal pads I carried constantly in those years. We generally were finished within forty-five minutes, after which I hosted a larger session for about thirty to forty presidential aides and advisers—those responsible for cabinet affairs, outside constituencies, special fields such as science, and the like. They got a short version of the earlier meeting and were invited to offer their thoughts on upcoming questions or issues. The larger meeting allowed people who were on the outer edges of the administration to hear and contribute to plans for responding to breaking news or controversies. And for big announcements—a bill being sent to Congress, the unveiling of an important initiative—it allowed us to streamline our message, so that the president's remarks on one subject wouldn't compete for attention with other announcements or comments by White House staff.

The latter group was too big for my office, so we met in the Roosevelt Room, just a few feet from the Oval Office. By 8:30 a.m. on most days, that second meeting was concluded, and all the key people in the White House understood our objectives and potential hazards, at least as far as we could anticipate them. None of that eliminated crises, of course. The White House is buffeted by them almost every week. But it gave us a sense of what we were trying to achieve, and prepared us for unexpected events rather than allowing ourselves to be bowled over by them.

Those sessions also allowed me to get to know the staff, many of whom were impressively intelligent and exceptionally devoted. One of the backbenchers in those days, attending the meetings but only rarely speaking up, was Rahm Emanuel. He didn't make an immediate impression. He was, as I said, more on the periphery in the early days, but when he did contribute I noted his forcefulness and incisiveness. At first the Clintons seemed wary of him. Just before I signed on as chief of staff, Bob Woodward had written a penetrating look at the budget deliberations of the Clinton administration, and though Woodward's work was spot-on, it had upset Clinton, who was appalled to discover some of what he considered private conversations described in the book. Stephanopoulos was suspected of leaking, and some suspicion hovered around Rahm as well.

Indeed, Clinton was angry enough at first that he asked me to fire both of them; I pushed back, insisting that they deserved another chance and promising, particularly in the case of Stephanopoulos, to clip his wings a bit. George had been with Clinton for so long and had such a vague set of White House duties that he was accustomed to dropping in on meetings and offering his advice, sometimes unbidden. I was determined to impose greater structure on meetings generally, and one effect of that was to put a tighter rein on George. He resented it at times, but it saved his job.

As for Rahm, we gradually got to know each other, pushed along by the fact that he and Sylvia hit it off. We were often the first ones to arrive at the White House in the morning, and when Sylvia and I came in together, I'd head for my office and she to the cafeteria for a cup of coffee. Invariably, there was Rahm, poring over the morning papers and preparing for his day. I liked his toughness—which I would come to appreciate later, when we were reunited in the Obama administration—and I enjoyed his facility with profanity. I pride my-self in the felicitous use of the occasional four-letter word, but I was an amateur compared to Rahm.*

Unfortunately, time did not stop for me to get the White House organized, and we continued to struggle as I settled in.

By the summer of 1994, health care was in deep trouble. Republicans had united against it, deciding there was more political advantage in fighting Clinton than in enacting any type of bill, even one that expressed philosophies they once had argued for themselves. That left us looking for a win on Capitol Hill. Welfare reform had been submitted but was still on the distant legislative horizon, so the main event on the Hill during my early weeks as chief of staff was securing passage of a crime bill. Congress had previously rejected an attempt by Senator Joe

---

*Later, when Rahm became chief of staff to Obama, some pundits would suggest that he picked up his language from me. I deny it.

Biden to address multiple aspects of the national crime problem in a single bill, but Clinton continued to support the idea.

As Clinton envisioned it, the bill drew elements from all sides in the debate over how best to address crime. Community policing was popular with liberals but had its roots in the "broken windows" theory of conservative philosopher James Q. Wilson, so proposing to have the federal government subsidize the hiring and training of one hundred thousand new police officers and, through them, to expand community policing was an easy sell with both parties. Creating a federal three-strikes system for locking away repeat offenders and adding twenty-six new crimes that would be eligible for the death penalty played well with the right; banning assault weapons was an important ambition of the left.

But creating omnibus legislation of that type can be either the secret to compromise or a deal killer, and in this case some of our closest Democratic allies on the Hill worried that we were trying to do too much. Supporters of the assault weapons ban, for instance, urged its inclusion in the crime bill because they feared the National Rifle Association would push its allies to wage a filibuster in the Senate if the proposed ban went up on its own. Critics of that strategy countered that its inclusion could sink the entire package or at least cost some members their seats if the NRA decided to get even with them. One of those who argued that last point was Speaker Tom Foley. Foley supported the assault weapons ban, but he foresaw a huge political backlash and urged us to drop it from the bill. We considered that as a matter of political expediency, but I, among others, was puzzled by the appeal of assault weapons—these are not for hunters, after all, they are purely for killing people. We decided to stick with the ban and take our chances politically. Foley understood, but was so skittish of the package that he declined to help us lobby for it. Instead he found some office space for us off the floor of the House and we set up shop there.

As with the budget battle from the previous year, we were in a contest for every vote, with changes that might help us in one camp costing us in another. This time, though, Republicans decided not to take a walk, so our lobbying was genuinely bipartisan. Clinton himself committed extraordinary time and energy to the effort, traveling around the country in what we billed as a "summer of safety." He highlighted community efforts in St. Louis; Albany, Georgia; and Boston, among other places, and brought in survivors from tragedies in San Francisco, New Orleans, and Petaluma, California, to testify to the effects of assault weapons or to make the case for new sentencing laws.

Nevertheless, votes were hard to come by. We were particularly frustrated by the opposition of the Congressional Black Caucus, which had generally been supportive of Clinton's programs. We argued that the bill's greatest impact could be on largely African-American communities, since those areas often were the hardest hit by crime. I made that argument, and also pointed out that the additional officers paid for under the bill would in many cases benefit those same areas. I didn't make much headway. Members of the caucus were steadfastly opposed to the death penalty, and those provisions were a deal breaker for most, whatever the other potential benefits of the legislation

Then we had a breakthrough. Barbara-Rose Collins, a former Detroit city council member who was elected to Congress in 1991, had rebuffed all my attempts to persuade her to join us, explaining that the death penalty offended her conscience and she could not vote for a bill that would expand it. I respectfully understood that, and assumed she was lost to us. Then one day I was surprised to get a call from her, saying that she'd been thinking about the bill and asking to meet with me.

Bill Richardson, then a congressman from New Mexico and a supporter of the bill, offered to host the meeting, and we gathered in his Capitol Hill office. I asked what I could do for Collins, and she informed me that Jesus had spoken to her in a dream the night before.

"Really?" I asked calmly, as a few of my colleagues did their best to compose themselves. "What did Jesus say?"

"He told me I should consider supporting the president," she answered, then added, "I think God will allow me to support this bill if I get a casino for my district."

"I'm glad to hear that Jesus is flexible," I responded, while Richardson, standing behind Collins, rolled his eyes in amazement.

I told her I'd see what I could do about the casino, and as soon as she left I asked Pat Griffin to get Secretary of the Interior Bruce Babbitt on the phone and see what he could do to push along the casino project in Collins's district, which included some Native American land near Detroit. Griffin tracked Babbitt down and made clear we weren't looking for final approval, just a nudge to push the project forward and demonstrate our responsiveness to the congresswoman. I could hear Babbitt sputtering on the phone, incensed to be part of such naked horse trading. Griffin listened to the secretary for a couple minutes, then covered the receiver and informed me of the obvious: "Babbitt's going batshit." My response: "Tell him to get it done."

On August 21, ten days after narrowly voting down the Crime Bill, the House reversed itself and narrowly approved it, this time by a vote of 235–195, with 188 Democrats, 46 Republicans, and one independent voting yes (and 64 Democrats and 131 Republicans voting no). Collins was among the yeses.

Crime trends are notoriously difficult to examine for causality, as so many factors influence violent behavior. Given that, it's impossible to know just how much the crime bill contributed to the historic declines in lawlessness and violence that characterized the 1990s. So I'm not trying to claim credit for all of what followed, but it's worth noting that the numbers were staggering. In 1994, the year the crime bill became law, there were 13,989,543 violent and serious crimes reported in the United States, almost 5,400 per 100,000 residents.[8] That same year, there were 23,326 murders across the country. Six years later, in 2000, Clinton's last year in office, the number of total serious offenses had declined to 11,605,751, or roughly 4,100 per 100,000 residents.[9] Murders had declined to 15,517.

Crime was dropping before Clinton and it continued to drop after his presidency, but his efforts at least did not reverse those trends, and almost certainly helped propel them. Thousands of men and women are alive today—and thousands of families are intact—because of the historic turnaround in this nation's battle against violence. Clinton helped lead that. The crime bill was in my view an important piece.

I had barely taken my seat outside the Oval Office when we hit our first foreign crisis of my tenure as chief of staff. It erupted in Haiti, where pressure had been building for months as a stubborn military junta clung to power despite mounting international opposition. Lieutenant General Raoul Cédras headed that junta, as he had since 1991, when he and others overthrew the government of Jean-Bertrand Aristide. President Bush imposed an embargo in response, and after the United Nations banned oil and weapons exports to Haiti in 1993, Cédras agreed to cede power back to Aristide, partly in exchange for amnesty for himself and the other military leaders.*

That date came and went, and Cédras still refused to leave. Attempts to enforce the agreement were met with violence, and by the middle of 1994 the United Nations reported growing unrest, including the kidnapping, rape, and murder of political activists and their families. On July 31, 1994, the UN Security Council authorized formation of an international military force to "use all necessary means" to remove the military leadership.[10] Trying one last time to avoid blood-

---

*That agreement, signed on June 21, 1993, was known as the Governors Island Agreement because it was negotiated on Governors Island in New York.

shed, the UN dispatched a special envoy to Haiti the following month; the junta refused to meet with the envoy. That left one last option: an invasion. A force of twenty-three thousand soldiers, overwhelmingly Americans, was gathered.

All that occurred as I was moving from OMB into the chief of staff job, and it came to a head just as I took over my new duties. In fact, it boiled over on September 18, a Sunday, just as I was making my first appearance in my new job on the Sunday morning talk shows. I joined General John Shalikashvili, the chairman of the Joint Chiefs, and the topic of the day was the question of how Haiti would unfold. I wrapped up my appearance and headed for the office through a hot, rainy Washington morning. Arriving, I discovered the president and his national security staff gathered in the Oval Office, their faces drawn with anxiety.

Standing around the president's desk were Shalikashvili (he must have taken a shortcut from the studio), Secretary of State Warren Christopher, National Security Adviser Tony Lake, and his deputy, Sandy Berger. Clinton was seated, and as was often the case when he faced a tense or difficult decision, the president listened while working on a crossword puzzle—always from the *New York Times*—a form of doodling that helped him to concentrate. Other aides were milling around the corridors outside the office, and some tried to join the group. George Stephanopoulos, for instance, started to enter, but I waved him away.*

As the afternoon progressed, the stakes grew. President Carter, Senator Sam Nunn, and General Colin Powell were in Haiti attempting to negotiate with the junta to avert the invasion even as the force began to move toward the island. President Clinton was in constant

---

*I actually don't remember doing that, but George recounts it in his memoirs, and notes that he was hurt by it. I didn't mean to snub him, but I was trying to curb Clinton's unfocused meetings and also to protect George in those days from Clinton's suspicion that he was a leak. I have no doubt that George's account is correct.

touch with the delegation, communicating through Powell. At one point, Powell called to say that the junta had agreed to leave, but did not want to set a firm date for its departure. Clinton rejected that, saying a date was essential. Powell went back to work.

Shalikashvili, meanwhile, warned that the invasion force was fast approaching the point where it would need orders to move forward. Finally, we could wait no longer. Told that the junta still had not agreed to a firm date, Shalikashvili asked whether the 82nd Airborne was "go" or "no go."

In that long moment, I fully appreciated the weight that a president must carry. We were all there to advise, and the negotiators in Haiti were furiously trying to offer an alternative, but in the end, only one person had the authority to say yes or no to a war. Clinton had been considering the question for weeks, but now it was time to decide.

"Go," he said.

Planes scrambled in Florida. Men strapped parachutes to their backs. Two aircraft carrier groups swung about toward the island. Marines prepared their weapons. How much resistance would these forces encounter when they hit the beaches and ports of a small but furious nation? In the Oval Office, we waited anxiously for the first reports.

And then came the breakthrough. Powell suddenly called to report that the junta had caved. The generals agreed to leave by October 15 or as soon as the Haitian parliament could approve a general amnesty. Our forces landed the following day, but rather than have to fight their way ashore, they were greeted peacefully. Clinton's reluctant willingness to wage war had been enough to prevent its necessity. After three breathless days, we exhaled.

Midterm elections historically work against the party that holds the White House. Harry Truman's Democrats got clobbered in 1946, losing both houses to the GOP for the first time since the Depression. Dwight Eisenhower won a landslide in 1952 and brought Republican majorities to both houses that year; two years later, he lost those majorities for good. Even Lyndon Johnson's landslide in 1964 wasn't enough to protect the party two years later: Democrats lost three Senate and forty-seven House seats in that election.

We knew that in the summer and fall of 1994. We worried that we could lose the Senate and we feared significant losses in the House. We didn't know the half of it.

Indeed, I knew even less than that, because, unbeknownst to me, President Clinton had been secretly reaching out that summer to his old political adviser, Dick Morris, in an attempt to take stock of the nation's politics. Clinton surely sensed that I wouldn't like Morris—he was right about that—so even though Morris started doing polling on the very issues that the White House staff was working on, Clinton didn't share the results, or even the fact, of the polls with me.

I learned much later that it was actually Hillary Clinton who had asked Morris, who by then was mostly consulting for Republicans, to resume working for the president.[11] The Clintons admired Morris, and he did have a nose for the political center. Unfortunately, it was accompanied by an outsized personality. He wore big, bright suits, held forth with infuriating bombast, gestured wildly for emphasis, milked his exhaustive polls, and openly disdained the substance of policy. He was about winning, and he had a knack for it.

In his memoirs, Clinton wrote that Morris offered him a fairly specific strategy for the midterms based on his private polls. Morris's proposal: Stop talking about the economy and the deficit, focus instead on the hundred thousand new police officers in the crime bill, as well as school reform and a few other popular issues. Clinton wrote that Morris also advised him to stay off the campaign trail and to project himself as "presidential" on the theory that boosting his own popularity would help Democrats. "Morris believed that would do more to help the Democrats than my plunging back into the political fray," Clinton later wrote. "Neither recommendation was followed."[12]

That was news to me. As I mentioned earlier, an important principle of White House organization during my tenure was that recommendations to the president needed to come through me, or else he would be distracted and I'd be in the dark. That's exactly what happened in this case. I didn't even know Clinton was talking to Morris at that point, much less that Morris had done polling and made specific recommendations for how the president should schedule his time or present himself to the public.

Elections to the House and Senate are not national referenda. They are local and state contests, fought on ideological grounds but also on matters close to home for voters; my own entry into Congress, for instance, was made possible far more by my predecessor's inattention to his district than by the ideological gap between us. In 1994, however, Gingrich introduced an organizing device for Republican candidates, the so-called Contract with America. I doubt many Americans read the "contract," and much of it wasn't made to be taken very seriously—tort reform, term limits, a ban on U.S. soldiers serving under United Nations command, and repeal of the marriage tax penalty were among the grab bag of Republican mainstays and hardly constituted a new vision of government. But the effect of the contract was to unify Republicans and make them appear to be the party of ideas, while Democrats seemed weak and divided. I wasn't Gingrich's fan, but I did admire his tactical ability.

Election day approached with ominous speed. Clinton did his best, making trips to battleground areas and trying to boost the fortunes of struggling Democrats. None of it worked. We lost everywhere, a total of eight seats in the Senate and fifty-four in the House. Tom Foley, who had warned us of the NRA backlash from the crime bill, became the first Speaker of the House since 1862 to lose his seat. Dan Rostenkowski, our erstwhile ally on budget and tax matters (though one with some ethics problems), lost his too. Not a single Republican incumbent lost his or her seat in either house.

Bill Kristol, then a rising star among Republican intellectuals, said the returns demonstrated that "60 years of Democratic dominance of American politics, established by Franklin D. Roosevelt, have been effectively ended by two years of Bill Clinton."[13] That may have been a bit much, but the *New York Times* was not wrong to observe that "everything in Washington is changed."

Clinton took it hard. One of his greatest strengths as president was his ability to connect with the American people; now that turned against him. The public's affection had turned to rejection. He mouthed congratulations to Gingrich, then retreated, glum and distant. Gingrich gloated about the American people's endorsement of the "Contract with America," and we braced for the worst. The year ended in gloom.

EIGHT

"We Thought You Would Cave"

One awful event and one unlikely person catapulted Bill Clinton back from the depths of the 1994 midterms to the tactical victories of 1995 and his decisive reelection in 1996. The event was the bombing of the federal building in Oklahoma City, and the person, believe it or not, was Newt Gingrich.

I knew Gingrich well enough to know that he was going to be a difficult partner on anything that mattered to Clinton, but even I couldn't have predicted how quickly he would race for the bottom. On December 4, before the new Congress had been seated with Gingrich as its Speaker, Gingrich appeared on *Meet the Press* and leveled an outrageous accusation.

"I had a senior law enforcement official tell me that, in his judgment, up to a quarter of the White House staff, when they first came in, had used drugs in the last four or five years," Gingrich told Tim Russert on live television. "He's not, I'm not, making any allegations of any individual person, but it is very clear that they had huge problems getting people through security clearance."

I was watching that Sunday morning, and when I heard those comments, I lost it. For years, I'd been watching Gingrich smear enemies and whip up controversies just to advance his agenda and position, but this was a direct attack on my staff. I let him have it, responding in an interview to what I regarded as his personal attack on my colleagues. "The time has come when he has to understand that he has to stop behaving like an out-of-control radio talk show host and begin behaving like the Speaker of the House of Representatives." I challenged Gingrich to bring me the names of the people who had abused drugs, or to make those names public, and promised I would fire them if the evidence supported his accusations. In the absence of such evidence, I added, his comments were "reckless charges . . . reckless accusations that impugn people's integrity. No facts, no foundation, just basically smear and innuendo."[1] Needless to say, my remarks were gratefully received by the staff I was defending.

It almost goes without saying that Gingrich never produced any evidence to back up his comments. Instead, he called my remarks "nonsense," and maintained that it was inappropriate of me to suggest that the White House would have difficulty working with him as Speaker. It was an early taste of how partisan disagreement would descend into personal invective in the mid-1990s. It was ugly.

To give Gingrich credit, though, his theatrics did not prevent him from occasionally doing the right thing. That was evident in those same weeks when we were trying to develop a new political strategy for working with a Republican Congress, and Gingrich was charting the Republican attempt to turn the "Contract with America" into a working doctrine.

As is so often the case, a crisis that none of us had any role in creating suddenly threatened to throw us all off track. This time it came from Mexico, where the economy was failing fast. Mexico had suffered a series of political shocks in 1994—a rebellion in the southern state of Chiapas and the assassination of Luis Donaldo Colosio both spooked foreign investors. The government intervened to prop up the value of the peso, but that drained the country's reserves. More assassinations and government instability followed, and in December the government first tried a small devaluation of the peso, then was overwhelmed when the currency's value plummeted beyond its control. By early January, Mexico was within a few days of insolvency.

That may seem abstract—a currency devaluation of a foreign country is hardly the kind of thing that stirs panic among American voters. But the implications for the United States were profound. If Mexico were to collapse economically, it would plunge our most populous neighbor into a prolonged recession, disrupting one of our biggest trading partners and sowing chaos along our southern border. Cross-border trade would be severely impacted, hurting businesses throughout the United States and damaging other Latin American nations as well. A sharp rise in Mexican unemployment would almost certainly lead to a dramatic increase in illegal immigration, and the drug trade would explode as desperate people turned to it for a livelihood. And the issue was not something remote or far off: As of January 10, 1995, our economists estimated that Mexico was within a week of collapse unless some help could be offered.

The need was not just immediate, but gigantic. Bob Rubin estimated that Mexico needed $25 billion in order to pay its bills and remain solvent through the crisis. In return, we could insist on some economic reforms that might steer the country back onto a more sustainable path, but there was significant risk that Mexico would collapse anyway, taking our money with it.

Politically, the proposal was a loser. The public was not going to rally around a bailout for Mexico, and Congress was not much better. Gingrich and Bob Dole both supported economic intervention to keep Mexico afloat, but their colleagues in both parties balked. It was in their view too much money for too vague a mission.

On the evening of January 30, Bob Rubin came to my office—the president was out—and told me we were out of time. As he put it, "Mexico has 48 hours to live."[2] Congress would not act, but there was an alternative: The Exchange Stabilization Fund had enough money to cover what was now estimated to be about a $20 billion shortfall, and the president could access that money without congressional approval. When Clinton returned to the White House that night, still in his tuxedo from a dinner he'd attended, Rubin told him we couldn't wait any longer. The president asked for my analysis. I told him I thought we had to act, that we could not simply stand by and let Mexico collapse. But I warned him that we were in this by ourselves, and that if Mexico defaulted on the loan or went under despite it, it might cost Clinton his reelection. The president ordered the bailout, and announced it the following morning, with Dole and Gingrich, as well as the Democratic leaders of both houses, joining him in the statement.

We all watched Mexico nervously over the next few months. The nation wobbled a bit at first, but then it recovered, not only avoiding collapse but repaying our emergency loan ahead of schedule—and with interest.

Clinton has often been criticized for his excessive preoccupation with politics—with being, in the phrase his critics liked to use, "poll-driven" rather than the bearer of deep convictions. I don't know any politician who's indifferent to popularity, and, yes, at times Clinton was more susceptible than most. But his handling of the Mexico crisis was a powerful reminder that he was not a prisoner to polling. He took a stand that was unpopular with the public. He did so without the support or cover of Congress. And he did so despite a clear risk to his presidency. That's courage.

My early months as chief of staff had been spent trying to establish better internal organization and communication. For the most part I was satisfied by early 1995 that we were moving in the right direction. The president was less harried and more focused. Decisions were handled more crisply. We weren't being surprised as often.

Still, there were slipups, and the press pounced on them as evidence that I had not succeeded in bringing order to the White House. In February, for instance, Clinton announced the nomination of Henry W. Foster Jr. to serve as surgeon general. Foster was an articulate, respected obstetrician from Tennessee who was acting director of Meharry Medical College and ran a family planning clinic and a well-regarded abstinence campaign—perfect credentials to lead what the president hoped would be a national campaign against teen pregnancy. But when members of Congress started asking questions about his background, specifically how many abortions he had performed, Foster gave incomplete and even false answers. At first he said he had terminated "fewer than a dozen" pregnancies, then, when antiabortion groups challenged him again, he amended that to thirty-nine. He also acknowledged having supervised testing on about fifty-five women of a product that induced early abortions.

None of this would have been enough to derail Foster's nomination if we had known about it up front, but the story came out in bits and pieces, and began to raise questions about the doctor's forthrightness. Clinton stuck with him, and in May the Senate's Labor and Human Resources Committee narrowly voted in his favor, but Texas senator Phil Gramm filibustered his nomination when it reached the full Senate, and though fifty-seven senators voted to invoke cloture, that was three shy of the number needed. Foster's nomination was reluctantly withdrawn.

I took some lumps for that, since it was clear that had we done a better job vetting Foster we might have headed off the entire controversy by acknowledging at the outset that abortion, which was after all a legal procedure, had been a part of Foster's medical practice. The *Washington Post* referred to the "bungled handling" of the nomination, and suggested that it was evidence of "how little the White House operating style has changed despite the appointment of Leon E. Panetta as chief of staff."[3] That seemed a bit over the top to me then—still does, in fact—but the writer did have a point. I had allowed the Health and Human Services Department to do most of the vetting of Foster, and only brought the White House staff into the process very late. The shifting stories in the days immediately after we announced Foster doomed the nomination of a qualified man and infuriated our allies on the Hill.

Overall, I believed we were making progress, but we weren't there yet. As I said at the time, "It takes a lot of work to bring all the sheep into the corral."

Spring was a struggle that year. Gingrich was the nation's political story, while Clinton seemed to have been outfoxed. The news was dominated by the Republicans in Congress and their rush to pass the legislation that comprised their "Contract with America." Clinton, meanwhile, was distracted and unsure of himself. And in his desperation to get his program back on track, he was regularly consulting with Dick Morris. He took great pains to keep those contacts from me and the rest of the White House staff. He and Morris spoke only over the phone and only late at night; Clinton gave him a code name, "Charlie," so that operators or others who might overhear a snippet of conversation would not know with whom he was speaking.

With "Charlie" whispering in his ear, Clinton began wandering in uncomfortable directions. He wondered whether he ought to pull back on affirmative action, for instance, an idea that would help him with conservatives, always Morris's aim. To his credit, Clinton held fast there, but Morris, who consulted with a number of Republicans, including Trent Lott, kept pushing. I had a hunch that "Charlie" might be Morris, but I didn't know for sure.

Harold Ickes, who detested Morris and was one of the shrewdest political analysts I'd ever met, sniffed out what was going on and came to me. "You know damn well who this 'Charlie' is," he harrumphed. When I acknowledged that I had my suspicions, Harold forcefully made the point that we couldn't allow this back channel to remain open. "We've got to bring this under control," he said. "We can't just let that go freewheeling out there."

While I considered how to address this with the president, the matter came to a head. In early April, the president was scheduled to speak to the American Society of Newspaper Editors, and the White House speechwriting team had produced a draft of the talk for him to give. A day or two before it was scheduled, Clinton returned with an entirely new draft. Our version had him largely avoiding Gingrich and congressional Republicans, a tactic I assumed Clinton approved of. Instead, he now proposed to engage those Republicans and emphasize our points of commonality.

I sensed Morris's hand at work, and confronted the president with my concerns: I respected his right to seek advice, of course, but doing so surreptitiously undermined me and complicated our attempts to focus the White House's message and decision making. For the moment, our challenge was to rescue the speech and to find some acceptable language that would steer between Morris's draft and ours.

Unsurprisingly, the speech Clinton delivered drew a confused and confusing response. The *New York Times* led with Clinton's threat to veto elements of the "Contract with America" and noted that "the major purpose of his speech was to mount a counterattack." The *Los Angeles Times* led its story by quoting the president assailing Republicans in Congress for "ideological extremism" and described the thrust of the address as "a marked departure from the accommodating rhetoric that has predominated in White House statements recently." The *Washington Post,* on the other hand, emphasized that he was offering to "split the difference" with those same Republicans. Which of those was right? Sadly, all of them. Our message was unclear even to me.

I was eager not to have that experience again, so I invited Morris to drop the alias and join us openly. We set up a Wednesday evening meeting that combined White House and political staff, including Morris.

On balance, that was preferable to having him lurking on the edges and talking to the president out of my earshot, but he was a handful.

After the first of our Wednesday meetings, during which I'd had to endure Morris's theatrical bombast for a couple hours, I was trudging down the hall back to my office and I ran into Harold, who was fetching a cup of water. "Charlie," I said, "goddamned Charlie."

His eyes lit up. "Dick Morris?" he asked, knowing the answer. I didn't respond, didn't need to, because he then finished his own thought: "He's a sleazy little fuck."

I couldn't have said it better myself. I tried my best to corral Morris, to respect the Clintons' appreciation for him, and to take advantage of his skills. But there were days when I regretted it. He used his entree to try to weigh in on foreign policy until Sandy Berger and Tony Lake complained; I shut that down. He sought out White House aides to lecture them on policies that his polling data suggested would be good for Clinton—at one point, for instance, Morris was arguing that we should provide a free college education to every American. Needless to say, that's an idea that polls well. I had to go back to the president again.

"He can't do that," I insisted of Morris having his own contact with my staff. "If he has ideas, he's going to have to come to me." Clinton again agreed. We kept tussling.

Morris polled incessantly, and his data always seemed to support his theory of what the White House should be doing. Again with eerie coincidence, that bent policy toward the center, agitating the more liberal members of the staff, especially Harold, whose philosophical disdain for Morris was nothing compared with his visceral distrust of him. Unfortunately for Morris, Harold controlled the money on the polling, and he demanded that Morris produce cross-tabs—the underlying demographic data that make polls genuinely useful—so that he could check Dick's conclusions. Morris evaded over and over until Harold told him he was cutting off the money. The next morning, a mountain of polling cross-tabs suddenly appeared in our offices. Harold described it as a "dump truck." That wasn't far off.

The mixed signals about our approach to congressional Republicans and the botched Foster nomination convinced some people that the White House remained in disarray, and some commentators began to look beyond Clinton, assuming he was a one-term president and asking who might succeed him. Bob Dole announced his candidacy on April 10. The following week, the president held an evening news conference that two networks declined even to air. At the conference, one reporter delicately raised the question of whether Clinton was already fading from the scene. "Do you worry," the reporter asked, "about making sure that your voice is heard in the coming months?"

Clinton was reduced to insisting that "the president is relevant here." There would be more low moments in the Clinton presidency, particularly in the second term, but that was the lowest to date.

The news conference was on April 18. Just before 9 a.m. the following morning, Timothy McVeigh parked a rented Ryder truck in a handicapped spot in front of the Alfred P. Murrah Federal Building. Inside the van was a load of fertilizer, racing fuel, and dynamite. At 9:02 a.m., just after parents had dropped off their children at the building's day care center, McVeigh lit two fuses, locked the van behind him, and walked quickly away, not looking back. Nineteen children were among the 168 who died. It was the second anniversary of the shootout at the Branch Davidian compound in Waco.

There was a television set just outside the door to the Oval Office, and the first reports were so shocking that Clinton emerged and stood next to me in silence. We watched for a few minutes, and the president offered a few quiet thoughts—he wanted to be sure investigators were headed for the scene, and he asked about whether a disaster declaration would help those affected by the blast. We discussed who might be behind this, agreeing that it felt like an act of foreign terrorism. Only later, after McVeigh had been arrested on a traffic stop, did the possibility of domestic terrorism enter our thinking.

That Sunday, the president and first lady traveled to Oklahoma to participate in a nationally televised service of remembrance. The president was uncharacteristically brief, and he captured that complex welter of emotions that swept over the country after the bombing—the shock and grief, the bewilderment and anger, the desperate search for some meaning. Much has been written about that wonderful and moving address, and about President Clinton's unique capacity to empathize with people in trouble. It was a great moment for the country, a defiant refusal to allow violence to curdle into hatred.

Less noted has been the effect it had on Clinton himself. He and the first lady were shaken and noticeably sad in the days after the bombing. They met on Saturday with a group of federal workers' children, who sat on the carpet in the Oval Office. One of them suggested that the Clintons plant a tree in memory of the victims, and the Clintons did on Sunday, a white dogwood on the South Lawn, before leaving for Oklahoma. Images of the planting showed them drawn and tired, unusually uncomfortable, unsure what to do with the shovels.

Then they spent the day amid rubble and shattered families. The men and women whom they comforted were in a sense their employees. Those who died included agents of the Drug Enforcement Administration and the Department of Housing and Urban Development. There were army recruiters and employees of the Federal Credit Union. As the president put it, those were men and women who "served the rest of us, who worked to help the elderly and the disabled, who worked to support our farmers and our veterans, who worked to enforce our laws and to protect us. Let us say clearly, they served us well, and we are grateful."

Those notions—of service and gratitude—spoke tenderly to the president. Whatever his faults, his embrace of those ideas was deep and genuine, and it was powerfully reinforced by his experience in Oklahoma City.

Tragedy can focus the mind, and it did in this instance. Clinton's speech reminded the nation of the president's capacity as a leader. It reminded Clinton of something else: the duty and opportunity that leadership presented. He returned to the White House with a new confidence, hard to describe but obvious to all of us. We moved forward.

With Clinton back at full strength, we spent the summer and fall fencing with Gingrich and the Republicans in Congress. We proposed to balance the budget in ten years; they pushed for seven. We offered our version of welfare reform; they offered theirs. They proposed deep cuts in spending for health care; we vowed to protect the sick and elderly. We disagreed vehemently over Medicare, with the administration pressing to reduce the projected increases in the program and Republicans fighting to cut it far more deeply. Republicans voted to drastically reduce AmeriCorps, a work program the president was very proud of; we fought to restore at least most of that funding. They cut education; we tried to invest in it.

In the summer, they attempted to cut foreign aid and agencies of the State Department, preying on the broadly held misconception that foreign affairs represents a serious drain on the budget when in fact it comes to less than 1 percent. Clinton threatened to veto that legislation, and took a hard swipe at the proponents of it during a commencement address at Dartmouth College. "Look at the history of the twentieth century," Clinton told the graduates on a rainy morning in Hanover. "Every time America turned away from the world, we wound up with a war that we had to clean up and win at far greater costs than if we simply stayed involved in a responsible manner."

Internally, we spent a great deal of time during those months debating whether we should offer a counterproposal to the cuts being endorsed by Republicans in Congress. On the one hand, offering an

alternative was sound governance; it would give us a negotiating platform to debate our differences with Gingrich and his allies and push us
toward an eventual deal. On the other hand, I didn't have much faith
that Gingrich was interested in a responsible deal. It seemed to me and
others that this was gamesmanship, and his intention was to break us,
not meet us halfway. My counsel was to concentrate our fire on the
defects in the Republican plan and to chip away at it politically. Others
agreed, and we spread the word to the Hill, where members dutifully
toed the line.

Clinton was not thrilled by that approach. He wanted to present a
counterproposal—he felt obligated to propose a budget, and he was
tired of being treated as a sideshow to Gingrich. He appreciated the
political wisdom of lying low, but it didn't come naturally to him,
and in a May interview he let slip that he felt he owed the country a
"counter-budget," which he said could be balanced in less than ten
years.

I was furious. We had been urging discipline on congressional
Democrats, and now Clinton had done exactly what we'd pleaded with
them not to do. My phone rang off the hook with angry members of
Congress, dumbfounded that we'd changed strategy without bother-
ing to let them know.

Truth is, it was just Clinton chafing at a strategy he never really
accepted. Making it worse was Morris, who fervently urged the president to ignore the advice of his staff and instead make a major speech
on the budget, in which he would lay out his proposal for bringing it
into balance. I fought it out with Morris in meeting after meeting—he
specifically blamed me at one of them for being the impediment to his
good ideas—but I could see that his counsel was working on Clinton.
As Memorial Day weekend approached, Clinton abruptly instructed
me to have the speechwriting team work up a budget speech for the following Tuesday, less than a week away.

As I've already written, budgets were an important part of my political upbringing. To me, there were smart ways to put together spending plans, and there were dumb ways. But I can't think of a dumber way to draft a budget for the U.S. government than to throw it together over Memorial Day weekend in order to placate a self-absorbed political consultant. Clinton gave me those instructions on a Thursday evening, and I straggled into the office the next morning, unsure about how to proceed. I happened to run into George Stephanopoulos, who was as troubled as I was. He warned me that Laura Tyson, who headed the Council of Economic Advisers, might resign if we went ahead.

For a moment I wondered whether I might too. To be genuinely effective in Washington, it pays to know your limits. I'd hit them in my conflicts with the Nixon administration in 1970 and 1971, and I'd never regretted leaving. Would being forced to throw together a slapdash budget for purely political ends rise to that same level of offense? I pondered that question even as we worked through the weekend to get Clinton the numbers that would form the core of his presentation. Finally, Bob Rubin persuaded him that we couldn't manage it. The Tuesday speech was shelved. I, along with the rest of the economic team, felt that we now had a chance to stick with a strong economic agenda.

Throughout my career, I've always believed that it's important to look for points of agreement, to appreciate the ideas on the other side and meet them halfway. But that's not at the expense of principles; it's a recognition that progress is important too. Thankfully, Clinton's last-minute reconsideration of that budget speech did not force me to choose.

Pulled between Morris and his staff, Clinton settled for a hybrid— a speech to the nation that would present our broad principles and some specific targets but avoid commitments in other areas, maintaining our maneuvering room. He gave the speech on June 13. In that brief talk, televised from the Oval Office, Clinton laid out five priorities: We would protect education; we would cut Medicare costs but not services; we would support tax cuts for the middle class but not for high-income earners; we would cut welfare to push recipients back to work; we would resist an overall level of cuts that was so high it might slow economic growth. Beyond that, Clinton did offer a few specifics. He said he was willing to cut discretionary federal spending by 20 percent, though he exempted education from those cuts, and he promised, once again, to balance the budget within ten years. He closed by noting that there were some observers who believed gridlock might benefit one side or the other politically; Clinton said he disagreed, and vowed to try to avoid it. That was our hand; now it was time to play it.

Those tensions mounted through the fall, as Gingrich, followed by a reluctant Bob Dole in the Senate, girded for a showdown over the federal budget and debt ceiling. They were demanding deeper spending cuts than we were willing to give. If they failed to get their way, they vowed to reject the continuing resolutions that keep the government operating in the absence of a budget. Their other bargaining chip was the ministerial vote to raise the debt ceiling, which allows the government to pay its creditors for debts it has already incurred; failing to raise the ceiling would put the U.S. government in default. The same Gingrich who had recognized the calamity of allowing Mexico to default was now prepared to sanction just that fate for our own government and economy.

For me this was an especially tricky period, because I was fending off not just Gingrich and the House Republicans but also Morris, our own house Republican. Morris's job was to position Clinton for his reelection, and through that prism it made a certain sense to seek a middle ground over the budget fight. If Clinton were seen as governing in cooperation with Republicans, it would mute their argument that he needed to be replaced. Of course, that meant capitulating on matters central to Democrats and to the administration up to that point, but that wasn't Morris's concern. So as the showdown loomed, I worried not only that Republicans would force us over the cliff but that Clinton might willingly join them.

We had prepared meticulously for the confrontation. Two weeks after the president's speech to the nation, he wrote to congressional leaders to warn them that the budget they were considering cut too deeply into Medicare.[4] He welcomed leaders back to Washington from the Fourth of July break and suggested that it would be "in error" to let budget talks come to an impasse.[5] On July 26, he reiterated his refusal to sign the bill that would cut foreign aid and eliminate important agencies working in arms control and information; if Congress insisted on passing the bill, Clinton said, he would veto it.[6] On July 29, the thirtieth anniversary of the passage of the original Medicare bill, the president and first lady jointly delivered the weekly radio address, devoting much of it to the promise to defend that program against the proposed Republican cuts.[7]

With each of those statements and more through August and September, we drew our battle lines, clarifying what we were willing to discuss and what we would fight to defend. Behind the scenes, we were also preparing. I asked members of our staff to assemble concrete examples of what some of the consequences of the proposed Republican cuts would be. They were striking: Cuts to the national park system threatened more than one hundred rural communities near those parks across the country; cuts to Medicare would deepen the suffering of families from Fairfax, Virginia, to Los Osos, California. The Chrysalis StreetWorks project in Los Angeles, which was registering important successes in putting homeless people to work and in housing, would face possible closure if the Republicans had their way with the budget for Housing and Urban Development. Children everywhere would suffer if education money dried up.

We collected those stories, inserted some of them into the president's speeches, and banked the rest to be used in an emergency. We got one.

Both sides took a small step back in late September, when Congress passed measures to keep the government running while we hashed out our differences. But that postponed for only a few weeks the ultimate test. On October 19, with time running out to raise the debt ceiling, Clinton urged members of Congress not to "play political games with the good faith and credit of the United States." And he warned them that if they cut deeply into Medicare or shifted economic burdens away from the rich and onto the middle class, he would refuse to go along. They went ahead anyway, approving a series of continuing resolutions; some were unobjectionable, and the president signed those. But others were conditional on the very cuts we'd explicitly ruled out.

Just as the budget standoff built to a crescendo, on November 4 Clinton was interrupted by a tragedy. Yitzhak Rabin, whose courageous willingness to enter peace talks with Yasser Arafat produced a foreign policy highlight of the Clinton presidency—as well as the memorable image of the two old enemies shaking hands—was shot at a peace rally in Tel Aviv by a young right-wing opponent of Rabin's peace efforts. Rabin was struck by two bullets and died less than an hour later.

Clinton was staggered by the news. He had been with Rabin less than two weeks earlier, and he admired him as he did few other leaders. They had worked together, at considerable risk of failure, and come to trust each other. "By the time he was killed," Clinton later wrote of Rabin, "I had come to love him as I had rarely loved another man."[8] Clinton traveled to Jerusalem for the funeral, leading an American delegation that included Presidents Carter and Bush, as well as Gingrich, Dole, and other congressional leaders. Clinton delivered a mournful eulogy for his friend on November 6, and left the following morning, arriving in Washington before dawn and returning, tired and brokenhearted, to the White House.

On November 13, Clinton vetoed H.R. 115, the continuing resolution that included the conditions he had vowed to reject, and dared Congress to take the next step. "I will continue to stand for my principles," he said.

Would he? With Gingrich pushing him to the brink and Morris urging him to find a compromise, would Clinton risk his reelection on the gamble that he could back down his opponents? Not only was that a political risk, but it also cut against his natural tendency to search for a middle way. He liked the center, understood the value of cutting a deal. As I met with Alice Rivlin from OMB, Harold Ickes, and Erskine Bowles, my concern was that Clinton would give too much, and that it would backlash with Democrats. They shared my worry.

On the evening of November 13, with the budget veto still fresh, leaders of the House and Senate came to the White House to see if we could cut a deal that would prevent the government from shutting down at midnight, when the previous continuing resolution expired. Clinton asked me to open the meeting with a presentation of what we were prepared to offer. I outlined the specifics of our proposals, including an offer to cut Medicare more than we had previously proposed, though substantially less than Republicans were seeking. I spoke for a few minutes, and as soon as I finished, Gingrich chimed in to complain that the White House had poisoned our deliberations by airing television ads that made our case and accused Republicans of endangering Medicare. I couldn't believe it. This was the same Gingrich who'd accused our staff of abusing drugs, who described the president as "the enemy of normal people," and who liked to call the Clintons "McGoverniks."

"Mr. Speaker," I said, struggling to control my temper, "you don't have clean hands."

That gave the more reasonable Bob Dole a chance to interject, and for a moment I thought we might avert the crisis. Dole was receptive to the proposal I had just presented. So receptive, in fact, that he startled me. "That's fine with me," he said of my pitch. "Let's take it."

Not so fast. Gingrich jumped immediately back in and said it was unacceptable to him. He was joined by Dick Armey, who wanted to whine more about the television ads. They were, he said, alarmist, and they were frightening his mother-in-law. Clinton parried that, apologizing if she was upset but reminding Armey that the Republican cuts would hurt her worse than ours.

Armey then tried to threaten the president. Unless he backed down, the congressman blustered, the GOP would shut down the government and drive Clinton from office.

Clinton did not flinch. He fiercely told Armey that he didn't care what the political consequences were, that he would veto and keep vetoing the Republican plan "even if I drop to 5 percent in the polls." And, he added, "If you want your budget, you'll have to get someone else to sit in this chair."

From that moment on, I knew that we might lose the debate, but we would not sacrifice principle. We were going to fight it out. At midnight, much of the U.S. government shut down, with far-reaching consequences: The Centers for Disease Control halted disease surveillance; more than three hundred national parks closed; passport services were halted; federal courts cut back hours and services. Payments to government contractors were delayed, with those effects rippling outward. Hundreds of thousands of workers went without pay.[9]

Despite the brinkmanship that had brought us to that point, both sides continued to talk even as the government went into hibernation. Day after day, Gingrich and company arrived at the White House, and we looked for ways to cut a deal. Dole was acutely conscious of the toll a protracted shutdown could take on his presidential campaign, and he was looking for a way out from the beginning. The stakes were different for Gingrich, who had a safe seat in Georgia and was looking to elbow his way into history by knocking down the president. And having sized up Clinton over the two years of his presidency, Gingrich clearly thought that Clinton would cave if he just kept up the pressure. So we would talk, seem to make headway, and then, just before we broke up, Gingrich would offer some new idea or proposal, setting us back again.

Almost from the first day, however, public opinion sided with Clinton, who was seen as waging a principled campaign to defend Medicare against congressional Republicans perceived as angling for political advantage.[10] Gingrich helped our side immeasurably with a childish remark on the second day of the closure. The Speaker was meeting that morning with reporters, and was discussing the personalities surrounding the shutdown. He noted that he was insulted that Clinton had not bothered to invite him and other Republican leaders to join him in the front of the plane to discuss the budget during their recent trip to Rabin's funeral. He also said he was angered to be asked to exit the plane from the rear when it returned to the United States the next day.

"I think that's part of why you ended up with us sending down a tougher continuing resolution," he said, adding, "This is petty, and I'm going to say up front it's petty . . . but I think it's human."[11] He didn't even stop there, but continued complaining about his treatment, suggesting that the White House had deliberately sent him and Dole out the back door so that television crews at the airport wouldn't get images of the Republicans and Clinton together. All of that was ridiculous and borderline paranoid—the plane had landed before dawn, and no crews were there to greet it; Clinton actually had wandered to the back of the plane to pay his respects to Dole and Gingrich, and Gingrich had even been allowed to bring his wife on the plane, a courtesy not extended to other members of the delegation. But the big point was so obvious that I barely had to make it: Gingrich was suggesting that he was willing to shut down the U.S. government because his feelings were hurt. I couldn't resist making a comment, so when CNN called and asked for my response to Gingrich's claim to have been slighted by Clinton, I gave one: "This is bizarre. Even if that were the case, which it isn't, why would you want to shut down the government because you feel somehow as if you've been snubbed?"

The front of the next day's *New York Daily News* featured a full-page cartoon of Gingrich in diapers, holding a baby bottle, crying, and stomping his feet. The headline read, CRY BABY: NEWT'S TANTRUM: HE CLOSED DOWN THE GOVERNMENT BECAUSE CLINTON MADE HIM SIT AT BACK OF PLANE.[12] The shutdown now had a human narrative: Beleaguered president forced to endure spoiled brat Speaker. As Lars-Erik Nelson of the *Daily News* wrote, it was "junior high school cafeteria intrigue," handed to us, unbidden, by the Speaker. In politics, sometimes it's better to be lucky than good, and we were in many ways lucky to have Gingrich as an adversary.

The Speaker's snafu and the polling numbers made Republicans receptive to finding a way out, and we offered them one on November 19. In the weeks leading up to the shutdown, I'd been working with Rivlin to look at various economic models and their effect on the deficit. For months we had been saying our proposals would balance the federal budget in ten years, but as the economy continued to improve, we concluded that we might actually be able to get there more quickly. In fact, without having to make the cuts demanded by Republicans, we believed now that we might be able to balance the budget in the seven years they were advocating. In other words, we could meet their target without their cuts. At our regular budget confab that day, I suggested to our Republican counterparts that the president could submit a proposal to that effect if they would vote to reopen the government. We cut the deal right there, and the government reopened immediately, though temporarily, because the resolution carried us only to December 15. The idea was that we would use those weeks to hammer out a deal and leave the government in operation. It did not work out quite that way.

We met almost daily, refusing to give in to our exasperation with one another. Meanwhile, we turned up the outside pressure, creating a White House Budget Plan with events every day to highlight the differences between our budget and theirs, as well as op-ed submissions, meetings with constituency groups, and consultations with our allies in Congress. When Clinton left on a long-planned trip overseas, we had Gore standing by in case the Republicans chose that moment to pass another set of offensive appropriations bills. Even holiday receptions were laced with references to the budget and a possible shutdown.[13] The news drumbeat increasingly took the line that we were trying to keep the government open, while Gingrich was willing to close it down.

All of which was merely the symptom of the larger contest: Gingrich had decided to use this moment to break Clinton, and Clinton refused to break. Republicans mocked our new economic projections, insinuating that we'd merely tweaked the numbers to make it appear that we could balance the budget in seven years without their pain. So on December 15, when the stopgap funding bill expired, much of the government shut down again.

We were buoyed by the public's reaction. The president was gaining strength, and the Republicans were losing. Moreover, Dole needed this over to get on with his campaign. So Christmas came and went without a deal. Snow fell on Washington, and we still didn't have a deal. Then, on January 6, Gingrich threw in the towel. "We made a mistake," he told Clinton with me and others present. "We thought you would cave."

The Republicans removed the offensive cuts from the remaining appropriations bills, and Clinton signed them. The president agreed to some additional savings and cuts in Medicare and elsewhere, and submitted to Congress a proposal to balance the budget by 2002. Clinton wrote an open letter welcoming all federal government employees back to work, and the government returned to full operation.

Less than three weeks later, Clinton delivered his annual State of the Union address, and it bore the marks of the shutdown and its aftermath. It was that year that Clinton memorably declared that "the era of big government is over," a line that Republicans cheered lustily that night and have long since pointed to as evidence that the shutdown forced Clinton to rethink the place of government in American life. Less often quoted, however, is the balance of that sentence. "But," Clinton added, "we cannot go back to the time when our citizens were just left to fend for themselves."

Later in that same speech, Clinton pulled off one of the great head fakes in the history of the address. It came near the end of the address, as he told a story of heroism during the Oklahoma City bombing.

"His name is Richard Dean," the president began. "He's a forty-nine-year-old Vietnam veteran who's worked for the Social Security Administration for twenty-two years now. Last year he was hard at work in the Federal Building in Oklahoma City when the blast killed 169 people and brought the rubble down all around him. He reentered that building four times. He saved the lives of three women. He's here with us this evening, and I want to recognize Richard and applaud both his public service and his extraordinary personal heroism."

The audience jumped to its feet and gave Dean a sustained standing ovation. Behind the president, Speaker Gingrich was among those who applauded long and hard.

"But Richard Dean's story doesn't end there," Clinton continued. "This last November, he was forced out of his office when the government shut down. And the second time the government shut down he continued helping Social Security recipients, but he was working without pay. On behalf of Richard Dean and his family, and all the other people who are out there working every day doing a good job for the American people, I challenge all of you in this chamber: Let's never, ever shut the federal government down again."

The chamber again erupted in applause, accompanied this time by hoots of derision as Democrats lambasted Republicans for the shutdown. Gingrich sat grumpily, not flinching as Clinton received the applause, the traces of a smile on his face. I was sitting in the gallery that night, just two seats to Dean's right. I stood and applauded along with the rest of the Democrats in the chamber and realized then that we had won.

Looking back on the shutdown over those weeks, there are several things worth recalling. The shutdown did not need to happen; and those who forced it, Gingrich and his allies, were badly hurt by it. The public decisively blamed them and not Clinton, whose political fortunes and reelection were strongly enhanced by facing down Gingrich. The administration did not ask for the confrontation, but we were ready for it when it came to us, and we outmaneuvered our opposition.

There were also unexpected results of the shutdown. After all our struggling between balancing the budget in ten years or seven, and after the GOP's dismissal of my prediction that we could balance the budget in seven without their cuts, it turned out that we were both wrong, though they were much more wrong than I. In fact, we balanced the budget not in 2002, as I had proposed we attempt, but in 1998, when the government, for the first time since the 1950s, ran a surplus. From that point forward, Clinton would never log another deficit.

There was another consequence of those weeks. When we sent federal workers home during the shutdown, it meant that the White House was uncharacteristically quiet at night. On November 15, when the government was shut down for the first time, most of the secretaries and other White House staff went home. My staff stayed, because we were embroiled in the negotiations. What that meant was that my interns were working late, and had relatively easy access to the president. At about 9:20 p.m., a young intern in my office named Monica Lewinsky was working alone in the outer office that led to mine. I would learn only years later, in the context of the impeachment hearings, what happened that night.

Publicly, the shutdown illustrated Clinton's potential for political resolve and arguably secured his reelection; privately, it revealed his lack of personal discipline and planted the seeds of his impeachment.

Clinton's decisive victory in the shutdown meant that he entered 1996 in an entirely different political position from the one he'd been in a year earlier. His approval ratings were on the rise—after spending 1995 mostly in the 40s, Clinton hit 50 during the first shutdown, and after delivering his State of the Union address never fell below that mark again in 1996. The economy was healthy, and Republicans were badly divided between the Gingrich insurgents, now tainted by their failure in the shutdown, and the more moderate elements led by Bob Dole. Dole would go on to win the Republican nomination, but his age and the party's divisions alone probably were enough to keep him from being a serious challenge.

That hardly meant that 1996 was a coast for Clinton, however. We all recalled well Bush's tumble from the heights of post–Gulf war popularity to the lows of recession president, and Clinton was taking no chances; certainly Morris wasn't, and he continued to push Clinton to take away issues that Republicans once owned in order to secure his hold on the center. In 1996, that meant welfare reform.

Clinton's support for revamping welfare was not entirely political. He had argued for it throughout his campaign and sent bills up to the Hill earlier in his first term. Indeed, I believed then—and still believe today—that if we had pressed welfare reform in 1993 or 1994, we might have gotten a serious and compassionate bill out of the Democratic Congress. Now the calculation would be far different, but we still had a chance with welfare, because it was an area where many Republicans shared many of Clinton's misgivings. Ending "welfare as we know it" was an idea that Clinton embraced sincerely, not cynically.

Welfare was not the only item on Morris's to-do list that year, but most of his other suggestions were fairly inconsequential tidbits intended to appeal to one constituency or another—support for school uniforms, midnight basketball, the v-chip to let parents control their children's television viewing habits (a favorite of Al and Tipper Gore), abstinence education, programs to wean children from tobacco and drugs. None of those amounted to much, but they served their purpose politically, and were generally positive programs and ideas.

Welfare reform was far more controversial, and Democrats were deeply divided over it. For Republicans, welfare was offensive because it encouraged dependency and discouraged work—condemning the "welfare state" was a staple of Republican dogma. Those were valid criticisms in many ways, but also easy ones for the GOP, since few poor people affiliated themselves with the party anyway (notably, many of the same conservatives who attacked welfare were much less critical of farm subsidies, government aid whose recipients were far more likely to be Republicans).

Clinton shared some of the conservative critique of welfare, but he resisted withdrawing the safety net altogether, and also was bothered by some of the illogic that had become built up in the system over the years. It troubled him, for instance, that a welfare recipient who left welfare for a minimum-wage job would as a consequence often lose his or her health care, since Medicaid was available to those on welfare but often not for the working poor. It was perverse to think that the cost of health insurance would push people out of work and onto welfare— and that it would keep them there. Beyond that, Clinton's extraordinary capacity for empathy led him to deplore some of the personal ramifications of welfare—the shame that many felt for having to receive it. He would often argue that those most offended by welfare were those forced to rely on it.

So as we worked for an acceptable welfare reform package, there was considerable room for political accommodation but also wildly differing motives. That made negotiations both promising and perilous. In 1996, the Republicans went first, and Clinton vetoed their initial attempt, which he felt was too hard on children.

Working through the relevant committees on the Hill, we hammered out a bill that was widely popular in Congress and yet very divisive within the White House. It transformed welfare from a traditional federal social program into a set of block grants. The government would give each state a set amount of money and require the states to contribute as well. That gave states an incentive to push recipients, almost all of them single mothers, from "welfare to work," as the saying went. Unlike the Republicans' first effort, it increased support for child care—a major inhibitor for many poor women trying to get work was that child care ate up so much of the money they might make by leaving welfare—but it imposed caps on how long a recipient could receive money. After five years, federal support for struggling families would cease. The program's new name reflected its changed intentions. Once called Aid to Families with Dependent Children, it was now to be called Temporary Assistance to Needy Families. The emphasis was on "temporary."

If that was all it had done, I might have been able to support it. I understood that welfare had become a source of dependency for many recipients, and if we could combine a cutoff with support for reentering the workforce, that struck me as a fair balance. But in an effort to broaden conservative support for the bill, we allowed it to reduce support for food stamps, which I had long championed in Congress, and to deny many benefits, including food stamps and medical care, to legal immigrants. That last provision struck me as heartless and irrational. My mother and father came to this country young and poor and worked for decades, paying taxes, building a family, running a business. If they had fallen on hard times, why would we have denied them the same benefits we would have given to their neighbors, solely because of where they were born? The bill was predicated on the premise that immigrants, legal immigrants, were somehow less American than people born here. I didn't accept that premise, and I urged Clinton not to accept it, first in private and then at a meeting of his senior advisers on this issue on the morning of July 31.

"A provision that prevents immigrants from getting any kind of assistance just seems to me to be against everything we've stood for," I said. "And I have to tell you, Mr. President, as the son of immigrants, it's very hard for me to say that you ought to support this."

Clinton was plainly torn. In the end, it was the rare instance in which we ended up simply disagreeing. He viewed this as his best chance to do something about the problems of welfare, and though he had serious reservations, he refused to let the moment go. On August 22, he signed the bill, including its indefensible provisions on immigrants. Several important members of the administration, including Peter Edelman, a top official at Health and Human Services, resigned in protest.

By its own terms, welfare reform was a success. It removed millions of recipients from the rolls—about 12.6 million people received Aid to Families with Dependent Children in 1996; about 4.5 million received TANF ten years later. It saved billions of dollars in federal spending and helped push many recipients back to work. How much of that is to the program's credit is a more difficult question to answer. The reform obviously was aided by the booming economy of the mid-1990s; how many of those recipients would have been left with nowhere to turn in more dire economic times is impossible to know. And yet decades of experience under the revised rules convinced many early skeptics that the reforms did achieve important success. Moreover, Clinton went back to Congress the following year and cleaned up some of the more coldhearted aspects of the bill he signed in 1996. Immigrants were reinstated as legitimate recipients of aid.

Though I opposed it, I recognized the political appeal of welfare reform. I didn't believe Clinton needed it to beat Bob Dole—for me, that deal was sealed by the shutdown—but it certainly did let out any air left in Dole's tires that year. It's hard to argue that a president who produces a landmark social reform with the support of majorities of both parties in Congress is either ineffective or out of touch. In that sense, welfare reform was a victory for Morris and triangulation. If so, it was Morris's last such victory. In September, just hours before Clinton's speech to the Democratic convention in Chicago, a Washington prostitute revealed to a tabloid news show that she'd had a long dalliance with Morris and that he'd shared his work with her, even letting her listen in on his phone calls with the president. Morris resigned. I'm not one to pass judgment on his personal life, but it sure was a relief to have him out of the White House.

No election can be taken for granted, and Clinton worked hard through the fall to make his case to the American people. In October, he traveled to New York, Connecticut, New Hampshire, Maine, Tennessee, Ohio, Kentucky (those last three in one day), Colorado, New Mexico, California, New Jersey, back to Ohio, Michigan, Florida, Alabama, Louisiana, Georgia, Virginia, back to Tennessee, Missouri, Minnesota, Illinois, back to Ohio, Pennsylvania, back to Michigan, back to Colorado, Arizona, Nevada, and back to California. On election night he carried forty-seven million votes, beating Dole by twelve million. He won 379 electoral votes, 70 percent of the total.

Clinton and I spent much of that evening playing cards at his hotel in Little Rock, joined by his friend and lawyer Bruce Lindsey. Clinton is a ferocious hearts player, who can keep track of several games at once. It took his mind off the updates flowing in from across the country. After a while, history overtook cards. The networks announced that he'd won.

Although Clinton lost a few states in 1996 that he'd won in 1992—and carried two, Arizona and Florida, that he'd lost the first time—the only real disappointment of the election was that, for the second time, he won without carrying a majority of the popular vote. In 1992, Ross Perot had been a blessing, taking more from Bush than from Clinton;

this time, he did much less well, but just well enough to keep Clinton below 50 percent of the popular vote. The result was one of modern American politics' stranger oddities: Al Gore in 2000 got a higher percentage of the vote than Clinton got in either of his two elections, but Clinton won both and Gore lost his.

I had made it clear to Clinton from the start that I wanted to wrap up my work once the election was over, and we moved quickly in its aftermath to make the transition. I was happy that he selected Erskine Bowles to succeed me—and pleased that Erskine, after some hesitation, accepted.

For Sylvia and me, it was at last a time to go home to California together, to resume our life in Carmel Valley in a way we hadn't really done since I left for Congress in 1976. We packed up during those weeks after the election and headed west right after the inauguration.

As we did, I jotted down some parting thoughts to the president. Clinton and I had begun our association with only the barest sense of each other. We had grown to become admiring colleagues and had finished as friends. My respect for him was enormous, and my debt to him—for the opportunity to help him accomplish great things for the country—was deep and heartfelt. So I wrote in a spirit of humility but also out of a genuine desire to leave him with some thoughts to help. I offered five thoughts.

"Trust in your own judgment," I wrote. "This does not mean you should not listen to others. But be more confident of your own first instincts and your ultimate judgment. After all, the people elected you for *your* judgment. And for God's sake, once you've decided, do not revisit the decisions—move on."

Second, "You cannot let the bastards get you down." Surrounded as he was by critics and a dedicated special prosecutor, Clinton could become distracted or morose. I was sure the American people were as tired of this as he was. I urged him to shrug it off.

Third, "Speak to the people." Clinton almost always did well when he reached around Congress or any other adversary and connected to the people directly. I hoped he would do it more and remember how much power it gave him.

Fourth, "Do not forget your most loyal troops." Here I confessed I had not helped Clinton as much as I could have. "I felt it was important to meet often with the cabinet and staff to keep them informed of what was happening," I wrote him. "My regret is that I did not insist that you do more of that." This was a tension of my entire time as chief of staff—how to streamline decision making and still preserve Clinton's connection to those he most relied upon. I do believe we'd made it better, but I recognized that the difficulty would continue.

Finally, and somewhat cheekily, I added, "Lastly, for God's sake, get your rest and stay on time."

With that, my service to Clinton was concluded. I would, of course, watch with appreciation and some dismay as he bounded through his second term, where his achievements were more incremental than in the first but helped to institutionalize the work we had begun. His economic record was sterling, and the country prospered under his leadership. And yet there were the tawdry revelations about Lewinsky and the bewildering attempt to drive him from office over that embarrassing episode. On December 19, 1998, he became only the second president in American history to be impeached, charged with perjury and obstruction of justice for his evasive, misleading answers about his relationship with Lewinsky. On February 12, 1999, he was acquitted on both counts. To this day, it boggles my mind to think that the nation spent those months discussing whether to remove the president of the United States from office because he lied about an extramarital affair. The American people seemed to share my bafflement; they responded to the impeachment by siding solidly with Clinton.

Bill Clinton was not perfect, but he left a better country than he inherited. And, amazingly, he departed as a more popular leader than when he arrived.

Sylvia and I were home. I had always regarded Washington as my workplace and Carmel Valley as my home. Now, after decades of bridging that gap, we had the chance to enjoy life in one location.

I wasn't quite ready for a rocking chair, so after a period of decompression I began scouting out ways to continue contributing. Cal State chancellor Barry Munitz, who had been such a help during the decommissioning of Fort Ord and its rebirth as a Cal State campus, was among the first to reach out with an offer. He brought me on as a consultant, and provided Sylvia and me with an office on Cal State Monterey Bay's still-transforming campus. That gave us a much-needed base of operations, which still provides our anchor today.

Sylvia launched an "America Reads" program in Monterey, and I began teaching some classes at my alma mater, the now-coed Santa Clara University. Reconnecting with young people was exhilarating for both of us, but also discouraging. So many students whom we encountered seemed to have lost faith in their government. They were prepared to believe the worst about any public official, and resisted the idea that public service was a fulfilling way of helping those in need.

From those observations grew a plan. We set out to expand the lecture series into a full-fledged institute, which became the Panetta Institute for Public Policy. Cal State Monterey Bay provided office space and some support, and we developed a group of sponsors and fund-raising events to raise about $2 million a year. That supported the lecture series as well as leadership courses, a Washington internship program, and eventually a master's degree program. We haven't ended cynicism among young people, but we've sent hundreds of interns to Washington, and have, I hope, impressed on them some of the positive potential of government, not just the baser calculations of politics.

I suddenly had time on my hands and few limits on my interests. I joined boards and commissions—the boards of Blue Shield, Zenith Insurance, Fleishman-Hillard, and the New York Stock Exchange, as well as a Pew commission that examined and reported on the state of the world's oceans and California Forward, a group formed to make recommendations for improving California's gridlocked politics.

Both of those latter projects were immensely rewarding. I chaired the Pew Oceans Commission, and we looked broadly at the state of the world's oceans—from pressure on fisheries to the impact of coastal development and climate change. As it happened, I was in Washington delivering an update on our oceans work in September 2001 and was sitting at a witness table in the Cannon House Office Building when one of my colleagues, Marilyn Ware, received a message and whispered it to me: The Twin Towers, she said, had been struck by a pair of airplanes and were on fire. Two planes striking both towers in rapid succession could not, we realized, be an accident. Interrupting my testimony, I told the members of the committee that an attack appeared to be under way.

I remember thinking that it was probably not smart to be in a House office building under these circumstances, a thought that dawned on others in the room at the same moment. The meeting was abruptly adjourned, and as I made my way back to my hotel, the radio carried news that a third plane had struck the Pentagon. Not since Pearl Harbor had Americans felt so under attack.

I was desperate to get home to California, but of course, the airlines were grounded. I called my old friend Norm Mineta, then serving as secretary of transportation, and he warned me that flights would remain canceled for days. John Franzén put me up at his place while I pleaded with Hertz to find me a car; eventually they turned up a Lincoln, and I shoved off for California, snaking my way across the heartland and watching community after community absorb the news. Motels replaced VACANCY signs with GOD BLESS AMERICA. Flags fluttered from porches and decorated lawns. People seemed to speak in whispers, and to go out of their way to be kind to one another. Later that week, I pulled into the driveway in Carmel Valley.

The oceans report, released in May 2003, took me back to the work I'd done as a member of Congress protecting the California coastline (the cover photograph of the report was of the Point Reyes peninsula in Northern California). The report's recommendations, based on two years of study, called for a new ethic of stewardship over our oceans and forcefully made the point that the economic potential of the seas depended on their ecological protection. It was, in my mind, a smart synthesis, and a reminder that environmental protection is not the enemy of economic growth.[14]

Similarly, the California Forward studies helped propel initiatives to create the state's first-ever open primaries and to turn redistricting over to a citizens' commission, removing it from the politicized process that had distorted it previously. It's my hope that over time those reforms will bend California's politics toward the center, producing more evenly divided districts and more incentive for deal making rather than ideological posturing. We'll see.

One other opportunity floated my way in regard to California politics. Governor Gray Davis was elected in 1998 and reelected in 2002, but he'd never enjoyed the deep affection of Californians and was seen more as an effective politician than as an inspiring leader. Dueling crises—the burst of the dot-com bubble left the state's budget in tatters, and a misguided attempt at privatizing energy produced electricity shortages and blackouts—emboldened his opponents, who launched a campaign to recall him. That put Democrats in a bind: If no Democrat joined the recall campaign and Davis lost, we would lose the governorship, but if a prominent Democrat did join, it would give Democratic voters an opportunity to dump the incumbent, a precedent none of us wanted to set.

A number of people approached me to see if I would run, and I gave it serious thought. At the time, though, I didn't know whether Senator

Dianne Feinstein, an old friend and California's most popular political figure, might join the race. She was no great fan of Davis's, and had often been considered a possible governor. I told her I'd wait for her to decide, and would get in only if she declined. She pondered the idea for a while, and by the time she decided to pass on the race, I felt it was too late for me to run. In retrospect, I'm glad I didn't, as it almost surely would have put me on a path—win or lose—of involvement in state government rather than federal, and thus probably would have closed the door back to Washington that I would eventually enter.

One last project from those years bears mention. In March 2006, with the security situation in Iraq at a particularly delicate stage, Congress appointed a special commission to examine the issue and make recommendations for moving forward. Jim Baker and Lee Hamilton were named to chair it, and Baker asked me to become a member. I accepted, joining Robert Gates, Larry Eagleburger, Vernon Jordan, Ed Meese, Sandra Day O'Connor, Bill Perry, Chuck Robb, and Alan Simpson.* We spent the next nine months conducting hundreds of interviews, including a number during our trips to Baghdad. During one of those visits, Bob Gates and I ran into each other in the dining room of our hotel, as we both were fruitlessly in search of something stronger than tea to drink. Being more experienced than I in this particular field, Bob suggested that we try the Baghdad CIA station. We made it over there; he poured himself a vodka, and I took a scotch. It pays to know people.

Ultimately, the Iraq Study Group produced seventy-nine recommendations—all of them unanimously agreed to by the commission. The recommendations were too numerous, diverse, and detailed to recount here, but they ranged from the diplomatic to the economic to the military to the symbolic. They implicitly challenged President Bush by

---

*Bob Gates was part of the original commission but dropped off when he was appointed secretary of defense. He was replaced by Meese.

emphasizing the dangerous situation in 2006 and by advancing a far broader effort than he was presently undertaking, but we did not criticize him directly. Our intention was to encourage progress, not to place blame.

When we presented our conclusions to the president and vice president, it was clear to me that they did not welcome a report that raised questions about administration policy. Nonetheless, the president seemed genuine when he pledged to review and consider our findings. The vice president said nothing.

Of all the work that commission did and all the specific ideas it put forth, the language that most strongly conveyed my broader feelings about leadership appeared at the outset of our final report: "Our country deserves a debate that prizes substance over rhetoric, and a policy that is adequately funded and sustainable. The President and Congress must work together. Our leaders must be candid and forthright with the American people in order to win their support."[15]

Those were the ideas that had guided my service to my country since my first election in 1976. They were the principles that would, unbeknownst to me in 2006, bring me back for one more tour.

PART II

PROTECT AND DEFEND

NINE

"The Combatant Commander in the War on Terrorism"

Our youngest son, Jimmy, joined the service of his country as a Naval Reserve intelligence officer in February 2003. He explained to Sylvia and me that he felt a sense of duty, a commitment to service that he had long seen in both of us, and that he was compelled to follow it. We gulped hard. America was fighting two wars when he signed up, and the thought of him in harm's way was sobering, even frightening. We tried to ask the right questions, to understand his decision but not to challenge it. Were we afraid? Yes. But our anxiety paled next to our pride, and hearing my son proclaim his call to service made my heart swell.

Then, in July 2007, the other shoe dropped. Jimmy had volunteered to deploy and had been notified that he was to be sent to Afghanistan. He had two little girls at home by then, ages one and three, so any danger to him now had ramifications for them as well. Nevertheless, he explained that he could not bear to see his fellow reserves sent off while he stayed home—"I need to go forward," he told us—and he figured it was better to go while his girls were little, rather than when they were older and might have a harder time with him away. There was no arguing with his passion, his logic, or his resolve, not that I wanted to. But my heart was in my throat as we saw him off. "Go," I said. "Do your job. Keep your head down. And get the fuck home."

He was sent to Bagram Airfield, far inside the war. Not one day passed while he was gone that Sylvia and I did not pause to worry about him. But Jimmy served with distinction and came home safe. From then on, I understood the indescribable mixture of pain and patriotism that dominates the lives of families who offer up a son or daughter to their country.

Worry for Jimmy shadowed us, but it did not consume us. Sylvia and I were home in Carmel Valley, and the burgeoning Cal State Monterey Bay campus provided a picturesque and efficient base of operations for our various projects. We were working with students, exploring ways to encourage responsible citizenship. It was our little war against cynicism, and it wasn't easy, but both of us believed in it. That Jimmy was abroad defending his country only strengthened our conviction that this was a country worth fighting for.

As the Democratic presidential primaries took shape in 2007 and 2008, I supported Hillary Clinton. I knew her from my time in the Clinton White House, of course, and admired her intelligence, tenacity, and decisiveness. Yes, we had disagreed on occasion—I had favored deficit reduction over what I regarded as an uncertain course on health care reform, and she initially had watched over my work as chief of staff to make sure I was sufficiently protective of her husband—but we had come to trust each other, and there were few people in politics whose acumen I more admired. I hosted events for her in California and voted for her in our state's Democratic primary.

I did not know Barack Obama as well, but we had met a few times. We first literally bumped into each other at the Democratic convention in 2004, where I was doing some media interviews and he delivered the stirring speech that first brought him to national attention. As I was leaving the hall one evening, he was entering, and we got jostled in the crowd. Ever gracious, he introduced himself, generously complimenting me on my leadership and accomplishments. Afterward, as he settled into the U.S. Senate, he asked me to Washington to discuss budget issues with him. We met in his Senate office, and I was struck by his quick grasp of the budget and its broader implications for the economy.

Once Obama prevailed in the primaries, I was happy to support him, though I actually was far better acquainted with John McCain. John and I had worked together on many issues during my time in Congress and the White House, and I respected him as a man of conviction and principle. On immigration and campaign finance, for instance, he had taken stands that defied the party's conservative and moneyed bases out of his belief that they were good for America. As a candidate, however, he succumbed to the pressures that refashion so many centrists—particularly Republicans—when they set their sights on the presidency. Just as Dole had done in 1996, when he dropped health care in order to pacify the Republican right, McCain in 2008 reinvented himself as a more extreme conservative in order to win his party's nomination. Once a principled maverick, now John picked Alaska governor Sarah Palin as his vice president. I understand the pragmatic side of politics—you can't govern if you don't win—but McCain's pick was manifestly incapable of taking over the country should harm have come to him.

As a result, I was thrilled at Obama's ringing victory on election night, welcoming not only the return of a Democrat to the White House but also savoring the deep satisfaction of seeing my nation, less than sixty years after concluding that school segregation violated the Constitution, elect a black man as president. It was a stirring reminder of this nation's capacity to grow.

Just a day or two after the election, I was attending a conference in Wyoming and staying with my old friend and former colleague Alan Simpson at his ranch. It was there that the Obama transition team tracked me down and asked me to join a call with the president-elect and Erskine Bowles in order to talk about Obama's selection of a chief of staff. I agreed, and a few hours later the three of us were on the line, joined by John Podesta, who was then serving as Obama's transition chief.

Obama went first, and dispensed with the obvious question. "Are either of you guys interested in the job?" he asked. I said no. I felt I'd already done it and wasn't eager to take it on again. Erskine said the same was true for him. With that out of the way, we moved to a conversation about what the chief of staff's duties were, and what made for an effective person in that post. I emphasized the need for the chief of staff to be someone the president trusts completely and someone with the character and fortitude to be candid. Both Erskine and I also discussed the importance of scheduling and access and coordinating relations with Congress. When Obama turned to candidates, I mentioned Tom Daschle as someone he should consider—his background in Congress would, I argued, be helpful.

We chewed that over for a bit, and then Podesta asked our impressions of Rahm Emanuel. I'd known Rahm in the Clinton White House, and thought very highly of him. Like Daschle, he knew Congress, and he also was close to the president-elect. His politics were centrist—he had supported welfare reform and NAFTA during the Clinton years. Moreover, he was famously blunt. There are a million stories of his intensity and colorful language. One of my favorites involved a nameplate he kept on his desk. It looked official, a brass plate attached to a piece of wood, and it read, UNDERSECRETARY FOR GO FUCK YOURSELF. I thought he'd make a fine chief of staff.

The president-elect thanked us for our advice and ended the conversation without making—or at least sharing with us—any decision. I went back to my conference and wondered whether I would hear from him again.

I did not presume that I was in line for a top position. As noted, I liked and respected Obama, but we barely knew each other, and eight years of President Bush had left lots of Democrats craving an opportunity to return to power in the White House. Moreover, I was seventy years old, arguably on my way to retirement. I wasn't beyond wondering, though. My work on the oceans project for Pew had exposed me to issues related to the environment and trade, and I did ponder whether I might be considered for secretary of commerce. The Iraq Study Group had given me some background in the current debate over national security policy, but I didn't imagine a place for myself in that arena, though Podesta did at one point rather casually mention the possibility of it.

So it was without much thought of the future that Sylvia and I visited our son Carmelo in Minneapolis over New Year's. We were enjoying our grandchildren and relaxing as a family when Rahm, who had just accepted the chief of staff job, called to sound me out on an idea: "What would you think about being considered for director of CIA?"

Despite Podesta's hint of something like this, I still was surprised by Rahm's call. "I don't know, Rahm," I answered. "Most of my work has been on budgets. Are you sure you have the right guy?"

He acknowledged that it was unconventional, but said that Obama was convinced the CIA needed to regain credibility lost in the Bush years. The agency had a rich history, of course, and its officers had worked furiously since 9/11 to protect the country from another attack. But it also had troubles. First and foremost, the agency had misjudged the presence of weapons of mass destruction in Iraq. In addition, the administration's critics were blaming the CIA for engaging in the process of "rendition"—taking prisoners across borders for interrogation without legal process. Even more controversially, the administration had sanctioned "enhanced interrogation" techniques, the worst of which was waterboarding, a method I regarded as torture, though many others felt that it was the kind of aggressive interrogation method that was warranted to prevent another 9/11. Some of that predated

Bush—rendition, for instance—but the revelations about secret prisons and rough interrogations had become hotly debated issues in the presidential campaign and in my view badly damaged America's standing in the world. Though it was merely an agent of the administration's policies, the CIA was being vilified on Capitol Hill and was viewed by the public with even greater suspicion than normal. Rahm argued that I could help restore some of the agency's standing and therefore its effectiveness.

It still struck me as odd, and not necessarily a great fit, given my background. And yet the idea did intrigue me. There were few greater challenges for the new Obama administration than ensuring that we had the intelligence necessary to combat terrorism, and there was no better post from which to orchestrate that effort than the CIA. I hadn't had much experience with intelligence, but I had served as an intelligence officer in the military, and during my years as Clinton's chief of staff I often sat in on the intelligence briefing, when the president is informed of the panoply of potential crises that loom over the world every day. I hesitated a bit, but told Emanuel I'd think it over. Hanging up, I told Sylvia about our conversation. She was as surprised as I was. "Where did that come from?" she asked.

We went on with our vacation while I pondered the possible job, the idea steadily growing on me. On Sunday, January 4, I attended mass with Carmelo and prayed for guidance. We then headed to the Vikings playoff game—they lost to the Eagles—and as we were leaving, Sylvia called Carmelo's cell phone to let me know that the president-elect was looking for me. I hustled back to our hotel and called him from there.

He immediately proffered the job: "I'd like you to be CIA director."

By that point, I was ready to accept, but I felt I owed him the opportunity to consider my lingering reservations. "Mr. President," I said, "my experience with the CIA director is that this is the person who has to provide you with very objective intelligence. If I took this, I'd feel an obligation to tell you the truth, no matter how uncomfortable."

He acknowledged that and emphatically said he would expect nothing less. *Right answer*, I thought. So I continued, describing briefly my experience at the Office of Civil Rights, where my determination to do my job had so offended higher-ups in the Nixon administration. Obama interjected that he knew that piece of my biography and appreciated it.

"I remember that," he said. "That's one of the reasons I want you to do this, to restore the credibility of the CIA."

With that, I agreed. After I hung up the phone, I took a moment to marvel at this latest turn in my career, focusing not so much on what it meant for me as for what it said about my country. It had been more than seventy-five years since my father had arrived at Ellis Island, a peasant with twenty-five dollars to his name. The United States had given him the chance to make a living, raise a family, and become an American. And now I, a first-generation American, son of an immigrant peasant, was poised to assume command of the nation's premier intelligence agency. My previous jobs in government had involved significant responsibilities, but now I was being entrusted with a leading role in its protection, and in the midst of two wars, no less. It surely is a testament to this nation's appreciation of its immigrants that it would bestow that responsibility on one of their sons.

I didn't have much time to ponder those ideas. Word of my appointment began to leak almost immediately. Sylvia and I were headed home to Carmel Valley the following day when I heard it on the radio. By late afternoon it was being confirmed by sources on the transition team and in Congress, putting me in a bit of a bind, particularly because of one person who had not been told in advance: Senator Dianne Feinstein, who chaired the Senate Intelligence Committee, the very committee that would consider my nomination. As I noted earlier, I considered Dianne a friend—our politics were similar and our careers in California had often brought us together. But Dianne zealously guards her prerogatives as chairman, and she does not take kindly to slight. In other words, she's not a good person to overlook in naming a senior intelligence official.

She made her unhappiness clear. "I was not informed about the selection of Leon Panetta to be the CIA director. I know nothing about this, other than what I've read," she told the *Washington Post*. As for my qualifications, she added, "My position has consistently been that I believe the Agency is best served by having an intelligence professional in charge at this time."[1] And that was from my friend! Imagine what my enemies were thinking.

As soon as I heard the reports of Feinstein's displeasure, I got to Rahm. I scolded him and urged him to talk to her directly. Otherwise, I warned, "it could be trouble."

After a few minutes, I called Dianne myself as Sylvia and I drove from San Francisco down the Central Coast. I apologized for the way in which she had heard the news and said I hoped we could meet to discuss my appointment. As we talked, I felt some of her rancor subside, but she remained concerned about my lack of experience. We agreed to meet as soon as I returned to Washington.

The next couple of days were a whirl of phone calls. I alerted the Panetta Institute's board members that this assignment might take me out of our work for a while, which they accepted with grace; similarly, I detached myself from the various boards and groups with which I was then affiliated. Sylvia and I also had a long conversation about what this meant for us. Our work at the institute was important to both of us, and it would be difficult to drop it while I moved to the CIA. Moreover, we both knew that my new assignment would be consuming. We knew the difficulty of separation, but we also knew how to make it work. Sylvia would stay in California and run the institute while I returned to Washington to run the CIA—and I would come home as often as I could. A part of me did wonder who was getting the better deal: Sylvia would stay on our twelve-acre ranch in the Carmel Valley with our golden retriever, Bravo, while I again scrounged for a place to rent three thousand miles from home.

After a day or two at home, I packed my bags and made the familiar trip to Washington. On arrival, I went straight to the transition team headquarters in downtown Washington, two floors in an unremarkable office building at the corner of D and 6th Streets, NW, about a block from the federal courthouse. Though nondescript on the outside, the offices inside hummed with anticipation and energy. The lobby of the building was a hive of activity. Reporters were staked out, taking note of who came and went. Security was tight. Young campaign aides were jostling in from the cold to drop off résumés.

As I stepped off the elevator, I was greeted by a sturdy, grinning young man, hand outstretched. He introduced himself as Jeremy Bash, and before I'd settled into my office, he had presented me with the names and phone numbers of every living former CIA chief, thoughts on key people for me to meet, and a draft of remarks for me to deliver when the president formally announced my appointment later that week. Bash was the chief counsel to the House Intelligence Committee, and was on loan to the transition team. Over those first few days, I marveled at his crisp efficiency and encyclopedic knowledge of intelligence programs and principles. Within a week, I asked him to serve as my chief of staff. As always, he was both accommodating and strategic: He accepted tentatively, urging me to check him out before making a final offer, and counseled against assembling a large team to accompany me to CIA. "I'll be your chief of staff," Jeremy said, "on two conditions. First, I'm going to be more 'staff' than 'chief.' There are a lot of professionals there, and we should rely on them. And second, I need to be the only aide who comes in with you at the beginning. No entourage."

Specifically, Jeremy warned me not to repeat the mistakes of Porter Goss, who had chaired the House Intelligence Committee until being asked to take over the agency in 2004. Goss arrived with a large group of senior advisers, displacing the CIA's existing leadership. The result was a significant political blowup, contributing to years of turmoil and dissatisfaction, as well as the loss of important, senior people: Two of the CIA's most experienced operations officers, Stephen Kappes and Michael Sulick, had quit their posts rather than work for Goss and his inner circle. I took Jeremy's advice to heart, checked him out, and offered him the job again. He accepted. We would spend much of the next four years together, to my great advantage and satisfaction.

In the meantime, I moved into the transition team offices and plunged into the world of national security and intelligence. I was given an eight-by-ten-foot office, which I shared with another member of the transition. Thankfully, that was none other than John Brennan, soon to become Obama's chief counterterrorism adviser, and years later, one of my successors as CIA director. Jeremy was across the hall, where he was assisted by a young campaign aide named Elliot Gillerman. Elliot set to work right away getting me in to see members of Congress. Well, almost right away. First he performed one other important task: He taught me how to use the phones.

Down the hall were Susan Rice and Jim Steinberg, who were leading Obama's national security team. Susan would go on to become ambassador to the United Nations, and Jim landed as deputy secretary of state. Many of us thought that Jim was in line to become national security adviser, a job he had prepared for as deputy to Sandy Berger during my years in the Clinton White House. But Obama did something that I'm sure he came to regret. Instead of relying on close advisers for his top national security positions, he reached for two seasoned military men he did not know well, Jim Jones and Dennis Blair. Jones, a decorated former marine, had served as Supreme Allied Commander of Europe, and Obama selected him as national security adviser. Blair, a cerebral and respected naval officer who had led Pacific Command, was nominated to be director of national intelligence. Placing military men in those positions gave Obama cover from those prepared to pounce on any mistake as evidence that the president's lack of national security credentials rendered him unfit for his office. Unfortunately, it also meant that he lacked rapport with the advisers responsible for some of his administration's most difficult and delicate decisions. In time, Obama would undo both of these personnel moves.

By contrast, two of Obama's other appointments in the foreign affairs and national security arenas were ringing successes. The president persuaded Bob Gates to stay on as secretary of defense, an important gesture of continuity as the country continued to fight wars in Afghanistan and Iraq. Moreover, Gates was a Republican, so his appointment—and willingness to accept the post—underscored the nonpartisan nature of America's approach to those conflicts. The other clear star of Obama's first cabinet was Hillary Clinton, whom he named as secretary of state. Known around the world, she was a luminous representative for the United States in every foreign capital, as well as a smart, forceful advocate in meetings of the president's top advisers. An additional benefit of her appointment was that it helped heal the wounds from the hard-fought campaign between her and Obama during the Democratic primaries. Democrats now could unite behind this presidency.

With Jones in as national security adviser, Jim Steinberg was assigned to Hillary Clinton to be her deputy, a prestigious and important post. The critical job of deputy national security adviser—the orchestra conductor for national security decision making in the White House— went to Tom Donilon. I had known Tom for a long time and respected him. He had served as Warren Christopher's chief of staff at the State Department in the 1990s and was a careful lawyer and a student of national security decision making. He had written about the way the job was handled under various presidents and was determined to make the National Security Council a highly functioning staff, as it was under president George H. W. Bush and his national security adviser,

Brent Scowcroft. Tom, whose brother Mike was a senior political adviser to Biden, would play perhaps the most important role in foreign policy decision making over the next four years. Intense and serious-minded, Tom immersed himself in the details of policy making. Sometimes he would push hard, but in my experience he was always willing to listen to counterarguments and to reconsider his position.

Two congressional aides who had served with then senator Obama on Capitol Hill were given prominent roles on the NSC staff. Denis McDonough, a hard-charging, creative, and whip-smart strategist, was assigned to oversee strategic communications; Mark Lippert, a naval reservist who had served in Iraq and was a master of the national security issues on the president-elect's desk, was given the job of NSC chief of staff. Both McDonough and Lippert enjoyed broad authority in the White House—the president listened to them and trusted them. McDonough would go on to become an effective deputy national security adviser and later the White House chief of staff. Lippert would later be confirmed by the Senate as assistant secretary of defense, traveled with me to Asia, and became my successor's chief of staff at the Pentagon.

A few days after settling in, I was visited by two men, one six foot five, the other six foot seven. They were Rich and Dan, who ran the protection detail for CIA directors and deputy directors. They folded themselves into the chairs in my shoebox office, their knees bumping up against the desk, and gave me the rules of my new life. First, a protective detail would follow me wherever I went. I would ride in the backseat of an SUV. I could not fly on a commercial flight, both for security reasons and to ensure I was reachable at all times. The agency would rent a charter aircraft for me everywhere I went. Finally, they assigned me a code name. From that moment on, I would catch snippets of them announcing the movements of "Eagle," as in "Eagle, en route, grocery store."

Most of the other senior government officials who joined the

Obama administration were moving to D.C. with their families and were in the hunt for homes to buy or rent. But since I was coming by myself, I didn't want to spend money on a house. Instead, I went back to my longtime friend and first campaign manager, John Franzén, and his good old house on Massachusetts Avenue. Overnight, that walk-up apartment on Capitol Hill became a place where I could command operations half a world away. The agency brought in security measures— video cameras and guards, among other things—and installed an important piece of spy gear, a secure phone, so that I could be in contact with the office at any hour.

I was eager to learn the history and nuances of the agency I was being asked to head, and, fortunately for me, one of those who knew it best was assigned to a desk less than six feet from mine. That was John Brennan, who had been considered for the CIA job but withdrew because some senators questioned whether he had effectively countenanced rough interrogations or rendition during the Bush years. In fact, John had opposed some aspects of those policies internally, but the prospect of liberal senators rising up in opposition to Obama's first nomination to head the CIA was enough to persuade him to back off, clearing the way for my nomination.

Soon after arriving in Washington, John, Jeremy, and I met over dinner in a private space at the Caucus Room, a steak restaurant near the headquarters of the FBI. As we talked, I was struck by Brennan's lifelong commitment to public service as well as his great abilities—he was a veteran of the CIA and spoke fluent Arabic, among other things. I was grateful that he would be serving on Obama's team as the administration's chief adviser on counterterrorism, a position formally known as the Deputy National Security Adviser for Homeland Security and Counterterrorism and one for which he was eminently well suited (and which did not require Senate confirmation). John's essential advice to me that night was that I needed to take the time to learn the culture of the agency, which he had served for nearly a quarter of a century. Moreover, John made clear that my focus had to be on terrorism and that there were, despite the criticisms, dedicated professionals at the CIA who deeply cared about the safety of the country.

The controversy around Brennan was a reminder of a particular challenge that I faced as I moved to take over at CIA. The fierce debate during the campaign over the tactics used in the response to terrorism created a gloomy sense at the agency that its people were tainted. No matter that the CIA itself had not advocated secret prisons or torture. Its men and women were given the job of protecting America and assigned the tools with which to do it. For those efforts, many now believed that the new president regarded them with suspicion, and might even authorize prosecutions of some officers. As the president's nominee, I understood that I too might be received warily.[2]

I was determined to make it clear that I was not among those who would demonize the agency or its officers. Before my confirmation hearings began, I met with Steve Kappes, the agency's deputy director since returning to the CIA under Mike Hayden. Plainspoken, direct, and imposing, Steve was a model officer, a former marine who easily cleared six feet. His graying beard, square jaw, and bald head made him stand out in almost any group. Steve had joined CIA out of the military, rising to become a station chief and head of the Directorate of Operations, now called the National Clandestine Service. Steve had also conducted sensitive discussions with the Iranians over the years, and was fluent in, among other things, the Libya file. He had helped negotiate with Qaddafi to rid that nation of weapons of mass destruction in exchange for the easing of sanctions.

Kappes was inclined to retire and allow me to name my own deputy, but first he agreed to walk me through the agency's history, major challenges, and key personnel. We spent ninety minutes together that first day, and he invited me to dinner the next week at "Scattergood," a handsome old house on the CIA campus. We continued our conversation there, and I asked him to stay on. He wanted seventy-two hours to think about it. When they were up, he informed me that he would agree to keep serving as the CIA's deputy director, to my pleasure and relief.

Steve's decision went a long way toward helping me secure the support of other agency veterans, most of whom I first met around a conference table at the transition offices. Chief among them was Scott White, the agency's associate deputy director, or number three, a linebacker of a man who had served in the navy and as a career analyst and administrator. Meanwhile, the heads of the four directorates—or the "Four D's," as they were called—brought deep, diverse talents: Mike Sulick, who returned along with Kappes in the Hayden years, now served as director of the National Clandestine Service, "the spy guy," responsible for espionage and covert action; Stephanie O'Sullivan, director for science and technology, oversaw our technical side, everything from concealing microphones in furniture to spy satellites; John, director for support, ran the main administrative functions of the agency, including communications, security, and personnel; and Michael Morell, director of intelligence, was responsible for creating the agency's main product—timely, accurate, policy-relevant analysis for the president and other "customers."

I introduced myself to this extraordinary group, told them a bit about myself, and shared my initial thoughts about the agency's role in protecting the country. Scott and the D's briefly described their mission areas, and pledged to support me internally. The meeting was warm and cordial, even personal. Realizing that many of them wondered whether I intended to replace them with my own team, I closed by trying to set their minds at ease. "We're going to work really hard together," I said, "but I hope we'll have some good times and become friends."

The meeting ran so long that I kept another visitor waiting. In retrospect, that was a mistake, because this next visitor would be my notional boss in the intelligence community—Admiral Blair, the nominee to be director of national intelligence. Blair had graciously run to the local Subway sandwich shop to grab us lunch, but after half an hour he impatiently knocked on the door of my meeting with the D's and announced, "Party's over, Leon and I have a meeting." It was the first time I met him, and it foreshadowed what would be at times an uncomfortable relationship.

On Friday, January 9, President-elect Obama somewhat anticlimactically announced my nomination along with that of Blair. Reports had been circulating for days, so no one was surprised, though one aspect of the news conference was portentous. Blair was generous to me in his remarks that day, but also made a point of asserting his place atop the nation's intelligence apparatus—correct in theory, though, as we would discover, not always in practice.

In the midst of those briefings and business lunches and dinners, I received a call from Sylvia. Sadly, she broke the news that her mother, long ailing, had died. Benedetta Crosetti had lived a long life, long enough to see not only her children grow to adulthood but her grandchildren as well. And yet even in celebrating her life, it was wrenching to lose her. For the first time in our lives, Sylvia and I were without any of our parents. I flew home immediately, attended the funeral, and returned to Washington later that weekend. I was back at work on Monday.

Of my initial conversations, none was more illuminating than that with my predecessor, Michael Hayden. Hayden had hoped to be retained as director, and privately he derided my nomination, referring to me as "Rahm Emanuel's goombah," an insult I learned of only much later.[3] By contrast, I admired Hayden, whom Jeremy and others credited with restoring the agency's morale and confidence after Goss's unsuccessful tenure.

My first meeting with Hayden was at transition headquarters inside the "SCIF" (a "sensitive compartmented information facility").

The SCIF had our secure computers and safes where we could store our classified notes and daily intelligence briefings. It also had a secure video hookup to the Obama team's transition office in Chicago, where the president-elect was receiving intelligence briefings. Hayden was eminently professional and determined to see that our transition was thorough, if for no other reason than to protect the agency, to which he was very loyal. Our first conversation was brief, mostly to introduce ourselves, and we agreed to talk later in greater detail.

Soon after, we did, meeting this time at Langley. Hayden had a stack of notes and methodically ticked off his points, emphasizing the quality of the CIA's staff and its need for independence. He said he thought Iraq was on track and wouldn't require much attention from me. He urged me to stay close to the Israelis on Iran and to keep up the pressure against Tehran. And he said that more needed to be done to truly make CIA the "national human intelligence manager," the coordinator for all human spy operations across the government, as the post-9/11 reforms had dictated.

I didn't need any convincing on those points, but Hayden also sternly warned me that the president-elect shouldn't back off from the aggressive counterterrorism policies of the Bush administration. He beseeched me to urge the president to protect the CIA's right to detain and interrogate terrorism suspects outside of the judicial "read them their rights" context. And he warned against suggesting that officers had ever engaged in torture—a matter that would present itself to me again in various controversies during my first year as director.

What really staggered me in Hayden's briefing, however, were his revelations about the CIA's growing involvement in the effort to locate senior members of Al Qaeda. Likening the mission of the CIA director to a military commander, he explained the important role the agency played in the broader national effort to prevent another 9/11. I was to be, in effect, "the combatant commander in the war on terrorism."

Our conversation that day was a sobering introduction to the difficult responsibilities that awaited me. Any person in those senior jobs—at CIA or elsewhere—carries a heavy burden; these operations require literal life-and-death decisions, sometimes on a daily basis. My rosary was never far away in those years, and I said more Hail Marys than I can recall.

First, though, I needed to be confirmed by the Senate. I didn't really doubt that I would get through—President Obama was riding a wave of popularity, and Democrats controlled the Senate. Still, Feinstein's initial skepticism at my appointment was a reminder not to take anything for granted. I meticulously visited members in their offices, introducing myself to those I hadn't met, catching up with those I'd known for many years. Those sessions were almost without exception cordial and friendly, though occasionally odd. When I referred to West Virginia's legendary Robert Byrd, whom I'd known for more than twenty years, as "Bob," he sternly corrected me. "It's Senator Byrd," he said. And when I met with Hawaii's Daniel Inouye, he vigorously supported my nomination, but seemed most interested in hearing whether as CIA director I would be allowed to carry a sidearm. I told him I didn't expect to. He seemed a bit disappointed. Notwithstanding those unusual moments in our conversations, both senators were strong supporters of the CIA mission and would lend valuable help to the agency during my time there.

The hearings began on the afternoon of February 5. I was pulled between Republicans who worried that I would impose limits on the agency that would inhibit its effectiveness and Democrats who worried that rough techniques were compromising American values and undermining our international moral authority. One thing both sides agreed on was that the CIA needed to do a better job informing them of its efforts and making sure that there was broad political support for that work. That was the easiest concern for me to dispense with, and I did so in my opening statement. "Keeping this committee fully and currently informed is not optional," I assured the members on the first day of my hearings. "It's the law, and it's my solemn obligation to fulfill that requirement."[4]

Under questioning about waterboarding and other techniques of enhanced interrogation, I firmly denounced them—President Obama had just days earlier issued an executive order prohibiting the use of such methods. Yet I did concede that in a so-called ticking time bomb scenario in which a suspect was withholding information that might imminently result in a catastrophe, I would "not hesitate to go to the President of the United States and request whatever additional authority I would need."[5]

I was also asked about rendition, a practice that dated to the Clinton years (though after I had left the administration), but that had become far more controversial under Bush, especially because the assumption was that the United States was intentionally moving suspects to countries where the interrogation methods would be more brutal than those the United States was prepared to employ. I promised the committee that should I be confirmed, the CIA would not authorize the transfer of any person in our custody to any other country "for the purposes of torture."[6] Hayden blew a gasket over that comment, which he said implied that the CIA had countenanced such torture in the past. He complained to Jeremy, and the next day, under additional questioning from the committee, I cleaned up my comments, clarifying that we might continue to divert some detainees to other countries after receiving assurances that they would not be treated "inhumanely." That was enough to mollify Hayden, and my testimony continued without further hiccups.

Her earlier concerns having been alleviated, Senator Feinstein endorsed my appointment, complimenting my integrity, drive, and judgment and expressing confidence that I would balance national security and national values. Kit Bond, the committee's ranking Republican, also supported me and said he was confident I would "use all appropriate and lawful means" to protect the nation from harm.[7] That was enough to bring along the committee, which supported me unanimously. The full Senate approved me by voice vote the next day.

On February 13, 2009, I stood in front of twenty senior officers in the Director's Conference Room on the seventh floor of CIA headquarters, placed my left hand on a Bible, raised my right hand, and repeated the oath that I had taken so many times before: to "preserve, protect, and defend the Constitution of the United States against all enemies, foreign and domestic." Steve Kappes did me the honor of administering those words. We were now partners in what was a lifetime's work for him and a new undertaking for me.

TEN

"Tell It Like It Is . . . Our National Security Depends on It"

The Central Intelligence Agency was founded in 1947, part of a restructuring of American defense and intelligence services under President Truman. The act created the U.S. Air Force, as well as the Department of Defense and the National Security Council, and it consolidated intelligence gathering under the auspices of the new CIA. The CIA would become the nation's first permanent intelligence agency—the Cold War made it more difficult to distinguish between war and peace—and this new entity was authorized to conduct clandestine activities, though to what extent was murky.

Some limits were clear: The CIA was forbidden from conducting domestic intelligence, was given no policy-making authority, and was denied the power to issue subpoenas or otherwise compel testimony. To emphasize its independence from the policy-making branches of the government, its headquarters were built outside the District of Columbia. That served two purposes: Land was cheaper in the suburbs, and, the thinking went, it was better to have spies kept at arm's length from the government.

Today, the George Bush Center for Intelligence—named after the only director to become president—sits on a busy thoroughfare, Route 123, which bisects the tidy neighborhood of McLean, Virginia. From my office, I could see Virginia, Maryland, and the District of Columbia through the canopy of shade trees and over the glimmering Potomac River. It was a beguiling setting, and in a sense a misleading one. In February 2009, the agency I now headed still was physically far from removed from Washington, but was now at the center of its debates over war, peace, and politics. It stood at a defining, challenging moment, as critics questioned its values, its professionalism, and its capacity.

I settled into a routine. Each morning, I awoke by 6 a.m., watched some TV as I dressed, and then met my lead security agent in front of my house. Without fail, he opened the door of the waiting SUV at 7 a.m. sharp. I rode in the back, and next to me was a brown leather-bound binder prepared by a young analyst named Amy. It was a version of the President's Daily Brief (PDB), and contained twenty to thirty pieces of raw traffic—reports of intercepts of key targets overseas (known as signals intelligence, or SIGINT), and from assets or friendly intelligence services (known as human intelligence, or HUMINT). The traffic was followed by short "articles" dissecting a particular question or problem raised by a senior government official. After culling through the PDB, I turned to a compilation of news clips about the CIA and foreign policy issues, also waiting for me in my car. In front of me was a secure cell phone, though the truth is that I rarely used it. The phones were clunky, and the sound quality was poor.

The motorcade flew up the GW Parkway, banked into the CIA campus, and flashed our sirens to signal to the gate guards to wave us through. Then the vehicles made a sharp left into a driveway and plunged into the underground garage for the executive officers. I hopped out of the car, walked ten steps, and entered a small elevator, operated by another security officer, which took us directly to the seventh floor. Before walking into my office, I relinquished one possession: my cell phone. No phones were allowed inside the agency. The director's office was no exception.

Greeting me each day were my two special assistants, Mary Jane Scheidt and Mary Elfmann. Mary Jane was the gatekeeper, sitting just outside my office, turning away anyone without a proper appointment. She also kept my schedule and handed it to me each morning on a printed card in a plastic sleeve. The proof of her indispensability was the fact that there were two peepholes in my office door—one for most people of normal height and one about six inches lower, for Mary Jane. Mary Elfmann and her successor, Dora Kale, kept the office humming. I was also supported by a pair of midcareer executive assistants who were on a one-year rotation in the office supporting Hayden. In addition to accompanying me to all my meetings and taking copious notes, they helped brace me for the tough decisions I would be asked to make. One, Sheetal, agreed to stay on with me through my first year; she was determined to teach me what it took to be director.*

At 7:30 a.m., a small team gathered for my morning intelligence briefing, which I held at the conference table in my office. Amy sat to my right. Steve Kappes typically took the seat at the other end of the table. Jeremy was part of this small group, which regularly also included Mike Morell, or a senior member of his team, and later his successor, Fran Moore. Later, that group also was expanded to include Stephen Preston, the agency's brilliant general counsel, whom the president nominated on my recommendation.

I discovered right away that it was hard to be casual at the CIA. Entering the briefing on one of my first days, I asked Mary Jane for a cup of coffee. Before I knew it, the kitchen staff wanted to know how

---

*The executive assistants who worked with and followed Sheetal were outstanding professionals: Jan, John, Amy, Gerald, Vince, and Maggie. One deserves special mention. Shana, a career analyst, started as my executive assistant and then became my deputy chief of staff. She was by my side during the entire bin Laden operation and helped ensure a smooth transition between me and David Petraeus.

I took my coffee, what kind of cup I preferred, how hot it should be. The next morning, a full coffee service arrived in my office on the CIA's finest blue-and-gold bone china for everyone in the meeting. The coffee was good. That was the good news. The bad news was that I had to reimburse the government for the cost of the service. I canceled it. Instead, I brought my own mug—it said CIA—CALIFORNIA ITALIAN AMERICAN—and poured my own coffee in the staff kitchen.

My credentials for running the CIA were not in the area of covert action or intelligence gathering. I was put there because I knew something about how to run an organization, and two things I recalled from my time with Clinton were the value of a defined daily schedule and the necessity of including key staff members in decision making. Beginning my first week, I convened my top staff every morning at 8:30 a.m. We met in a wood-paneled room, with the CIA seal at one end and a picture of the president at the other.

I sat in the middle of the table, Steve and Jeremy to my left, and Scott White to my right. Filling out the table were the four directorate heads, along with a three-star air force general, Mark Welsh, who was our main liaison to the Pentagon; our public affairs chief, Paul Gimigliano (later George Little); our congressional liaison, Bill Danvers, who worked with me in the Clinton White House and who I specifically picked for the job given the importance of that role; our general counsel, first John Rizzo, later Stephen Preston; and the agency's comptroller, Susan Bromley.

I opened the meeting each day with a report of any meetings or interactions I'd had with the White House or foreign leaders. Then Jeremy would read the schedule for the day. Steve and Scott would give brief reports on items they were working on. Then we went around the table, starting with the National Clandestine Service chief, Mike Sulick.

That may not sound revolutionary, but those sessions represented a cultural change at the CIA, and the senior staff didn't immediately know how to respond. At first the staff was aghast that I would discuss sensitive operational details in front of the comptroller or the public affairs chief. But I knew from my White House days that the most important thing I could do was to get the senior team on the same page. If an officer screwed up overseas, I wanted to know about it. If a technology demonstration had failed, I expected to be told—before reading it in the morning clips. And if the White House was hassling us during a policy meeting downtown, I wanted to know, so I could raise it at the appropriate level.

"I'm going to be honest with you," I said at one meeting. "I need you to be honest with me. The last thing I want is for something to be going on in the bowels of this place that I don't know about."

Two days a week, we'd follow the general staff meeting with an "NCS update"—a deep dive on operational activity that had occurred during the previous forty-eight hours, including any important reports from our assets. Truth is, I didn't find these meetings terribly illuminating. The reports were laden with jargon and code names. It was hard to divine the larger significance of these single updates wholly ripped from their context. They did, however, educate me on the painstaking and complex work of espionage. Our officers operate undercover overseas, requiring the agency to build multiple aliases and cover organizations for them. A simple meeting in a European capital may require our officer to travel to three or four cities before meeting her asset, so she can definitively establish whether she's being followed. "Surveillance detection" is a building block of any good espionage operation.

The days were filled with briefings from various agency components, meetings with visiting heads of foreign intelligence services, and meetings of the National Security Council Principals—the top brass of the administration's national security team—usually in the White

House Situation Room. Once a week, on Tuesdays, we briefed the president himself on counterterrorism issues. Brennan organized that session, and I prepared for it by bringing in the relevant case officers and letting them walk me through the issues.

For lunch, I made it as often as possible to the agency cafeteria on the first floor. I stood in the salad bar line with everyone else and paid for my meal. I genuinely enjoyed the chance to bump into the people of the agency and hear what they were thinking. It may sound like a small gesture, but it kept me in touch with our employees and let them see that I was at work. And by the way, the food in the cafeteria was not too shabby—CIA stations around the world are generally recognized for the quality of their food, and the cafeteria's cuisine offerings were as diverse as the world that the CIA covered.

The days were long, but I made a point of huddling with Jeremy and the immediate office staff before any of us left for the evening. We called this "EA time" (for "executive assistant"), because it was the best chance for my two executive assistants to catch me up on what I could expect in tomorrow's meetings. They ran through the schedule. I usually had a few questions, and then we broke for the evening.

My nights often continued from there, and many evenings included an official dinner in my dining room, down the hall from my office. These were white tablecloth, bone china affairs, usually for a visiting intelligence chief. Three or four from our side would dine with three or four from theirs. If I was lucky, no interpreter was needed. I got to select the menus, and I had an Italian chef—Freddie—so the food was outstanding.

One of the first issues to confront me in the new job was a holdover from the Bush years that had been a prominent part of my confirmation and that now posed complicated problems for the CIA. The issue was enhanced interrogation, and the problem that confronted Obama early in his presidency was how much of that program—its legal and moral underpinnings, as well as its efficacy—should be made public, now that he had ordered a stop to it. Bringing that question to a head was a lawsuit filed by the American Civil Liberties Union demanding the release of memos that provided the legal underpinnings of the program. Specifically, the ACLU, using the Freedom of Information Act, was seeking copies of three Bush-era legal memos that analyzed various interrogation techniques in terms of American law, international norms, and American obligations under its membership in the United Nations, as well as a fourth memo that analyzed those same techniques if used in combination with one another. They were known colloquially in the press, if somewhat misleadingly, as the "torture" memos. I say misleadingly because the bottom line of the memos was to uphold a number of rough interrogation tactics as not violating American or international prohibitions against torture.

Soon after I arrived in my new office, Greg Craig, then serving as White House counsel to President Obama, asked whether I would object to the release of the memos. Candidly, I didn't give it much thought. I told him I believed their release would help put the past behind us and move on, and therefore I had no objection. I figured that was the end of it, but a few days later, Acting CIA General Counsel John Rizzo learned that the president was preparing to make the memos public. I was out of the country on CIA business when Rizzo got the news, and he was alarmed enough to take the matter to Kappes. Unable to reach me, they decided they should at least alert the former CIA directors who had had a role in the interrogation program, so Rizzo called George Tenet, Porter Goss, and Mike Hayden. All three shared Rizzo's concern, and before I had heard that a decision was imminent, they had begun marshaling supporters of the program to lobby the White House against its chosen course.

I liked John Rizzo. He was Italian, which of course I appreciated, a bit of a character, and an unusual sight to behold. Barely five foot five, with a snow-white beard, he dressed like he had walked right out of *Esquire*—pink socks, orange pocket squares, ornate cuff links, Gucci loafers, and hand-tailored suits. Despite his somewhat outlandish look, John was well respected in legal circles and an iconic presence at the CIA. He had been on the verge of leaving when my appointment was announced, but I'd asked him to stay until his successor could be confirmed, and we'd struck up a professional friendship; I was grateful to have his knowledge of the agency's history and command of the legal issues it confronted.

Which does not mean that I was happy with him when the White House tracked me down and brusquely demanded to know why my predecessors were stirring up trouble over the release of the documents. I called Rizzo and told him to knock it off. I then called Rahm Emanuel and asked him to put the release on hold until I could get back to the country and confer with Rizzo and others at the agency. Rahm agreed.

Back at Langley, Rizzo opened our meeting by profusely apologizing for unleashing the former directors. He had meant only to extend them a courtesy so that they were not surprised by the memos' release, he said, not to provoke them into challenging the decision. I told him to forget it, though I did make clear I'd rather he not do that again. We then turned to the substance of the issue. Rizzo knew this subject intimately—in fact, he was the one who had requested the legal review, and the memos were addressed to him. He vehemently insisted that releasing the memos would damage agency morale and undermine American commitments to allies to keep this program secret. After hearing him out, I was convinced that he was right and I'd been wrong. I alerted John Brennan that I had changed my view of the memos, and I laid out for him in writing my view of the issue. Yes, there was the value of transparency, I acknowledged, but I also concluded, repeating some of Rizzo's arguments, that releasing the documents could expose agency methods and operational details, as well as abrogating promises of confidentiality to friendly countries, including those that had allowed the CIA to conduct interrogations within their borders. Beyond that, Rizzo persuaded me that it was unfair to our officers to expose these methods; the officers who had applied the techniques had done so only after being assured that they were legal. To make public these documents retroactively would only reinforce the demand for the officers to be punished. It seemed wrong to me to ask a public servant to take a risk for his country and assure him that it was both legal and approved, then, years later, to suggest that he had done something wrong.

The debate over the release of the memos was hard-fought internally. Rahm Emanuel agreed with me. Dennis Blair, whom I initially thought shared my view, unexpectedly came down on the side of releasing them. The president kept his own counsel.

On the afternoon of April 15, with a court order pending that required the administration to turn over the documents, I learned that the president was close to deciding the issue. Obama was scheduled to leave for Mexico the next day, and I worried that he might announce a decision to make the memos public before leaving on his trip. I felt it imperative that he not do that without at least hearing the case from my people. I called Rahm, explained the situation, and suggested that the president meet with some senior CIA officials before making a final decision. Rahm's response: "Bring 'em down."

Jeremy quickly rounded up seven of our top people in the relevant parts of the agency—the head of our Counterterrorism Center and chief of operations for the center, the deputy director of our Clandestine Service, deputy chief of the Near East Division as well as that division's chief legal officer, and our deputy general counsel. We piled into two SUVs and drove from our Langley headquarters straight past the White House gates. We bounded up the stairs from the West Wing basement to the area outside the Oval Office, where the president greeted us as we entered, cheerfully calling out, "Come on in, fellas."

Obama sat in a wingback chair, and I sat on the couch to his left. The officers also sat on couches. Jeremy pulled up a chair, and we were joined by one other White House aide, Deputy Chief of Staff Mona Sutphen.

The president spoke first. "Look," he said, "we have a court hearing tomorrow, and our lawyers think we are going to lose this case. I basically agree with them. And then not only will we have to turn over the memos, but we'll be accused of being obstinate. If we are going to get the same result, I'd at least like us to get the credit for being transparent."

He then turned to me.

I began, "I brought these guys here because I want you to hear about the *impact* of revealing interrogation memos." Then I summarized my concerns about the release of the memos. Most important, I added, I wanted the president to have the benefit of the agency's best minds on this topic.

The president had already told us what he was thinking, but he stressed that he was open to input. Every person from the agency who was with me that day spoke against the release, some cautiously, others vehemently. The president listened. He never looked at his watch or showed any sign of impatience. He asked a few questions and seemed genuinely to appreciate the depth of conviction, sincerity, and anxiety that our people conveyed. Once everyone had spoken, he paused for a moment. "Let me take this one back," he said. He did not promise to change his mind, but he did listen, and his willingness to consider those objections impressed my colleagues immensely. Before we left, he also accepted my invitation to come visit the CIA at the earliest opportunity.

The following day, he ruled against us and released the documents. In doing so, however, the president took great pains to avoid jeopardizing his relationship with the CIA, which he recognized was crucial to his success. He carefully balanced his remarks, noting that while he believed "strongly in transparency and accountability," he also recognized the need to protect certain classified information in a "dangerous world." The "exceptional circumstances" surrounding these memos compelled their release, he insisted. He also had comforting words for officers of the CIA: "In releasing these memos it is our intention to assure those who carried out their duties relying in good faith upon legal advice from the Department of Justice that they will not be subject to prosecution."

Despite those assurances, and even though many of the techniques described in the memos had already been publicly reported, their release created the expected stir. There was something chillingly banal about the methodical detailing of "dietary manipulation," "nudity," and other techniques leading up to waterboarding, which the lawyers approved even though they recognized that it induced the sensation of drowning and thus did "cause fear and panic."[1]

I wasn't surprised at the president's decision. I recognized that the concerns of the CIA had to be balanced against other imperatives of the administration, and I understood the president's rationale. In addition, the president's decision was considerably softened by the other news I got that day: He intended to visit the CIA as soon as he returned from Mexico. On April 20, he did.

When the president arrived at Langley that afternoon, he rode up the elevator and I met him when he got out at the seventh floor inside my office suite. First the president joined me on the couches in my office for a short discussion with Steve Kappes, whom Obama had personally called before releasing the memos. Joining us from the White House were Rahm Emanuel and John Brennan. Denny Blair was also there. We chatted about the memo release, but quickly pivoted to the importance of keeping the pressure on Al Qaeda. Obama knew the agency well enough to know that if Kappes had doubts about his resolve, others would share them; alternatively, Kappes's endorsement would persuade many of our colleagues that the president could be trusted. The president addressed Kappes directly and made clear that he was not shrinking from the fight against Al Qaeda.

Next we gathered a few dozen officers from across the agency for the chance to speak with the president. The officers selected for this meeting were in their seats thirty minutes prior to the event, which was held in a conference room in my office suite. They waited in silence. As he entered, they stood politely, but there was uneasiness in the room. The president spoke first, standing behind a small lectern in the front that had been brought by the White House advance staff. He acknowledged that his decision to release the memos had come over my objections, and stressed that he understood the reservations CIA officers had regarding a review of practices that he had deplored but that they had undertaken with authorization. As he had a few days earlier, he stressed that no one would be prosecuted who had stayed within the legal authority laid out in the memos.

The president's ease and confidence, coupled with his clear appreciation of the equities at stake, went a long way to mollifying the concerns in the room. A number of officers asked cautious questions, and then one mustered up her courage and said what many were undoubtedly thinking. Her voice quavering slightly, she pleaded with Obama to recognize her commitment and that of her colleagues to protecting the country from a genuine threat. For her—and for many of my new associates—the underlying fear of the new president and his administration was not so much that Obama would put CIA officers in jail but rather that his unwillingness to condone rough interrogation reflected a larger sense that Al Qaeda wasn't really that grave a threat.

"Al Qaeda is dangerous," this officer said emphatically. "We need to keep after it."

Obama nodded, plainly moved. "I get it," he said.

It occurred to me in that moment that the workforce could handle revelations about the prior administration's counterterrorism policies. Our employees even could withstand investigations and recriminations. What they could not abide was any suggestion that we were flinching in our commitment to the mission.

A few minutes later, the president appeared downstairs in the grand entryway of the CIA, familiar to every viewer of *Homeland* or any one of dozens of CIA-based dramas. There, on the iconic tile floor and before the wall on which the names of fallen officers are inscribed, he and I were greeted to a raucous, warm welcome—so warm, in fact, that it took both of us slightly by surprise. The CIA is a unique agency with a singular mission, but its employees are no longer just the Ivy League spies of the early Cold War. Today's CIA draws from all walks of American life, and the boisterous applause for the new president—from seasoned CIA officers, cafeteria workers, gift shop employees, and security guards—was a reminder of the exuberance so many Americans felt for this young, inspiring new chief executive.

I laughed that the crowd seemed awfully loud for a group known as "silent warriors," and the president was interrupted time and again by laughter and applause.

The heart of his speech deserves to be quoted at length:

There have been some conversations that I've had with senior folks here at Langley in which I think people have expressed understandable anxiety and concern. So I want to make a point that I just made in the smaller group. I understand that it's hard when you are asked to protect the American people against people who have no scruples and would willingly and gladly kill innocents. Al Qaeda is not constrained by a constitution. Many of our adversaries are not constrained by a belief in freedom of speech or representation in court or rule of law. So I'm sure that sometimes it seems as if that means we're operating with one hand tied behind our back or that those who would argue for a higher standard are naive. I understand that. You know, I watch the cable shows once in a while.

What makes the United States special, and what makes you special, is precisely the fact that we are willing to uphold our values and our ideals even when it's hard, not just when it's easy, even when we are afraid and under threat, not just when it's expedient to do so. That's what makes us different. So, yes, you've got a harder job, and so do I. And that's okay, because that's why we can take such extraordinary pride in being Americans. And over the long term, that is why I believe we will defeat our enemies, because we're on the better side of history.

So don't be discouraged by what's happened in the last few weeks. Don't be discouraged that we have to acknowledge, potentially, we've made some mistakes. That's how we learn. But the fact that we are willing to acknowledge them and then move forward, that is precisely why I am proud to be President of the United States, and that's why you should be proud to be members of the CIA.[2]

Before I leave the discussion of enhanced interrogation, let me add a personal note. As director of the CIA, I never had to grapple with the legal and moral implications of extracting information from a prisoner by stripping him naked, slapping him, depriving him of sleep, or making him think he's drowning. President Obama abolished those practices before I was even confirmed. I do, however, believe he was right to take that action, even if it has consequences that many critics of the practices would prefer not to acknowledge.

Extremists on both sides of the interrogation debate avoid subtleties and prefer to shade the conversation in their favor by ignoring what they dislike to hear. Proponents, such as former CIA counterterrorism chief Jose Rodriguez, maintain that without those techniques, America will be helpless against fanatical enemies such as Al Qaeda.[3] Rodriguez is an admirable public servant, and he makes a good case, but his analysis underplays the important intelligence leads gained without resorting to harsh interrogation and pays too little heed to the damage done to American values by stooping to the practice. On the other side, many critics of those same techniques contend that humiliating or inflicting psychological pressure on a prisoner yields little and that the same information could be gotten through strong questioning pursuant to military guidelines—a position that Bob Mueller of the FBI made to me in one of our early conversations.

In support of that position, some critics of enhanced interrogation argue that none of the harshly interrogated suspects coughed up information that led directly to the eventual elimination of, most notably, Osama bin Laden. That's true, but only up to a point. Harsh interrogation did cause some prisoners to yield to their captors and produced leads that helped our government understand Al Qaeda's organization, methods, and leadership. The interrogation techniques so coolly described in those memos are not intended to jolt a prisoner into a sudden admission, but rather to break him down and convince him that he has no choice but to cooperate. In many instances, that is precisely what happened. No one shouted out bin Laden's address when strapped to a waterboard. Rather, it was the slow accumulation of leads, one building on the last, some extracted, unfortunately, after unsavory techniques were used.

At bottom, we know we got important, even critical intelligence from individuals subjected to these enhanced interrogation techniques. What we can't know—what we'll never know—is whether those were the only ways to elicit that information.

If a future president ever asked me whether we should go back to those techniques, I would say no. I believe they cut too deeply into America's sense of itself. We take deserved pride in being a country devoted to decency and respect for human dignity, and shoving a man into a box is incompatible with those ideals. It is foolish to maintain that those interrogations did not achieve anything, but it is also callous to pretend that we did not sacrifice idealism in return for those leads. Similarly, we should be clear-eyed about the fact that we gave up those practices at a cost—that there is information we might never have received had interrogators not been allowed to inflict pressure, anxiety, and even pain on subjects. I believe we must pay that cost anyway. We are truer to our ideals now that we have renounced enhanced interrogation, and in the long run it is our ideals that will cause us to prevail. As the president said, our ultimate victory against those who seek to destroy this country will be won not just by force but by our determination to stay true to the "better side of history." That will make it a victory worth savoring.

Although the president ruled against me in the debate over the memos, my defense of the CIA's position helped make clear that I was willing to fight for my new colleagues. That went a long way toward establishing my leadership internally. Externally, however, we still had a big challenge. That was especially true on the Hill, where the CIA has historically served as a convenient whipping boy, and it was certainly the case in early 2009. Democrats were in control of both houses of Congress and thus controlled both intelligence committees, and Democrats are not famously supportive of the CIA. By the end of the Bush years they had so thoroughly honed their attacks on the agency that they seemed incapable of shifting gears.

My first trips to the Hill to meet with the committees reflected the built-up mistrust between the members and the agency. We met in formal hearing rooms, with the members seated above and before me and my deputies. They would take turns barking questions at me, demanding documents, and openly displaying their skepticism of my answers. Pete Hoekstra, the ranking Republican on the House Intelligence Committee, was a particularly aggressive questioner, lacing his queries with partisan innuendo. Democrats were not immune and often used the hearings to lob partisan volleys at their Republican colleagues. At times I felt like shaking them and saying, "People, the election is over. Time to move on."

Bill Danvers, my able congressional liaison, had an idea to change the format of the meetings, moving from the hearing-style venues to gathering around a table. We drank coffee and talked as colleagues rather than talking up or down to one another. Right away the atmosphere changed from a grilling to a conversation, and we established a tone of respectful engagement. I painstakingly briefed the committees on anything that seemed germane to their oversight and attempted to answer all questions. As I reminded them, I came from Congress, and I knew the importance of its function.

There is a difference, however, between respect and subservience. I was not prepared to simply roll over. In May, House Speaker Nancy Pelosi, a leading critic of Bush-era intelligence activities who had chaired the House Intelligence Committee in the early 2000s, spoke at a press conference and, in response to a question from Jon Karl, stated that she had been briefed on waterboarding but that the agency had assured her it had not engaged in that practice. That seemed hard to believe. We had records that she and her colleagues were briefed on September 4, 2002, and were told in that session that Abu Zubaydah, the CIA's very first detainee, was subjected to waterboarding.

I watched Pelosi's press conference from my office with Steve Kappes and Jeremy. Both thought we would have to respond publicly. As Pelosi well knew, it's a crime to lie to Congress, so she was accusing top officials of the CIA not only of having concealed a matter of intense national security importance but also conceivably of having committed a federal offense.

I had no particular desire to wage war with the Speaker of the House—a fellow Democrat and a fellow Californian whom I had known since my days in Congress, when we often got together for dinner—but I certainly was not going to let my deputies be accused of lying when the record so clearly contradicted the claims against them. I prepared a chart of forty congressional briefings, including the one from 2002, and released it publicly. I also invited members of Congress and their aides to review the full notes of the meetings, which remained classified. Most important, I worked with Jeremy and our public affairs chief, Paul Gimigliano, to craft an e-mail to CIA employees that we also released to the news media. It read, in part:

> There is a long tradition in Washington of making political hay out of our business. It predates my service with this great institution, and it will be around long after I'm gone. But the political debates about interrogation reached a new decibel level yesterday when the CIA was accused of lying to Congress.
>
> Let me be clear: It is not our policy or practice to lie to Congress. That is against our laws and our values. . . . Our contemporaneous records from Sept 2002 indicate that the CIA officer briefed truthfully on the interrogation of Abu Zubayda, describing the "enhanced techniques that had been employed."
>
> My advice—indeed, my direction—to you is straightforward: ignore the noise and stay focused on your mission. We have too much work to do to be distracted from our job of protecting this country. . . . We are an Agency of high integrity, professionalism and dedication. Our task is to tell it like it is—even if that's not what people always want to hear. Keep it up. Our national security depends on it.

"Tell it like it is"—if ever there was a shorthand for the CIA mission, that was it. Pelosi amended her story in the face of our response, but continued to insist that while she was present at the briefing when waterboarding was mentioned, she was told only that the method had been authorized, not that it had been used.* I let the matter drop, be-

---

*That claim has since been challenged as well. Jose Rodriguez, in his memoir, says he provided the briefing and that not only was Pelosi present for a full discussion but that she participated fully and asked a number of questions that to him made it clear that she understood the range of interrogation techniques that had been used.

lieving that I had done what I could. That ended the flap, and I reached out to her a few weeks later. "I regret we went through that," I told her, "but I hope we can work together." Pelosi knows politics better than just about anyone; she agreed to put the issue behind us.

The dispute with the Speaker notwithstanding, relations with the Hill gradually improved, both in tone and substance. I traveled often to Congress personally, and I worked to unearth any operations or policy matters that deserved the attention of the committees. One of those has recently become the source of some controversy, so it bears special mention.

In June, a couple of our people in the National Clandestine Service somewhat sheepishly informed me of a program they felt they should bring to my attention. As they explained it, it was a counterterrorism program designed to locate terrorists across the world. Even though the program had only been planned—that is, it had not gone "operational"—it was still an important change in the way the CIA would do its business. The Bush White House had blessed the program. But the agency had not briefed the congressional intelligence committees about the training that had been done, the money spent, or some of the people the agency was working with in this effort, which some agency officials justified because the program was still not operational. Yet I was concerned, because I knew Congress would hit the roof if it found out about this activity from a press leak or through some other channel.

At the end of our meeting, I directed that the program be suspended and that we conduct a full review of its activities. And I asked for time the next day to meet with the full membership of both intelligence committees in the House and Senate. Briefing them, I told them of the program, as well as my decision to end it. The leaders were supportive and grateful that nothing had come of this ill-conceived idea.

My decision to end the program was not popular with senior people in the agency, even Kappes, but I felt it was important to do because allowing it to continue risked further undermining our credibility with Congress.

In addition to canceling that program, I also ended other contractor work for the CIA, including an agreement we had had with another firm since 2002. As President Bush disclosed, the CIA had operated "black sites" to interrogate Al Qaeda detainees. This contract pertained to the operations at these sites. Since President Obama had ordered them closed, there was no need for these contracts. Again, some people were upset, but I thought it was an important step in putting the past behind us.

In the aftermath of 9/11, Congress, as it is wont to do, went searching for explanations for how such an attack could have slipped through American defenses. The impulse to uncover mistakes and correct them was commendable, but rarely do lawmakers content themselves with just acknowledging slipups. Instead, they fix systems, and in this case they attempted to fix our national security apparatus by creating a new position, the director of national intelligence. In theory, that person acts as a coordinator between the various intelligence agencies, making sure that the National Security Agency, FBI, and CIA, for instance, share relevant information, so that a person or plot under scrutiny by one agency doesn't slip by the others.

That's all well and good, but the problem with the position is that the director of national intelligence doesn't really have a staff to produce his own information, so he is regularly caught between wanting information and having to rely on others to get it. In the case of Blair and me, that resulted in an ugly struggle for control over certain CIA assets. It was during the spring of 2009 that Blair first raised an idea with me: Because CIA station chiefs around the world also had a line of responsibility to the director of national intelligence, Blair proposed that he be allowed to name those officers. I told him I was willing to talk about ways that the station chiefs could represent the director, but I was strongly opposed to letting him pick those chiefs. They worked for the CIA, were paid by the CIA, and had come up through the ranks of the CIA. Their job, fundamentally, was to manage the liaison relationship—the relationship with the host government's intelligence service—a classic CIA mission. I could not relinquish my authority over them, nor was he in a position to judge them. What I suspected was that in some cases, Blair intended to select officers from other intelligence agencies to serve as his representatives.

Blair took me aside at a lunch honoring the judges of the Foreign Intelligence Surveillance Court and brusquely let me know that he was going to send out his directive to the intelligence community instituting his change. I asked him not to and requested a meeting to discuss it further. Then Blair invited me to attend a ceremony at the DNI offices at which he would announce the new titles for our station chiefs. I debated refusing to attend, but went and used the opportunity to warn Blair that I remained opposed to his idea. He ignored my request and that same day signed the new policy, which was forwarded to the field by his staff that evening as "Intelligence Community Directive 402," containing the changes.

There was no way I could stand for that—his unilateral action had not been through the National Security Council process, and he took it knowing of my objections. I called in Kappes and directed him to send all our people a follow-up to Blair's e-mail. The cable, dubbed a WWSB ("World Wide Stations and Bases"), was terse and direct. It stated that the DNI's revisions to Directive 402 were to be ignored. Period.

Needless to say, that left things in an uncomfortable position, and I followed up by explaining to Jim Jones and Tom Donilon what I'd done. They agreed that Blair had bypassed the process, but did not immediately take my position on the substance of the issue. Instead, the matter was sent to Vice President Biden to investigate and decide. The vice president met with Blair and me separately, and though I don't know precisely what Blair told him, I made myself clear. "I'm prepared to work this through," I said, "but I'm not about to let the DNI name my station chiefs."

About a week later, Biden summoned all of us together and gave us a short memo. It provided some of what Blair was after—assurances that station chiefs would represent his office—but made clear that naming them remained a function of the CIA. I responded that I still had a few reservations, but that I accepted the conclusion and was ready to move on. Blair, on the other hand, curtly announced, "No, I can't accept it."

I was slack-jawed. A little note on Washington politics: When the vice president of the United States is assigned the job of mediating a dispute and announces his decision, your job is to accept it. Instead, Blair asked for an audience with the president, effectively seeking to overrule Biden. Donilon told Blair that was not going to happen, and Blair went away mad. Shortly thereafter, Biden made his recommendations final. In early December, the fax machine outside Mary Elfmann's desk whirred with an "urgent" fax from the Situation Room. It contained a memo from Jones clearly stating that the CIA retained authority to name station chiefs. Case closed.

That wasn't the only instance where Blair and I disagreed. Apparently after a series of meetings with a foreign ambassador, he concocted the loony notion that we should enter into an agreement with that country under which both countries would agree not to spy on each other. That may sound appealing on the surface—we're ancient allies who don't wish each other harm—but it's shortsighted to forswear gathering intelligence from anyone, since you don't know when you might need to know something that's not publicly available. Moreover, entering into such an agreement with one country would invite others to make the same request. How could we justify not calling off spying in other countries? And would we really expect those countries to honor those agreements? When Blair presented this idea to the National Security Council, it was met with embarrassing silence; Jones put the matter to a vote of the National Security Council Principals, and Blair was the only one to favor it. Jones and Donilon directed him to dial it back, deepening Blair's discomfort, as he'd already led the other country to believe we had a deal.

There was at least one good outcome from that dustup. Donilon, recognizing the need for better communication between the CIA and the office of the DNI, chaired a weekly intelligence meeting at the White House. That was helpful on sensitive operational issues, and made sure the White House was aware of what we were up to.

In the middle of 2010, Blair was replaced by Jim Clapper, who was deft and scrupulous. In fact, Clapper may be the perfect person to serve in the difficult position of DNI. Although he's been criticized for testimony he gave to Congress regarding the work of the NSA, he's an intelligence expert, and he's open-minded, forceful, and yet respectful of the agencies he's asked to coordinate. I am still not sure whether the position is worth it, but if the government has to have it, Clapper is ideal for the job.

Although the White House backed me in those disputes with Blair, I had my differences with the president's senior national security staff. Our most frequent flash points came over the issue of how much of the agency's work I could share with the press, public, and Congress. I felt that I should reveal as much information as was prudent, especially since the rationale for putting me in charge of the agency was in part to restore confidence in its work. Secrecy hardly fostered that confidence.

The White House, particularly NSC chief of staff Denis McDonough and Tom Donilon, were of the view that the CIA director should not deliver major speeches or give press interviews. (Part of their concern stemmed from their discomfort with the way my predecessor, Mike Hayden, had so publicly defended enhanced interrogation.) I understood their point, but I felt the White House was clamping down too hard and did not trust its senior officials enough. Moreover, it meant that those officials who knew the most about certain subjects were excluded from important public debates, skewing the conversation in ways that sometimes did the administration's policies a disservice. Some of my colleagues on the national security team, notably Bob Gates, found the restraints insulting; for me, it was not so much an insult—I didn't take it personally—as it was a bother. I had to submit speeches for White House approval, and when I would forward requests for interviews, the White House would take weeks to respond, effectively killing the idea without ever saying so directly. That penchant for control may have been an understandable reaction to the problems of the Bush years, but it was in my view an overreaction that deprived the White House of some of its more capable public spokesmen. An additional consequence was that David Plouffe or David Axelrod—political advisers—were most often those who represented the administration. They were capable spokesmen, but because they came out of politics, their highly visible role had the effect of overemphasizing the political side of important policy decisions.

Some of the same undermined the administration's relations with Congress. Among those close to him, the president was believed not to have found his time as a senator very rewarding and to be disdainful of Congress generally. I never witnessed that disdain directly, but I did pick up evidence of it within his senior staff. They often made it clear that they didn't want any agency head revealing executive branch deliberations to members of Congress or cutting their own deals with members on policy questions.

One example sticks out. Chairman Feinstein, with ranking member Kit Bond's reluctant concurrence, decided early in the Obama years that she wanted to launch a comprehensive study of the Bush-era interrogation policies. She requested access for her staff to every operational cable regarding the program, a database that had to be in the hundreds of thousands of documents. These were among the most sensitive documents the agency had. But Feinstein's staff had the requisite clearances, and we had no basis to refuse her.

Still, I wanted to have some control over this material, so I proposed a deal: Instead of turning over the documents en masse to her staff, we would set up a secure reading room in Virginia. Her staff could come out to the secure facility and review documents one by one, and though they could take notes, the documents themselves would stay with the CIA. I thought it was a sound compromise and a good deal for the agency, so I didn't think to clear it with the White House. I soon found out they saw it differently.

I was summoned down to a meeting in the Situation Room, where I was told I would have to "explain" this deal to Rahm. About a dozen of us—including Blair, Brennan, Preston, Donilon, and McDonough—piled into one of the smaller side conference rooms off the main Situation Room. It did not take long to get ugly.

"The president wants to know who the fuck authorized this release to the committees," Rahm said, slamming his hand down on the table. "I have a president with his hair on fire, and I want to know what the fuck you did to fuck this up so bad!"

I'd known Rahm a long time, and I was no stranger to his language or his temper, so I knew when to worry about an outburst and when it was mostly for show. On this occasion, my hunch was that Rahm wasn't that perturbed but that Obama probably was and that others at the table, particularly Brennan and McDonough, were too. Rahm was sticking up for them by coming after me. Before I had a chance to defend myself, Blair chimed in.

"If the president's hair is on fire," he retorted, "I want to know who the fuck set his hair on fire!"

It went back and forth like this for about fifteen minutes. Brennan and I even exchanged sharp words when I, unfairly, accused him of not sticking up for the agency in the debate over the interrogation memos. Finally, the White House team realized that whether they liked it or not, there was no way we could go back on our deal with the committee. And just like that, the whole matter was dropped.

That was the end of that, but it belied a deeper disagreement over how best to manage our relations with Congress. In my view, the administration's reticence to include Congress was shortsighted. Because of my background, my inclination was to bring Congress into sensitive matters, both for its input and as a defensive measure to prevent later second-guessing. Those impulses were not often shared by the White House in those early months.

Having cut the deal to let Feinstein's aides review the interrogation materials, I then set up a task force to manage the process—organizing the documents and creating procedures for accessing them. I also asked the task force to prepare summaries of the material so we would know what had been read and what implications the documents might have for the CIA. Importantly, those summaries were supposed to be just that—not analysis of the material or conclusions drawn from it, merely synopses to help us stay on top of the process.

Those synopses subsequently have come to be known as the "Panetta Review," though I was not aware of what the final review concluded beyond the summary of the documents. Since then, the oversight committee and the CIA have publicly fought over the handling of the material. That's a shame, because both have important responsibilities. Congress is entitled by law and common sense to provide oversight to the work of its intelligence agencies, and the CIA and other agencies have an equally serious duty to protect classified information. Neither of those responsibilities need come at the expense of the other.

I firmly believe that American national security is best protected when there is a partnership between Republicans and Democrats and between the executive and legislative branches. When trust breaks down, as it did in the spring of 2014 when Chairman Feinstein accused the CIA of spying on her staff conducting the review, it erodes the effectiveness of our intelligence operations and inhibits sound congressional oversight. The focus turns to finger-pointing and investigating past actions rather than to cooperating to protect the national security. As Winston Churchill once said, "If we open a quarrel between past and present, we shall find that we have lost the future."

Mending relations with Congress, elbowing for position within the administration, and ridding ourselves of a destructive relationship with certain contractors were among the more important Washington tasks I faced in those early months. But the CIA's real work was across the globe, identifying threats to American security and, where possible, neutralizing them, either on our own or in cooperation with the many intelligence agencies with whom we were allied. The threats to security were dizzying in number and complexity.

Late that summer we received a particularly unnerving one. One well-known terrorist—a short, grandiose brute thought to command some sixteen thousand Pakistani and foreign fighters in the area of South Waziristan—was believed to have acquired an extraordinarily dangerous weapon and was boasting his intention to use it.

The terrorist was well known to American officials, but in the Bush years officials had not pursued him because his terrorist energy was directed at Pakistan, not the United States. In May 2008, however, he invited Western journalists to a feast and then announced before them his jihad against American forces in nearby Afghanistan. After that, he began sending fighters across the border to kill Americans.

Worried that he was preparing an even more lethal attack, I alerted my counterpart in Pakistan, Ahmad Shuja Pasha, then the head of Pakistan's main intelligence service, the ISI (Inter-Services Intelligence).

Pasha and I would become well acquainted over the next few years, but at that point we had met only twice—once during my first trip as CIA director, which included a stay in Pakistan, and once when Pasha visited the United States in April 2009, when we met at Langley.

Pasha was an intriguing, enigmatic figure who carried himself with a military bearing, perhaps the result of having served as a general in the Pakistani military before being handpicked by Ashfaq Kayani, then the chief of army staff and the most powerful man in Pakistan, to run ISI. Pasha understood English perfectly, though his spoken English was often halting and too soft to hear. Like others in the officer corps, he had a whiff of a British accent.

I was impressed by his moderation, sense of history, and worldliness. During dinner with President Asif Ali Zardari on my first visit to Pakistan, Pasha told me that the problem in western Pakistan stemmed from the replacement of the malik, the secular tribal leader, with the mullah, the religious authority. He inveighed against the number of madrassas in which poor Pakistani youth were being molded, and yearned to draw his country into the future. Yet for all of Pasha's charm and sincerity, what I did not know was how much he was willing to take on militants within his own country.

What I had to tell Pasha in the summer of 2009 was a matter of common concern for both of us. Pakistan was waging its own battle with the Tehrik-e-Taliban (TTP), the Pakistani Taliban group responsible for the assassination of former prime minister Benazir Bhutto. In 2008, a leader of that group was believed to have orchestrated the bombing of the Marriott Hotel in Islamabad, killing more than forty people, including Americans who were staying at the hotel; one guest whom I knew personally barely escaped with her life. On my first trip to Islamabad, I drove by the site, but it still was too dangerous for me even to stop and observe a moment of silence.

Now, we had reason to worry that one of the TTP's leaders had a "dirty bomb." If so, no one doubted whether he would use it. I warned

Pasha that our intelligence analysts were divided about how seriously to regard this threat, but that some considered it realistic. Pasha agreed to treat the matter with vigilance. Meanwhile, I alerted our military and other forces of the possible menace.

Those pursuing this terrorist were aided by a few factors: Although he did not court publicity in the manner of some of his compatriots, his public declaration of jihad against the United States meant that U.S. officials had a good sense of his appearance, as well as his curious habit of wearing a distinctive cap. In addition, he suffered from an illness that apparently produced pain in his back and legs; he treated those pains with regular massages.

A few days later, someone matching his description was staying at the home of his father-in-law. There were other people in the house, however, making it a complicated operation to capture or kill the terrorist without harming others. If his identity could be established, it would be difficult to let him get away, given his record, threats, and possible capacity. A man wearing the hat he often wore appeared on the roof, accompanied by another person—it appeared to be his doctor— who massaged his legs. I was at the White House attending a meeting of the National Security Council while that was unfolding. A call came in during the meeting about the sighting of our target on the roof and I, along with my staff, asked some critical questions.

What were the odds that this was the right man? Answer: 70 to 80 percent.

What about others in the house? Would the building collapse if it was hit, killing innocents? The answer: There were others inside, but the mission, according to the operators, could be accomplished without killing noncombatants.

Sometimes it takes weeks to know whether an operation has been successful. Not this time. After a day or two of confusion, press reports confirmed that he was dead. His wife had been killed in the operation as well.

Despite the death of the terrorist's wife, the president was pleased at the demise of this dangerous man. On the next Saturday, Jeremy received a call from the White House Situation Room operator, saying that the president wanted to thank the officer who helped track the terrorist. "Where can the president reach him?" the operator asked. "First," Jeremy said, "it is a *her*, not a him. Second, here is the phone number in her car; she's driving." The officer later told us that when the call came in, she nearly drove off the side of the road.

There was, however, another consequence of our work during those months. Al Qaeda, recognizing that its strongholds in Afghanistan and Pakistan were becoming increasingly insecure, began searching for redoubts in other parts of the world. Our mission, hard enough to fulfill in South Asia, with its rugged terrain and mystifying allegiances, was about to become much, much more complicated.

ELEVEN

"Disrupt, Dismantle, Defeat"

The war against Al Qaeda was—still is—waged around the world, in airports, Arabian deserts, the heart of Manhattan, Afghan mountain ranges, and the Horn of Africa. But during my time at the CIA, the strategy for that war was plotted every Monday, Wednesday, and Friday afternoon in a conference room in suburban Virginia. There, at 4:30 p.m., a dozen or so of the CIA's most accomplished officials, analysts, and operators gathered for the "CT-ME" (short for Counter-Terrorism and Middle East) update. Three times a week, month after month, those men and women filed in, took their seats around a cherry table, opened their binders, produced their notes, and conducted a war.

The meeting's agenda was set by Roger,* the director of the CIA's Counterterrorism Center, or CTC.[1] Roger was a veteran of CIA activities in North Africa and Iraq, a cerebral student of Islamic ideology. Nobody had done more to understand, analyze, chase, and eliminate

_____
*Not his real name.

Al Qaeda. As CTC director, he commanded the largest office at CIA and had the biggest budget. As the name implied, the Counterterrorism Center was the heart of the agency's counterterrorism effort, fusing together operators and analysts who directed our worldwide campaign against Al Qaeda.

Stephen Kappes and Michael Morell often reminded me that when they began their careers at the agency three decades earlier, operators and analysts didn't mix. They ate in separate cafeterias; that's how distrusted the analysts of the Directorate of Intelligence were by the old hands of the Directorate of Operations. Today, operators and analysts not only talk and eat together, but they collaborate, work side by side, and even serve in the field together. Both sets of officers were represented at the CT-ME update.

The update provided an opportunity for Roger's officers, together with those in the Near East Division and the respective analytic offices, to brief me on important developments from Marrakesh to Bangladesh. We made resource and budget decisions about the footprint of the CIA in Iraq and Afghanistan—where we should open new bases; how we should coordinate with the intelligence services of allies; how we should analyze unfolding developments in the context of the broader effort against Al Qaeda. We discussed the analysis that would be presented to the president during his wide-ranging review of the Afghanistan war during 2009. And we reviewed reports from our officers' meetings with sensitive assets who were working to penetrate the plots against America.

The last item on the agenda was always the same: operations along the Afghanistan-Pakistan border and elsewhere—the operations about which so much has been written. The effort was led by Emma,* who knew the back alleys of Waziristan better than I knew Monterey. With

---

*Not her real name.

her flat, professional affect, she carefully walked me through the detail of every proposed operation. I studied maps and videos and reports from the field, information from other agencies, and our best assessments of where Al Qaeda and its associated militants—the Haqqanis, the Taliban, Commander Nazir—might try to move their hideouts. The meeting often ended with an apology from Roger: "Sir, we may have to call you late tonight for approval to go forward; I apologize for the hour."

Though the format of that meeting was predictable, the contours of the conversation were ever-changing, as we responded to an evolving, metastasizing enemy, whose bases of operations shifted in response to our work and larger geopolitics, ever in search of chaos to exploit.

In the years since 9/11, Al Qaeda had morphed. U.S. forces chased bin Laden and his henchmen out of Afghanistan in the fall of 2001. Bin Laden himself slipped into the ungoverned spaces in western Pakistan, and Al Qaeda's leadership followed. For several years, the Federally Administered Tribal Areas (FATA) in Pakistan became Al Qaeda's safe haven. Situated west of the Indus River and east of the Durand Line, the FATA was the badlands of Pakistan. Barely governed by Pakistan's central government in Islamabad, the Tribal Areas, particularly North and South Waziristan, and the villages of Miram Shah and Mir Ali, provided protection for Al Qaeda to regroup and restart its campaigns against the West and Western values.

In 2006, Al Qaeda senior leaders operating from the FATA planned and nearly pulled off a spectacular terrorist plot. Directed by Rashid Rauf, a British Kashmiri born in Pakistan but raised in Birmingham,[2] the plot sent operatives to Europe to hijack ten airliners bound for the United States and explode them in midair with an ingenious liquid bomb hidden in soft drinks and Gatorade bottles. If you ever cursed an airport security guard for preventing you from taking your water onto an airplane, you can thank Rashid Rauf. Intelligence cooperation between the CIA and the British stymied the plot. British authorities were able to sneak into the bomb factory in Britain, record the activities, and arrest the ringleaders. Pakistani authorities arrested Rashid Rauf, but in December 2007 he mysteriously escaped from a Pakistani prison. Free again to go about his work, he began to develop cunning and diabolical new plots against the West. As was the case before his arrest, he operated from the ungoverned areas of Pakistan, beyond the reach—at the time—of American power.

That's because until mid-2008 the Bush administration had a policy not to conduct unilateral counterterrorism operations inside Pakistan unless the Pakistanis granted permission. And they never granted permission. The Bush administration acquiesced, reluctant to push the Pakistani government too hard given that country's strategic importance to the region. That's understandable in some respects, but one consequence was that by 2007 the efforts to dismantle Al Qaeda were largely stalled. American officials referred to 2007 as "0 for '07." We had driven Al Qaeda from its haven in Afghanistan, only to have it set up shop again just across the border.

Granted effective protection, the militants grew bolder. They started streaming across the Afghanistan-Pakistan border to attack our forces, and their enemies grew to include not just Americans but Pakistanis as well. Finally, in July 2008, the Bush administration lifted the restrictions on unilateral operations in the FATA. By then, many plots were under way. The 2008 bombing of the Marriott Hotel in Islamabad was one such attack; both Americans and Pakistanis died in that blast, reminding our countries of our common interest in combating these terrorists.

The 2008 policy change paid off. The question in the spring of 2009 was whether the United States would continue or whether we would scale back. My instinct was to push forward.

The visitor in my office in the summer of 2009 wore a long white robe with gold trim, comfortable thick-soled sandals, and a black braid rope around his head to hold in place a long white ghutra.

His Highness Prince Muhammad bin Nayef was the head of Saudi Arabia's internal intelligence service, known as Mabahith. He was also the son of the interior minister and a nephew of the king. In the complex world of Saudi royalty, the betting money was that Prince Nayef, his father, would ascend to be crown prince and Muhammad bin Nayef, or MBN, as the son was universally called by U.S. officials, would become interior minister. There were even those who suggested he could become king. Of the next generation, he was among the smartest and most accomplished.

His prominence and effectiveness made him a threat to many. Bin Nayef had been the victim of repeated assassination attempts—terrorists planted a car bomb outside his offices in Riyadh, others fired a missile at his plane. In the summer of 2009, a third attempt was made, this time by a terrorist claiming to be giving himself up and submitting to Saudi Arabia's fascinating repatriation program, under which extremists could seek and receive forgiveness in return for renouncing violence and pledging loyalty to the regime. Bin Nayef's administration of that program had been far more successful than the efforts of other governments, where hard-line tactics had created deep animosity and helped cultivate new generations of terrorists. By contrast, bin Nayef had largely driven Al Qaeda in the Arabian Peninsula out of Saudi Arabia.[3]

In our initial meeting, bin Nayef recounted for me his latest near-death experience, just a few weeks earlier. It began as part of his repatriation program and involved a potentially significant surrender. Abdullah al-Asiri, a scruffy young terrorist who was among Saudi Arabia's most wanted enemies, sent word that he was prepared to turn himself in and renounce his attacks on his country. Bin Nayef welcomed the news, and agreed to accept Asiri's surrender personally.

Asiri arrived on schedule for their meeting, and bin Nayef greeted him politely, leading him to a set of pillows on the floor, where the two sat, their shoulders nearly touching. As they did, Asiri began to shake and cry. Then he reached under his robe, briefly alarming bin Nayef. But instead of drawing out a weapon, he emerged with a cell phone, saying that he wanted to call his family and tell them that he was turning himself in. The sight of the cell phone was a relief, bin Nayef told me. But then, before he could fully process Asiri's actions, a huge explosion ripped through the room.

It blew a crater in the reception area, but apparently because the force of the charge faced downward, it left bin Nayef with only a few cuts to his hands and other minor injuries. The bomber was blown into nearly a hundred pieces; bin Nayef did not spend so much as a night in the hospital. Asiri had hidden the bomb in his rectum and detonated it with his phone.

The attempt on bin Nayef's life had its roots in Yemen, and that's what he had come to discuss with me. As effective as bin Nayef had been at diminishing Al Qaeda's presence in his country, he was stymied by the problem of how to attack it across the border in Yemen. In fact, Asiri's older brother, working in Yemen, had built the bomb that vaporized his brother and left the prince standing; the brother, Ibrahim al-Asiri, was still at work in Yemen even after he reduced Abdullah to scraps. And behind him was an even more sinister force: Anwar al-Awlaki, the American-born cleric turned terrorist leader.

A native of New Mexico, educated at Colorado State University, Awlaki was a powerful radicalizer of young men. He had served as an imam at mosques in San Diego and Falls Church, Virginia, both of which were visited by the 9/11 attackers, and was among the first Al Qaeda propagandists to make creative use of the Internet, exhorting his listeners to violent jihad and distributing his message internationally. Even after he left the United States, first for England and later Yemen, distance did not deter him from encouraging others in their hatred toward America. He ran a Web site where he posted frequent sermons; it included a tab, "Contact the Sheikh," through which readers could pose questions to him.[4] Beginning in late 2008, he received his first of many e-mails from U.S. Army major Nidal Malik Hasan. Although Awlaki was guarded in his responses, Hasan's decision to contact him reflected his growing renown. On November 5, 2009, three months after Abdullah al-Asiri nearly killed Prince bin Nayef, Major Hasan leaped atop a desk at Fort Hood, shouted, "Allahu Akbar!" and opened fire on those inside the Soldier Readiness Center. Thirteen people died and forty-two more were injured. As with the attack on Prince bin Nayef, this tragedy connected back to Yemen.

The Yemeni government wanted these terrorists out, but Al Qaeda effectively established tribal areas of its own, settling in beyond the reach of that country's limited government, which lacked the technical and human resources to eject a hardened bunch of criminals from their encampments. If we were going to dismantle and defeat Al Qaeda, we needed to conquer it not just in Afghanistan and Pakistan, but in Yemen as well. Bin Nayef made that case to me in 2009. He was right.

Nor was Yemen the only new destination for this spreading threat. In Somalia, a small government held court in Mogadishu, but it controlled almost nothing outside the city and even struggled to manage some of the city itself. That gave yet another nascent terror group with aspirations of mayhem an opportunity to seize power, land, and control.

Known as Al Shabaab ("the Youth"), it was an outgrowth of a system of sharia courts that took root in Somalia during the chaotic attempts to unite that country's rival clans and warlords in the late 1990s.

The courts imposed a semblance of order in areas otherwise reduced to anarchy—any law being better than none. But the courts lacked the ability to compel obedience, so to enforce their orders they created their own militias.[5] Of those, Al Shabaab was among the most radical, and it solidified its standing among the Somali people during the 2006 Ethiopian invasion of the country, when Al Shabaab fighters waged an insurgency that harassed and distracted the Ethiopians and their surrogates. In time, the Ethiopian forces crushed the constellation of sharia courts that had founded Al Shabaab, but the group itself survived, and more radical elements within the organization took control. Beginning in 2008, Al Shabaab turned on the Somali government itself, transforming the group from a defender of that country into an outpost of Al Qaeda. From that point on, Al Shabaab became a focal point for violence in the region, launching terrorist attacks inside and outside Somalia, offering haven to foreign fighters, and—of particular concern—attempting to lure young Somali expatriates, including those who had settled in the United States—back to its camps for training in the global war against the West.

The Somalia affiliate, dubbed Al Qaeda in East Africa, had ties back to the cell that had bombed two American embassies in August 1998, in Nairobi and Dar es Salaam, killing more than two hundred people. In September 2009, acting on an intelligence tip, U.S. special operations officers swooped down into a lawless section of Somalia via helicopter and killed Saleh Nabhan, a member of the FBI's most wanted list.

Confronted with these expanding threats into new areas, those of us responsible for our national security had to disrupt terrorist plots in multiple countries. In some places the military took the lead while in others, the CIA was out front. I wanted us to work together better. I directed our NCS leadership, together with the associate director of the CIA for military affairs, General Welsh, to strengthen cooperation between the CIA and special operations forces. Together, we would confront Al Qaeda wherever we found it.

And then there was the United States itself. During one of my first intelligence briefings during the transition, I had been told that the FBI's assessment was that there were no Al Qaeda cells operating in the country. But both FBI director Bob Mueller and Mike Leiter, the head of the National Counterterrorism Center, warned me that we didn't know what we didn't know—and that we should assume that Al Qaeda was trying to recruit operatives who could operate in the West.

At a regular CT-ME update in the summer of 2009, I received a briefing about one of Rashid Rauf's operatives who had made it into the United States and was embarked on a potentially devastating mission. Najibullah Zazi was a twenty-four-year-old Afghan who immigrated to the United States with his family when he was fourteen. His father became a U.S. citizen and found work in New York. Zazi lived for ten years in Flushing, Queens, and at some point became sufficiently radicalized to take up arms against his adopted country. He traveled to Pakistan and was provided explosives training in 2008. In 2009, his Al Qaeda masters, including operations chief Saleh al-Somali, directed him to bomb the New York City subway system, providing him with a special explosives recipe.

Using some of the authority that Congress had granted the National Security Agency to monitor terrorist e-mails, the U.S. government was able not only to track those communications but also to see the bomb recipe, which was shared with the FBI so that agents here would know what materials Zazi was likely to purchase. When Zazi left his home in Aurora, Colorado, in August 2009 on his way to New York to carry out his mission, he was followed the entire time by the

FBI. Apparently spooked by reports from relatives and others that agents had been asking about him, he called off his plans and flew back to Colorado. Roger's team kept me apprised. On September 22, 2009, Najibullah Zazi was arrested; he remains in custody today.[6]

Time and again, we were successful at stopping terrorist attacks. But even success in this area was a cause for alarm, as each of these operations reminded us of the spread and lethality of Al Qaeda. We were fighting around the world, against a determined, creative, and merciless enemy. There was no rest.

It was against this background that I paid a visit to MacDill Air Force Base in Tampa, Florida, headquarters of U.S. Central Command and U.S. Special Operations Command. My host was General David Petraeus, the affable, disciplined, and confident commander who had helped turn the tide of the Iraq war with his famous "surge." He first welcomed me into his office, which was nothing short of a shrine . . . to him. To be fair, we all collect so much bric-a-brac in these jobs—coins, awards, and photos of ourselves—that our walls become covered with the stuff. I did it too. But David set a new bar. Every inch of flat space in his office was covered with a military challenge coin he had received. Every bit of wall was covered with a picture of him flying in a helicopter, wearing shades, surveying his battlefield—Iraq, or wherever—below. He also had a huge coterie of advisers, people who were loyal to him and whose careers he had carefully looked after. I had Jeremy with me, along with General Welsh and one of our liaisons to Petraeus's command. David had two or three flag officers, several field-grade officers, and even enlisted women and men there to help him with the briefing.

He had recently returned from Pakistan, where he had met with General Kayani, and he had immersed himself in the nuances of the region. He deftly walked me through the Pakistani military's advances in western Pakistan, jabbing a 3-D map of the North-West Frontier

Province with what looked like a pool cue. David knew the name of every battle, every township lost and gained in the fight against the militants, and every stronghold of the leading terrorists.

The next day—and the real purpose of my visit—I cochaired with David a meeting of all of the senior officials in the U.S. government responsible for counterterrorism. Once, the concern about the American government approach to terrorist threats had been that it was conducted by agencies in silos, barely communicating with one another. No more. The State Department's ambassador at large for counterterrorism, Dan Benjamin, was there, as were Stuart Levey and David Cohen from the Treasury Department. All of the major military commands were represented. Mike Leiter led off with a briefing on the U.S. government's overall strategy against terrorism—a complex web of responsibilities that stretched from diplomatic initiatives and monitoring the money behind the groups to military and covert action.

I was particularly impressed with a briefing from a three-star navy admiral, Bill McRaven, who led the Joint Special Operations Command. Bill made a big impression with his booming baritone, wide smile, and huge biceps. He methodically went through all of the terrorist hot zones around the world, detailing U.S. military activities in each of these places. Bill's forces were responsible for, in military parlance, "finding, fixing, and finishing" terrorist targets. They had proved decisive in the efforts against Al Qaeda in Iraq.

CIA's briefing was much different, at least in appearance. It was led by Norm, one of Roger's deputies and a rumpled, soft-spoken career analyst in his fifties, sporting thinning hair, thick glasses, a bit of a paunch, and a loosened tie. But, like McRaven, Norm also brought his A game, quickly breaking down the agency's efforts against Al Qaeda senior leaders. In essence, he said, our strategy was to put enough pressure on the leaders of Al Qaeda to force them to burrow further underground, take more risks with their communications, or make a mistake. We needed to keep the pressure on. On that point, everyone agreed.

At the end of the daylong session, the CIA team packed our bags and headed for our charter plane. Jeremy offered to give Mike Leiter a ride, since we had one extra seat in the sixteen-passenger jet. I sat in my usual spot, facing forward on the right side of the aircraft. I asked Mark Welsh to sit across from me so we could review the day. A thunderstorm was booming over Tampa, but Mark assured me it was nothing to worry about. He was an F-16 pilot and one of the air force's best, so I allowed myself to relax. A few minutes after takeoff, as we were in a steep ascent, the plane bumped violently, a loud "ding" rang out, and the oxygen masks dropped from the ceiling. I looked at Mark.

"Okay, that's not good," he said, not the words one hopes to hear from an F-16 pilot during a bumpy flight. "We should put these on," he added, gesturing to the masks. For a moment, it occurred to me that this could be how it ends. Thoughts of Sylvia and the boys bounced in my head as I breathed through the mask. The air force steward came racing down the aisle with a heavy binder in his hand, urgently flipping pages in a manual. It didn't make me feel much better to think that in the middle of an emergency the pilot apparently wanted to look something up.

And yet I guess he found it, because the plane slowly leveled off. After a minute or two, the captain assured us that all was okay. The oxygen masks dangled there during the entire two hours back to D.C.

When we got off the plane, Mike Leiter looked at me, white as a sheet, and deadpanned, "That's the last time I ever ask *you* for a ride."

Through the summer and fall of 2009, President Obama and his national security team aggressively searched for a new approach to the war in Afghanistan. The options were infinite in theory, limited in practice. Obama had campaigned as a critic of the Bush administration's overreliance on military solutions, particularly its conflation of Islam and terrorism. The war in Iraq had been easier to dismiss—"a war of choice" as he called it, distinguishing it from the war in Afghanistan as a "war of necessity." Now, as president, he sought a new way to prosecute the necessary war. He was prepared to add resources, including troops, but he wanted a plan to end the conflict, leave behind a stable nation, deny refuge to Al Qaeda, and eventually to bring home American forces from the longest war in this nation's history.

In one sense, I was peripheral to that debate. It largely centered around troop strength, obviously a matter for the military and the president to decide. And yet the CIA was integral to our efforts in Afghanistan. As a result, I participated in most of the major meetings, particularly at the outset of the review.

Those conversations touched on many nuances and complications, but they largely boiled down to two questions: How many troops were needed to stabilize Afghanistan, and how long would they have to stay? In turn, both of those questions demanded identification of an objective: Were we in Afghanistan until it was a fully functioning democracy, with respect for human rights and sectarian differences? Or would we be satisfied with a country that could sustain itself and hold its own against the blandishments of current or future terrorist organizations that sought protection there? Finally, what was our posture toward the Taliban? Was it inextricable from Al Qaeda, or could we live with a restored Taliban if that group—whose subjugation of women and imposition of distinctly anti-Western Islamic codes were offensive to most Western values—nevertheless governed without threat to its neighbors or others?

As those debates occupied the administration in the fall of 2009, I had some distinct advantages over many in the room. While there was disagreement about how to approach the Taliban, there was universal consensus that we needed to spare no effort against the leadership of Al Qaeda; I didn't need to argue much for our work. I prepared a list of items that I believed could help the CIA replicate and extend such operations. I proposed a buildup of CIA operations in the region, continued work on the border between Afghanistan and Pakistan, and the expansion of our capabilities that would allow us to find more Al Qaeda fighters in the region.

I presented our suggestions at a meeting with the president and his national security advisers on October 7, 2009. The general nature of those meetings was that proposals were made and taken under advisement, and that was expected. The president, after all, needs to consider any significant policy determination in the full light of his responsibilities. Commitment to spending in Afghanistan has to be weighed against domestic priorities and competing demands from across the government. In this case, as was often his practice, he jotted notes as I spoke. When I finished with my list of requests, however, the president's reaction was uncharacteristically and bracingly decisive. "The CIA," he said, "gets what it wants." That settled it. I had permission to proceed with my full program.

Two days later, General Stanley McChrystal's vision for Afghanistan got its first full airing before the National Security Council. McChrystal, who had submitted his classified review of the war at the end of August, argued for a surge of forty thousand troops. He'd been making that case in sessions with the president and others for weeks, but in response to demands from the White House that he not present the president with just a single proposal, he had—somewhat artificially, in my view—broadened his recommendations to include three: an increase of either ten thousand, forty thousand, or eighty-five thousand soldiers. The last, he said, would allow for a more aggressive and sustained counterinsurgency campaign, while the lowest number would be only enough to provide training for Afghan troops to take the job forward.[7] Moreover, Obama had already agreed to an increase of twenty-one thousand troops early in his term, so whatever surge he authorized now would be the second major increase in forces in less than a year—from a president committed to winding the war down, not ratcheting it up.

Although McChrystal's options had the appearance of offering the president a choice, there was less of a choice than it seemed. If Obama opted for the increase of ten thousand, the military warned that it could not guarantee Afghanistan's continued stability, nor train its forces fast enough to let the government there defend itself. That was a trap that Obama could not afford to fall into. At the other extreme, sending eighty-five thousand more soldiers to Afghanistan was beyond the political pale. Authorizing it on top of Obama's earlier deployment would have meant that the president would have, in a single year, sent more than one hundred thousand soldiers to that war. The cost would be astronomical, the president would break faith with his supporters, and Congress would almost surely reject it.

The overall picture was that the ten-thousand-troop option wasn't enough to do the job, and the eighty-five-thousand-troop surge wasn't economically or politically feasible. In effect, then, the military was giving Obama one choice and making it look like three.

Making matters worse, McChrystal and other generals had been publicly campaigning for a buildup even as they professed to be giving neutral advice to the president. McChrystal was particularly visible. He had given an interview to *60 Minutes* in which he seemed to imply that President Obama was detached from the particulars of the Afghanistan war, and then on October 1 he had delivered a speech in London about the state of the conflict. Afterward, he was asked whether a limited campaign could be successful. "The short answer is no," he responded. "A strategy that does not leave Afghanistan in a stable position is probably a shortsighted strategy."[8]

Setting aside that McChrystal may well have been right about that, it nevertheless was an ill-advised remark at a time when the president was still considering his options. The military, or at least some of the military's leading generals, were effectively boxing in their boss. The White House saw this as a coordinated effort to limit the president's decision space, while Gates saw it as evidence that the Pentagon brass was unable to stay on message. For my part, it seemed that the leading generals saw the problem the same way and weren't good about keeping quiet, but not that they were organizing a campaign against their president.

At the meeting on October 9, I tried to draw a distinction between our approach to the Taliban and to Al Qaeda. Yes, they were intertwined, I argued, but our real enemy was Al Qaeda. The Taliban's affront to the United States was not so much its backward domestic policies—denying girls the right to go to school, for instance. The reason we were at war was because the Taliban had offered Al Qaeda safe haven. If we could grind down Al Qaeda, we'd have much less to fear from the Taliban. That focus, I argued, made some of the other concerns less troubling. Afghan president Hamid Karzai was unpredictable and widely regarded as corrupt, but our mission didn't need to wait for a perfect president or a flawless government. We needed stability, influence, and a functioning state in order to prevent the lawlessness that would provide fertile earth for dangerous seeds. That was more important than the precise number of troops on the ground or the schedule for the surge and eventual drawdown.

Others staked out a variety of positions in that and subsequent meetings. The generals consistently maintained that anything less than a surge of forty thousand troops would doom the mission. Vice President Joe Biden challenged that presumption again and again. More than anyone else in those conversations, Biden raised the specter of Vietnam, of incremental increases in commitment without a clear plan or exit strategy. Hillary Clinton, by contrast, was an enthusiastic champion of the military's proposed increase. She conceded that stepping up America's military commitment to Afghanistan was no guarantee of victory, but she also forcefully argued that failing to do so virtually guaranteed failure. Gates argued for the surge but, late in the debates, proposed that it could be carried out with between thirty thousand and forty thousand troops, a modest scaling back that helped calm the conversation.

To me, the debate over troop levels took too long and was too public, especially given that I believed it was destined to end pretty much where the military wanted it to end. Obama was a new president, a Democrat without military experience. For him to defy his military advisers on a matter so central to the success of his foreign policy and so early in his presidency would have represented an almost impossible risk. Bob Gates might have resigned. Worse, the war might have soured, and Obama surely would have been blamed for losing the gains Bush had fought so hard to achieve.

In the end, Obama accepted Gates's recommendation, settling on thirty thousand new troops with an emergency reserve of three thousand more, and, more important, moving away from the notion that our mission was to destroy or eliminate the Taliban. Rather, he adopted the formula that our mission was to "disrupt, dismantle, and defeat" Al Qaeda. That struck me as a more focused and achievable aim, and it better reflected America's interest in the region. We were not there to dictate the specifics of Afghan government; instead, our objective was to prevent the country from lapsing back into the environment that had allowed Al Qaeda to operate there. When Obama lit upon "disrupt, dismantle, and defeat" as our approach to Al Qaeda, I adopted that same language to frame the CIA's role.

As for the matter of troop strength, I wasn't at the table for the final deliberations. That's mainly because the administration excluded Denny Blair, the director of national intelligence, from the military conversations, and because Blair was responsible for coordinating the intelligence services, protocol prevented me from attending meetings if he was not included. That had the strange effect of forcing the administration to consider the appropriate strategy and staffing for Afghanistan without direct input from the CIA, an unwise example of personnel questions trumping the need for thorough discussion.

Despite that, I thought the resolution was thoughtful and balanced, even if it was largely preordained. Presenting it to the public for the first time, on December 1, President Obama eloquently explained his rationale—his reluctance to commit more men and women to a long fight, but also his determination not to walk away too soon, before America's objectives had been met.

Obama delivered his address at West Point's Eisenhower Hall Theatre, and with the cadets before him, he acknowledged that his decision would have profound implications for many of their lives. "I know that this decision asks even more of you—a military that, along with your families, has already borne the heaviest of all burdens," he said. He described writing letters to the families of fallen soldiers, visiting the wounded at Walter Reed, greeting the caskets at Dover. "If I did not think that the security of the United States and the safety of the American people were at stake in Afghanistan, I would gladly order every single one of our troops home tomorrow."

But that security was paramount, he explained, and was threatened by instability in Afghanistan and Pakistan. "This is the epicenter of violent extremism practiced by Al Qaeda. It is from here that we were attacked on 9/11, and it is from here that new attacks are being plotted as I speak. This is no idle danger, no hypothetical threat."[9]

Nine days after announcing his intention to send thirty thousand more soldiers to Afghanistan—and after eleven months of a presidency that had waged a strenuous campaign to thin the ranks of Al Qaeda—Barack Obama received the 2009 Nobel Peace Prize. The announcement of that prize had been greeted with a bit of disbelief in Washington, but to his credit, President Obama's speech accepting it powerfully expressed the truth that peace, sadly, is too often secured only by force.

That same month, the winner of the Nobel Peace Prize presided over a concerted campaign to bring down Al Qaeda's leadership. Two high-ranking Al Qaeda leaders were taken off the battlefield in quick succession. We were recapturing momentum, and I wanted our foot on the gas.

Meanwhile, Petraeus and McRaven were stepping up the fight in their theater. In mid-December, cruise missiles slammed into Al Qaeda training camps in Yemen. I was grateful to see that we were getting more aggressive in Yemen, as I was deeply concerned about Anwar al-Awlaki. But I privately worried that cruise missiles were not the right tool. We needed more precision and better intelligence. What America would need against Awlaki was an armed drone. But that's not what was in place.

Still, we were exerting precisely the pressure we had discussed a few months earlier with our military counterparts, and we were doing so across the region, denying Al Qaeda quarter and respite. But Al Qaeda was not only malevolent, it was cunning and resilient. We would not win easily, and not without scars and sacrifice, as we were soon reminded.

It was Christmas morning, and our family was gathered, as usual, in the house my father built in the Carmel Valley. Our family and my brother's family enjoyed a traditional Christmas Eve dinner the night before and ended the night with ten games of bingo. Christmas Day began with mass, followed by a big breakfast and then presents—the same rituals we have observed in that house since I was a boy.

Breakfast had just ended when the house phone rang. It was Jeremy. "I am so sorry to interrupt your Christmas, Director," he began. "But there was an attempted bombing of an airplane as it was landing in Detroit. There may have been a small explosion or fire. The plane is on the ground. Everyone is safe. The guy is in custody."

The guy was Umar Farouk Abdulmutallab, and he had boarded Northwest Flight 253 in Amsterdam after beginning his travels in Yemen. He passed most of the long flight without attracting much attention, but as the plane began its descent into Detroit, he complained of feeling sick and covered himself with a blanket. People sitting near him heard a noise and saw smoke and sparks. They jumped Abdulmutallab and wrestled him to the ground, preventing a bomb in his underwear from exploding. Had it gone off, the plane almost certainly would have been destroyed, killing hundreds, perhaps more—and on Christmas Day. It did not, so only he was hurt, but it was obvious that our systems for keeping terrorists and bombs off airplanes had failed.[10]

Months later, our technicians demonstrated for me a bomb similar to the one he had used. They gave me a pair of goggles and stood me in a bunker more than a hundred yards away. When the bomb went off, it rocked the bunker, and debris rained down over my head. I'm no bomb expert, but it was powerfully clear what would have happened to that airplane.

The incident caught the administration off guard, and we did not respond well, at least initially. President Obama was in Hawaii, and initially elected not to comment publicly on the near miss. Homeland Security secretary Janet Napolitano strangely proclaimed that "the system worked," when plainly it had not.[11] A review of Abdulmutallab's history later revealed that the CIA was among the agencies that had failed; our files had information that should have placed him on a no-fly list, but the person responsible for handling that information hadn't flagged it promptly, allowing Abdulmutallab to board the plane even though his own father had tried to warn us that he was dangerously unstable.

"John Brennan has asked us to come down to the White House and explain how this happened," Jeremy told me the next day. Brennan chewed him out and was critical of the CIA's lapse. We couldn't do anything but take it. We took our lumps, and redoubled our efforts to tighten scrutiny.

We were lucky in this instance. Not only did alert passengers prevent a catastrophe but Abdulmutallab turned out to be an important source of information. Immediately after his capture, he was interrogated to determine whether he was part of a larger plot along the lines of 9/11. Those interrogations were done under the national security exception that allows federal agents to grill a suspect without warning him of his right to remain silent or to have a lawyer present. Abdulmutallab talked and gave up some information, though not much. Then, convinced that no larger plot was under way that day, the FBI read him his Miranda rights, and he stopped talking.

That became a cause célèbre, as conservative critics of the administration, led by the predictable Dick Cheney, seized on the decision to read him his rights as proof of Obama's naiveté. Cheney released a statement roundly castigating the president: "As I've watched the events of the last few days, it is clear once again that President Obama is trying to pretend we are not at war. He seems to think if he has a low-key response to an attempt to blow up an airliner and kill hundreds of people, we won't be at war. He seems to think if he gives terrorists the rights of Americans, lets them lawyer up and reads them their Miranda rights, we won't be at war."[12]

Within the administration, the decision to read Abdulmutallab his rights was hotly debated afterward. Some, including me, argued that there was simply no constitutional way to arrest a person within our borders and indefinitely deny that person the rights afforded by the Constitution; others argued that we needed more flexible rules to protect the country from attack, that enemy combatants, even within the United States, were fundamentally different from criminals. Congress couldn't resist getting in the act, with various members floating ideas for depriving anyone accused of terrorism of their most basic rights.

Thankfully, the furor gradually subsided without any fundamental re-jiggering of constitutional protections.

Less noted was what happened after Abdulmutallab was informed of his right to remain silent and to have a lawyer. After first shutting up, he then relented and talked at length. It was Abdulmutallab who revealed that Anwar al-Awlaki had personally sent him on his terrorist mission. And it was Abdulmutallab who told FBI agents that the person who made the bomb that he carried in his underwear that day was Ibrahim al-Asiri, brother of the young man who had tried to kill Prince bin Nayef. Those statements helped us better understand the workings of Al Qaeda in Yemen and ultimately led to Awlaki's elimination. Importantly, investigators coaxed those admissions from Abdulmutallab without duress. He was not denied sleep or stripped naked, much less waterboarded. His confessions were the result of patient, clever interrogation of a suspect who had been read his rights and who nevertheless elected to cooperate with skillful questioners— proof that civil liberties and expert, aggressive investigations can and do coexist.

Less than a week after the Christmas Day attempt, we were hit again, this time with much more tragic results.

Throughout the fall of 2009, CTC had briefed me during the CT-ME update on a tantalizing lead. A Jordanian doctor named Humam al-Balawi had inserted himself into the top ranks of Al Qaeda in Pakistan and was offering to help us find none other than Ayman al-Zawahiri, the Egyptian doctor who was second only to bin Laden in the Al Qaeda leadership. Balawi had been a minor celebrity of the jihadist underground, writing under an assumed name and posting Internet pieces that encouraged martyrs and generally railed at the West. Jordanian officials tolerated it for a time, but when Balawi seemed to drift from commentary toward possible action, they arrested him and subjected him to a rough interrogation at the kingdom's infamous security headquarters.

While in their custody and immediately after his release, Balawi appeared to rethink his jihadist inclinations and responded warmly to encouragement by his Jordanian handler, a highly respected intelligence officer. Balawi left Jordan for Pakistan in the spring of 2009. There, he was to attempt to infiltrate Al Qaeda, a mission that would allow him to redeem his family name with a demonstration of loyalty to his king and country. The promise of a significant reward also sweetened the pot.

Balawi made it to the tribal areas of South Waziristan, and after a few months of cautious but growing contact with local terrorists, the Pakistani Taliban invited him to come live with some of its leaders. We briefly worried that he might have been killed that summer, but no harm came to him, though he disappeared for a time.

When he resurfaced, Balawi produced a short video that created a whirlwind of activity in Washington and Amman. In it, he was shown sitting near a top associate of bin Laden's, incontrovertible evidence that Balawi had, in fact, inserted himself into the innermost reaches of Al Qaeda. A few weeks later he followed that up with an even more astonishing report: He had just met Zawihiri himself—the Egyptian terrorist needed medical attention, and Balawi was a physician. Balawi's account included a number of details about Zawihiri's medical and personal history; they were consistent with other information, and there seemed no doubt but that Balawi had secured the confidence of one of the most wanted men on earth.

This was a very big deal, and I personally briefed the president about our new lead. He shared the enthusiasm that our officers felt, though he, like many of our top people, wanted to know more about Balawi. What motivated him? How had he been so successful at infiltrating a notoriously suspicious terror group? I told Obama that we were pursuing those questions, and as we did, I kept in close touch with John Brennan, both to keep the White House informed and also to seek his counsel.

One thing that all our people agreed about was that we needed a face-to-face meeting with Balawi. He was amenable, though he had several conditions. He insisted that his Jordanian handler be present, and he initially proposed locations that we rejected as too dangerous. Instead, his Jordanian handler proposed, with our support, that the meeting take place at the U.S. base in Khost, Afghanistan. Security was tight, so he could do so without being observed by spies on the periphery of the facility, and it was safely under our control. After some hesitation, Balawi agreed to a plan whereby one of our people would pick him up and deliver him for a debriefing at the base.

Then another round of hiccups ensued, as he missed one scheduled meeting time after another. As the year drew to a close, we didn't know precisely what to expect when we finally met Balawi in person. In the predawn dark of December 30, a sharp rap on the door of my room from a member of my security detail brought the answer crashing home.

It was Amy, my former briefer and now one of the senior aides in my office, on the line. Her voice was trembling. "I need to talk on a secure line," she said. "There's been an attack in Afghanistan, and some of our officers have been hit." She called me back on my secure line and told me that our meeting with the source had gone terribly wrong and that he likely had been wearing a suicide vest.

Jeremy raced in to the office, and I stayed on the phone with him much of the morning. The initial reports were gruesome—some killed, others maimed, some in surgery. Fragments and body parts everywhere.

I was so staggered that at first I didn't put it together with Balawi, but as I conferred with Jeremy and Steve Kappes and we received the reports coming from the field, it became clear that Balawi, whom we'd imagined as our double agent, in fact had been working with Al Qaeda. We had been so excited by the prospect of inserting an agent into the highest ranks of our enemy that we let down our guard. Treated as a visiting dignitary rather than as a possible attacker, Balawi, unsearched, was waved through to the inner compound, where more than a dozen officers eagerly looked forward to greeting this electrifyingly significant asset. Instead, as he stepped out of the car and the security officers ordered him to show his hands, he blew himself to pieces. The specially made suicide vest ripped through the semienclosed area.

By midafternoon, the toll was clear: Seven CIA officers had been killed in the explosion. The Jordanian case officer died too, as did the driver of the car.

As the magnitude of the tragedy became clear, I called those who I believed needed to hear the news directly from me: Dennis Blair, then still the director of national intelligence; Vice President Biden; Admiral Mike Mullen, chairman of the Joint Chiefs of Staff; and the president of the United States.

"This guy turned out to be a double agent," I began. "We lost seven people."

Obama was quiet at first. He expressed his sorrow, offered to help any way he could. Just days after the Christmas bomber had nearly brought down an American airliner, the president was understandably concerned that we were experiencing something larger. I promised him we were investigating as we spoke and would report anything we learned to him. He thanked me, again expressed his regrets, and we hung up.

The explosion at Khost was one of the largest losses of life in the history of the CIA. I had been director for nine months, and suddenly the agency for which I was responsible was profoundly shaken. Men and women bound by common patriotism and dedication to service grow very close, and those who died in Khost had affected many, many colleagues. I returned to Washington immediately, reaching out to families and employees at all levels of the CIA even as I asked myself the same hard questions many of them were confronting. I too had been swept up in the promise of this extraordinary source, had allowed myself to jump ahead to the capture or elimination of a potent enemy. Had I missed clues that should have warned me and others earlier? For days I was tormented by the thought that I had let my colleagues and agency down.

But my job was not to wallow. It was to comfort those who were suffering and to press ahead despite our grief. At our first staff meeting following the explosion, I asked that we honor our colleagues with a moment of silence. There in my office sat the senior leaders of the agency, those who I had come to know over the past ten months, who had joined me every morning in this conference room at this hour. We had come to trust one another. Now we had suffered together. Some cried silently. All looked downward. Then I spoke briefly:

"When you are at war," I said, "there are risks that you take, but we are a family—we have to be a family. We now have to pull together to not only deal with the pain of this loss but also to pull together that we fulfill the mission. We hit them hard this past year, and they're going to try to hit us back. But we have to stay on the offensive."

The next day, I stood in the bitter cold at Dover Air Force Base to welcome home the bodies of our colleagues. The senior CIA team was there, as was General Jim Cartwright, vice chairman of the Joint Chiefs. With so many victims, the families were forced to gather in a multipurpose room because they overflowed the base's chapel. As I introduced myself and expressed my condolences to the families, not one voiced anger. Not one person questioned the security arrangements or demanded an investigation or complained. Their loved ones had chosen this work, entered it with full appreciation of the dangers involved, and yet entered it nonetheless. To a family, each of them voiced the pride they felt in their husbands and wives, sons, daughters, parents. And without exception, they asked me to be sure to take the fight to those who had killed their loved ones. I promised that I would.

And of course we had wounded colleagues as well. I visited them at Bethesda Naval Hospital, some with mangled limbs, many with serious head wounds, all badly hurt. One young man asked me about his colleagues, and I told him several had died, only just then realizing that his family had been sheltering him from the news. He stared blankly; I prayed that the revelation would not hamper his recovery. Another of the injured, our deputy chief of station for Afghanistan, I knew from the CT-ME updates. He too was badly hurt, but surrounded by family grateful to still have him. Still another one of our officers greeted me with a smile and told me he knew my son from Afghanistan. "Please give my regards to Jimmy," he said. Every one of our wounded officers returned to duty.

We quickly learned the details of Balawi's betrayal, in part because his terror allies released videos boasting of their role in Balawi's attack, praising him for his martyrdom, and featuring Balawi himself denouncing the United States and vowing that his death would bring vengeance. Hakimullah Mehsud, a cousin of Baitullah Mehsud's who had taken over when the latter was killed, had helped train Balawi for his mission, and said it was done specifically in retaliation for the killing of his cousin. Sheikh Said al-Masri, Al Qaeda's number three leader, supplied logistical support and money, and crowed afterward about Balawi's "successful epic."

I commissioned a special study of the episode, not to affix blame but rather to ensure that we might learn from it. Internally, that caused some anxiety, as officers and supervisors worried either that they might be unfairly singled out or that the agency might try to heap all responsibility on the officers who died, blemishing their sacrifice. In the end, we concluded that some agency officers did miss red flags, and were nearly blinded by their belief that we were dealing with an exceptionally valuable source. Still, it was hard to find that those failings merited disciplinary action. At the same time, I was determined that the agency not become paralyzed or overcautious. There are certain risks that can't be eliminated in the work of espionage and counterterrorism, and retreat to safety would mean the end of our effectiveness. I need not have worried. The officers of the CIA rose bravely and dramatically to the occasion.

We shook sources, worked overtime, scoured electronic intelligence and surveillance. Al Qaeda members scrambled for safety, unsure who to trust or where to hide. A few weeks after the bombing, U.S. officials spotted a senior Taliban leader involved in the Khost attack. He survived, but the United States was on his trail.

The president came to Langley on February 5 for a memorial service for the Khost victims, and I joined him for the solemn duty of saying good-bye to our fallen heroes. Steve Kappes had arranged for an Irish tenor to sing "Danny Boy," and each of the officers was eulogized by a friend from within the agency. With snow falling outside the tent in which families and colleagues gathered, the president spoke movingly, addressing the families, speaking most earnestly to the young children who had lost parents. And he addressed the larger CIA family as well, urging its officers to continue their work in tribute. "There are no words that can ease the ache in your hearts," he acknowledged. "But to their colleagues and all who served with them—those here today, those still recovering, those watching around the world—I say: Let their sacrifice be a summons. To carry on their work. To complete this mission. To win this war, and to keep our country safe."[13]

At the end of the ceremony, I asked Bill Danvers, my congressional liaison, to pull aside the chairmen and ranking members of the intelligence committees. Danvers escorted that small group—Senators Feinstein and Bond, Representative Hoekstra, Staff Directors Mike Delaney and David Grannis—into a small waiting room off the marbled lobby on CIA's first floor. I joined them a few moments later. Earlier that day, the national security staff had formally approved an effort to kill or capture Anwar al-Awlaki. The discussion focused on that decision.

That crossed a significant threshold. Awlaki, though a committed enemy of the United States, was also an American citizen, raising significant questions about our responsibilities under the Constitution and our obligations to ensure the nation's safety. Those issues had been carefully debated inside the government and among the agencies—the Justice Department had considered the question at length—and final approval from the president now had been given.* The members of Congress and their aides voiced strong support for the president's decision. They appreciated the special process that was undertaken to ascertain the legality of the operation and were supportive of the outcome.

America was hitting Al Qaeda hard, but Al Qaeda and its allies were fighting too. On May 1, Faisal Shahzad, a thirty-one-year-old naturalized American citizen born in Pakistan, parked a Nissan Pathfinder in Times Square. He had packed it with gasoline, fireworks, three propane tanks, and a couple of clocks with batteries attached. It wasn't the world's most sophisticated bomb, but Shahzad turned on the hazard lights, lit a fuse, and walked away. Fortunately, a T-shirt vendor was concerned and called over a mounted officer, who quickly began moving people away as the NYPD's bomb squad rushed to the scene.[14]

As with the Christmas Day underwear bomber, alert citizens combined with inept bombers prevented anyone from being hurt that day, but as we dug into Shahzad's past—after being read his Miranda rights, he willingly cooperated with investigators—we learned that he had received explosives training in Waziristan from the Tehrik-e-Taliban. The same group supplied him with $12,000 to carry out his mission.[15]

In the wake of the Times Square attempt, the president asked me to

---

*In his May 23, 2013, speech, President Obama publicly noted his role in the Awlaki case. "As president," he said, "I would have been derelict in my duty had I not authorized the strike that took him out."

go to Pakistan to confer with officials there about what we knew. More specifically, National Security Adviser Jim Jones and I were on a mission to deliver a warning. I told Pasha when we met in mid-May that if another terrorist act or attempt on our soil had its roots in Pakistan, it would invite the gravest response from our country. We would, under such a circumstance, reserve the right to conduct our own military operations, with or without Pakistani permission, in order to protect ourselves. He protested that Pakistan could not be held responsible for every lunatic who passed through it, but Jones and I were unyielding. Either Pakistan did its part to combat terror operations within its borders or we would. I then turned around and flew home, arriving before dawn on May 21.

That morning was the last of the funerals for the officers who died at Khost, this one for Elizabeth Hanson. Though she was not a veteran, she had died in the service of her country fighting a war, and her family wanted her interred at Arlington. At first the military authorities balked, understandably if stubbornly citing the rule that only veterans may lie at Arlington. I interceded, however, and Bob Gates granted permission; he too attended her funeral. Not long after she was laid to rest, one of her killers would die in a missile strike in a South Waziristan village.

The strike that killed him was not an act of vengeance. It was one of national security. But I hope that those who felt relief from his removal from this earth included the families of those whose lives he had wantonly taken at Khost.

The deaths at Khost haunted me, as they did so many of my colleagues, and I felt compelled to see the scene for myself. I asked our staff if I could visit the base, and at first met resistance, as it was very much on the front lines. After elaborate security precautions were arranged, however, I made the trip. When I found the scarred CIA post within the military base, the pockmarks from the ball bearings contained in the suicide vest were still visible on the walls. I ran my fingers over them. And I placed a small plaque there; it included a quote from Isaiah:

> I heard the voice of the Lord, saying, Whom shall I send, and
>   who will go for us?
> Then said I, Here *am* I; send me.

No words better express the selfless heroism of the men and women of the CIA, including those who died for their country on that frigid afternoon in a windswept, dusty village in Afghanistan, thousands of miles from home, fighting for the security of their country. I asked for copies of the plaque to be made, and I presented one to each of the families. The names of these young men and women deserve to be remembered. They are:

Harold Brown Jr., age 37
Elizabeth Hanson, age 30
Darren LaBonte, age 35
Jennifer Lynne Matthews, age 45
Dane Clark Paresi, age 46
Scott Michael Roberson, age 39
Jeremy Wise, age 35

TWELVE

"Everywhere in the World"

M y first goals as director of the CIA—the tasks that President Obama assigned to me at the outset—were to restore its standing with the American public and political leadership and to hone the agency's capacity for fighting terrorism. But those weren't my only jobs. The CIA's original purpose was to supply American leaders, especially the president, with clear, insightful intelligence—"the most accurate and up-to-the-minute information on what is going on everywhere in the world," as Truman said.[1] That intelligence is produced by officers and analysts, and it's enhanced by our relations with other services on every continent. As a result, those interservice relationships are vital to our knowledge of foreign affairs, and tending to those relationships is an essential duty of the director of the CIA. As director, I traveled to dozens of countries, usually without much fanfare, and glimpsed some of the world's most delicate operations.

Early in my tenure I visited the Middle East, for the obvious reason that so many of America's security interests connect back to that region in one way or another. It is of course a breeding ground for much anti-Americanism, including terrorism, and in 2009 thousands of American forces remained in Iraq, where they confronted an increasingly complex sectarian conflict. Israel is America's most stalwart ally in that part of the world, and it was among my first stops on this visit in the spring of 2009.*

Upon arriving in Tel Aviv, I was taken directly to the headquarters of the Mossad, Israel's legendary intelligence service, housed inside a series of modern, low-slung buildings along Israel's coast. I was greeted by Meir Dagan, an intelligence operative as legendary as his agency. Short and paunchy with an easy smile, he seemed benign at first, almost a kindly grandfather. But Kappes had warned me not to underestimate him. As Kappes noted, above Dagan's desk hung a photograph of his grandfather kneeling before a Nazi guard, who had a billy club dangling from his right hand. Moments after the photograph was taken, Dagan's grandfather was executed. This was the image Dagan used to remind himself of his duty. He himself had been born on a train between the Soviet Union and Poland. After surviving the Holocaust, he and his family made their way to Israel in 1950. He served thirty-two years in the Israel Defense Forces, rising to the rank of major general. He was, in short, not to be taken lightly.

Meir and I were scheduled to have dinner that night, but before the meal began we were joined by General Amos Yadlin, head of Israeli defense intelligence. Amos is an intense general, whose wire-rimmed glasses and gentle manner mask an inner toughness that has made him one of Israel's most influential military men. He came armed with a stack of charts, graphics, and maps—the topic was Iran.

---

*My first trip as director was to Afghanistan, Pakistan, and India to take the measure of the war and our campaign against Al Qaeda along the Afghanistan-Pakistan border. This was my second.

F or President Obama's national security team, an increasingly ominous centrifuge facility near the city of Qom was a significant and long-running source of concern. In September 2009, President Obama would describe this work to the world at the G-20 meeting along with our allies. The Fordow Fuel Enrichment Plant, as it was called, was being built underground.

There was much about it that was troubling. Fordow was built on a base of the Iranian Revolutionary Guard, the elite commandos of the Iranian state responsible for its campaign of terror around the world. Moreover, the facility was buried under a mountain, deep inside a hardened bunker. The size was also alarming, though for a paradoxical reason: It was too small to produce nuclear energy, and yet perfectly sized to create a stockpile for weapons use.

Iran's two enrichment facilities, Natanz and Fordow, both could produce highly enriched bomb-grade uranium. Israel's security would depend in part on the willingness of the United States to help prevent Iran from obtaining a nuclear weapon.

The intelligence community assessed in 2009 that Iran already had the ability to produce enough highly enriched uranium for a nuclear weapon in a few years, and the completion of the facility at Qom would advance that timeline. Iran also had, and was continuing to develop, missiles capable of carrying a nuclear weapon. With the Qom facility under construction, the clock was running on Iran's achieving a capability to enrich uranium to the point where it could not be stopped with an airstrike.

Meanwhile, the Iranian people were becoming restless with their country's growing international isolation. During the June 2009 election, the Green Movement nearly brought historic change to Iran. But the regime cracked down and crushed the dissenters. In a sense, then,

Iran's leaders were running two races, one to build a bomb, the other to hold on to power. The question became: Could the ayatollahs build a weapon before history caught up with them?

That topic dominated much of my time in the Obama administration, until my final hours as secretary of defense. Ultimately our strategy was to pursue a resolute diplomatic approach—sanctions and negotiations—while also trying to demonstrate to Israel and the world that we were serious when we said we refused to let Iran develop a bomb.

That first dinner with Israel's military and intelligence leadership was notable for its level of shared trust and even intimacy. On top of that, one moment in particular drove home to me the stakes of these conversations and the seriousness of my Israeli counterparts. It occurred late in the evening, after the conversation had drifted away from Iran. I used the opening to ask Meir for some advice:

"Look," I said, "we're dealing every day with Al Qaeda. What would you do?"

He didn't hesitate. "I'd kill them," he said. "And then I'd kill their families."

One of his aides gently interjected, sensing how impolitic that was. "You can't do that," he began.

"Why not?" Dagan asked. I don't know whether he was serious, but I wouldn't want to be the one to doubt him.

Anyone who has traveled to the Demilitarized Zone that separates North and South Korea knows what it is like to look back in time. Around the rest of the globe, the Cold War has receded. The great superpower standoff that tensely held the peace from the end of

World War II to the fall of Soviet communism has been replaced by plenty of stress and tension, but at least the threat of imminent attack by the ally of one superpower against the ally of another is for the most part a remnant. Not so along this border, the world's most heavily guarded.

I got my first look at the barricades and barbed wire and the almost theatrical hostility between the North and South during a visit to Seoul in 2010. We approached from above, and I gazed from the window of my helicopter as we choppered in from the airport to a U.S. military helipad in downtown Seoul. To fly over Seoul is to witness one of Asia's modern marvels. A sprawling city of almost ten million people, it is as dense and modern as lower Manhattan, but spread out for miles and miles. It is industrious and thriving, in stark contrast to the plight of its neighbor to the north.

General Skip Sharp, commander of U.S. Forces Korea, soberly briefed me that day on the contingency plans that governed our more than 28,500 men and women on the peninsula. If North Korea moved across the border, our war plans called for the senior American general on the peninsula to take command of all U.S. *and South Korean* forces and defend South Korea—including by the use of nuclear weapons, if necessary. Our forces maintained a readiness posture that allowed them to "fight tonight." I left our meeting with the powerful sense that war in that region was neither hypothetical nor remote, but ever present and imminent.

After a meeting with South Korea's president, Lee Myung-bak, at the Blue House—South Korea's White House—I boarded a U.S. military Black Hawk helicopter again, this time for the brief ride from Seoul up to Camp Bonifas, about four hundred yards south of the DMZ. From there, a bus took us into Panmunjom where the 38th parallel divides North from South Korea.

The DMZ is about as far from Seoul's Blue House as Dulles Airport is from our White House. And in that zone, two lines of enemy soldiers spend all day, every day, staring across a four-kilometer divide that has separated the two countries since an armistice was struck in July 1953 bringing to an end the Korean War. To this day, that conflict remains halted by a truce, but no peace treaty has ever been finalized, so the armistice in theory could fail at any time, and both sides keep a wary watch on one another in Panmunjom.

Standing on a bluff on the southern side of the line, I looked across the border at a North Korean soldier, who in turn used his binoculars to watch me. He probably had no clue who I was. The blankness of his stare was as inscrutable as the regime behind him.

At Panmunjom, there is a row of buildings used for the rare talks between North and South. One straddles the border itself, with a line running down a square table to mark the actual boundary. We entered, and for a moment I crossed the line, putting a toe into North Korea. As I did, guards outside on the North Korean side of the border pressed against the windows, menacingly glowering and brandishing their weapons.

That regime has been a principal focus of American concern for more than fifty years, but even as I took the reins of the CIA, I realized that we knew precious little about it. Its severe isolation from the rest of the world and its highly insular power structure—the only three presidents it has known have been father, son, and grandson, each more eccentric than the last—have made it an exasperatingly difficult culture to observe and understand. In 2009, Kim Jong Il, the second of those three leaders, was in failing health, and we were anxious to learn more about who might take over after his death and what that might portend for the future of the Korean Peninsula. Those uncertainties were magnified by North Korea's determination to cause trouble: In July 2009 it launched two sets of missile tests, the latter on the Fourth of July, no less.

Unfortunately, our insights into the regime were few and shallow. Our only real ability to understand and influence North Korea was through China, its lone source of support, and even China's reach was limited. First as CIA director and later as secretary of defense, I would persistently push the Chinese to rein in their North Korean allies, or at least to give us assurances that they would intervene if the regime suddenly collapsed, as it realistically could. Still, the regime remained infuriatingly hard to penetrate. When Kim Jong Il began to send signals that he would empower his son to be his successor in 2010, it took us almost completely by surprise.

North Korea remains one of the most problematic and dangerous nations on earth as far as the United States goes. Virtually all of our two-war scenarios involves one war between North and South Korea and another somewhere else, so we devote considerable time and energy to anticipating the potential for trouble in that part of the world. And, of course, we station nearly thirty thousand American soldiers along the border to repel an invasion should that day ever come. North Korea is locked in the past, desperately attempting to cover its inadequacies, squash free expression, and spend the little money it has on nuclear weapons. It's hard to believe that such a government will find its way easily into the present; while it flails about, the United States is forced to remain vigilant and to cultivate our other relationships in the region, to at least contain the potential damage that this backward country might someday attempt to inflict.

The CIA's history in Latin America is not entirely a proud one. In 1954, CIA officers, with the approval of President Eisenhower, staged a coup against Guatemalan president Jacobo Árbenz, a reformist leader wrongly believed by some in Washington to be a communist or at least to tolerate communists in his government.[2] That covert action and the CIA-led toppling of Iranian prime minister Mohammad Mossadegh in 1953 are mainstays of the critique of the CIA's adventurism and have left bitter feelings in both countries for decades.

So it was with some uncertainty that I traveled to Latin America during my CIA tenure, visiting Colombia, Mexico, Peru, and Argentina. Somewhat to my surprise, I was warmly received in each country. Our cooperative work in the region to combat the narcotics trade was appreciated and even admired, as were other aspects of our alliances. America was helping Argentina fend off Hezbollah in the region where Argentina, Brazil, and Uruguay share a border (Hezbollah was smuggling in the area to raise money for its terrorist work there and elsewhere), while also helping Peru in its long battle against the Shining Path. We were keeping tabs on Venezuela's brusque and combative leader, Hugo Chávez, and those in Nicaragua and Ecuador who were following Chávez's lead. And we were recalibrating our relationship with Honduras, where a coup had led to turmoil in that country's politics and a breakdown in civic order that was allowing crime and drug trafficking to flourish.

In Colombia, that country's long fight against the rebel group known as the FARC—the Revolutionary Armed Forces of Colombia—had been waged in part with assistance from the United States. Originally the military arm of the Colombian Communist Party, the FARC fluctuated in size and influence throughout the 2000s, but its methods were a continuing source of regional instability. It secured funding by trafficking in drugs and kidnapping for ransom, and Colombia wanted help in thwarting the group's efforts. The campaign against the FARC received a boost in 2008, when Colombian forces located and freed Íngrid Betancourt, the former presidential candidate, who had been taken hostage in 2002. Betancourt's rescue, along with fourteen other hostages, including three Americans, was a powerful demonstration of the government's growing capacity to take on the FARC and helped erode the organization's fearsome image. By 2010, when I visited, peace talks were under way, and the FARC's capacity to inflict violence was much diminished, though it still remained a fighting force of several thousand.

While in Colombia, I visited the Macarena region, where the FARC remained active. Military commanders there performed a demonstration of their methods for raiding FARC compounds, and we discussed the accelerating tempo of those raids. It was clear to me that under President Álvaro Uribe, with whom I met, the government was committed to keeping up the pressure and that progress was being made.

In Mexico, the issues were very different, and mostly connected to our extensive trading ties and long border. President Felipe Calderón hosted me during my time there, and he was anxious about growing violence near the border, particularly in Juárez and, on our side of the line, El Paso. He complained that U.S. gun laws allowed weapons to flow easily into Mexico, which in turn made Mexico's job of controlling drugs more difficult. I sympathized and pledged to do all I could to improve the situation, but I had to admit that gun control was a powerfully difficult problem to confront in the United States, as I knew going back to my days in the Clinton White House, when our success at including modest gun control measures as part of the crime bill was believed to have contributed to the political wipeout we suffered in the 1994 midterm elections. Ever since, Democrats had been skittish about gun control, with the irrational consequence that our nation refuses to take steps that would help fight drugs and save lives. Calderón had extended himself at political risk to fight drug trafficking, and had worked closely with the United States to do so.

For decades, the then Soviet Union and the United States invested heavily in spying on each other, producing some of the most memorable moments of the Cold War. There was the downing of Gary Powers's U-2 flight in 1960, which badly embarrassed the Eisenhower administration and contributed to the collapse of a summit conference in Paris. There was the turning of Aldrich Ames, a CIA officer who sold the KGB the names of our assets inside the Soviet Union, betraying his country for nothing more exotic than money. There was the arrest and conviction of Robert Hanssen, an FBI agent who spent more than twenty years spying for the Soviets. That's a lot of history to put behind us, but it was the past, after all; by 2009, the superpower conflict of the Cold War had been replaced by a wary sizing up of each other and a cautious search for common purpose.

The end of the Soviet empire also meant the end of the KGB. It split in two: The SVR handled the external spying, including its presence in the United States. The FSB handled internal security, including counterterrorism, fighting the Chechens, and running aggressive counterintelligence efforts against American officials in Russia.

My first meeting with my Russian counterpart, SVR director Mikhail Fradkov, took place at CIA headquarters in Langley, and reminders of the Cold War jumped out right from the beginning. When he arrived, Fradkov was escorted upstairs to the suite where my office was located. He spent a few minutes in the outer office while I wrapped up some business, and when I came out to greet him he was standing next to one of the many photographs that line the walls of the suite. It was an old black-and-white picture of Oleg Penkovsky, a colonel in the Soviet Union's military intelligence agency who supplied invaluable information to the CIA and British intelligence in the early 1960s, including secrets about Soviet missile systems that helped the Kennedy administration recognize the significance of construction activity in Cuba in 1962; that information helped Kennedy chart his course during the Cuban Missile Crisis and may have averted a nuclear war. Penkovsky is still considered one of the greatest assets the West ever acquired inside the Soviet Union. He was arrested by the Soviets in 1962 and executed on May 16, 1963. Staring at his picture, Fradkov winced.

That night, I took Fradkov to dinner at Restaurant Nora, one of Washington's finest eateries. Thank goodness the food was good, because the conversation wasn't. Fradkov seemed determined to stay with his talking points rather than engage in any serious conversation, so the evening dragged on, dull and ponderous. My aides had warned me of this, but I thought, perhaps naively, that we could look for ways to cooperate in areas such as Chechen terrorism, where we had common enemies. I tried, but it wasn't going anywhere. Fradkov said over and over that he wanted to cooperate with us, but he wouldn't say how. It was tiresome, and I was wearing thin. Just when I was about to give up, Fradkov seemed to drop his guard. What, he asked me, did I think had been America's worst intelligence or foreign policy mistake? I thought for a brief moment and told him I thought it had been the mismanagement of the Iraq war. I then asked him the same question about the Soviet Union. He paused for a long moment, and then answered simply, "Penkovsky."

That was the beginning of a tentative, occasionally candid relationship that Fradkov and I developed in meetings and over dinners in Washington and Moscow, each time blending overtures of friendship and overtones of animosity. Fradkov wanted to create a joint SVR-CIA working group to share information and collaborate on some common operational activities. The old Cold Warriors in the CIA's Clandestine Service—including Mike Sulick—told me I was wasting my time. The Russians would never share, and they'd use the whole thing as a ruse to get close to our officers and try to recruit them as spies, they said. Perhaps, I thought. But we would also look small if we rejected an offer to work together. Let's say yes, I argued, and see where it takes us. If we got nothing out of it, so be it. We moved forward, tentatively.

Our next set of meetings was in Moscow in 2010. Fradkov hosted me for dinner at SVR headquarters in Yasenevo, a southwestern suburb of Moscow, and the next day at the famed Central House of Writers dining room in Moscow. The food was horrendous—I'm not much for boiled fish and vodka—but the conversation was slowly getting better. Fradkov launched into one monologue about Russian accession to the World Trade Organization, but otherwise stayed focused on how the

United States and Russia could share intelligence on issues of common interest.

Still, the vestiges of the Cold War loomed. My meeting with my FSB counterpart, Alexander Vasilyevich Bortnikov, occurred at FSB headquarters in the infamous Lubyanka Building, the dark baroque edifice that once housed the KGB and its famous dungeon prisons. When we entered, the first thing that caught my eye was a bust of Lenin. We were escorted through the building's historic lobby, and Jeremy whispered to me, "I think I can still hear the screams from the basement."

As with our conversations in Washington, my talks with Fradkov on that visit produced only glimmers of possibility. Moreover, just weeks earlier I had received a private briefing from the FBI informing me of a ten-year investigation it had conducted regarding a ring of deep-cover SVR agents living inside the United States and awaiting activation.

The program was a classic piece of Cold War theater. Men and women were brought to the United States and encouraged to make their way through life as everyday Americans—taking classes, getting jobs, raising families. Some posed as immigrants from Canada, others stole identities from children who had died many decades earlier. For years, they were to live normal lives and try to develop contacts that could someday be useful. Two were real estate agents, one worked for a travel agency, another for a telecommunications firm. One was a teacher, another wrote occasional columns for a Spanish-language newspaper, another gave tax advice. Their affiliation with the Russian government was so secret that even their children did not know their true identities. In this case, however, the FBI had been keeping tabs on these "illegals," as they called them, for more than a decade, patiently waiting for the right moment to swoop in.

I first learned of the FBI's operation to track the illegals—dubbed "Ghost Stories"—in early 2010, but at that point the issue was simmering fairly slowly. The surveillance had been under way for years, and there was no need to change anything. Then in the spring the FBI learned that one or more of the sleeper agents was preparing to leave the country. If that happened, they might not return, and we might lose our chance to capture them. The trouble was timing: It came just as President Obama was preparing to welcome Russian president Dmitry Medvedev on a state visit to Washington in late June. On June 18, we briefed the National Security Council and the president—the FBI played the lead role, but I attended because of the implications for the CIA and our intelligence operations generally.

The main point of that day's discussion was whether the diplomatic fallout from busting up this ring was worth the security advantages of doing so. As far as the U.S. government could tell, no secrets had actually been passed back to Russia through these agents, and arresting them, especially on the eve of a Russian state visit, was sure to be provocative. But as I told the president that day, our officers believed it could be handled without much long-term consequence. I argued that the operation could proceed without impacting the broader relationship with Russia. The group generally agreed, and suggested that if the FBI successfully rounded up the agents, one way to minimize the fallout would be to quickly propose a swap, so the Russians would get their people back, we'd get some the United States wanted in return, and Russia would be spared the embarrassing spectacle of multiple criminal trials for their sleeper agents. Mueller and I argued for the arrests to go forward, with a swap as the ultimate goal, but the vice president and Tom Donilon asked the right questions: Would this operation undermine Medvedev, or would the overall relationship with Russia withstand this temporary setback? The meeting began to break up, but Donilon stayed. I could see he was struggling with this one.

I pressed the point that the relationship could sustain this hit. We also agreed that Congress, which we would be briefing about the operations, would strongly rebuke us if we failed to arrest the spies. Tom agreed, and we had consensus. Shortly thereafter, President Obama green-lighted the operation.

President Medvedev arrived in Washington on June 18, and the meetings were productive. There was of course no mention of the secret operation we were planning against the illegals. As soon as Medvedev boarded a plane to leave, however, the FBI carried out simultaneous raids and arrests, picking up ten sleeper agents and leaving their families and neighbors in a state of genuine shock. The first Russian reaction was predictable—they claimed there was no basis to the charges and denounced our efforts with the usual hyperbole.

The Justice Department moved to do its job. The U.S. attorney for the Southern District of New York charged the illegals in his jurisdiction with fraudulent immigration. He did not accuse them of espionage, but the indictment was intentionally exhaustive, so that the Russians would realize that we knew what was up.

Once we had the Russians, the question was what to do with them. Acting on the president's behalf, as a diplomatic back channel, I agreed to reach out to Fradkov—not because of the intelligence relationship we were developing, but because this was now an issue between our countries, and I thought we had developed the trust to handle it together. The mission was to explore the possibility of a swap. It was certainly possible that Fradkov would simply disavow the illegals and make counteraccusations, standard operating procedure for Cold War relations. So when I dialed him to make my pitch, I did so with low expectations.

"Mikhail," I began, using a speakerphone and surrounded by some of the government's top officials and Russia experts, "we have arrested a number of people, as you saw in the press. Those people are yours." Our interpreter gave it to Fradkov in Russian.

There was a long pause, reminiscent of our first dinner when he contemplated my question about the Soviet Union's worst intelligence failure. Then, at last, he spoke. The translation: "Yes, they are my people."

The men and women around me had to stifle themselves to keep from cheering out loud. Instead, a silent round of raised eyebrows and high fives ran through our room as we realized that we were already past denial and into negotiations. So I offered our bid: "We're going to prosecute them. If we have to go through trials, it is going to be very embarrassing for you."

Another long pause. "What do you have in mind?" he asked.

"You have three or four people who we want. I propose a trade."

He didn't agree on the spot. He said he first needed to check with Russian leaders, including—I'm sure—Putin, who had worked the illegals program during his KGB years. After we exchanged some draft agreements, a deal was struck. The United States would return their ten agents, and they would give up four Russians who were in prison for allegedly working with the United States or Britain. He agreed, and we had a deal.

There still were details to resolve. Among other things, a number of the children of the sleeper agents had no desire to go to Russia. They'd grown up in the United States believing that their parents were teachers or writers or real estate agents, and now they were bound for Moscow, a city that meant nothing to them. Understandably, they weren't thrilled. But America wasn't going to take custody of the kids, so the sullen youngsters were reunited with their parents and the whole lot of them were put on a plane for Vienna. And there, in perfect Cold War fashion, the prisoners from both sides crossed on the tarmac, trading planes. A few minutes later, everyone was headed for their new homes.

The Cold War was over, but the scene in Vienna was proof that the old games were alive and well. All that was missing was the sound of the zither playing the theme from the movie *The Third Man*.

After the exhaustive debate that President Obama's advisers, including me, conducted during 2009 over the Afghan surge, monitoring the progress of that war was obviously of central importance—we needed to know whether the surge was working, how long to let it play out, and when to begin to draw back down. All of those were mostly questions for the military, but they were shaped by diplomatic imperatives and informed by intelligence, most of which came from the CIA. I credit Tom Donilon for ensuring that every meeting began with an intelligence estimate. And he included not only Denny Blair, the director of national intelligence, who provided the intelligence community's view, but also me, for the CIA's analysis and operational vantage point on the war.

Just after noon on March 10, 2010, the National Security Council Principals gathered in the White House Situation Room for the first in a series of sweeping reviews that would examine our Afghan efforts from every angle. As was usually the case, the report was mixed. On one hand, I could confidently tell my colleagues that efforts against the Al Qaeda leadership along the Afghanistan-Pakistan border were producing results. One report I shared at that session, for instance, concluded that the "deaths of numerous Al Qaeda personnel in Pakistan's North Waziristan Agency (NWA) since November 2009 are reducing the viability of the NWA safe haven." Al Qaeda, I told the group, was suffering from low morale and recoiling from disarray in its leadership. At the same time, Karzai continued to demonstrate the qualities that made him so frustrating to the United States—he had not yet completed filling out his cabinet, which still had eleven vacancies among the twenty-five positions—and insurgent attacks were on the rise, nearly doubling from February 2009 to February 2010.

The State Department, meanwhile, was looking for a way to separate the Taliban from Al Qaeda, an ambition that I had endorsed in principle during the Afghan debates in 2009. It was time, State recommended, to encourage the Afghan government to engage with the Taliban on certain conditions: that the Taliban leadership renounce Al Qaeda, recognize the Afghan constitution (including its provisions protecting the rights of women and minorities), and abandon its armed struggle against the Afghan government. If it would agree to those conditions, it would create the possibility of a peace agreement that would sideline Al Qaeda, our real enemy. I was skeptical of this so-called Taliban reconciliation. I thought we had to hit them harder on the battlefield and coerce negotiations. At times I feared that the U.S. embassy in Kabul was too eager to cut a deal with the Taliban. But despite my reservations, the decision was made to begin to open discussions with certain Taliban leaders to see if they were serious.

Through the summer and fall, we continued to make headway in Afghanistan, while also encountering obstacles and setbacks. The military, under the leadership of General Petraeus and with the help of the CIA, was battering the Haqqani network. Devastating floods in Pakistan were occupying that government, but also provided us with a welcome opportunity to provide relief and thus bolster our case that we could be regarded as a friend. At the same time, corruption continued to undermine Karzai's government, to the point that Attorney General Eric Holder proposed having the Justice Department put together a brief on the evidence of corruption in order to get Karzai's attention.

Those sessions culminated with a pair of meetings, both attended by the president. The first took place on December 14, almost exactly a year from the day that he had approved the surge and announced it at West Point. The second occurred the following month, on January 24, 2011. Both were largely positive, though again not without caveat or qualification.

"Specific components of the strategy are working well, and there are notable operational gains," the national security staff reported at the first of those sessions. "Al Qaeda's senior leadership in Pakistan is weakened and under more sustained pressure than at any other point since it fled Afghanistan in 2001." For the first time, it was realistically possible to foresee the destruction of Al Qaeda's core. Meanwhile, the Taliban's momentum had been seized and reversed in some parts of the country. Our forces, Petraeus reported, were "hitting on all cylinders."

That created an opportunity, and President Obama wanted to seize it. As he put it during the January meeting, 2011 presented the possibility of moving to the political aspects of our mission and to encouraging reintegration and reconciliation within Afghanistan; the military would provide backing, but its work would be guided by a larger political strategy. All of this seemed reasonable and promising.

Then Vice President Biden introduced a sobering note. How long, he asked, would Afghanistan require significant American aid? Karl Eikenberry, our ambassador to Kabul, responded that it would be at least another ten to fifteen years, and both Biden and Jack Lew from OMB estimated that the amount of aid needed to sustain this security operation would be $6 to $8 billion a year. That put things in perspective.

"We must adjust our sights," the president remarked cautiously, reminding the group that support for Israel and Egypt was about $5 billion a year and adding, though it was hardly necessary, that there was "substantially more support in Congress" for Israel and Egypt than either Afghanistan or Pakistan. Without that aid, would Afghanistan fall backward? What level of support did it require to survive, and what constituted sufficient stability for the purposes of the United States?

In other words, the White House staff argued, we should aim for what was "good enough" for Afghanistan. The president explained the approach succinctly, and in my view correctly. The goal was, he said, a nation that did not harbor terrorists capable of striking the United

States and one with a government sufficiently supported by the people that it could remain stable into the future. That's well short of nation building.

The descriptor—Afghanistan "good enough"—never sat easily with me. It struck me as insulting to the Afghans, and sounded defeatist and therefore not sufficiently respectful of all those who had died in the war. But that was a disagreement about language, not policy. I was pleased that we were coming to the realization that we had a sound benchmark for American involvement in a troubled country that we will never make modern, but we might at least make safe and stable.

My job in that context was fairly specific: It was to batter Al Qaeda and prevent it from regrouping or reemerging as a force in Afghanistan. As I reported to the National Security Council on March 3, Al Qaeda's leadership was being removed faster than it could be replaced; if permitted to keep up the pressure, the United States "could inflict irreparable damage." But beyond simply thinning Al Qaeda's ranks, there were two targets whose elimination would have more far-reaching consequences: Osama bin Laden and Ayman al-Zawahiri. And of those, bin Laden had special significance, for "remnants would cling to Al Qaeda as long as Osama bin Laden is at large." Our part of the fight, then, was to find and either kill or capture Osama bin Laden.

THIRTEEN

"Go In and Get Bin Laden"

Osama bin Laden was the ubiquitous face of terrorism. He was the person chiefly responsible for the deaths of three thousand Americans, the most wanted man on earth. And as of early 2009 we had absolutely no idea where he was. When I arrived at the CIA, the last reliable information we had had of bin Laden was during the battle for Tora Bora, a fortified set of caves and trenches in the thin air of the Afghanistan-Pakistan border. A ferocious, frigid struggle for that complex in late 2001 resulted in its capture, but not before bin Laden, who knew those mountains intimately, snuck away—an escape that reinforced his mythic status among his followers. We had a few reports of him in Afghanistan's Kunar Province in mid-2002. And then the trail went cold—so cold, in fact, that the Bush administration, once enthralled by the hunt, reversed itself entirely and worked to downplay any expectations. In 2006, Bush declared that the capture of bin Laden was no longer a "top priority."[1]

By contrast, as a senator and a presidential candidate, Obama had made it clear that the search for bin Laden *was* a top priority for him.

He memorably and portentously proclaimed during a presidential debate with John McCain that he would not hesitate to act if given the opportunity to strike at bin Laden, even if it offended Pakistan, where it was often assumed bin Laden was hiding. "If we have Osama bin Laden in our sights and the Pakistani government is unable or unwilling to take them out, then I think that we have to act and we will take them out," he said on October 7, 2008.² Soon after I was confirmed to my position, the two of us met, and he stressed that he'd meant what he said. He was emphatic and unambiguous: Killing or capturing Osama bin Laden was to be the single most important mission for the CIA. I understood and agreed.

Beyond the question of justice, bin Laden's continued freedom and the Bush administration's resigned acceptance of it seemed to crystallize much of what Obama was determined to change in the areas of national security and intelligence. He was convinced that the war in Iraq had distracted the United States from the genuine threat to our security—that of terrorism generally and Al Qaeda specifically. He argued repeatedly in the campaign that while the Bush administration was pursuing phantom enemies and nonexistent weapons of mass destruction in Iraq, we had lost our focus on those who actually had attacked the United States. Even the war in Afghanistan, launched to roust Al Qaeda, had by 2009 become mired in debates over nation building, the reliability of Karzai, and other complications. For the new president, nothing was more symbolic of that misdirection than bin Laden himself, who had killed more Americans than any terrorist in history, was actively attempting to kill more, and yet was still at large. This mattered to the new president.

The agency I inherited was gamely pressing on, though without much support or sense of direction. In the years before I arrived, the CIA had surged officers into the area along the border between Afghanistan and Pakistan, hoping to recruit agents to find someone— anyone—who knew where bin Laden was hiding. Not much came from it. The agency had also carefully scrutinized bin Laden's videotaped messages, trying to cull information from the background noise and images. Steve Kappes reluctantly conceded that we'd not learned much from those efforts either.

We theorized that bin Laden operated within a very tight circle of trust, communicating to his forces through people he personally knew and had confidence in. That helped shape our efforts, which I laid out for the president in June 2009 when I took a counterterrorism team with me to the White House to brief him. At that point we were pursuing three principal lines of effort: We were analyzing bin Laden's media communications, looking for members of his family, and trying to penetrate his courier network. We also operated under the assumption that bin Laden was not moving around but rather had holed up somewhere. He was, after all, one of the most recognizable people on earth, with a bounty on his head. He would, we speculated, flee if he believed he was in danger, but otherwise he would probably remain in whatever safe location he had secured.

Bin Laden's family offered one possible way to connect to him. We identified one of his sons, for instance, and discovered that he had been held under a form of house arrest in Iran. But by that time, we discovered that the son, Saad bin Laden, had been released, so we tracked him to Pakistan, hoping he would reach out to his father now that he was free. That lead dried up when the younger bin Laden was killed. The world would not much miss him, but our chance to follow him to his father evaporated as well.

The courier line of inquiry held out possibility too, though our efforts there were similarly stymied. One of the slides I presented to the president in June 2009 listed as one possible courier the name "Abu Ahmed al-Kuwaiti." No other information was provided, and neither I nor the president elaborated on it that day.

If the significance of the courier at that point eluded us, the priority of the effort was crystal clear: President Obama had ordered that capturing or killing bin Laden was to be the most important objective of America's intelligence services. I understood the order, and recognized that it came directly from my commander in chief. With the president's clear direction, I thus set about to recapture the agency's dissipated urgency with respect to bin Laden. I began to ask for regular updates on the hunt for HVT1 and HVT2—High Value Targets 1 and 2, our shorthand for bin Laden and Zawahiri. At the end of each CT-ME update, I asked the specialists assigned to bin Laden to stay after the conclusion of the main meeting, and probed them for details on our hunt for Al Qaeda's chief.

Those discussions were frustrating, more a description of what we didn't know than what we did. At our weekly briefings, when I would ask for signs of progress, too often the response was, "Nothing to report, sir." They were enlivened by the prospect in late 2009 that we had a bead on Zawahiri, but, sadly, that ended with the tragedy at Khost. We climbed back into action afterward but remained hampered by unclear lines of authority and responsibility.

Soon after the Khost bombing, I asked a senior group of CIA officials who the person responsible for finding bin Laden was. The head of the National Clandestine Service raised his hand. So did the head of the Counterterrorism Center. So did the head of the center's Pakistan-Afghanistan Department. So did a few others. If I've learned one lesson in management over the past forty years, it's that if everyone is in charge, nobody is.

From that day on, I ordered that a single person, or two at most, be placed in charge of this hunt. It took some internal discussions to figure out who that would be, but the Counterterrorism Center eventually settled on two people: Gary, the head of the CTC's Pakistan-Afghanistan Department and a career officer with deep knowledge of the Middle East; and Sam, an analyst who was immersed in Al Qaeda and regarded as the agency's leading expert on the organiza-

tion.* I directed that Gary and Sam report to me weekly with updates on the search.

In the movies, plots turn on big moments, epiphanies where a suspect breaks or a mystery is revealed. In the real world of intelligence,
by contrast, breakthroughs are the result of patient and resolute work,
the slow accumulation of facts, each of which may seem ambiguous but
that collectively add up to a hypothesis. That was the case in our search
for a courier who might be working with bin Laden.

The first information we had received about couriers came to the
CIA in 2002 when a detainee associated with Al Qaeda identified a bin
Laden courier by the nickname of "Abu Ahmed."

The following year, Khalid Sheik Mohammed (better known as
KSM) was arrested in Rawalpindi, Pakistan. He was turned over to
the CIA and subjected to extensive interrogation, including waterboarding. KSM did confirm that someone he called "Abu Ahmed al-
Kuwaiti" had been a courier for bin Laden, but he did not provide us
with the man's true name. We suspected he was lying, which made us
all the more interested in his account—why bother to lie?—but we still
did not have a real name, much less a whereabouts for this possible
courier.

Then another detainee confirmed part of what we suspected: Abu
Ahmed did, in fact, work closely with bin Laden and had not, as far as
the detainee knew, ever retired from that work. We now believed Abu
Ahmed represented an important lead, but we still did not have his
real name.

And then in 2007 another source passed along information that
closed that gap: Abu Ahmed's name, Ibrahim Sa'id Ahmed Abd al-
Hamid, a native of Kuwait who had joined Al Qaeda in Afghanistan.
At last we had the real name of a real courier, but there were two more

*These are not their real names.

questions: Was he alive, and if so, where was he? Detainees either did not know or would not say.

We searched the world, and at first received discouraging information that Ibrahim had been killed fighting in Afghanistan. That sidetracked us for a while, but it turned out to be wrong. It was instead one of his brothers who had died. Ibrahim remained alive and was said to be living and working in Pakistan.

What followed was a methodically constructed attempt to figure out where Ibrahim lived and worked, a plan designed with utmost care to minimize the possibility of tipping off the courier that we were on to him. We knew that Ibrahim periodically arrived in a certain city, but we didn't know where he was coming from. We considered following him, but he was careful and alert to any hint of surveillance. Finally, we tracked him all the way to a dead-end street on the outskirts of Abbottabad. That seemed to be the end of the line, so we dispatched an agent to see what lay at the end of that road.

On August 27, 2010, at the end of our regular CT-ME update, Gary and Sam stayed behind for my bin Laden briefing. They told me that afternoon that we had followed Ibrahim's car to what our officers described as a "fortress." My ears pricked up. "Fortress?" I asked. "Tell me about this fortress." Beginning that day, we spared no resource—human or technological—in determining what lay behind the twelve- to eighteen-foot walls of that home in Abbottabad. It became known as AC1 (Abbottabad Compound 1).

Michael Morell, whom I appointed deputy director after Steve Kappes retired in the summer of 2010, helped me analyze what exactly this compound represented. Mike was the agency's brightest analyst and was deeply respected by the operators. Through the entire operation, I never wanted Michael far from me. The house itself was curious. It was by far the biggest in the neighborhood—eight times the size of the next largest. Property records indicated that Ibrahim and his brother were the owners, but neither was wealthy enough to afford a property valued at roughly $1 million. Moreover, Ibrahim appeared to live not in the main residence but in a guesthouse inside the compound's walls, strange if he was the principal owner. The main home was three stories tall, and the top floor had a balcony, but the balcony was enclosed by a seven-foot-tall wall. Who puts a privacy wall around a balcony? Barbed wire topped the perimeter wall. There was no Internet connection or landline telephone at the house. It seemed clear that someone inside this compound had gone to extraordinary lengths to secure his privacy, but that could mean many things. It could be a criminal, a drug dealer, even another high-value terrorist.

We clearly needed to know more, but there was enough to suggest that something significant was going on inside this compound. In September, less than a month after we identified the compound as being potentially important, I briefed the president for the first time about our mounting suspicions. I told him about the compound's security and privacy structures, as well as the unusual ownership situation. He asked what we were doing to collect more information about the house, and I told him we were devoting every effort to finding out more. He urged us to step up our efforts.

It was not easy.

Our surveillance revealed that a man would periodically emerge from the house and rapidly pace around the compound, not so much strolling as seeming to quickly try to get a little exercise, a little like a prisoner in a yard. We dubbed him "the Pacer."

We could not tell much about him. We discussed mounting a telescope on a nearby hill, but the sightlines were not good, and our people worried that it might be noticed. I suggested putting a camera in a tree at the edge of the compound, but the trees were deciduous, and the camera would certainly be noticed if attached to bare limbs. The residents burned their own trash—intriguing in a neighborhood with trash service, but not helpful in identifying the residents.

We were, however, able to develop some information about the compound and those inside it. We determined that there were three families inside the walls, and as we watched their movements, we gradually developed a roster of those who occupied the compound and their habits. Ibrahim and his family lived in the guesthouse, as did his brother and his brother's wife. In the main house were an adult male, at least one adult female, and an adolescent male. There were six children living in the compound as well. That hardly sealed the case that it was bin Laden, but it did conform to other intelligence regarding him, as we believed he was probably living with the youngest of his three wives, a teenage boy, and three young children born in the years since 9/11.

It occurred to me that it would be helpful to determine how tall that man was, since bin Laden was well over six feet. We brought in analysts who were experts at measuring shadows in photographs. But they couldn't tell his height.

In November, we received enticing information that gave us a strong sense that Ibrahim was still working with his former colleagues. To us, that meant he was back with bin Laden.

Now we had a suspicious fortress and an evasive courier. That courier practiced extraordinary security, lied to his family about where he was, and was believed to have once worked for bin Laden.

Just before Christmas, I again briefed the president on our surveillance of the compound and the courier. By now our view was hardening that we had located an important target, but as the president pointed out, we still did not really know who it might be. We knew that a family was living inside and never stepped out of the walls and that great pains were being taken to protect their privacy. We did not know who they were or why they were so secretive. I returned from the briefing that day and told our team that the top priority of the CIA, the most important mission of the most important intelligence service in the United States, was to figure out who lived in that house. I urged the team to think broadly about what it needed to fully comprehend who was behind those walls. I told them not to worry about budgets and urged them to produce new ideas for figuring out who our suspect was.

They had been working at this long and hard, and my demand that they dig deeper at first produced a weary resignation. Understandably, they felt they already had used every tool in their toolbox and could not imagine what else to try. I would not accept that we were out of ideas. Frustrated, I told them I wanted ten new thoughts at our next meeting. I was openly angry, furious at their seeming acceptance that we had done all we could. They left in silence. My Italian blood was up.

Jeremy and Mike Morell stayed behind after that session. As my temper cooled, I asked them whether the time had come to replace Gary, who it seemed to me had grown discouraged. Jeremy urged me to wait and see what the group produced in response to my demand for fresh ideas. Meanwhile, he met with Gary and the rest of the group and made it clear to them that their jobs were on the line. Just dismissing ideas as impractical was not enough. He prodded them to suggest anything, no matter how outlandish, in order to get their thinking going and to reassure me that they weren't out of gas. "This is like math class," he told them, as he later reported to me. "You need to show your work." I'd asked for ten ideas; he pressed them to come up with twenty-five.

When we met next, they had thirty-eight, and it was clear that they'd been energized by the effort. Some of the ideas were impractical or risked tipping our hand—one proposed throwing a stink bomb into the compound and photographing the residents as they exited; another was to put listening devices in the grocery packages that were delivered to the compound; a third, particularly amusing one, was to broadcast a booming voice over a loudspeaker proclaiming that Allah wanted them to leave the house. But wild ideas are far better than no ideas. We were being creative, and I could feel the energy surging back into the group. I kept Gary in place, and was glad I did.

These meetings, it almost goes without saying, were held in the utmost secrecy. We deliberately kept the circle of those involved in the bin Laden case extraordinarily small, even within the CIA. The only participant in those sessions who lacked a top security clearance was my dog, Bravo. It tickled me to watch these tough, intense CIA officers debate the most secret mission of our agency, then pause to scratch Bravo's head. Bravo heard a lot in those months, and never leaked a word of it.

But some people had to be told. As we devoted more and more resources to this operation, we needed the support of Congress, which had to authorize a "reprogramming" of funds to continue our surveillance that was supplying our only real insight into the compound. That meant taking the risky step of briefing the relevant congressional leaders. The White House was petrified that news of the operation might leak, but I saw no choice. I had promised to keep Congress abreast of our operations, and I needed congressional support to pay for this increasingly complicated and costly undertaking. Accordingly, I briefed the chairs and ranking members of the intelligence and defense appropriations committees, as well as the congressional leaders, in December. A few weeks later, when Republicans took over the House of Representatives, I invited Michigan congressman Mike Rogers, the new chair of the House Intelligence Committee, and the committee's new staff director, Michael Allen, to join me for dinner at Langley. We met in my office, the dark woods and quiet Potomac beneath my window, and I personally explained to them our suspicions about the house in Abbottabad and our efforts to discern who was there. They listened in respectful, slightly amazed silence. We had dinner afterward, an unusually subdued meal in my private dining room.

When the White House learned of those conversations, the president's staff was incensed. The White House demanded a list of everyone I had briefed, and warned me that I had endangered this vital operation. I did as I was told, but had no regrets. The leadership was entitled by law to know, and as a political matter it was better for them to own it than to be able to distance themselves from it later if something went wrong. Despite the apprehension at the White House, not one word of those briefings trickled out, proof that Congress actually can be trusted, even with what was probably the biggest secret we had.

By the end of 2010, we were so convinced that the house in Abbottabad harbored a valuable target that we began to fashion a plan for taking it. Up to this point the entire effort had been run by the CIA, and the first option naturally was that CIA officers would conduct a ground raid—perhaps by working their way gradually into position near the compound, then raiding it late at night and secreting bin Laden back out of the country. Institutionally, that was appealing—it was our hunt, and we would finish it. But John Bennett, a veteran CIA official and the head of the Clandestine Service, advised me that he did not believe CIA officers, acting alone, could take the compound and capture its occupants. An operation of this size and complexity, well within the borders of Pakistan, would require the specialized skills of the military's special operations forces. Mike Morell strongly agreed.

That raised a host of logistical and diplomatic difficulties—invading a sovereign country is hardly something to do casually. Thankfully, the chief of the Joint Special Operations Command, which would supply the military personnel for any such undertaking, was Vice Admiral Bill McRaven, whom I knew from our meetings with the military in Florida and who was widely regarded as one of the most capable leaders anywhere in our armed services. At my request, Mike Morell asked McRaven to come to the agency in late January.

In the office next door to mine, Morell told him what we'd found, and who we believed might be inside. McRaven listened with rapt attention. When Morell concluded, the admiral nodded appreciatively. "Congratulations," he said. "This is an incredible piece of work." More important, he expressed complete confidence that his forces could carry out the mission being discussed—flying into a village, dropping from a helicopter, capturing or killing the inhabitants, and returning to safety. That was reassuring, of course, but also underscored the special complexity of this operation: It would not be in Afghanistan but rather in Pakistan. If something went wrong, our special operations forces would be far inside a country where they had no right to be. Getting out might prove harder than getting in. McRaven did not flinch at the danger. He proposed a navy captain to oversee the planning and named a commander whom he believed was well suited to conduct the operation itself. We left the option of a CIA raid on the table, but now we added a special operations forces alternative as well.

The risk to our forces could of course be vastly reduced if we conducted this as a joint operation with Pakistan. With that in mind, we thoroughly discussed whether to involve Pakistani authorities. But the ISI's reputation for leaks and divided loyalties—many ISI agents had ties to the Taliban—made it difficult to trust others with this information.

One day, we received information that a helicopter had flown directly over the house. That reminded us that this compound was in plain sight, less than two miles from Pakistan's main military academy and nestled within a residential neighborhood. If Pakistani authorities were genuinely curious, they could have found this compound as easily as we had. It could mean that our intelligence was simply better than theirs; it could mean that we were wrong about who might be in the house; or it could mean that they lacked the desire to get bin Laden. Additionally it showed that this was an area where helicopters did occasionally operate, so an incoming helicopter would not necessarily be so unusual as to cause residents to immediately sense an alarm. Soon enough, we would come to appreciate the significance of that.

The Abbottabad compound was the consuming focus of my work in those months, but the rest of the world did not do us the favor of standing still. On December 17, 2010, a street vendor in Tunis, angered that authorities had confiscated his vegetable cart and worn down by a lifetime's worth of petty insults inflicted by a corrupt regime, set himself on fire. Tarek al-Tayeb Mohamed Bouazizi died three weeks later, on January 4. His dramatic act ignited repressed fury across the Middle East.

On January 1, 2011, a bombing in an Egyptian Coptic church killed more than twenty people and set off protests that pitted Christians and Muslims in conflict; President Hosni Mubarak pledged to "cut off the hands of terrorists," and Egypt descended into political and sectarian violence. Protests soon spread to Algeria and then Libya, and the Arab Spring was under way.

The uprisings that convulsed so much of the Arab world beginning at the end of 2010 represented in one sense a fulfillment of American intelligence and in another sense a failure. For years, CIA analysts had warned of the building pressures across the Middle East and North Africa—increasing numbers of young people unable to find work; rising income disparities; deepening anger at corruption; alienation from ossified regimes. Those were the underpinnings of the Arab Spring, and the CIA, true to its mission to provide policy makers with insights into the world, identified them as sources of pressure long before they blew.

At the same time, we did not anticipate the flash points or the speed with which events might unfold. On January 14, 2011, less than a month after Tarek al-Tayeb Mohamed Bouazizi set himself on fire, Ben Ali ended his more than two decades' rule in Tunisia and fled for the safety of Saudi Arabia. That marked the first successful uprising of the spring, and fueled further action across the region. We scrambled to keep up.

By the end of 2010, the combination of rapidly unfolding world events and the pressure and secrecy of the bin Laden case was wearing on me. I was looking forward to a brief respite. I traveled home to Monterey to spend the holidays with my family—painfully recalling that it was at this time the year before that the Christmas bomber and Khost attack had brutally interceded. This year was more restful. I chopped some wood and tended to the walnut grove, and celebrated New Year's Eve with Sylvia and old friends in Monterey.

There, one of my oldest friends and the owner of one of Monterey's best restaurants, Ted Balestreri, welcomed the new year with an extravagant suggestion. He showed off an 1870 bottle of Château Lafite Rothschild—the finest in the cellar of the Sardine Factory—and announced, "If Leon catches Osama bin Laden, we'll open that bottle!"

"You're on!" I answered.

There's no question I had some inside information on that bet.

One of my first trips as CIA director included a stop in Egypt, where I met with President Hosni Mubarak in 2009. We already were acquainted. During Clinton's presidency, Mubarak was at the White House for the final stages of a peace negotiation between Israel and the PLO over the West Bank, and during a last-minute snag, Clinton asked me to keep Mubarak entertained in the Oval Office while he shuttled between Yitzhak Rabin and Yasser Arafat.

That was fourteen years earlier. In my conversation with Mubarak this time, he was stern and serious, arguing that he was now America's essential ally in the region, the person best poised to keep the peace— his government was stable, his relations with Israel solid, his credibility among other Arab leaders strong as well. I didn't argue with any of that, though I did note some worrisome signs. Mubarak was protected by legions of security guards—the approach to his office was cleared for blocks, emphasizing the distance between Egypt's president and his people.

Once events in Tunisia took hold at the end of 2010 and began to inspire other young, disaffected people across the region, Mubarak's confidence suddenly seemed misplaced. Ben Ali's decision to flee Tunisia changed the calculus not just in that country but across the region, as dissidents smelled the possibility of reform, and even actual regime change. That possibility, underappreciated by the CIA's intelligence from the region, now moved to the center of events.

What's more, our insights into those events—particularly into the protest groups—deteriorated as quickly as the demonstrations accelerated. That's because in many cases we relied on the intelligence services of the government for our understanding of the events and actors inside those countries. The Arab Spring was blooming quickly, and our view of it was narrowing fast.

On January 25, a gigantic, coordinated protest brought thousands of Egyptian demonstrators into violent confrontations with the police and military. Not content to ask for reform, these protesters explicitly demanded that Mubarak step down. That placed the United States in a precarious position: Mubarak was an old ally and abandoning him would not only turn our back on decades of cooperation but would also signal to other Middle Eastern regimes that we were abandoning them to dissidents. Moreover, there was always the question of who would come next: It's one thing to deplore Mubarak, another to feel confident that his successor would be an improvement. On the other hand, Mubarak was a fairly ruthless leader and those protesting his government had a strong moral basis for their complaints—and certainly felt entitled to be understood and supported by the United States, which was born amid similar dissatisfactions not so long ago, at least in historical terms.

Attempting to find some way to ease Mubarak from power without nudging Egypt toward chaos, we reached out through intermediaries. The White House directed my deputy, Mike Morell, to reach out through intelligence channels and deliver to Omar Suleiman, the head of Egypt's intelligence service, a stark message: that Mubarak's attempts to hold on to power were becoming self-destructive. We proposed some talking points that might guide Mubarak toward relinquishing authority without simply fleeing the country. Suleiman agreed to communicate those points to Mubarak, and when the Egyptian president announced plans to address the nation on the evening of January 28, we were optimistic that our message had been received.

On the afternoon of January 28, I joined my colleagues in the White House Situation Room to listen as Mubarak delivered a much-anticipated address to his people. Mubarak spoke late at night in Egypt, and those of us in Washington anxiously hoped he would announce his intention to step aside and turn over power to a successor. He did not. He adopted half-measures, sacking his cabinet and offering not to run again for president but continuing to hold on. In the Situation Room, the mood was bleak. Even from thousands of miles away, it was obvious that this would not placate the demonstrators. The following day, Mubarak named Suleiman as his vice president, suggesting a transition. Again, however, it was too little at that late hour. By February, President Obama sided firmly with the protestors, and on February 11, Suleiman announced that Mubarak had stepped down. It had taken less than six weeks from the first major protest for one of the Middle East's most stable governments to fall. The Mubarak I had first met more than a decade earlier in the Oval Office of the White House was sent off to jail.

As the situation in Egypt careened toward its conclusion, the United States confronted yet another challenge. In the city of Lahore, long regarded as the cultural and intellectual capital of Pakistan, a young American named Ray Davis pulled into a jammed traffic intersection on January 27 and was accosted by two men on a black motorcycle. They had guns, and one jumped off the bike and pointed his weapon at Davis, who was stuck at a traffic light behind the wheel of a Honda Civic. Davis drew and fired a Glock 17 nine-millimeter pistol and shot them both. He then pulled out a camera, photographed the man with the weapon as he lay in the street, and called the local American consulate. A crowd gathered and surrounded Davis, preventing him from leaving. Making matters worse, a car rushing from the consulate struck a pedestrian, killing that person as well.

Before any help could make it to Davis, police came on the scene and took him into custody. When they searched his car, they found the pistol, five magazines, and seventy-five rounds of ammunition, as well as a GPS device, a Motorola radio, a cell phone, a digital camera, a first aid kit, batteries, a passport, and $125 in U.S. currency.

Davis was in the country on a diplomatic passport and assigned to the embassy in Islamabad. The Pakistanis concluded that he was a CIA officer and assumed the worst—that we had officers crawling all over the country and that they had just happened to stumble upon this one. Davis was a security officer, assigned to protect American officials. He was not collecting intelligence. He was, however, well trained and had followed that training when confronted by armed gunmen. The question was: What to do with him? The Pakistani public, egged on by extremist elements in that country, clamored for Davis to be executed, ignoring that the men he killed had been involved in thefts before and had provoked the incident. The United States demanded Davis's release under diplomatic immunity, which the Pakistanis rejected. The crisis steadily grew.

President Obama directed that various members of his cabinet reach out to our counterparts in Pakistan as we searched for levers that might spring Davis from prison. In my case, that meant appealing to Pasha and imposing on our already fragile relationship. I both presumed on Pasha and broadly hinted to him when I emphatically warned him that I would hold him personally responsible for Davis's safety.

As the senior officials in the U.S. government considered various options, we knew there was an ancient Islamic tradition of restitution in cases of serious crimes, even murder. If the families of the men killed by Davis would accept a payment for the loss of their loved ones, perhaps the courts could be persuaded to accept that as a just conclusion of the affair. The diplomatic efforts that followed focused on determining whether the families might accept such a settlement. As the president's senior advisers became more focused on the bin Laden hunt, rescuing Davis became more urgent. We did not want him in Pakistan on the night that U.S. special operations forces were going to be raiding that country.

Friday, February 25, was a balmy day in Washington, warm and windy, a whiff of spring in the air. It had been just over a year since we at the CIA had lost our colleagues at Khost. Memories of the president's mournful visit the previous February weren't fresh, but they lingered, as did the urgency to deliver justice. That evening, after most of the government had closed for the weekend and even our building was largely quiet, the senior ranks of the U.S. military, led by James Cartwright, vice chairman of the Joint Chiefs of Staff, quietly paid a visit to the CIA, where we met in a conference room down the hall from my office. McRaven attended, as did Mike Vickers, Defense's undersecretary for intelligence and a former CIA operative whose gentle, owlish look belied his fierce commitment to the destruction of Al Qaeda. There, for the first time, we shared with them the entire sum of our knowledge about the Abbottabad compound. Our analysts had built a scale model of the compound, and we placed it on the table. Throughout the briefing and discussion, we circled the model, imagining what was inside, contemplating what it would take to breach its walls and confront its occupants. By the end of the evening, top officials of the American defense and military establishment were transfixed by a three-story home at the end of a dead-end street in a small town nine time zones away.

If it was bin Laden, and if we got permission to go after him, how would we do it? That question was on all our minds, and it led to the development of what we called the "COAs," courses of action. Initially there were five, or rather five and a half. COA 1 was a bomber strike that would wipe out the compound and all those inside; COA 2 was a helicopter assault by special operations forces, who would swoop in, raid the compound, and capture or kill our target, if he was there; COA 3 was a raid by CIA officers, an idea already viewed with some skepticism inside the CIA but on the table to consider; COA 4 was a joint raid with Pakistan; and COA 5 was to simply tell the Pakistanis what we knew about the compound and urge them to act. There was, in addition, what one might consider COA 4a: If word of our suspicions were suddenly to leak, we were prepared to alert the Pakistanis and scramble immediately toward the compound, presumably in conjunction with their forces. That was to be activated only in an emergency, but we worried throughout those weeks that we might have to act on a moment's notice or risk losing bin Laden forever. Notably, we did not consider the use of an unmanned aircraft as a viable option at first, for reasons I'll return to in a moment.

One week later, I delivered the same briefing for an even larger group, this time at the White House and headed by Donilon. Admiral Michael Mullen, chairman of the Joint Chiefs, was present, as were Cartwright and Jim Clapper, the director of national intelligence, and Deputy National Security Adviser Denis McDonough, who played an essential role through the operation keeping the process running. Once again, I laid out the evidence that we believed clearly identified the compound as housing a significant target, and once again, I conceded that we could not be entirely sure who the occupant was. Nevertheless, as I concluded that day, there was a real chance that this was bin Laden. And if it was, it was our first opportunity since Tora Bora to get him. We finished that meeting and returned to our offices. I was barely back at Langley when Donilon called to say that the president "believes we need to move very quickly." He authorized me to develop an operation and asked how soon we could put one together. I told him I would start that minute and have him something as soon as the president was ready.

Working with McRaven, we refined the ideas that so far had been presented. In the first, a B-2 Stealth bomber would blow the compound to smithereens. In the second, special operations forces aboard helicopters would raid the compound, either with or without help from the Pakistanis. We also retained the alternative of using CIA officers to conduct a ground raid on the compound.

Options in hand, I returned to the White House Situation Room on March 14, this time to brief the president. Vice President Biden attended, as did the military leadership, including Secretary of Defense Bob Gates. I began with a review of what we knew about the compound:

Ibrahim had led us there, and we had intelligence that he had once worked for bin Laden. The house was fortified and shielded from view in a way that strongly suggested someone was hiding inside. "The Pacer" lived in the main house, came outside only for hurried laps around the yard, and never left the compound. All that pointed toward the possibility of bin Laden, but it was not, I acknowledged, conclusive. It could be that Ibrahim was protecting bin Laden's family but not bin Laden himself; it could be another terrorist or criminal hiding behind those walls. The uncertainty of who was inside only made more serious the risks of any action. We could blow up this house and damage our relations with Pakistan, only to discover we had taken out a drug dealer. But there were risks to not acting as well. We could miss our best chance in a decade to capture or kill Osama bin Laden.

The president listened without interrupting, then asked a few questions and offered his thoughts. First, he said he did not believe we could afford to share this intelligence with any other nation, including Pakistan. There was too much danger of leakage from that country's intelligence services, and Obama did not want to jeopardize a chance to snare bin Laden. Moreover, there was another problem with notifying

Pakistan: What if we shared our evidence, and they declined to act? Would we go on our own over their objections? There was simply too much risk at stake to trust an untrustworthy partner. No matter what we decided to do, we would do it alone. That ruled out COA 4 and COA 5.

Once we had resolved that question, the president asked a number of questions about COA 2, the helicopter raid. He was especially focused on the issue of how much time the occupants of the house would have to escape once they heard the approaching helicopter. Would our teams get there only to find that the target was gone? We couldn't answer that definitively, and Obama, understandably, instead turned to the airstrike alternative. As he noted, that seemed least likely to endanger American forces and most likely to destroy the target without warning or chance of escape.

The president did not reach a final decision that day, though his comments suggested to me that he was inclined to favor the bomber option. Before doing so, however, he wanted to know more about what a bombing raid would entail, and he asked to have the other options fully developed. Wrapping up, the president directed us to move "with haste."

Events elsewhere also demanded attention. Japan was struck by an earthquake and tsunami on March 11, and was still struggling to recover as we met that afternoon. Then, on March 16, two days after my meeting with the president, Ray Davis was hauled before a judge.

Davis appeared in court for a scheduled appearance and sat through a brief session at which he was confined inside a cage while the judge and lawyers discussed his case, all in Urdu and thus unintelligible to him. It appeared he would be bound over for trial, and the judge announced that he would soon take up pretrial matters such as Davis's claim for diplomatic immunity. But then the same judge abruptly cleared the courtroom and brought in the victims' families. The families were offered compensation for their loved ones. They accepted, and Davis was whisked away, first to an airfield, then into American hands, then home.

The release infuriated those Pakistanis who saw him as a CIA assassin, and my relations with Pasha entered a decidedly cooler phase. Some of my administration colleagues and many outsiders later questioned why the government had worked so hard for Davis's return. The answer is simple: Davis was in Pakistan because America sent him there, doing a job his country asked him to do. He may not have done it perfectly, but the United States does not leave its people behind. It was his government's responsibility to bring him home. On May 16, Davis returned to America.

Across the Middle East, meanwhile, the Arab Spring continued to accelerate, particularly in Libya, where a reasonably coherent group of insurgents sought Western aid in toppling Muammar Qaddafi, the aging and eccentric leader who had once been a major sponsor of international terrorism but who in recent years had directed his paranoia toward oppressing his own people. Qaddafi struggled to maintain power by unleashing violent attacks on his fellow Libyans, and America, along with our NATO allies, was compelled not to simply stand by. Troubled by what Qaddafi might do, President Obama knew that the only way to prevent a massacre was for the United States to play a role. Three days after Davis's release, a NATO coalition including American forces launched Operation Odyssey Dawn with a fusillade of cruise missiles intended to cripple Qaddafi's air defenses.

President Obama was in Brazil when that assault began, so his international relations calendar for April included summitry on one continent, war on another, riots and natural disaster on a third. It was, to say the least, a busy month. And it wasn't over yet.

Those crises erupted and subsided, and we were back to peering down into the yard of that mysterious compound in Abbottabad,

My office at the Pentagon. The portraits of Dwight Eisenhower and George Marshall were left over from Bob Gates's time; I kept them because I shared Bob's admiration for those two leaders. The retriever is Bravo; he came with me.

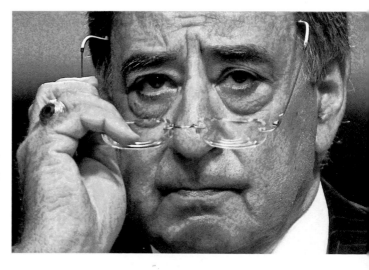

At my confirmation hearing for secretary of defense. I was confirmed by a unanimous vote, no doubt in part because we had successfully concluded the bin Laden operation five weeks earlier.

ABOVE As secretary of defense, you get to see some impressive
hardware. Here I am aboard the USS *Enterprise*.

OPPOSITE, ABOVE As he entered the House of Representatives to deliver
his 2012 State of the Union address, President Obama complimented
me on a "good job tonight." The microphone at the left of this photo
caught the remark and sent reporters scrambling. The president was
referring to our successful rescue of Jessica Buchanan and Poul Hagen
Thisted, a pair of aid workers kidnapped in Somalia and freed by a
U.S. special operations team that same day.

OPPOSITE, BELOW As CIA director and secretary of defense, I traveled
to more than fifty countries. This shot is from 2012, as we were
wrapping up a trip in Afghanistan.

ABOVE The president and I marking the eleventh anniversary of the 9/11 attacks.

OPPOSITE, ABOVE One of the great pleasures of serving as defense secretary is meeting our men and women in uniform. Here I'm speaking with a group of them in Kandahar, Afghanistan, in late 2012.

OPPOSITE, BELOW I was proud to help end the military's long ban on women serving in combat, and I was moved to do so in part by women I saw around the world serving our country in perilous positions. Pictured here are First Lieutenant Kelly Boak, Lance Corporal April Whitham, and Lance Corporal Elisabeth Reyes, all serving in Afghanistan.

OPPOSITE, ABOVE Afghan president Hamid Karzai was a difficult partner, though we actually hit it off on occasion. Here he visits the Pentagon in early 2013.

OPPOSITE, BELOW Meeting with NATO leaders in Brussels. That's Jeremy Bash, my chief of staff and partner through my time at the CIA and Department of Defense, to my left. The Marine is John Kelly, my military aide at the Defense Department.

ABOVE Israeli defense minister Ehud Barak and I collaborated on a number of issues of great importance to our countries. He was a reliable ally, a trustworthy counterpart, and a friend. Here we enter the Pentagon together in April 2012.

Meir Dagan, Israel's legendary former director of the Mossad. I once asked him how he would deal with Al Qaeda. His answer: "Kill them."

 In June 2012, I had the rare opportunity to visit Vietnam. We exchanged artifacts from the war, discussed America's commitment to Asia, and held a number of ceremonial affairs, including this review of Vietnamese troops.

On a visit to China in September 2012, I met with my counterpart, Defense Minister Liang Guanglie. He gave me a plate with my face on it. I was flattered, but really, what do you do with such a gift?

ABOVE I started life in my dad's restaurant, and have always appreciated a good meal. Here I'm dining in the mess hall of the PLA Engineering Academy of Armored Forces in Beijing on September 19, 2012.

OPPOSITE, ABOVE I am Catholic. I carry a rosary, attend mass every Sunday, and say my Hail Marys when the occasion arises. It was thus a special honor when on January 16, 2013, on a trip to Italy, I had the opportunity to meet the pope. He thanked me for my work in keeping the world safe.

OPPOSITE, BELOW My final round of European visits was a pensive one, and included a stop in Britain, our most enduring ally. Here I'm leaving 10 Downing Street after meeting with Prime Minister David Cameron.

OPPOSITE, ABOVE One of my last trips as secretary of defense took me to Tripoli (I was the first defense secretary ever to visit Libya) and to this graveyard, the oldest resting place of American servicemen outside the United States.

OPPOSITE, BELOW Wrapping up. My staff gave me this cake as a farewell gift (the meat-axe is meant to symbolize my work cutting the Pentagon budget).

ABOVE General Martin Dempsey, chairman of the Joint Chiefs, was a friend and ally through my time at defense. He helped end the bans on gays openly serving and on women in combat. Here we prepare to testify regarding the attack on the U.S. facility in Benghazi, a topic that holds endless appeal for some members of Congress.

ABOVE I've known Hillary Clinton for more than twenty years. I served with her in the Obama cabinet and beside her in the Clinton administration. She is smart, principled, and decisive, a magnificent public servant.

OPPOSITE, ABOVE Heading home. Here I'm boarding the plane for California after concluding my tenure as secretary of defense.

OPPOSITE, BELOW President Obama had brought me back to government service in 2009 and did me the honor of attending my farewell when I wrapped up that service in 2013.

Back in Monterey, Sylvia and I oversee the Panetta Institute for Public Policy at Cal State Monterey Bay. It's our hope to give young people some of the same sense of mission and possibility that have guided us through our lives in government.

BELOW Our family celebrated Sylvia's and my fiftieth wedding anniversary in Hawaii. Here we are surrounded by our sons—Jimmy, Carmelo, and Christopher—their lovely wives, and our grandchildren. And, of course, Bravo.

contemplating two questions: Who was inside, and, if we determined there was enough evidence to risk that person's capture or killing, how would we do it?

I recognized the appeal of the bombing option and sympathized with President Obama's inclination in that direction. I felt, though, that we needed to know more about exactly how it would play out, so I asked our people to bring in the experts. Not long after, a group of airmen from the 509th Bomb Wing from Whiteman Air Force Base near Kansas City—we called them the "flyboys," and they looked every bit the part, with leather jackets and crew cuts—came to my office to describe what they would need to do to eliminate "the Pacer." Their mission would rely on two B-2 bombers. They would take off from Whiteman, fly halfway around the world, track the Afghanistan-Pakistan border, then "stealth up" and bank right. Minutes later, they'd be over the target.

To eliminate the compound, each bomber would release sixteen JDAMS (Joint Direct Attack Munitions), each one a two-thousand-pound bomb. Those thirty-two bombs would reduce the compound to dust and rubble. If Osama bin Laden were inside, he'd be killed, but so would many noncombatants, including all the women and children living inside the compound and possibly neighbors as well. The tentative casualty estimate was fifty to one hundred people, most of whom, of course, would be innocent civilians in a country with whom we were not at war. Moreover, the chances of our later proving that we had killed bin Laden would be remote. It would be hard to recover DNA evidence given the obliteration of the site, and because we would have just conducted an unannounced bombing raid of a nominal ally, it seemed unlikely that Pakistani officials would be eager to help us dig through the rubble for our proof.

I had my doubts, but the flyboys were eager to do the job, and I knew the president liked the idea in concept, so we took it to John

Brennan and laid it out for him. He winced at the fallout from such a raid. "This," he said, "sounds like a bad plan."

But if we were to rule out the bomber option, that would leave the president with just one alternative to consider—the helicopter raid by special operations forces. It is never desirable to give the president only one course of action, so it was then that Cartwright proposed the possible use of an unmanned aircraft. The drone would target "the Pacer" during one of his exercise rounds, but those were fleeting trips around the courtyard. The weapon would have to be ready to fire at a moment's notice, and it might miss. If "the Pacer" was shot at and missed, he would surely go into hiding elsewhere, and we would be back to the days following Tora Bora, chasing a wisp, encouraging his followers to believe in his invincibility. In addition, there was one of the same problems that bedeviled the bomber option: If a U.S. missile successfully hit bin Laden, there would be remains, but we would get only what the Pakistanis shared with us; given the state of our relations, we had no reason to believe they would go out of their way to reward us.

At our next meeting with the president, he reviewed the B-2 proposal and announced that he shared our reservations and those of Brennan. He took it off the table. At the same meeting, I made the case that this job was ill suited to a CIA ground raid, eliminating it from consideration. That left either the helicopter assault or the use of the drone.

Despite McRaven's confidence and the undeniable skill of our special operations forces, the helicopter option was very dangerous. Abbottabad is more than one hundred miles from the Afghan border, so helicopters bearing the team would have to cross a large swath of terrain, conduct a loud and violent operation in a residential neighborhood, and then hustle back out of the country before Pakistan's military could detect them and scramble their fighters. On the ground, there were the risks of resistance from the inhabitants of the house or from neighbors alarmed by the sight of foreign forces swarming their community. And of course there was always the possibility of equipment failures. No one involved in our operation needed to be reminded of the 1980 attempt to rescue the American hostages in Tehran. That noble effort ended in the crash of a helicopter, the deaths of eight soldiers, and the release of not a single hostage. Bob Gates, who had participated in the planning for the 1980 attempt, was particularly determined not to repeat it. "It's the unexpected you have to fear the most," he said.

Nevertheless, we wanted to know what such a raid would look like. We brought in the SEALs for an initial briefing, telling the operators that they would be conducting a mission in Libya. Once there, Gary, our CIA team leader, stood before the group and announced, "This isn't about Libya. We have found Osama bin Laden, and you guys are going to go get him." Cool as ever, the SEALs absorbed that news without comment.

Working with CIA officers, the SEALs developed a detailed plan for raiding the compound, created two mockups of it, and drilled their assault relentlessly over a period of about four weeks. On April 7, the team was confident enough to conduct a rehearsal, this one in the eastern United States. That first rehearsal was conducted with helicopters on a mockup of the compound surrounded by a fence. The team was practicing ways to enter, but the observers were also focused on how much time would lapse between the first sound of the helicopters approaching and the entry of the team into the building—the question President Obama had raised a few weeks earlier. Jeremy attended the rehearsals on my behalf, and reported back that it appeared we would have about ninety seconds. Beyond that, he noted that the team seemed professional and capable and that McRaven pointedly deferred to the members to develop their own operation. This was not to be micromanaged, a clear statement of his confidence in his men.

Six days later, the assault force performed another drill, this time with the military command, including Mullen, in attendance and held out west at a high-altitude location that better simulated the conditions in Abbottabad. This was a full drill, with the team simulating the entire hundred-mile trip to the target and then the assault itself. Now it was under a minute—precious little time for a houseful of sleeping residents to awake, react, and escape. Gary and his team, along with Jeremy and CIA general counsel Stephen Preston, watched the rehearsal through night-vision goggles. Afterward, they reported to me that the operation was risky, but they were also convinced that it was feasible.

At this point I was briefing the president or his national security team every day, updating them on the planning and desperately hoping to produce definitive evidence of who was occupying the compound. Even as we edged toward launching a strike, we still could not say for sure who "the Pacer" was.

That was particularly worrisome to some members of the CIA's National Clandestine Service, the agency's espionage arm. They are instinctively skeptical of intelligence gleaned through technical sources, and inclined to give more weight to that from human intelligence. Several senior officers—some of the most experienced intelligence experts in our government—argued to me that we should not conduct the raid but rather should wait for more information. They developed a last-ditch plan to try to get eyes inside the compound, but that effort failed to provide the confirmation we sought

So when I gathered our principal bin Laden analysts and operators in mid-April to get their assessments of who lived in this much-studied house, I began by recognizing that we did not have proof, but I wanted to know what each member of our team thought of the evidence. I went around the table. Most rated the odds of its being bin Laden as greater than 50 percent, but conceded that it wasn't rock-solid. Then Sam, one of the team's two leaders, surprised me by declaring that he rated it at 80 percent. Sam was cautious by nature and I had relied on him daily as we intensified the fight against Al Qaeda, so his level of confidence impressed me greatly. And then another of our officers, whom I'll call Maya, went even further. Maya had an encyclopedic knowledge of the bin Laden case and the compound. She was quick, incisive, and utterly dedicated to the mission, and she had the job of briefing the SEALs on what to expect inside the compound. When I called on her and asked what she rated the probability of bin Laden being "the Pacer," she did not hesitate: "Ninety-five percent," she answered.* The CIA team overall was less sure, but we had a strong case.

Internally, the circle of CIA officers and officials aware of the operation was gradually growing. I was eager to make sure we acted lawfully, of course, so I asked Stephen Preston, the agency's exemplary general counsel, to review our operational plans. Normally that would involve a number of lawyers working in consultation, but this operation required special treatment. Preston said afterward that it had been "not heavily lawyered but thoroughly lawyered." Similarly, I knew that if we went ahead with this, it would be a matter of intense international interest, and the press would clamor for details—a complicated situation because we would want to be responsive but also to zealously protect against the release of information that might compromise any prosecutions (if we captured bin Laden) or future operations. I had great confidence in our lead communications person, George Little, so I brought him into the circle as well.

On April 19, the president reviewed the rehearsals. He was as impressed as the rest of us, but worried about what might happen if the teams were caught on the ground and had to fight their way out of the country. Based on those concerns, which Bob Gates echoed, the president suggested adding two backup helicopters to the mission. They were to cross the border with the strike teams and then land nearby, to

---

*That exchange is captured in the movie *Zero Dark Thirty*. The film centers on "Maya" to the exclusion of work done by others; she was a vital part of the hunt for bin Laden, one of the many people in a gigantic team effort.

be called upon only if something went wrong. We also prepared a special diplomatic team to stand by to intervene with Pakistani authorities in the event of a conflict on the ground.

Having heard the options and amended the plan, the president authorized the assault team to move into position in Afghanistan. Accompanied by McRaven, those Navy SEALs and the army pilots from the 160th Special Operations Aviation Regiment, as well as a CIA officer and a military dog named Cairo, deployed on April 25. They were to be ready to launch on a moment's notice, though the drone option remained on the table as well.

The following day, with McRaven joining by secure videophone hookup, the Principals Committee met yet again, this time with Donilon chairing. We had a few new nuggets of intelligence—we discovered, for instance, that the brothers living at the compound were using assumed names, an incremental bit of information but one that continued to reinforce the conviction that something surreptitious was going on there. We also shuffled through some operational details—how the team would fight its way out of Pakistan if confronted there by Pakistani forces; how to dispose of bin Laden's body if he was there and killed; what to do with prisoners if they were taken. One contentious question was whether and when to inform Congress that the operation was under way. Several participants naturally worried about leaks, and since we were now aiming to launch over the weekend, there was the additional complication of how to make notifications over secure lines to members presumably not in their offices at night over the weekend. I proposed that we notify members late in the week to be ready for a secure call over the weekend. Yes, that raised the risk of a leak, but bringing in Congress, I argued, as I had before in defense of my earlier briefings, was both the right thing to do and tactically important so that members could not later claim to have been left in the dark. "Keeping Congress informed is to our advantage," I said, noting that if the operation were a success, they would want to share credit; if it failed, at least they couldn't complain that they were left out. The group agreed. The calls went out.

As if all this weren't enough to keep me busy, the president had one other piece of business that week involving me. On Tuesday, April 28, President Obama nominated me for secretary of defense, replacing Bob Gates. The president and I obviously had worked closely together over that same time—especially, though the public did not yet know it, over the past few months—and when he raised the idea of my moving to Defense, I accepted despite some reservations. I had not expected the timing to coincide with the launch of this delicate and difficult operation, however, and the two crashed together in those final days in April.

After the president made the announcement—which also included the move of General Petraeus to replace me at the CIA, and General John Allen to replace Petraeus—Jeremy and I retired to the White House Situation Room to call the chairs and ranking members of the House and Senate Armed Services committees. Barely had I finished those calls before we headed into the climactic meeting of the preparations for our imminent assault on Abbottabad.

This meeting of the National Security Council Principals included the full team: the president, the vice president, Defense Secretary Gates, Secretary of State Clinton, DNI Clapper, National Security Adviser Donilon, and Joint Chiefs chairman Mullen. President Obama opened the meeting at 4:45 p.m.

I updated the group on our latest fragments of intelligence—the news that the courier and his brother were using assumed names and that sources in Abbottabad "consistently comment on the secretive and suspicious nature of [the house] and its occupants." In addition, we had learned that the women who lived at the house would not answer the door unless the men were present, and we were told that dogs could be heard barking inside. That last point seemed marginally relevant because earlier intelligence indicated that bin Laden had kept guard dogs at previous locations. We estimated that seventeen people were inside the compound, but Ibrahim was away only temporarily. If he returned with his family before we carried out our operation, the number would jump to twenty-two.

And then I concluded. "The bottom line, Mr. President: This information confirms what we know—the secretive nature of the compound, the security precautions, the living under aliases. We have no contrary information. Our basic assessment remains the same."

McRaven then briefed the group on the status of our team and the options for action. Like me, he reiterated that this was the best intelligence we'd had in years suggesting bin Laden's presence. And yet it was far from unambiguous. Still, McRaven's recommendation was to go, and to go with the assault team.

As others chimed in, the doubts and worries were heavy. Gates raised questions about the strength of our information, noting that our evidence remained entirely circumstantial. Clinton acknowledged that more time might give us better intelligence, a sentiment others advanced as well, but she concluded that this was a rare opportunity and believed we should seize it. Biden argued that we still did not have enough confidence that bin Laden was in the compound, and he came out firmly in favor of waiting for more information.

Moving to the question of which course to pursue if the president authorized a strike, the group was similarly split. Gates continued to have reservations about the helicopter assault, and Cartwright favored relying on the drone. I argued against using the drone, repeating my concern that it might miss and cost us a unique opportunity.

As for whether we should go ahead at all, I strenuously said that I believed we should act. Any delay risked a leak. This was our best chance, and we needed to take it. "There's a formula I've used since I was in Congress," I said. "If I asked the average citizen, 'If you knew what I knew, what would you do?' In this case, I think the answer is clear. This is the best intelligence we've had since Tora Bora. I have tremendous confidence in our assault team. If we don't do it, we'll regret it."

The president promised to decide the matter within a day. The next morning, Donilon called to say the president had approved the operation and had opted for the assault team. "It's a go," he said.

I called McRaven on a secure line, told him we had approval and the operation would go that weekend. He was to judge the best day based on weather conditions. He said he was leaning toward conducting the operation on Sunday, as opposed to Saturday, and that he'd let me know that afternoon. Before hanging up, I left him with my prayers and a last piece of advice: "Get in, get bin Laden, and get the hell out of there. If bin Laden's not there, get the hell out of there anyway."

Hanging up, I was struck by the enormity of what the president had just approved. The lives of two dozen men would be at risk, and the Obama presidency, including his prospects for a second term, could well turn on the outcome. My own place in history would almost certainly be defined by what transpired over the next forty-eight hours. With such stakes, it seemed worth memorializing this point in time, so I took a moment to jot out a note for the file. It is dated Friday, April 29, 2011, 10:35 a.m. It reads, in its entirety:

Memo for the Record—

Received phone call from Tom Donilon, who stated that the President made a decision with regard to AC1. The decision is to proceed with the assault. The timing, operational decision making and control are in Admiral McRaven's hands. The approval is provided on the risk profile presented to the President. Any additional risks are to be brought back to the President for his consideration. The direction is to go in and get Bin Laden and, if he is not there, to get out. Those instructions were conveyed to Admiral McRaven at approximately 10:15 a.m.

Leon Panetta, DCIA

The president and I attended the White House Correspondents' Dinner that Saturday night. He was gregarious and funny, unfathomably cool under the circumstances—he used the occasion to trumpet the release of his birth certificate and to witheringly mock Donald Trump, who was in the audience and who had waged a sustained and weird campaign to challenge the president's place of birth. The audience, save Trump, reeled in laughter, none aware of the historic drama unfolding beneath Obama's remarks. He was light and jovial. I was seated at *Time* magazine's table, and though I was tense, I tried not to show it.

The dinner, incidentally, had produced a minor disagreement regarding the timing of the raid. I and others had warned that if the operation were conducted on Saturday night, it would be hard to explain the absence of the president and other key officials from the event, a high-profile evening that brings together Washington journalists and political figures and one that we had already committed to attending. That rankled some of the military leaders, who groused about having to accommodate the "Washington social schedule" in a matter of national security. That wasn't my intention. I was happy to skip the party, but I worried that the operation might leak if the press suddenly started asking questions about where the president and others were or if we suddenly got up and left. Fortunately, we avoided a clash when McRaven concluded that the weather was slightly more advantageous on Sunday than Saturday.

Sunday morning, May 1, I went to mass and offered unusually directed prayers. "I hope this works," I offered to God. "And I hope it works well."

I headed for the office and joined a Principals Committee meeting by secure video link. The president was not present yet, but Donilon wanted a last check of where everyone stood. "Absent some change," he said, "the president's decision stands." He then asked for any new information. "Does anybody want to register anything to make this a no-go?" he asked. There was silence. "The president has made his decision, and it's a go," Donilon concluded. It was 1:24 p.m.

Twenty minutes later, the video link from Afghanistan lit up at Langley, where Mike Morell and I anchored our communications from the conference room across the hall from my office, which had been converted that day into an operations center. I was joined at CIA by Admiral Eric Olson, commander of U.S. Special Operations Command; Roger, the head of our Counterterrorism Center; Tish Long, director of the National Geospatial-Intelligence Agency; and several senior CIA and NSA officers. We hooked up the Situation Room at the White House. The president now joined the rest of his national security team gathered there.

The helicopters lifted off precisely at 2 p.m., 10:30 p.m. in Afghanistan (and 11 p.m. in Pakistan), flying low and fast to the east. The total flight was 171 miles. The first twenty minutes or so were in Afghan airspace, but then the two helicopters bearing the assault teams crossed into Pakistan, followed by two backup CH-47 Chinook helicopters that would land in fields outside Abbottabad and proceed to the compound only in an emergency. Two more helicopters stood by at the border, prepared to enter Pakistan if our teams needed to battle their way out.

It took one hour and forty minutes for the helicopters to reach Abbottabad, so those of us in Washington fell into a nervous silence as they crossed into Pakistan. I fingered my rosary beads, and members of the president's team in Washington, at Langley, and in Afghanistan spent those fretful minutes reviewing final details. Assuming we found bin Laden, we were prepared to take him prisoner, but we anticipated resistance and were prepared to capture him only if he conspicuously surrendered. This was a military raid, not an arrest. If he was killed, we would bring his body with us to photograph it, measure it, and secure a DNA sample. Within a few hours, we felt we could be 85 to 90 percent sure of his identity; within a day or so, we would know conclusively.

At 3:30 p.m., or 12:30 a.m. in Abbottabad, our helicopters arrived on target. Within seconds, things began to go wrong. According to the plan, the first helicopter was supposed to hover over the compound while twelve team members rappelled into the courtyard. Instead, it swung over to an adjacent animal pen and set down. The rotors abruptly stopped turning. Then the second helicopter also deviated from the script. Rather than drop six Navy SEALs on the roof, as planned, it skirted over the compound without stopping, circled, and headed for a spot outside the walls.

The tension in our operations center, already on a knife's edge, now crested. Two helicopters were bouncing around the compound, and none of our team was yet inside the house. Surely the residents were up and either preparing to defend themselves or fleeing.

"Bill," I said, addressing McRaven on the screen, "what the hell's going on?"

Unflappable as ever, McRaven briefly disappeared from the screen and then returned. "It appears we have a helicopter down in the animal pen," he announced. "All of the guys are okay. They are exiting the helicopter and moving to the objective."

The wounded helicopter hung in the yard, and the president's insistence on supplying a backup in case the team needed to fight its way out now seemed brilliantly prescient. "No problem," McRaven added. "Backup helicopter on the way."

Undeterred by the rough landing and change in plans, the SEALs adjusted and moved to blast their way inside from the street. Six members of the team went to the guesthouse, six to the main house, and six to the north entrance of the main house. Pouring inside the compound, they dropped out of our sight, since we were watching from above.

One of the first people they encountered at the guesthouse was the courier who had led us there. Ibrahim fired on one of the team members, and was killed instantly. His wife shouted that he was dead, and that she and her children were the only ones left in the guesthouse. She was ordered to remain there, surrounded by her children, with the door open. At the main house, other women and children were moving about in confusion; our team members, shouting in Arabic, sent them to a secure room, where they were not allowed to leave but where they were protected from harm.

The courier's brother suddenly appeared with something in his hand. He and a woman next to him were shot and killed. She would be the only woman killed that night.

As the teams moved up the stairs of the main house, they encountered gates at each level and broke them down to move on up the stairs. Between the second and third floors, a bearded young man whom the assaulters recognized as Khalid bin Laden, bin Laden's son, was shot and killed. As the SEALs moved to the third floor, a tall, bearded man poked his head out of a doorway. A member of our team, recognizing him instantly, shot at him and missed. The man disappeared back into the room, and an AK-47 was visible in the doorjamb. Team members moved toward the door. As they moved inside the room, two young girls and an adult woman rushed the SEALs. Our operator grabbed the girls and shoved them to the side as they screamed in fear. One woman shouted at the man upstairs, calling him "sheikh." Our team members saw the bearded man and shot him twice, once above the left eye and once in the chest. A woman in the room, whom we later learned was bin Laden's third wife, was shot in the leg, but not seriously wounded.

All of this took about fifteen minutes. I and the other members of the security team watched in excruciating anticipation. At 3:51 p.m. our time, just before 1 a.m. in Abbottabad, McRaven relayed word that the team had sent a preliminary call of "Geronimo," our code word for the successful killing or capture of bin Laden. I was not clear in that moment whether that meant we had taken bin Laden prisoner or killed him. I asked for confirmation. "Geronimo," he repeated. "EKIA." Enemy Killed in Action. A few moments later, the SEALs reappeared on the screen, six of them dragging a body bag to the helicopter.

In our operations center, that was a long-anticipated moment, but no one rejoiced. There was no high-fiving or triumphant whoops. Our men were still deep in Pakistan, surrounded by danger, a long way from home.

And the situation on the ground was growing more tense and complicated by the minute. The explosions and gunfire from the compound had begun to draw the attention of neighbors, and they came into the street, some venturing toward our forces. One member of our team, assigned to keep an eye on the neighborhood, saw them approaching and worried that we were in for a fight.

"Brothers," he yelled in Pashto, "please go back inside. This is government business. Please go back in your homes."

Most stopped, but two kept coming. "Stop," he yelled, more forcefully this time. "Go back. This is government business."

That was just enough to hold them off. Our team members scrambled inside the compound to scoop up computers, hard drives, files, anything that might have value. Outside, our Pashto-speaking officer bravely held the crowd at bay. Then it was time to go. The backup helicopter and surviving helicopter swooped into position, and our team rigged the wounded chopper with explosives and blew it up in the compound, creating a fireball that lit up the screen we were watching. There was no further disguising our presence, so our troops hastily boarded to hightail it back for the border and the safety of Afghan airspace. They were accompanied by one body bag, and they took DNA samples as they flew. When the Chinook lifted off with all our forces on board, it was a huge relief.

At 5:41 p.m. in Washington, we received word that our helicopters and team members were out of Pakistan. They had killed three men and one woman, and injured one other woman, bin Laden's wife. We lost a helicopter, but not a single member of our team was hurt. Then it was time for joy.

"From now on," I told McRaven over the link, "any problem I have, I'm going to assign it to you and your forces." My colleagues laughed with amazement and relief. At 5:50 p.m., our helicopters touched down in Jalalabad, Afghanistan.

There, the team unloaded the choppers and focused on the question the world would want answered momentarily: Did we have the right guy? Two women in the compound had identified him as bin Laden before we left, but we wanted more than that, especially since they were no longer available to us and we weren't planning to be back in Abbottabad anytime soon. A team member took photographs of his face, immediately subjecting them to photo authentication. Others tried to measure the corpse, but no one had thought to bring along a tape measure—proof that no matter how much anyone plans, something is always forgotten. Instead, a member of the team who was just over six feet tall lay down beside the body and determined that it was a few inches taller than he.

All that took less than half an hour, and at 6:20 p.m. McRaven declared that there was a "high probability" that it was bin Laden. The DNA samples from the corpse later would establish beyond any doubt that we had in fact killed Osama bin Laden.

We closed up the link to Afghanistan, and Jeremy and I hopped into one of the CIA's SUVs and rode from Langley to the White House. The sun was setting, and it strobed through the trees as we made our way down the parkway. Washington was quiet. It was a Sunday evening, May Day 2011. Usually a trip to the White House was a last-minute opportunity to make sure we had our facts and issues in order; we would tick off items, shuffle through papers. Today we rode in silence.

When we arrived, Mike Morell joined me in the Situation Room, where the president was already meeting with his team. As Mike and I entered, the others looked up and extended their congratulations. "Great job," the president said. "Everyone at the CIA who worked on this deserves the nation's thanks." It was a special moment for me and the CIA—nothing makes a fight more worthy than the joy of winning.

The topic of discussion when I arrived was how, when, or even whether to announce what we had just done. We proceeded with the plan to conduct a burial at sea, so the body was transported by marines flying an Osprey to a waiting aircraft carrier, the USS *Carl Vinson*.

Bin Laden's body was prepared for burial according to Muslim traditions, draped in a white shroud, given final prayers in Arabic, and then placed inside a heavy black bag. Three hundred pounds of iron chains were put inside as well, to ensure that the body would sink. The bagged body was placed on a white table at the rail of the ship; the table was tipped over to drop the body into the sea. It was so heavy that it dragged the table in with it. As the body sank quickly out of sight, the table bobbed on the surface.

At the White House, President Obama's initial impulse was to say nothing for the moment. He was acutely conscious that if we announced this to the world, we could not be wrong. We should wait for the DNA analysis, he suggested. That struck me as sound reasoning, but probably unrealistic. "This is going to come out," I interjected. We'd set off explosives, fired lots of shots, and left a burning helicopter in a suburban neighborhood a mile or two from Pakistan's West Point. It seemed to me unlikely that this secret was going to hold very long.

Obama acknowledged that I had a point there, and my standing was pretty high at just that moment. "Today, anything you say I'm prone to agree with," he said, chuckling. He quickly turned serious again, and added, "But we have to get this right. I want us to have thought through *everything*."

Gates, Clinton, and McDonough argued that the president, having made the courageous call to approve the operation, should be the one to announce it. The president continued to mull his options, wanting to make sure we handled this correctly with Pakistan while also holding back until we were absolutely sure it was bin Laden whom our forces had killed.

The meeting was about to adjourn so that Admiral Mullen could call his counterpart, General Kayani, in Pakistan. As we were breaking up, Jeremy entered the room carrying the report of the facial recognition analysis. It was built on points of comparison developed by the agency's technical experts—details such as a facial mole, the curvature of his ear, the space between his eyes, the shape of his earlobe. Every one matched. "We got him," the president said. He struck me in that moment as deeply satisfied but in no sense joyous and not yet convinced he should announce it to the world.

Mullen enjoyed a strong personal bond with Kayani, though one that had already been tested that year with the Ray Davis matter. With Undersecretary of Defense for Policy Michèle Flournoy listening in and taking notes, Mullen placed the call and informed Kayani that we had conducted a covert operation against bin Laden. "It is very good that you arrested him," Kayani responded. "He's dead," Mullen said. That seemed to take Kayani aback, as did the information that bin Laden had been living in the compound for five years. Somewhat to our surprise, Kayani responded by asking us to make the announcement, figuring that at least that would leave ambiguous the question of Pakistan's participation in the raid.

After that call, we reassembled in the Situation Room and reviewed what we knew. The president was now convinced. "We shoot for tonight," he said, regarding the plan for announcing the action. "Let's have a draft within an hour."

Obama then called Pakistani president Zadari and Afghan president Karzai, and I made a similar call to Pasha. He had just heard of the raid, and his response to me was largely one of resignation. I told him that we had made the deliberate decision to exclude him and his agency from our planning, and hoped that it would relieve them of any blowback from having cooperated. He wearily replied that "there's not much to say. I'm glad you got bin Laden." I reminded him that two American presidents had vowed to take this action unilaterally if we had the chance; he acknowledged that, again with more resignation than anger. Our friendship would never recover, and relations between our countries were undeniably strained, but it was a price we had to pay for an action we had to take.

I called home to share the news with Sylvia, and we enjoyed a quiet moment of reflection, reminding each other of all the work that had brought us to this point in our lives and the nation's history. I couldn't stay on long, but I suggested that she call Ted Balestreri, tell him to watch TV, and let him know that he owed me a bottle of wine. After we hung up, Sylvia tracked down Ted at his club, where he was finishing dinner. She reminded him of his New Year's offer.

"Turn on CNN," she instructed him. "And get the wine opener ready."

His response: "The son of a bitch set me up."

Shortly after 11:30 p.m., President Obama addressed the nation and announced what we had done. He mentioned me by name, which I found overwhelming, and poignantly acknowledged the work of our intelligence and counterterrorism officers, which was wonderfully deserved. And his reflection on this moment as a pivotal episode in a long and devastating war perfectly captured the sentiments of me and my colleagues as we watched from the East Room:

> The American people did not choose this fight. It came to our shores, and started with the senseless slaughter of our citizens. After nearly ten years of service, struggle, and sacrifice, we know well the costs of war. These efforts weigh on me every time I, as

commander in chief, have to sign a letter to a family that has lost a loved one, or look into the eyes of a service member who's been gravely wounded.

So Americans understand the costs of war. Yet as a country, we will never tolerate our security being threatened, nor stand idly by when our people have been killed. We will be relentless in defense of our citizens and our friends and allies. We will be true to the values that make us who we are. And on nights like this one, we can say to those families who have lost loved ones to Al Qaeda's terror: Justice has been done.

Tonight we give thanks to the countless intelligence and counterterrorism professionals who've worked tirelessly to achieve this outcome. The American people do not see their work, nor know their names, but tonight they feel the satisfaction of their work and the result of their pursuit of justice.[3]

I congratulated the president on his speech. George Little took me to Jay Carney's office, and we conducted a conference call with reporters to share what information we could. Then Mike Morell, Jeremy, and I left the White House. As we crossed the lawn to our car, I could hear the crowds outside the gate. They were chanting, "U.S.A., U.S.A., CIA, CIA." It was the proudest moment of my professional life.

I called an all-hands meeting of CIA employees the next day, and hundreds gathered in the Bubble, as we called the auditorium that sits just outside the main entrance to the headquarters. As I stood up to speak, officers were laughing, cheering, and applauding. "What the hell are you all excited about?" I asked, to roars of more laughter. "What a great day."

Everyone there, I noted, shared in this victory, one that would "go down in history as one of our greatest achievements." I mentioned the chants that I had heard as I left the White House the night before and noted that they were "for every officer who has ever worked in a war zone. They were for every officer who ever helped thwart an Al Qaeda attack, whether it's Europe or Africa or South Asia, the Middle East or here at home."

After describing the evidence that led us to bin Laden's compound, I acknowledged that we had launched our mission without knowing with complete certainty who we would find inside. "Yes, it's dicey," I said, recounting the deliberations with the president and his team, "yes, there are risks, and yes, you don't know how this is all going to work out. But the bottom line was that we thought we had an obligation to act."

Finally, I read to them one of the many e-mails and messages we had received since word of bin Laden's death had rocketed around the world. "I am an Australian citizen who lived in New York City from 1997 to the end of 2000," one correspondent wrote. "I worked at Deutsche Bank in midtown. The guy who sat behind me . . . died in the South Tower on 9/11. From the bottom of my heart, thank you . . . just THANK YOU . . . I have closure." My colleagues erupted in applause. They had done their jobs.

Over the next few days, we tidied up the loose ends of our operation. McRaven and I briefed the Hill. One memorable moment from those sessions came in response to a question from Senator Bill Nelson. "What in the training of those SEALs taught them to push these two young girls aside?" Nelson asked of the team member who put the children into a safe room during the raid.

"Senator," McRaven responded, his voice trembling with emotion, "these are Navy SEALs, but first they are people. They are people who value life. They have wives, kids, mothers, and fathers. That's what taught them."

The team had seized four weapons in the assault, and now I had to dispose of them. I gave bin Laden's AK-47 to the CIA Museum, where it is today, and presented a second AK-47 to the SEAL team (they, in turn, brought me a brick from the compound; it sits in a glass case outside my office in Monterey). The last two were pistols, and I sent one to the CIA's Counterterrorism Center and one to the Pentagon.*

The two shots that ended bin Laden's life did not vanquish the threat of terrorism or even Al Qaeda. They did not ensure this country's safety. Nothing can. But they denied Al Qaeda its founder, its functional leader, and its mythological figurehead. More important, his death proved that America was resolute. It took years of work and a brave call by the president of the United States. But the end of bin Laden firmly proclaimed that no matter how long it takes or how much risk is involved, this country will not let others do violence to us without repercussions. To the victims of 9/11, the victims of Khost, the victims of terrorism anywhere, we proved that we will fight until justice is done.

---

*A few months later we held an event at the CIA and recognized some of those who participated in the operation. I was under the impression that everyone in the audience enjoyed a security clearance, but learned later that one of the producers of Zero Dark Thirty was allowed to attend. Some critics pounced on that; all I can say is that my shout-out to the SEAL team member that day was meant to congratulate him, not to expose him, and was made only because I had been assured that everyone in the audience was cleared.

FOURTEEN

"To Be Free, We Must Also Be Secure"

P resident Obama's decision to nominate me to the CIA was the single most surprising appointment I received during my years in government, but his suggestion to move me over to the Department of Defense was a close second. The first hint I had of it came in late 2010 at the conclusion of one of the periodic meetings of our intelligence team. They generally occurred, as this one did, in Bob Gates's Pentagon office, and featured the chairman of the Joint Chiefs, the director of national intelligence, myself, and a few other representatives of the intelligence agencies. We sat at a large rectangular table in Gates's enormous office—Eisenhower used to point out that his Pentagon office was larger than his boyhood home—and shared our work, trying to avoid duplication between the Pentagon and the CIA and figuring out ways to extend the reach and sophistication of our agencies.

This time, Bob asked me to stay for a minute as we all got up to leave. Curious, I sat back down and waited. Once the others were gone, Bob returned to the table.

"Leon," he said, "I'm about ready to go, and I just want you to know that I'm going to recommend you to succeed me."*

I was unsurprised at the first part. Bob had already stayed beyond the year that he had promised Obama, and I knew he was ready to leave. The second half, however, floored me.

"Bob, at some point, I gotta go," I said. I'd promised Sylvia and the institute that I would not stay in Washington beyond four years, and I didn't think it was right for the president to name one secretary to replace Gates and then have to turn right around and name another two years later if he was reelected. I shared those reservations with Bob.

"I don't agree with that," Gates responded. "You are the one person around here who understands loyalty and support for the troops." My budget experience would also be valuable, he added, as the pressure for cuts was mounting.

It was my turn to disagree. "I'm sure there are others out there," I said. "And I'm not sure this is the right thing for me."

After leaving him that day, I told Sylvia and Jeremy, but then didn't think much more about it. I was plunged back into the details of the bin Laden planning, which picked up steam in early 2011. But the White House kept poking at the idea. Bill Daley, who succeeded Rahm Emanuel as chief of staff, insisted that I should take it and that no one else could do the job. That was ridiculous and I told him so, specifically suggesting that they call Colin Powell and interview him for the position. I did agree, however, that if they couldn't find anyone else suitable, I'd be willing to consider it.

That was the last I heard of it until I arrived for a meeting with Joe Biden in the early spring of 2011. I visited him at the White House, and we sat down for what I thought would be one of our regular catch-up sessions. Instead, he came at me regarding the Defense job. He insisted

---

*I did not know then, and only learned from Bob's memoirs, that he had also suggested Hillary Clinton, Colin Powell, and New York mayor Michael Bloomberg as possible successors.

I was right for it, that it would make the transition smoother to replace Gates with an existing member of the national security team, that it would represent the capstone of my career.

As we batted the idea back and forth, I asked who might replace me at CIA. Biden told me they were looking at David Petraeus. That gave me pause. I had worked well with David, but worried more than a bit about whether a four-star general—who was so used to entourages and perquisites and a strict chain of command—could bond effectively with the agency staff, who it seemed to me thrived in a more casual and freewheeling and less hierarchical environment. The agency's senior officers were sensitive to manipulation—they weren't spies for nothing—and if they sensed that Petraeus was there to advance his standing or agenda, not theirs, they'd have a tough time adjusting. I tried to raise my concerns gingerly.

"Are you sure you want to do that?" I asked. Biden did not answer. I suspect that the White House shared at least some of my apprehension about Petraeus; he and the president had danced around each other during the Afghan surge debate. But my guess is that Obama's advisers were taken with the idea of moving the general to the CIA in part for political reasons: Placing him atop the agency almost certainly would distract him, at least for a while, from the presidential ambitions he was believed to harbor. And of course, he was qualified and had the stature for the post.

As for me, I was convinced that the president would eventually find someone else to replace Gates, and I openly downplayed speculation that I would get the job. Mike Morell told me one day that he'd heard a rumor I was being considered. I acknowledged that I'd talked it over with the White House, but I insisted to him that I was staying. He seemed relieved. Meanwhile, Gates's chief of staff, Robert Rangel, made clear to Jeremy that Bob was pushing for me, undeterred by my ambivalence. A few days later, when press reports began to suggest that I was a candidate, I announced in our CIA morning staff meeting that

I did not expect to be offered the post, and intended to turn it down if I was.

For the moment, that settled it. I flew home for Easter weekend on Friday, April 22, staying in touch with the office regarding our surveillance of the compound in Abbottabad. McRaven's forces were setting up at the base in eastern Afghanistan, and all was proceeding according to the plan.

On Sunday, April 24, I was flying from Monterey to D.C. when the phone rang in the plane. That didn't happen very often. The communications specialist on board quickly grabbed it and handed it to me. It was the White House Situation Room, and the president was trying to hunt me down. We were on an open, unclassified line, so we didn't discuss the planning of the mission; instead, he turned straightaway to the Defense job. He told me what I already knew—that Bob was leaving and that he wanted me to consider the post. He didn't press me hard to say yes right away—that's not Obama's style—but he made clear that his expectation was that I would come around. I told him I thought there were others who could do the job, and that in any event I needed a day or two to talk to Sylvia and make a considered decision. Although technically I didn't accept anything, I hung up thinking that the president believed he had secured my agreement to join his cabinet as secretary of defense.

Back in the office on Monday, I pulled in Jeremy to seek his advice. He suggested that before I formally accepted, I should lay down some conditions, which I jotted down on a notecard. First, I should have the same access to the president that Gates had, including a weekly private meeting. Second, I should have the authority to pick my own team, including my own deputy secretary and chief of staff, and to make whatever military personnel changes I thought were necessary. Third, I needed to be involved in every decision about the military or the deployment of military forces. (This should have been unnecessary, but Bob had often complained about what he regarded as meddling from the White House, and I wanted to be sure not to replicate those frictions.) Finally, and perhaps most important because of the long separations, I needed to be able to go home on a regular basis. That had been my practice during most of my time in Washington—the only exception being my years as Clinton's chief of staff, when Sylvia joined me—though the reasons for it had changed a bit over time. When I was in Congress, I considered it important for my constituents that I be in regular contact with the district and its issues. In the executive branch, it was important for my sanity—it kept me grounded in real life and connected to my family. Without those trips, I could not have functioned effectively.

I took these conditions to Daley on Tuesday, and he didn't flinch. Instead, he launched the vetting process that same day. Not much had changed over the past two years, so examining my background this time was relatively routine. Jeremy organized my tax returns and some other basic information for the White House lawyers. I was brought down to the White House counsel for the ritual interview: Did I have any skeletons in my closet, old or new, that would embarrass the president? I said no, and that was that.

On April 27, just four days before the raid on Abbottabad, the White House leaked the news, and we assembled the next afternoon in the East Room for the presidential announcement. Joining Bob and me were: Petraeus, who would be leaving Afghanistan to run the CIA; General John Allen, who would replace Petraeus as commander in Afghanistan; and Ambassador Ryan Crocker, whom Hillary Clinton had convinced to come out of retirement and take over as our ambassador in Kabul. Clinton and Tom Donilon joined us onstage with the president and vice president.

The president was gracious as always, thanking Gates for his long service under eight presidents, and praising my patriotism, management skills, leadership, and knowledge of budgets—all of which, he noted, would be required in my new position.

Despite the success that came later that week in killing bin Laden, I knew better than to take my confirmation for granted, so I spent much of May and June meeting with senior people from the Department of Defense to better understand that enormous operation and with senators to field their questions about my qualifications and plans for the department.

Gates asked Robert Rangel to oversee transition briefings for me, and Robert directed that the Pentagon's legislative affairs chief, Liz King, guide my nomination through the Senate Armed Services Committee. Marcel Lettre, a former national security aide to Senate majority leader Harry Reid, was deputized by Rangel to organize my introduction to the department and handle all aspects of the transition. Marcel worked hand in glove with Jeremy, as well as with Gates's senior military assistant, Lieutenant General John Kelly.

John would prove an especially valuable friend and assistant during my Pentagon years, as he more than anyone helped guide me through the intricacies of military leadership and command. A marine's marine, affable and bluff, John understood how the Pentagon worked. More important, he grasped the true nature of service and sacrifice: He was the seniormost general officer to have lost a child in the wars since 9/11. His son, Robert Michael Kelly, was a second lieutenant in the Marine Corps, and was leading a patrol of forty marines and a navy corpsman in Afghanistan in November 2010 when he was killed by a roadside bomb. His family was of course devastated by their loss, but John stayed with his duties and helped Bob Gates and then me throughout my tenure at Defense.

First things first, I had to decide where to live. Gates had occupied a large home on Navy Hill, near the Department of State, and all of the four-stars lived in palatial houses at Fort Meyer, the Marine Barracks, or the Navy Yard. Bob urged me to take over his place, which he had set up so that the department wouldn't have to incur the expense every few years of installing secure communications and security in the new secretary's house. But while the homes were smart and economical for the uniformed leadership, which received a housing subsidy, that didn't apply to the civilian secretary, so I'd be stuck with paying full market rate. I didn't need a four-bedroom house, so after mulling it over briefly, I elected to stay put in my Capitol Hill walk-up.

We held the initial briefings at my office at CIA. First up were Undersecretary for Policy Michèle Flournoy and Director for Operations of the Joint Staff Lieutenant General Bob Neller, who briefed me on where our forces were deployed, the current operations in Iraq and Afghanistan, and some of the key policy issues, including NATO, missile defense, our force posture in Germany, Japan, and South Korea, and our major war plans. Flournoy's role was at the core of the Pentagon's mission, working with the White House and foreign leaders to ensure that our military power was being deployed in support of our foreign policy objectives. She helped me supervise the deployment and assignments of our troops around the world. Those briefings were my first look into the enormity of my new job. Flournoy and her deputy, Jim Miller, who would later succeed Michèle as undersecretary for policy, were two of the most critical advisers I had during my time as secretary.

Next came Ash Carter, the Pentagon's top weapons buyer and acquisition guru—someone I wanted to consider to be my new deputy. Ash had been a protégé of former secretary Bill Perry, whom I always admired, and Ash had made strong gains over the past two years—helping Bob Gates rapidly field mine-resistant vehicles in Afghanistan and Iraq and smashing some old bureaucratic totems. That's no small feat, for one early lesson of those briefings was that the Department of Defense not only operates around the world, it also spends money like crazy. One example: At the height of the Afghanistan war, the department was spending $2 billion *a day*.

Mike Vickers, the highly capable undersecretary for intelligence, was someone who had been integrally involved in the Abbottabad planning, so I knew him well when he came to update me on defense intelligence issues. Mike was a former Green Beret and CIA officer who had overseen covert actions in Afghanistan; his previous job at the Pentagon had been to oversee special operations and counterterrorism, and he brought me up to speed on the areas of the world where the Pentagon was playing the lead role in the fight against Al Qaeda and other terrorist organizations. I immediately asked him to stay on, and he agreed.

I did not know Jeh Johnson, the department's general counsel, but he also impressed me from our first conversation. He walked me through a range of issues, including the legal basis for using military force, the chain of command, and the major legal questions the department was facing. Chief among those were the pending repeal of "Don't Ask, Don't Tell," and the military trials being planned for the Al Qaeda leaders held at Guantánamo.

On the military side, I spent considerable time with Mike Mullen, the chairman of the Joint Chiefs, with whom I had worked closely the previous two years. I admired him immensely, and had been especially impressed with his management of the U.S.-Pakistan relationship in the aftermath of the bin Laden raid. Our conversations focused on the pace of the drawdown in Afghanistan—which the president was about to sign off on—but more generally about how to take care of the troops in an era of declining budgets and changing priorities. Like any good chairman, Mike kept his finger on the pulse of the rank and file, regularly consulting with the senior enlisted advisers from the various military departments.

Gates, meanwhile, took one big issue off my hands by concluding a critical piece of business before he left: pushing for the nomination of General Martin Dempsey to succeed Mullen, and for Admiral James "Sandy" Winnefeld to succeed the vice chairman, Hoss Cartwright. Though Hoss had many friends at the White House, he and Mullen did not work well together—barely speaking even—and Gates rightly worried about whether Hoss would be a team player if he became chairman. I liked Hoss, but I trusted Bob's instincts, as did the president. He elevated Dempsey and Winnefeld, effectively ending Hoss's distinguished career.

When Marty and I met, I already felt a kinship. Marty was as New Jersey Irish as I was California Italian, and we shared a common religious faith as well as immigrant pride in our country. He carried no party affiliation, only a lifetime devotion to the army and the United States. He had led troops in the fight in Iraq, but utterly lacked bravado—referring to himself occasionally as a "poet"—and believed that military force was not to be used casually. I trusted his uncanny ability to size up situations that called for military force and relied on his guidance. He became a trusted partner in addressing defense questions at the National Security Council.

Those briefings left me with a profound sense of the range and depth of the responsibilities that awaited me—assuming, of course, that I was confirmed by the Senate.

Even as my nomination was pending, Bob Gates was grappling with the White House and OMB on how to fulfill the president's promise to cut $400 billion from defense over the next decade, a concession to growing pressure from the Republican right, especially the Tea Party, to find reductions throughout the federal budget. I was okay with a large cut, and so was Bob. What we worried about was the pace and nature of the reductions and their impact on the readiness of the force. If we were to absorb such large cuts without damaging our military readiness, DoD needed flexibility about where and when to make them—neither of which would be the case under sequestration.

In order to manage those cuts responsibly, Gates had launched a "strategic review" of the department's missions and capabilities in order to determine what types of activities the department would have to keep doing and what we could scrap. Gates and his team—he called his closest civilian and military advisers the "small group"—walked me through some initial thoughts about where to get savings, which included such difficult areas as military pay and benefits, never an easy sell on the Hill. Still, it was doable, I thought, if we could control the pace and type of cuts. In my view, the way to do that was to get ahead of the debate, offering our own proposals and not letting Congress assert itself early.

After one of my sessions with Gates and the budget team, I walked down the outer hall of the Pentagon to a secure conference room. Joined by Kelly and a few others, I met Sandy Winnefeld for the first time; he was then serving as commander of U.S. Northern Command, making him the military officer responsible for the defense of North America. A gifted presenter, Winnefeld had a knack—unusual in high government and military circles—for speaking in English and making complex matters simple. Good thing, because he was charged with briefing me on my so-called crisis authorities. As secretary of defense, I had specific responsibilities under certain crisis conditions. What to do if a terrorist hijacked a plane and flew it toward the Capitol, or a ballistic missile was shot from North Korea, or, heaven forbid, a nuclear-armed enemy launched a full-scale attack on the United States?

In the least likely but most consequential scenario—nuclear war— there was a decades-old protocol with well-established lines of authority. Down deep inside the National Military Command Center, under the Pentagon, the watch team ran through a nuclear drill three times a day, at the turn of every eight-hour shift. My role as secretary was not to launch a nuclear weapon—only the president can authorize that— but rather to join a secure conference call of the president's senior advisers during a crisis, receive advice about attack options from the military leaders, and provide the president with my personal views. From the day I was sworn in, I would never be far from a proverbial "football"—in my case, essentially a notebook of various nuclear attack options. The air force assigned me a "strike adviser," a colonel whose sole job was to stand by and be prepared to walk me through the book in the event of a catastrophe. The multitude of options was dizzying, but I took comfort in knowing that the likelihood that I would have to recommend a nuclear strike was infinitesimally small.

A more likely but still exacting challenge involved how to respond if an enemy such as North Korea launched a ballistic missile or two at the United States. It would be up to me to decide whether—and how—to shoot it down. By the time the watch officers at North American Aerospace Defense Command (better known as NORAD) at Peterson Air Force Base in Colorado got me on the phone, I might only have seconds to decide. Russia, China, and North Korea were all potential attackers in these scenarios, but North Korea was by far the most worrisome: Under reckless leadership, that country had repeatedly tested its TaePoDong II missile, and now reportedly had a mobile missile launcher that could fire a weapon at the United States with little to no warning. The North Koreans had not yet mated a nuclear warhead to the ICBMs they were developing—as far as we knew—but the prospect of an intercontinental missile streaking toward an American city and exploding its warhead, even a conventional warhead, was awful to contemplate. In one sense, the decision to shoot down an enemy missile is simple: If anyone fired a ballistic missile at the United States, we would of course attempt to defend ourselves. The problem arises with the fact that the decision would have to be made so quickly. If the object hurtling through space turned out to be not a missile but rather, say, a just-launched satellite, we would have committed an act of aggression against a hostile and unpredictable foe. For that reason, our 28,500 troops on the Korean Peninsula kept a watchful eye on North Korea's missile launch program, and also for that reason, I listened carefully to Winnefeld's description of our system and my place within it.

Closer to home, the department was responsible for a program to keep civilian aircraft out of restricted zones—around Washington and wherever the president traveled. We dubbed this program Operation Noble Eagle, or ONE. This operation bothered me no end, and overseeing it was one of my most unhappy jobs. Every week or so we'd get a report of a small plane violating flight restrictions in the National Capital Region. The watch center would call my office on a secure line to make sure they knew where I was in case I needed to make a decision about the fate of the plane. Sometimes we would scramble fighter jets to fly alongside the plane, tip wings, shoot flares, or in some cases "head bump" the offending pilot by flying right up next to him—anything to get his attention and alert him that if he failed to turn around, he would be shot out of the sky.

These mishaps occurred so frequently that I was petrified we would eventually shoot down some clueless amateur pilot out for an afternoon in his Cessna. Our fighter jets were too fast for these small planes, and our system for warning pilots about airspace closures was no more sophisticated than a dog-eared "Notice to Airmen" pinned up over the coffee machine at private airports every few days. One of my first acts was to direct General Kelly and Paul Stockton, who ran homeland security affairs for me, to come up with recommendations for a better system. As a result, we did make some improvements, working with trade journals and pilot organizations to better inform pilots about the closure rules.

The close calls continued, however, with one particularly dicey situation arising during the presidential campaign. Because the airspace near the president is always closed, it's hardest to control it when he's moving around, as is the case during a campaign. One day while Obama was out west, a pilot innocently strayed into the airspace and somehow missed attempt after attempt to turn him around. The call was placed to my office for me to authorize shooting him down, but just as my aides prepared to interrupt my meeting so that I could give the fatal order, he got the message. I've long wondered whether he realizes that he came within seconds of our shooting down his plane.

During my courtesy calls on Capitol Hill, the senators weren't much trouble, though a few did press me on the budget cuts that the Pentagon would be absorbing, and some used our conversations to lobby for their ideas or issues. Jon Kyl of Arizona, for instance, pulled out some old comments I'd made expressing skepticism about missile defense; I assured him I would do everything I could to pursue those programs.

On June 9, I made the now-familiar trip up Capitol Hill to face members of the Senate. The questioning focused mostly on Afghanistan. The surge had ended and the total number of American forces was scheduled to begin decreasing the following month. John McCain and I tussled a bit as he tried to debate me over the difference between "significant" reductions, as the president had promised, and "modest" reductions, as outgoing secretary Gates preferred. I wouldn't give him the answer he wanted, so we went back and forth before he eventually moved on.

The matter came to the full Senate on June 21, and the discussion there was, as the *New York Times* described it, more of a "celebration" of my career and bin Laden's death—that operation's success clearly put a shine on my nomination—than a hard-hitting challenge to my credentials or plans. South Carolina Republican Lindsey Graham, who could be rough on the Obama administration, went so far as to call my selection a "home-run choice."[1] New York Democrat Chuck Schumer, one of my housemates during my time in Congress, joined Graham to "add my accolades," and Graham remarked that it wasn't every day that the two of them voted together: "Graham and Schumer," he joked. "That shows you the depth and breadth of Leon Panetta—the way people view him here."[2] McCain, after venting at me for a bit, came around too. The final vote was 100–0. I was at the CIA when the roll was called, and Jeremy brought me the news of the tally. "You gotta be kidding," I said. Republican senator Mitch McConnell, the minority leader, kindly thought to save the original roll sheet and had it delivered to me. It's one of my proudest possessions.

Moving from the CIA to the Pentagon was just a few miles—both sit on the Virginia bank of the Potomac River, looking back across it toward Washington—but the scale of the two operations was incomparable. It was, I said at the time, like moving from the local hardware store to Home Depot.

The U.S. Department of Defense in 2011 employed more than 2 million servicemen and -women and another 800,000 civilians. It included an additional 1.1 million men and women in the National Guard and Reserves. Yet another 2 million retirees received benefits through the Department of Veterans Affairs. The Department of Defense is the largest employer in the United States, and it owns more real estate than any organization on earth. It maintains hundreds of bases around the globe, and employs thousands of people to staff them.

Like any large employer, it must confront the myriad problems of its workers. The men and women of the armed services have families, kids in school, doctors' appointments, and day care; they get into accidents and fall ill; they get married and divorced; they're involved in lawsuits; and they need time off. The tasks of managing such an immense organization are thus monumental.

At the CIA, I oversaw thousands of employees (the exact number is classified) and a major, international organization, but it was dwarfed by the size and range of the military. At the Pentagon, roughly 23,000 people worked in the main building alone. From the first day, my greatest fear was that the size of the Defense Department would overwhelm me, that I would never be able to truly take command of it. Many a secretary of defense has been swallowed up by the job, and I was determined to fight against that pull. It was a concern that dogged me throughout my tenure at the department.

Moreover, the Department of Defense is unlike most employers in one respect: Its workforce fights wars. A total of 4,476 American servicemen and -women, as well as 13 civilian employees of the Defense Department, died in the Iraq war; as of late 2013, another 2,299 soldiers and 3 civilian Defense employees had died in Afghanistan. More than 50,000 were wounded in those conflicts.[3]

The military services are intended to operate in unison (thus the "Joint Chiefs"), but they also are distinct organizations, with their own histories, specialties, and priorities. I learned those distinctions in my meetings with the service chiefs, as I asked each of them for their assessment of their services and their needs, especially in light of cuts we knew were coming. The air force was focused on modernizing its fighter fleet and developing a Joint Strike Fighter that was long delayed and horribly over budget; Gates had essentially canceled another high-end fighter, and the air force wanted assurances that I'd keep this program alive. The navy's primary concern was that we protect shipbuilding and the shipyards that support it; if we cut back too far, Navy Secretary Ray Mabus warned me, the yards would close and we'd lose the infrastructure necessary to keep our navy afloat—an infrastructure far too big and complex to start up in wartime. The Marine Corps, meanwhile, had borne heavy burdens in the Afghanistan war—the Marines were given lead responsibility for Helmand Province, among other things—and General Jim Amos emphasized the personnel and equipment needs of his force. In addition, he was intent on returning the Marines to their amphibious roots, arguing for a "middle-weight maritime force," using aircraft such as the V-22 Osprey and the Marine version of the Joint Strike Fighter, both of which he argued were integral to that mission.

Of all of them, however, it was the army's presentation that was the most striking. When we sat down, I asked Army Secretary John McHugh for his thoughts on where the army was today. I'll never forget the first words out of his mouth. "Mr. Secretary," he said, "the army is tired." The army, he explained, had lost more soldiers than any other service during the Iraq and Afghanistan wars, and it was showing the strain. Yes, the army needed state-of-the-art equipment, but more important, its soldiers also needed health care and mental health services. The main weapon of the army was the soldier, and those soldiers were worn out. Implicit in McHugh's analysis was another warning: If we tried to balance the budget by making excessively deep cuts to the army's ranks, we'd make those problems worse, as already tired soldiers would be forced to make more tours and would take on even more strain.

I arrived at my new post on July 1, unloading my personal things into my office, with its sweeping views of the Potomac and the monuments on the other side. In one corner I set up a few reminders of the bin Laden operation, highlighted by the brick our team had presented to me. A large piece of granite taken from the Pentagon after 9/11 occupied a prominent place in my office as well, giving special poignancy to the bin Laden items. I put a Remington statue of a cowboy on horseback in one window—Remingtons have always appealed to my sense of the West and of an American spirit—and a bust of Lincoln in another. And yes, I put up the requisite mementos of a life in government—photographs of me and various presidents, Democrats and Republicans, and other dignitaries and leaders. No Washington office is complete without them. To remind me of home, I brought over some family pictures and a prized photograph of the Pacific Ocean.

Finally, there were two portraits behind Bob Gates's desk when he had the job, and I left them: One was of Eisenhower and the other of General George Marshall. I've already described my long-standing admiration of Eisenhower, and I regarded Marshall as the model public servant. I was pleased to have the two of them looking over my shoulder.

Jeh Johnson, general counsel of the department (and later the secretary of homeland security), administered me the oath of office at 8:45 a.m. on Friday, July 1. I then received my daily intelligence brief—similar to that which I had been receiving as CIA director—and plunged directly into my first meeting with my senior team. Fortunately for me, Bob Gates had built an exceptionally capable team of military and administrative staff, and I supplemented it with a few people of my own. Jeremy was sworn in as the department's chief of staff. Marcel Lettre became his deputy. We promoted a talented policy assistant, Bailey Hand, to coordinate all of my briefing materials and prepare me for meetings with the president and national security policy makers. General Kelly ran the office with two military assistants—for the bulk of my tenure, air force colonel Jeff Taliaferro and navy commander Larry Getz. Delonnie Henry, who had served under Don Rumsfeld and Gates, stayed on to run my schedule. Shelly Stoneman, who had joined the Pentagon under Gates, oversaw the personnel process and was a link to the White House.

In discussions with Tom Donilon and Denis McDonough at the White House, we settled on Ash Carter, my first choice, to succeed Bill Lynn as my deputy secretary. Bill was a good man but hadn't clicked with Gates, and I wanted a fresh start in that important post. Carter was a veteran of the department who had worked for and advised many secretaries, and was the rare leader who understood both the policy and budget sides of the agency. He was a wonk, a nuclear physicist and author, but he's also a compassionate commander who would slip out on weekends to visit wounded soldiers at Bethesda and Walter Reed.

Bill Danvers, who'd been with me back in the Clinton years, came over with me from CIA to help on special projects, and eventually I brought George Little over from the agency to take over the department's sprawling public affairs apparatus. George would travel with me all over the world and would become one of my closest advisers.

On that first morning, I gathered together the senior civilian and military leaders—service secretaries, undersecretaries, and chiefs, about twenty people in all. We introduced ourselves, and I laid out for them what seemed to me to be the broad parameters of our mission. Drawing from my recent briefings, I identified nine important priorities: achieving the strategic defeat of Al Qaeda; prevailing in Iraq and Afghanistan; preventing Iran and North Korea from building nuclear weapons capabilities; effectively responding to cyber attacks; continuing to protect American power and values; maintaining our nuclear arsenal; strengthening and reforming security cooperation with our allies; protecting our troops and their families; and making smart decisions about our budget. A full plate. There was broad agreement that those were the right challenges. Before concluding, I added a bit about me: I warned my new colleagues that I'd spent forty years in public life and over that time had developed a pretty sharp bullshit detector. I wanted to know of problems before they showed up in the news, and I valued frankness and directness. I didn't want to be misled. There were nods around the table, and I felt I'd made my point.

I followed up that meeting with a note to all the department's personnel so that they too would have some sense of where I hoped to take the organization—as well as an appreciation of my commitment to our work. "As Secretary of Defense, I will do whatever is necessary to protect America and to meet the needs of the men and women who serve in harm's way and the families who support them," I wrote. "Even as the United States addresses fiscal challenges at home, there will be no hollow force on my watch." That phrase, "hollow force," was an important one to the military; officers who had lived through the Vietnam War remembered the gutting of budgets that went on in those years to keep troop levels high and expenses down. Units often had inadequate weaponry and support, rendering them ineffective and at risk in battle. It took decades to recover from that period, and I hoped my words would at least assure my new colleagues that I understood that history and was determined to avoid repeating it.

I reminded the troops of my background in Congress, at OMB and the Clinton White House, and at the CIA, and noted that I had wrestled with tough budgets before. Finally, I concluded with a little reminder of my personal history and values, which seemed relevant as the country prepared to enjoy the Fourth of July weekend: "My parents, immigrants from Italy, came to the United States to seek a better life. They taught me that it was important to give something back to the country they adopted. I will never forget my father's words: 'To be free, we must also be secure.' As Americans come together to commemorate what we and those before us have accomplished, and as I take on my new role, my thoughts are with you and your families. You are making personal sacrifices to preserve our liberty, serving on front lines around the world. You are fighting to keep America safe. Rest assured that I will fight with you and for you."

As the message went out, so did copies of my picture. It is customary for defense installations to display a photograph of the commander in chief and the secretary of defense, so my portrait would now hang beside that of President Obama. On July 1, 2011, thousands of commanders around the world took down Bob Gates's picture and put up mine.

After lunch, I made my first visit to the Tank. It is on the Pentagon's first floor, and it's where the Joint Chiefs meet every week to discuss everything from troop deployments to service pay and benefits. I entered for the first time at 1:30 p.m. on my first day, and the first thing I noticed was a painting of Lincoln meeting with his generals during the Civil War. Called *The Peacemakers,* it seemed to capture the essence of the Joint Chiefs and their mission.

I knew a few of the men around the table. Mullen and I had worked closely on bin Laden and policy matters involving defense and intelligence. Hoss Cartwright, then still Mullen's deputy, was someone I also knew well from those same operations. Most of the others were less familiar, so I introduced myself and briefly expanded on the nine priorities I had shared that morning. I tried to strike a tone that was both appreciative and serious, stressing my great respect for each of them and also my insistence that they be candid with me. "I'm not going to pull any punches, and I expect you to do the same," I ended by saying. "If you're not honest with me, you're not going to be in your job for long."

They seemed to like the straight talk.

In retrospect, that first day was something of a portent of my tenure. It combined serious policy discussions (the challenges before us), ceremony (I visited the National 9/11 Pentagon Memorial), congressional interaction (I had a brief phone call with Carl Levin, chairman of the Senate Armed Services Committee), professional socializing (Sylvia, who was with me for the swearing in, joined me and Admiral Mullen and his wife, Deborah, for lunch), and an overarching preoccupation with moving the U.S. military out of war and into the future.

After wrapping up my first day on the new job, Sylvia and I headed home to celebrate the Fourth of July in Carmel Valley. Although I had warned the White House that I needed to return home frequently in order to stay connected with my family and keep my balance, I was not allowed to fly commercially, both for security reasons and because I needed to be reachable in an emergency. So whenever I traveled as defense secretary, I did so in a military plane.

Under a formula devised by the government long before me, I was required to reimburse the Treasury for my travel. Typically that meant writing a check for about $630 each time I traveled home and back, more if I had family or Bravo with me. That was about what I would have spent flying commercially, which I would have been happy to do if allowed to. I dutifully paid my bills.

The problem was that the military plane that carried me, usually a small air force business jet specially outfitted with secure communications equipment, cost $3,200 an hour to operate. That meant my travel was expensive for taxpayers, and after a year or so I'd paid $17,000 for my trips but the actual cost was about $860,000.[4] The press reported that in the spring of 2012, but I explained that I had been making this trip all my life and that I'd reimbursed the government all that I had been asked to pay. That seemed to satisfy everyone, and thank God it did. I'm not sure I could have been CIA director or secretary of defense without being able to go home at regular intervals.

Some of my early moves at Defense may seem minor, but they were intended to emphasize action over inertia and candor over jargon. I gave Ash Carter wide latitude to make change and encouraged him to trust his own instincts; he knew I would back him up. Together, we renamed the "Deputy's Advisory Working Group," recasting it as the "Deputy Management Action Group," in order to emphasize that we wanted action, not just advice. Carter proved to be a masterful deputy, managing such projects as the development of the defense budget and the drawdown in Afghanistan. I had complete confidence in him. As he liked to say: I worked on the bridge, while he manned the engine room.

Chief among the responsibilities I was assuming was the management of two wars, in Iraq and Afghanistan, and I wanted, for both substance and symbolism, to visit those countries as soon as possible. I did so at the end of my first week.

Traveling as secretary of defense was a whole different undertaking than it was as director of the CIA. As I wrote earlier, I traveled extensively during my CIA years, visiting every continent but Antarctica and developing important contacts and friendships. But those trips, by necessity, usually were done in secret. I flew on a specially outfitted airplane with communications gear, but I was accompanied by a small retinue of aides with me, and of course, no reporters. The emphasis was on convenience and maintaining a low profile.

The Department of Defense was another matter. The plane was an E-4B, a windowless, hardened 747, which could sustain the electromagnetic shock from a nuclear blast. It included not only communications equipment but also war-fighting gear. In an emergency, I could advise the president on the launch of a nuclear strike from the cabin of my plane. With proper aerial refueling, this "Doomsday Plane" could stay aloft for days. My cabin had a desk, a couch, an array of phones, a bathroom, and bunk beds. I must admit, my favorite piece of gear was one of the plane's least grand accoutrements: a small DVD player on which I watched movies between meetings and phone calls. The staff knew to pack my bag with classics—Humphrey Bogart and Ingrid Bergman accompanied me on many a mission to far corners of the world.

Once on board, I'd meet with the travel and policy team to review the agenda for the trip and prepare for my meetings with foreign counterparts. We'd review points I needed to make, and try to crystallize pages of briefing books about, say, Afghanistan, onto a four-by-six card that I could use to jot down the key messages for President Karzai.

I usually held a press conference with the reporters on the plane to preview the themes of the trip and to take questions on the issues of the day. Then I'd allow myself a glass of scotch with John Kelly, Jeremy, and the team; we'd eat well, and hit the hay for a few hours before landing.

Traveling with reporters was an important aspect of my new job and a good way to signal our priorities. At the same time, it had its downsides. Even casual comments found their way into news stories, and I learned quickly that I needed to watch my mouth. As I've made clear, my language runs to the salty end of the spectrum, and I was hardly alone in that in the councils of government. On that first trip, however, I was reminded that it did tend to stand out in other venues.

I joked with our troops at Camp Victory, Iraq, that the country where they were stationed would bounce back, in part because "this damn country has a hell of a lot of resources." I also vented about the uncertainty that Iraqi officials were expressing with regard to the presence of U.S. troops after 2011. Prime Minister Nuri Maliki was dragging his feet, and my message to the Iraqis was, "Dammit, make a decision." That quote made the cover of *Stars and Stripes*. In Afghanistan, I misstated our position on how fast we'd be bringing troops home, and I said what everyone in Washington knew but we couldn't officially acknowledge: that our goal in Libya was regime change. None of that did much damage, but it was distracting. Elisabeth Bumiller, a reporter for the *New York Times,* accompanied me on that trip, and put together a lighthearted look back at my foibles, concluding that I was "another species entirely" from my more taciturn predecessor.[5] Guilty. As I told the press, I'm Italian, and that's who I am. George Little had his hands full cleaning up after me, but I wanted to be candid with our troops (many of my quoted remarks came from meetings with soldiers), and on balance I think my ease with reporters and others was helpful in making relationships.

While in Kabul, I stayed at "Bader House," the Distinguished Visitor Quarters at Camp Eggers—military accommodations about as nice as any in Afghanistan; at least there were carpets and air-conditioning— and held three important meetings. The first was with Petraeus, who updated me on the progress in training Afghan army and police forces. Our goal was to train 352,000 of those forces, and Petraeus told me we were ahead of schedule, but he emphasized the challenge involved. For many of these young soldiers, we weren't training them on sophisticated weapons or tactics. We were starting at the very beginning. As Petraeus described it, we'd hand them a map and begin to discuss ways of capturing and holding terrain, and the first question would be: What's a map? Many young recruits were illiterate, so our job began with teaching them to read, moved to teaching them to use maps and fire weapons, and only then on to fighting battles and wars. Basic training was truly basic.

Some of those same issues came up in my conversation with my Afghan counterpart, Abdul Rahim Wardak, a veteran of the mujahideen fight against the Soviets. Wardak was a fascinating combination of grizzled and polished: He spoke with a faint British accent and had gentle mannerisms, but he was tough and seasoned. He survived an assassination attempt in 2005 and pressed on. He encouraged the United States to remain in partnership with Afghanistan, for the sake of his country. He emphasized that the training needed to continue and that the United States needed to resist the temptation to leave.

Those temptations were real, as were the hardships faced by our servicemen and -women. On that first trip, I visited Camp Dwyer in the Helmand River Valley to observe our troops training Afghan forces. The heat was blistering—we had a thermometer that topped out at 120 degrees, and the needle pegged that. Still, our troops stood at attention and greeted me graciously even as they melted in the heat.

Finally, I met with Hamid Karzai himself, this time over dinner at the presidential palace. As was our custom, we spoke privately before sitting down for dinner, and he complained to me that he did not feel he was trusted by President Obama or other senior officials in Washington. He was particularly frustrated by the American embassy and Ambassador Karl Eikenberry, who he said ignored him. That relationship, according to Karzai, had simply collapsed. I'd heard some of that during my time at the CIA, so I wasn't entirely taken by surprise. Responding, I suggested that Karzai could reach out directly to me. In the early days after 9/11, the CIA had helped Karzai regain control of Kabul, and legend held that a CIA officer had saved his life. That gave Karzai a comfort level with the CIA, and when I offered to serve as a channel for him going forward, he seemed eager to have someone he could turn to.

When we moved to dinner, I nevertheless braced myself for him to tongue-lash me—he often held forth for public consumption—but he was gracious, though he would occasionally lead the conversation in strange directions. He reflected at considerable length on his knowledge of the American family, which he attributed to a visit he made to New Hampshire years earlier during which he briefly lived with a host family. Then, toward the end of the evening, he bluntly asked me, "What is the secret of the success of the American military?" I was at first taken aback, unsure how to answer. But then I suggested that perhaps it began with George Washington, who resigned his commission upon entering politics. That moment, I suggested, established the precedent of civilian control of the military, and it demonstrated that effective leaders need not control every aspect of their societies.

I flew on to Iraq, where the focus was now on our drawdown there—how many troops should remain as we finished up our work. General Lloyd Austin, our commander in Iraq, argued for a residual force of more than ten thousand, and I generally agreed, feeling that we should not undermine the progress we'd made by simply walking away. Later, in a conversation with Maliki, I urged him to take the necessary legal steps to secure a Status of Forces Agreement that would make the maintenance of such a force possible. He was noncommittal, as he often was—hence my "Dammit, make a decision" comment.

All in all, it was a productive trip, but also a reminder of the difficulties our military was shouldering. We were still engaged in two countries that were ambivalent about our presence—on one hand, eager to see our troops leave; on the other, fearful of what might come after. Ending wars can be very difficult.

Nevertheless, I returned from Iraq and Afghanistan convinced that we had made strong progress in both places, and that we could leave those countries in better shape than we found them—if only we could consolidate our gains, strengthen the capabilities of their governments, and maintain a sizable force in both places to continue to train and advise the militaries. I knew that would be a tough sell in Iraq, which Obama had opposed from the start, but thought it might be easier in Afghanistan, where the president had shown a willingness to beef up before drawing down. I was half wrong. It was a tough sell for both places, and the trouble in Afghanistan began within weeks.

On August 6, a Friday evening, I had just landed in Monterey for a weekend visit at home when John Kelly called. A Chinook helicopter had been shot down on approach to a landing zone where our forces were conducting a counterterrorism raid in Wardak Province in the eastern part of Afghanistan. The helicopter was struck by a rocket-propelled grenade, which had not been designed as an antiaircraft weapon. That was hardly consolation. Thirty American service members and eight Afghan soldiers were dead. It was the largest single loss of life of the entire Afghanistan war.

Twenty-five of those who died were members of our special operations forces, including twenty-two Navy SEALs, many from the same unit that had taken down bin Laden.[6] As I hung up the phone, I realized that families across the United States were about to receive word that they had dreaded more than anything. At that moment, they still believed everything was fine; within hours, they would know otherwise. John and Jeremy kept me apprised of events through the night as the recovery mission continued and eventually concluded.

I flew to Tampa the following day to attend a change-of-command ceremony at our Special Operations Command, whose forces had borne the brunt of the casualties in that attack. Admiral Bill McRaven, who had led the bin Laden operation, assumed command that day, as he well deserved, but the solemnity of the moment overtook any enthusiasm Bill had for earning his fourth star.

On Tuesday, I made my second trip to Dover Air Force Base. Twenty months earlier, it had been bitterly cold when the bodies of our

CIA officers killed in the Khost bombing came home. As cold as that day was, this August day was oppressively hot, and aides circulated among the grieving with bottled water and Gatorade. Soon after I arrived, the president landed, and I met him as he strode down onto the tarmac. We first made our way into a lounge area where the families of the deceased were gathered, some three hundred people from every corner and walk of life in the United States. There were mothers in walkers, babies in strollers, wives and girlfriends with heads in hands, fathers with hollow eyes, sons fighting back tears. They were strewn across couches, pacing aimlessly, sitting on tables or lying on the floor.

Quietly and with great dignity, the president circulated through the grieving Americans. They stood as he approached, and he made time for every family, hugging, patting people on the shoulder, speaking softly to each parent, each child, and letting them tell him about their loved ones. President Obama's critics sometimes suggest that he does not connect with people, that he is aloof or standoffish. I wish all Americans could have seen him that day. He was sincere, strong, and genuine. The grieving families turned to him, and he reassured them that their loved ones had died for a purpose, in defense of their country and their families. Nothing could restore the lives of those servicemen, but President Obama that day helped heal the wounds of their absence.

At the ceremony inside a giant hangar, the president, the service secretaries, and I stood at attention for nearly two hours while the flag-draped transfer cases were taken from aircraft into waiting hearses. The families waited quietly in the wilting heat, the silence interrupted only by soft sobbing. Those parents and children, brothers, sisters, and loved ones were strong and determined even in the face of such loss. Every member of Congress who ever complained that he couldn't take a stand on an important issue because he feared the political consequences at home should meet these families. One conversation with a grieving family beside a flag-draped casket would put that fear in perspective.

Each week on Thursday afternoon, about a dozen senior military officers would file into my conference room at the Pentagon. The chairman and I took our places on one side of the table, facing our briefers from the Joint Staff. The briefers then would open each session by sliding a notebook across the table. It was classified "Top Secret" and was full of "deployment orders" awaiting my signature. Every time a unit—no matter how small—was sent anywhere in the world, it required an order, and all major orders (and many minor ones) required the approval of the department's top official, in this case me. Some of the deployment orders were straightforward; most required some discussion about the rationale and risk. We would talk for a few minutes and I'd ask questions, especially if there were disagreements about the need for a transfer or movement. And then I would decide with a signature on each order.

From July 2011 to February 2013, I reviewed and approved the orders that deployed our forces in such a way as to provide, to the best of my ability, the most effective protection for our country. Every one of those orders was based on a judgment of how best to defend our country, and many of them put men and women at risk. After I returned from Dover, I never looked at a deployment order book the same way again.

FIFTEEN

"A New Defense Strategy for the Twenty-first Century"

T he men and women of the Pentagon began their working day on the morning of September 11, 2001, like many other Americans. They parked their cars or emerged from the subway, passed through security, and made their way to their offices. By 9 a.m., thousands were at work, attending meetings or pouring a cup of coffee or moving through the layered corridors of the storied building. They were doing their best, as they do every day, to defend the United States, to protect a people and a way of life. Unbeknownst to them, American Airlines Flight 77, bound from Dulles Airport to Los Angeles, had changed course in the air over Kentucky and was hurtling back toward Washington, inexplicably refusing to acknowledge attempts to reach it over the radio. The plane carried more than ten thousand gallons of fuel and, more precious, fifty-eight passengers and six crew members.

At 9:37 a.m., it struck the west side of the Pentagon, smashing through the outer ring, known as the E Ring, and into the D and C Rings. Confused employees at first did not know what had happened, but the deafening noise, erupting flame, and powerful smell of jet fuel soon erased all doubt. One hundred and twenty-five Pentagon employees died that morning, along with every person on board Flight 77. For the Pentagon, 9/11 was personal.

Every anniversary of the event brought a new wave of reflection, and the tenth such commemoration fell soon after I became secretary of defense. President George W. Bush and Laura Bush joined me in laying a wreath at the spot where the plane crashed. Afterward, the Bushes and I retired to my office for coffee. President Bush spotted a photograph of me with his mother and father and thanked me for displaying it. We'd had our differences, and I'd worked for the man who beat his father in 1992, but there was never rancor between me and the Bush family, and on that day we wondered at the extraordinary events of the past decade. He was affable as always, and unusually reflective. Bush had devoted his life and presidency to defending the country after 9/11, and I appreciated his support for the work of the CIA and the Pentagon.

Later, I spoke to Pentagon employees, along with members of the families of the victims and firefighters who pulled wounded workers from the burning building. A light rain was falling, adding to the somber mood as those assembled reflected on that day ten years earlier, a day that, as I said during the ceremony, transformed "this building . . . into a battlefield." I asked those present to join me in a pledge to "keep in our hearts the sacrifices of those who gave their lives for this country on 9/11 and during a decade of war." I'm confident that the men and women who stood before me in the rain that morning did just that.

That evening, as I was preparing to leave my office to attend a memorial service at the Kennedy Center, my assistant rushed in to tell me that Ehud Barak was on the phone from Israel, and it was urgent. I knew Ehud well enough to know that he did not sound the alarm lightly.

"What's going on, Ehud?" I asked.

"There is a problem in Cairo," he said, his voice discernibly anxious. "A mob of Egyptians has surrounded our embassy, they've attacked it, broken through the walls, and are making their way up into the building. We got most of our people out of there, but there are still six Israelis locked behind the last door. We have to get them out."

It took me a moment to process what he was telling me. I had forgotten that Israel maintained a small, heavily secured embassy in Cairo; it was one of the more tangible symbols of the Israel-Egypt peace accord that the United States had helped broker under President Carter. Ehud's plea reminded me of that, but I still wasn't sure what I could offer. "What do you want me to do?" I asked.

"I need you to call Tantawi and tell him to get his security forces to the scene and to let our people go," he answered sharply. Field Marshal Mohammed Hussein Tantawi was a career officer in the Egyptian army, the head of the Supreme Council of the Armed Forces (SCAF), which took over rule after the fall of Mubarak. He was the ruler of Egypt in every sense—at least until an election could be held—but because he was the military chief, he was considered my counterpart. I might not be able to turn away a mob in Cairo, but Tantawi could.

The stakes were even higher than the fate of the Israeli embassy employees. Tripoli had fallen the previous month. Tensions were rising in Syria. The king of Jordan, my friend Abdullah, was on shaky political ground. Our partners in the Gulf—Saudi Arabia, the United Arab Emirates, Bahrain, and others—were nervous about our plans to cut defense spending and impatient for us to confront Iran more forcefully, an anxiety felt in the Gulf even as acutely as in Israel. Amid those strains, a blowup between Israel and Egypt could have frightening ramifications for the entire Middle East.

We needed to act quickly. One important feature of the secretary's Pentagon apparatus is a large windowless room down the hall from my office. Dubbed "Cables," it is a personal watch center that allows the American secretary of defense to monitor global events and reach leaders almost anywhere. On most nights, the calls it placed were routine;

now it snapped into action to try to save lives. Cables, with our Middle East team packed inside, went to work to size up the situation in Cairo and to get Tantawi on the line, but the first response from his staff in Cairo was that he was "not available." No further information was provided. For the next hour, we kept dialing. Each time: "Not available."

Increasingly anxious—and more than a little angry—I wondered aloud why he would refuse to come to the phone.

"He's not going to talk to you until he has the situation under control," John Kelly suggested. "He is trying to get his arms around this. Let's keep calling, so he knows how urgent this is."

Bailey Hand, my policy aide, poked her head in the door of my office to inform me that the White House was now on the phone. Israeli prime minister Netanyahu had called President Obama with a similar request for help. Obama too had reached out to Tantawi, only to be put off. The president's staff made clear that the United States expected a call back immediately. We kept dialing to emphasize the point.

I was running late for the ceremony at the Kennedy Center, and I couldn't keep the crowd of a thousand family members waiting any longer. I jumped in my SUV and told John Kelly and Jeremy to get me on the phone as soon as he called back. At the center, I settled into my seat while my military assistant, Commander Larry Getz, took a place backstage with the mobile team from Cables.

Finally, the call came, and Larry pulled me out of my seat in the front row. Backstage, I grabbed the phone and wasted no time with pleasantries.

"Field Marshal, there is a crisis in the streets of your city," I said. "The Israeli embassy in Cairo is being attacked. There are six innocent people in there. I need your personal assurance that you will do everything you can to get them out alive." I had never spoken to the man, and here I was barking orders at him on behalf of America—not usually the way I like to do business, but I had no choice.

He was as calm as I was brusque. "Secretary Panetta," he began, as if he hadn't heard a word. "It is a great honor to speak to you. I look forward to welcoming you to Egypt. Our great country and your great country enjoy a very special relationship." My frustration mounted as he continued to pile on puffery and avoid the reason for our conversation. I needed assurances that the situation was under control, not an invitation to visit Cairo. Finally, he came to the point, telling me that his security forces were on the scene and that the Israelis would be rescued.

Later that evening, Egyptian security forces battered their way into the building, broke up the attack, arrested the attackers, and ferried the Israelis to safety. Once the crisis was resolved, I took up Tantawi on the invitation he offered that night, visiting him in Egypt. We worked closely together thereafter.

I n some respects, the military is a great American equalizer. It takes men and women from all parts of the country, from all ethnic and religious backgrounds and economic strata, and joins them in common purpose. In 2011, however, that fundamental egalitarianism had an exception: Under the tenuous doctrine of "Don't Ask, Don't Tell," gays and lesbians were allowed to serve in the armed forces, but only if they were willing to conceal their orientation.

That was a residue of the Clinton years, and a particularly unstable one. In those first, disorganized months of Clinton's tenure, one entirely self-inflicted controversy grew out of the new president's well-intentioned attempt to create a rational and fair approach to the treatment of gays in the armed forces. As a candidate, Clinton had promised to end the military's ban on gays within its ranks, a position I supported as a matter of simple fairness. But his timing and handling of the issue once he won the election left a lot to be desired.

From the start, Clinton was regarded with some suspicion by the military—the "draft dodger" label was hard to shake. And when he tried to turn his campaign promise into a change in military policy, his chiefs rebelled. Colin Powell, then the chairman of the Joint Chiefs, warned that it would be "prejudicial to good order and discipline," and other military leaders raised practical and even moral objections.[1] Congressional leaders echoed some of the same concerns, and the new president could hardly afford a showdown with the military so early in his administration, especially one that he was sure to lose on the Hill. The result was a wobbly compromise: Gays would no longer be hounded out of the military merely for being gay—or for going to a gay bar or living with a person of the same sex—but they could still be removed if they openly acknowledged their orientation. I wasn't part of the debate that produced "Don't Ask, Don't Tell"—I was still budget director at the time—and in one sense it did represent progress. It did for the first time allow gays to serve in the military, and it ended some of the witch-hunt efforts to ferret out the sexual habits of service members. Still, it rested on soldiers' concealing their identities, even lying about them. That's hardly a strong foundation for an organization that demands integrity from its employees. I thought even then that it was not destined to last.

To his credit, President Obama wanted to complete the work that Clinton began. In his State of the Union address at the beginning of 2010, he vowed to end "Don't Ask, Don't Tell," announcing that he would "work with Congress and our military to finally repeal the law that denies gay Americans the right to serve the country they love because of who they are. It's the right thing to do." Gates and I reacted differently to that pledge. Gates was conflicted, generally supporting the president's goal but also feeling blindsided by a policy position he'd only been notified of the day before. I had not been privy to those conversations, but my view was that the old law should be repealed and that gays should be allowed to serve openly.

As promised, the president did spend 2010 working out the details, and Gates supported the effort, though wanting to be sure that the

Joint Chiefs were fully consulted and on board. In order to assess the impact that integration would have on our forces, Gates asked Jeh Johnson and army general Carter Ham to cochair a study; they began their work in March 2010 and conducted a thorough and insightful analysis, interviewing hundreds of men and women in the service and retired from it, as well as hosting focus groups and soliciting opinions through a major survey of the force. Among their many findings was that 70 percent of those questioned believed ending the ban would have no effect, a mixed effect, or a positive effect on their unit's ability to "get the job done." About the same percentage indicated that they had worked at some point in their military career with someone they believed to be gay—a surprisingly high number, given that disclosing one's orientation in those days often led to dismissal. In the 1980s alone, the military estimated that it had spent roughly $500 million to expel seventeen thousand gay soldiers from the ranks.[2]

In addition, the report highlighted the military's experience with racial integration begun after World War II. No less than George Marshall, perhaps the most revered American military man of his day, had argued in 1941 against racial integration of the services, warning that "experiments within the Army in the solution of social problems are fraught with danger to efficiency, discipline, or morale."[3] Five years later, a survey of enlisted men found that more than 80 percent opposed integrated training, housing, or assignments.[4]

Despite those reservations, in 1948, President Truman issued an executive order mandating the end of racial segregation in the armed forces, at a time when southern schools, buses, and other public accommodations still were segregated by race. It did not happen quickly or without incident—a year after Truman's order, a majority of servicemen and -women still opposed integration, and compliance was spotty. And yet change did come: By 1953, some 95 percent of servicemen and -women served in integrated units.

The bottom line of the report:

We conclude that, while a repeal of Don't Ask, Don't Tell will likely, in the short term, bring about some limited and isolated disruption to unit cohesion and retention, we do not believe this disruption will be widespread or long-lasting, and can be adequately addressed by the recommendations we offer below. Longer term, with a continued and sustained commitment to core values of leadership, professionalism, and respect for all, we are convinced that the U.S. military can adjust and accommodate this change, just as it has others in history.

That report was finished and submitted in November 2010, and helped the proposal overcome resistance in Congress, particularly the Senate, which soon after passed legislation to end the ban. On December 22, 2010, the president signed the law that struck down this remnant of antigay bigotry, pending completion of training to prepare the services and certification that we were ready to go ahead. That certification was broken into three segments, the last of which was given to me just three weeks after I took over from Gates.

There were some lingering concerns. Despite the strong majority of service members who did not anticipate any problems with ending the ban, a significant minority, roughly 30 percent, did believe it would undermine cohesion or discipline. Those concerns were amplified by the fact that we were at war, so any negative impact of integration could have battlefield consequences. General Jim Amos, commandant of the Marine Corps, had publicly warned that allowing gays to serve openly could cause "disruption" in smaller units, and he remained wary of the idea almost to the end. But the Johnson-Ham report had impressed him as well as others. When I joined with the chiefs in late July in the conference room outside my office, I wanted to hear any specific concerns that any of them had; I did not want to sign off on the proposal and then have my subordinates publicly denounce it. Amos was my main worry.

He surprised me. "I've seen these briefings," he said that day. "I've read the report. I'm now convinced we can do this. We are prepared to implement repeal." The navy and air force were also on board; the army had concerns and reservations. But they all repeated the refrain, "We are prepared to implement repeal." I knew that this represented a dramatic change from the military in which these men were raised, and I knew that they were worried about whether the rank and file under their command would react negatively. But I was also proud of their workmanlike professionalism. The mission was repeal. They would carry out that mission without hesitation.

With that, we had consensus, and I certified that the military was ready to go ahead. In the Oval Office on July 22, with Mike Mullen and me on either side of him, President Obama signed the certification. Sixty days later, the ban ended.

Most of the hard work on this issue had been completed before my arrival, but I was gratified to play the small but important role of wrapping it up. I released a statement expressing appreciation for the work that so many had done to bring about this achievement. "Thanks to the professionalism and leadership of the U.S. military," I said, "we are closer to achieving the goal that is at the foundation of America—equality and dignity for all." Personally, it was especially gratifying to contribute to a historic civil rights milestone, having worked early in my career to enforce school desegregation. The story of American civil rights is one of the noblest in our country's long history. I'm very proud of the small part I played at those two junctures—and at one more before I wrapped up my service the following year.

There was one last piece of business to conclude once "Don't Ask, Don't Tell" was repealed. Having ended that doctrine, we were now faced with the difficult question of how to extend benefits to the partners of gay service members. Military spouses are eligible for all manner of benefits: access to commissaries, health care, educational opportunities, even burial in veterans' cemeteries. Gays and lesbians could now serve openly as members of the military, but those who were legally married to those service members had no spousal rights. And because the Defense of Marriage Act was still the law of the land, the federal government couldn't officially recognize marriage even in those states that allowed same-sex marriage.

The White House was putting enormous pressure on all departments and agencies to ensure that every person who stepped forward to serve his or her country, gay or straight, would have the same benefits for their loved ones. At the White House, Denis McDonough and White House counsel Kathy Ruemmler were strong champions of extending these benefits. I supported that goal wholeheartedly. But we struggled with the legal question of how to recognize a relationship between two people who weren't married under federal law. Having pushed the chiefs on "Don't Ask, Don't Tell," I was worried that they would revolt. After hours of consultations, I hammered out an agreement with the chiefs that would allow gay service members to sign affidavits that they were in a long-term, committed relationship, and to allow those partners the same benefits as other military spouses. The memorandum implementing those changes and extending those benefits was distributed over my signature just days before I concluded my time as secretary of defense.

Interestingly, for all the debate and worry over ending the ban on gays in the military, the actual implementation was strikingly without incident. Beginning with the formal abandonment of "Don't Ask, Don't Tell" on September 20, 2011, I received monthly reports from the field on the new dynamic and its effects—if any—on units around the world. There was virtually no protest or complaint. A major obstacle to equality fell almost silently.

During my tenure as secretary of defense, Washington and the world sometimes seemed to be moving in opposite directions, placing special tension on the Pentagon. On one hand, as the helicopter crash on August 6 powerfully underscored, we were fighting in Afghanistan and Iraq. And we were fighting fires breaking out across the Middle East—challenges for a military that had spent nearly a decade at war. All of that required staggering investment; the 2009 surge in Afghanistan alone, which we were now gradually tapering off, cost nearly $50 billion a year. Maintaining those forces without conceding other strategic areas to adversaries argued for steady, even increased defense spending, an argument Gates had made in support of the modest increases he sought.

But the politics of Washington pulled the other way. Democrats believed that the large troop deployments were no longer achieving important objectives—and often with very high costs—and wanted to bring troops home, sometimes without sufficient concern for what troubles we'd be leaving behind. And the Republicans were torn between establishment figures such as John McCain who remained committed to the national defense and the emergent members of the Tea Party who wanted to cut government down to a new size, irrespective of the vulnerabilities that such an action might create. In a town where the two parties agreed on almost nothing, they suddenly settled on the consensus that we could dramatically cut defense spending during wartime.

Compounding all that was the more than doubling of military spending in the Bush years, which made sustaining the current levels of funding hard to justify. Before 9/11, the United States spent about $287 billion a year on its military. By the time I became secretary of defense, that number had grown to more than $718 billion.* The growth in spending meant that the United States had spent more than an additional $2 trillion on defense over that decade, much of it to fight the

---

* The number includes spending for the wars in Iraq and Afghanistan; technically, those were budgeted separately from general defense spending, but that was largely an accounting fiction. The fact is that money spent to fight those wars was military spending no matter how it was labeled.

wars in Iraq and Afghanistan. By 2011, the United States spent more on its military than the next thirteen highest-spending nations—*combined*.[5]

At the same time, just slashing—in the form, say, of across-the-board cuts—was guaranteed to damage America's military readiness. As I had long learned, the problem with cutting programs across the board is that it makes everything less effective. It does not distinguish between programs that are valuable and should grow and programs that are underperforming or no longer relevant and should be shed.

One Saturday in July, I got an urgent call from Jack Lew, then the OMB director and soon to become White House chief of staff, tracking me down to alert me to a development in the talks between the White House and congressional leaders. The Republicans had manufactured a crisis around the routine matter of approving an increase in the nation's debt ceiling, which allows the government to pay lenders for money it has already borrowed and spent. Without budget concessions, Republicans were threatening to refuse to raise the limit, potentially forcing the U.S. government into default on loans it owed. That was playing with fire, but it had brought the White House reluctantly to the negotiating table on spending cuts. Under consideration, Jack told me, was a deal whereby the White House would agree to strict caps on discretionary spending for a decade in return for the support of Boehner and congressional Republicans on the debt ceiling vote. That seemed to me a lot to give in return for a ministerial vote, but I was okay with the caps in theory—the real question was how they would be set and applied.

Then came the kicker: The defense cut, Lew told me, would be about $500 billion (it turned out to be $487 billion) over ten years. The Pentagon forecasts budgets only five years out, so some of this was guesswork, but the bottom line was that we would have to take our plan for fiscal year 2012 and slash it by about $50 billion every year. That's $1 billion a week, or almost $200 million a day, every day, for ten years. I warned Jack that we could endure those cuts for a few years, but after a while the fat would be gone and we'd be gouging into muscle.

And that wasn't even the whole story. Jack continued, saying the deal also included creation of a special "Super Committee" of senators and congressmen charged with finding an additional trillion dollars in savings. They'd get a few months to hash it out, and if they didn't reach agreement, steep across-the-board cuts would go into effect automatically, slashing yet another $500 billion from defense over ten years. To me, that was stunning, a return to the goofy, meat-axe approach that harkened back to the Gramm-Rudman automatic spending cuts in the 1980s, when I'd fought against automatic cuts as chairman of the House Budget Committee. I sputtered a bit, but Jack told me it was the best deal the White House thought it could get. In August, the president signed the Budget Control Act. God help us, I thought, if this committee failed to do its job.

In the following days, I huddled with my team, including the Pentagon's comptroller, Bob Hale; my director of cost assessment and program evaluation, Christine Fox; Ash Carter; Michèle Flournoy; the Pentagon's acquisition chief, Frank Kendall; and the chairman of the Joint Chiefs, General Martin Dempsey. We agreed on a two-pronged strategy. First, we would pick up the Gates strategic review and focus it on how to achieve certain priorities within these Budget Control Act levels. Second, I would rail publicly against sequestration and try to use my position and whatever standing I enjoyed to push the so-called Super Committee to cut the deal rather than give in to automatic cuts. I thought I might get some attention from both sides of the aisle since Republicans as well as Democrats would be reluctant to have us cancel troop training, mothball ships and airplanes, or delay acquisitions—all of which could slice deeply into readiness, something no one professed to want.

There are many reasons why defense spending increases over

time, and most relate to the size of the department. Pay hikes of just a couple percentage points can cost upwards of $2 billion; health care, fuel, insurance, building maintenance, the basic expenses of running a mammoth organization together add more than $15 billion a year of additional spending to the Defense Department budget, so holding it flat means cutting other spending in order to accommodate the natural growth of the budget. And you tinker with those expenses at some peril: Politicians don't like the idea of cutting military pay or benefits, especially in wartime, and that's particularly hazardous in the context of a volunteer military. If you make it unappetizing to join, young people will opt for something else. Alternatively, you can save money by shutting down bases, but as I'd learned during the Fort Ord experience back in Monterey, that's a complicated, politicized business.

An aversion to complexity and an abundance of politics are what drove the budget debate to the across-the-board alternative, and it had surface appeal: What could be wrong with cutting "across the board"? If everyone takes a modest hit, then no one has to take a huge one, or at least so the theory goes. In fact, it doesn't work that way. Let me try to illustrate the folly of the across-the-board approach with an example. Imagine you're looking over your family budget and trying to find ways to tighten your belt. You notice that you're spending a lot on fuel—gassing up your cars, running the clothes dryer, heating the house. And let's say you own two cars, one an old gas guzzler, the other a modern, fuel-efficient compact. You might conclude that you could save money by driving the gas guzzler less and using your compact for more errands. Or even that you'd be better off making a short-term investment for long-term gain, say, by trading in the gas guzzler and buying a second, more efficient car. You might have to put some money down for the new car, but you'd save every time you filled up and it might soon pay for itself. Or you might elect to turn down the thermostat and wear sweaters for the winter. All of those are potentially sensible solutions to a real problem, one best solved by thinking creatively and having the flexibility to implement the best solution for your particular problem.

What you almost certainly would not do is try to cut across the board. It makes no sense, for instance, to simply drive both cars 10 percent less; you might be better off driving the smaller car 10 percent more and the larger vehicle 20 percent less. You might have a child who's sick and needs to be in a warm house, so cutting there might be dangerous. Or last winter might have been especially mild and this one especially harsh, so you might have no choice but to spend more on heating and save elsewhere (one problem with across-the-board cuts is they reduce from arbitrary baselines). The best solution for you is not to cut everything the same—it might be to spend a bit more in some areas and a lot less in others. For you, targeted cuts could be prudent and save you money, even prepare your family for the future, while an across-the-board cut could be foolish, expensive, and even dangerous.

I fought as hard as I could to keep Congress from adopting that imprudent reasoning as the basis for a federal budget. On August 23, just a few days after the president signed the act, I warned in a speech at the Naval Postgraduate School that Congress's failure to approve thoughtful deficit reductions had encouraged it to create the "doomsday mechanism" of across-the-board cuts. "Hopefully the committee . . . will have the courage to be able to confront those issues if they're serious about trying to reduce the deficit," I added. "But I have to make it clear . . . that if it fails to do that, and it results in this sequester . . . it will be devastating to the defense budget. It will hollow out the force. It will weaken our national defense. It will undermine our ability to maintain our alliances throughout the world. And, most importantly, it will break faith with the troops and their families."

To bring that point home, I traveled to the Hill again and again, privately meeting with members to urge them to find a solution. House Speaker John Boehner was sympathetic, agreeing that across-the-board cuts would be devastating. But he was confident that wouldn't happen. "We'll find a way," he said. Senate majority leader Harry Reid wasn't so sure; he believed Republicans were already committed to letting the cuts take effect. Mitch McConnell and Nancy Pelosi, the minority leaders of the Senate and House respectively, were also worried about where this was headed. But no one had a plan to stop it. I was struck in those sessions by the absence of serious leadership in either chamber. Lots of members were talking in small groups, but there was no overall direction or urgency. I could feel Congress drifting toward the abyss, and no one on the Hill seemed to know what to do about it.

I was prepared to offer an additional $100 billion in defense cuts— beyond the $487 billion we already were implementing—if that would head off the sequester. The president and his advisers appreciated the offer, but didn't encourage me to pursue it, in part, I'm convinced, because they were worried that I would cut a separate deal to spare defense, since Republicans might come up with the votes for that. In fact, as my efforts to fight the sequester began to get some attention, a few congressional Democrats, including Maryland senator Barbara Mikulski, urged me to emphasize the danger of cuts to domestic programs, not just defense. To my amazement, the rest of the cabinet, including the members responsible for those parts of the budget, largely stayed out of the debate. That left me to argue for all of us, which I tried to do, even when I found myself frustratingly alone.

In some ways that was symptomatic of what I regarded as a problem with President Obama's use of his cabinet. Far more than in previous administrations that I'd witnessed—certainly more than in Clinton's, when I'd been near the center of the action—President Obama's decision-making apparatus was centralized in the White House. In the national security arena, that meant that aides such as Donilon and John Brennan played vital—and often highly expert and valuable—roles in coordinating policy and messaging. There's nothing wrong with that, but it did have the effect of reducing the importance of the cabinet members who actually oversaw their agencies. Those agency heads were rarely encouraged to take their own initiative or lobby for priorities. In fact, several times when I reached out to Congress or the press without prior White House approval, I was chastised for it.

The problem that created, unfortunately, was evident in the sequester debate. The agency heads who best understood how cuts would affect them and the services they provided opted to strike a low profile; as a result, neither Congress nor the public got the benefit of their insights into what was about to transpire. My colleagues in the cabinet knew the cuts would be decimating, but for the most part they waited for permission to object. It never came.

As I was trying to avert the sequester that fall, we were proceeding at the Pentagon with our strategy review, driven in part by the $487 billion cut that we'd already agreed to. Even without sequester, we recognized that we weren't going to be able to substantially cut defense spending by knocking out a cargo plane program or an amphibious vehicle here or there. We also weren't going to be able to reach these cuts by eliminating duplication or trimming staff—the idea of Pentagon "bloat" is a misnomer. The fundamental problem is not duplication or waste, though there was plenty of both. To really cut spending required tough decisions to give up some of what we were doing, and to decide what we could afford to do without. We needed, in my view, a global vision of our military priorities. Starting that fall, we picked up Gates's strategic review and put every program to the test: Did we need it, could we afford it, could we live without it?

The strategic review was led by Michèle Flournoy, Vice Chairman Sandy Winnefeld, and Christine Fox. I told them they were to project which missions our military had to perform over the next decade, which missions we could afford to sacrifice, and what a force of the future would look like.

I began to lay out my vision for the department with my first major public address as the new secretary. I'd been invited to give a talk at the

Woodrow Wilson Center in Washington that fall, and my speech on October 11 seemed like a good opportunity to put some ideas forward and generate some public discussion that might help shape our internal deliberations.

I acknowledged that we were facing difficult choices at the Defense Department and that we had to confront them directly or risk the ramifications of hollowing out our forces in order to achieve reductions. Rather than follow that path, I told the audience that we were "adjusting our strategy and balancing our military to better confront the most pressing security needs." What were those needs? Foremost, of course, was waging the war in Afghanistan and winding down our presence in Iraq. But those conflicts, as costly as they were and as much sacrifice as they demanded, would not go on forever. Combat operations in Iraq had already concluded, and negotiations were under way to determine what presence, if any, the United States would maintain after the end of 2011.

And then there were the challenges we could see forming on the horizon. First was nuclear proliferation. North Korea was actively pursuing a bomb and testing missiles, though not with much success; Iran was enriching uranium "far beyond its needs," and defying international obligations. Next was the growing threat of cyber attack, which confronted the United States with the "prospect of a catastrophic disruption of critical infrastructure." Especially nerve-racking in the area of cyber is that it was within the reach of not just governments but nonstate actors, terrorists. Finally, there was the emergence of China, which posed complex challenges for the United States, a relationship with tentacles of economic cooperation, regional rivalry, and geopolitical tension.

How then to respond to those challenges while also cutting spending? In the Wilson address, I suggested that we needed a force that was more agile, more technologically sophisticated, and more committed to efficiency, especially in weapons procurement. And then there was the inescapable: We needed to reduce the overall size of our military, "recognizing that a smaller, highly capable and ready force is preferable to a larger, hollow force."

But the strategy required more than general observations about evolving threats and capabilities. To be successful, it needed the insights of commanders at all levels, sufficient specific guidance to be implemented, and political buy-in at the highest levels. That fall, we set out to gather information and design a new look for the U.S. military.

One of the most complicated international relationships to manage in my years with President Obama was that between the United States and Pakistan. At their core, both countries realized we needed each other's help, but we didn't trust each other. It showed.

The United States' counterterrorism operations in the Pakistani tribal areas had done enormous damage to Al Qaeda and the Taliban by 2011, but our efforts there had aroused Pakistani opposition. Then there was Ray Davis, whose story was soon forgotten in the United States but bitterly remembered in Pakistan. And of course there was our decision to undertake the bin Laden operation without notifying, much less cooperating with, the Pakistani government. Each of those episodes was in my view handled correctly, but it's true that they took a toll on our relations with Pakistan. After bin Laden was killed, for instance, Pakistan expelled some of our military trainers, and the United States pulled back some of its military aid, then almost $2 billion per year.

For the most part, our uneasiness concerning Pakistan was unspoken. We grumbled about it in the inner circles of government, but made nice in public. Then, on September 22, Admiral Mullen, approaching the end of his tenure as chairman of the Joint Chiefs, told a blunt truth and did so publicly. Testifying before the Senate Armed Services Committee, and with me sitting beside him, Mullen announced that the Haqqani network, a leading insurgent group fighting against American forces in Afghanistan, was a "veritable arm of Pakistan's Inter-Services Intelligence Agency." That network, he added, was behind a recent attack on the American embassy in Kabul as well as a June 28 attack against the Inter-Continental Hotel in that same city. In effect, Mullen accused our Pakistani allies of suborning attacks on American forces, diplomats, and citizens.

That was sure to cause a controversy, and it did, but I was in some ways surprised by the expressions of shock. We had been discussing this for months, and it was an open secret that Pakistan's intelligence agency had ties to terrorist groups—that, after all, was a major part of our rationale for not sharing our bin Laden intelligence with the ISI. As he usually did, Mullen spoke the truth at the hearing that day; as is too often the case, there were repercussions. Pakistani officials called his testimony "irresponsible" and said his comments threatened to rupture relations between our countries.[6]

Things went from bad to worse over the next few months. On November 26, International Security Assistance Forces, the formal name for our coalition in Afghanistan, came under attack along the Afghanistan-Pakistan border, with incoming rounds emanating from the Pakistani side. The ISAF soldiers attempted to contact their Pakistani counterparts over the radio, but received no response. They then opened fire with a counteroffensive, calling in aircraft gunships to defend their positions. The battle ended with twenty-eight Pakistani soldiers dead. Pakistan was outraged.

I commissioned an internal inquiry to examine the actions of our forces even as tempers soared in Pakistan, where one senior official claimed that the attack was a deliberate invasion of Pakistan; in retaliation, the government closed supply routes into Afghanistan that our forces relied upon.

Within the administration, there was a pitched debate about whether to apologize. State Department officials responsible for managing our relationship with Pakistan wanted us to say we were sorry and get on with it, while I thought we should express our regrets but only apologize if we concluded we were to blame. I braced for the White House to side with State, but in this case McDonough told Jeremy that if we didn't think we had something to apologize for, we shouldn't. That gave me the political cover I needed to rebuff State's apology caucus.

After yet another round of tit for tat with Pakistan, we released our internal investigation, accompanied by a statement. It emphasized that ISAF forces had fired in self-defense and acted appropriately under the circumstances as they knew them. But the statement acknowledged that poor communications and faulty maps had contributed to the tragedy and added, "For the loss of life—and for the lack of proper coordination between U.S. and Pakistani forces that contributed to those losses—we express our deepest regret. We further express sincere condolences to the Pakistani people, to the Pakistani government, and most importantly to the families of the Pakistani soldiers who were killed or wounded."

That didn't please everyone. It didn't really please anyone, but the crisis passed.

The NATO assault on Libya, launched in March and supported largely by U.S. aircraft, succeeded in knocking out Qaddafi's air defenses and then conducted strikes on his forces throughout the summer, but by the time I became secretary of defense, the momentum seemed to be petering out. The rebels were disorganized despite the efforts by the United States to train them. They still lacked basic command-and-control and maneuver capabilities. Qaddafi was nothing if not determined, and was digging in. To me it seemed a stalemate was in the offing.

That summer, however, I sat down in my office with our Supreme Allied Commander Europe, Admiral Jim Stavridis. Jim was a modern warrior-intellectual. He'd commanded an aircraft carrier strike group and served as senior military assistant to Don Rumsfeld, and was now on his second tour as a combatant commander. He also held a PhD, was a prolific author, and would go on to become dean of the Fletcher School at Tufts. Well spoken and geostrategically sophisticated, he was universally admired by the leaders of European governments. Moreover, the Libyan war was a NATO campaign, and Stavridis was responsible for it. And he turned my head that day.

My worry that Libya was headed in a bad direction was based on our intelligence from the country, most of which indicated that the opposition was not strong enough to make a move on Tripoli. To my surprise, Stavridis thought differently. He told me he thought Qaddafi's regime was splintering and that the rebels were stronger and more determined than they appeared. I admit I was skeptical, but I recognized that Stav, as I called him, had a clear view of the situation and was smart enough to analyze it well. I left our meeting thinking there was hope after all.

It turned out that Stav was absolutely right, and soon proven so.

At the end of August, the rebels stormed Qaddafi's Tripoli compound. Qaddafi fled. Two months later, after our punishing air campaign, rebels found him hiding out in his hometown, Sirte. He was dragged through the street, dazed, blood pouring from the left side of his head and soaking his jacket. He stammered incoherently, then was stood up before a mob and executed. As with so many of the events of the Arab Spring, this was captured on cell phones and shared around the world. Libya's fate was now in uncertain hands, but the country had at least cast off a murderous and deranged dictator.

The Libya campaign was a hard one for the Obama administration. The president himself was conflicted about it—we were still trying to extricate ourselves responsibly from Iraq, and the last thing that President Obama wanted to do was launch another war in the Middle East. But the case for action in Libya was compelling: Qaddafi was demonstrably vicious, and the international community was solidly aligned against him, with NATO, the UN Security Council, and Arab leaders all united in calling for his ouster. If force could not be used under those circumstances, it raised the question of whether force could ever be used. Recognizing that, the president approved what I regarded as an intelligent compromise: We would not send in troops—no "boots on the ground"—but we would commit the forces necessary to play a decisive role in knocking down Qaddafi's air defenses, clearing the way for the rebels to take the lead.

The result was, in military terms, resoundingly successful. A dictator was dispatched, and the Libyan people were given a new opportunity to lead themselves. What they do with it remains to be seen, but the operation proved that not all American military engagements need to become quagmires or occupations. There are other ways to fight.

At home, my worst fears about the budget and Congress were realized just before Thanksgiving. On November 21, the Super Committee gave up, its leaders announcing that they could not find common ground to cut the budget and avert the sequester. Having put the gun to its own head and loaded it up, Congress decided to fire it.

The only consolation was that sequestration would not take effect for another year. Figuring we could return to that later, I decided to go ahead and complete our strategic review while continuing to work on members of Congress to find a way out of their self-inflicted wound. Those talks remained frustrating, but our strategy deliberations were producing a thoughtful new vision for U.S. defense—a defense strategy for the twenty-first century, as we called it. After much deliberation, the strategy boiled down to these essential elements:

1. The new military would be smaller and leaner; coming out of Iraq and Afghanistan, we would draw down our forces but mold them into more agile and deployable units, armed with the latest

technology. We would rely on the National Guard and Reserves and the country's industrial base to ramp up in the event of a major war or wars in order to supply forces and equipment.

2. We would "rebalance" our forces toward Asia in order to be able to project force quickly and powerfully from the Middle East to the Pacific, a recognition that future conflicts were more likely to spring from those parts of the world than from Europe, where NATO provided an umbrella of security for our interests.

3. Elsewhere in the world, we would adopt a new style of presence we described as "rotational deployment." No longer would we seek to put large occupying forces into a country for years at a time; instead, we would emphasize short-term deployments, exercises, training, technology, joint operations, and weapons systems— so-called small-footprint approaches. That reflected our economic realities as well as the political landscape in many of those countries. Emerging countries like Indonesia, for instance, do want our help and knowledge, but they don't want to host an American military base to do it. In addition, we would stress new alliances and partnerships to help others develop security capabilities.

4. We would continue to maintain a capacity to fight, as the saying goes, "two wars at once," but that would not mean the equivalent of World War II's European and Pacific theaters. In effect, we would work to be able to fight one full-fledged war while in essence "freezing" the second and imposing severe costs on the adversary. We would continue, however, to be able to confront more than one adversary at a time—as we had done in Iraq and Afghanistan and even Libya.

5. Finally, we would make key investments, recognizing that even as parts of our operation shrank, new demands required us to expand others. Special operations forces would grow; we would add

unmanned systems and intelligence capabilities; we'd invest in cyber warfare, both offensive and defensive; and we would continue the development of space-based systems.

Those principles drove certain decisions that made up our new strategy. We moved to reduce the size of the army to 490,000 troops within five years—a less severe cut than some had sought but one that brought it to the lowest level since 9/11, reflecting our determination to no longer serve as an occupying force in two locations simultaneously. We killed some weapons systems and found economical alternatives to some surveillance aircraft. We considered eliminating an aircraft carrier group, but elected to keep it, though we did trim the number of new ships we would buy. And we found money for new investments in cyber security, special operations forces, and new technologies.

By far the most important strategic decision we made was to rebalance the focus of our military toward the Asia-Pacific region. The rebalance reflected priorities outlined by the president and by Secretary Clinton to effectuate an overall "pivot" to the Asia-Pacific region. That meant sending more troops and naval forces to the area. Until then, our fleets were divided roughly fifty-fifty between the Atlantic and Pacific. Once it was complete, we aimed to deploy about 60 percent in Asia and 40 percent in the Atlantic region—a decision I announced on June 2, 2012, at the annual gathering of Asia defense leaders at the Shangri-La Hotel in Singapore.

In announcing this new orientation, I began by emphasizing the common interests of the United States and its Asian allies: stability, security, prosperity. Ever since it reached the West Coast in the nineteenth century, I emphasized, the United States has "been a Pacific nation." I stressed the value of partnerships and presence and sought to reassure any doubters that our commitment would survive our budget challenges. "Through times of war, times of peace, under Democratic and Republican leaders and administrations, through rancor and comity in Washington, through surplus and through debt, we were there then, we are here now, and we will be here for the future," I concluded. Our partners were encouraged—and relieved.

Those were the mainstays of our new defense strategy, but just as important as the substance was the process. First, I held numerous meetings with our senior military and civilian leaders to get not only their input but their buy-in. Involving them in the process ensured that they would be advocates for the outcome. Even more important, President Obama participated throughout—rare for a commander in chief on a matter of strategic planning—and thus not only approved of the result but also had a direct hand in shaping it. He hosted a series of meetings to develop the strategy in the Oval Office and Situation Room, and he invited all the combatant commanders, service secretaries, service chiefs, and civilian leaders to join him in the East Room, where the president called on each of the twenty or so participants and asked for their input. In those sessions, he insisted that at the end of the process we remain the strongest military in the world, but he embraced the goals of the strategy—he was, for instance, a strong supporter of the rebalance to Asia—and he helped refine other aspects of the proposal. Above all, he insisted that troops be protected—I could see in his adamancy the influence of the first lady and Dr. Jill Biden, both of whom were leading efforts to care for military families—and he made the brave call that we could afford to reduce the size of our armed services. Cutting back the size of the military is hard for any president, especially a Democrat, but President Obama was persuaded by the idea that we needed a new type of military for a new mission. His engagement shaped the outcome, and his support made it possible.

In February 2010, the president had agreed to add Anwar al-Awlaki to the list of approved targets, concluding that he was a high-level Al Qaeda operative, that he was directing attacks against the United States, and that he was thus a military enemy of his native country. As noted earlier, congressional officials were advised of this on February 5, 2011. Though the Awlaki case was different from most of those targeted in that he was an American citizen, the underlying rationale—that he was an enemy combatant waging war against the United States—was identical, and that position was supported by the Justice Department.

Adding him to the target list and actually finding him, however, were two different things. He was difficult for U.S. officials to track down. At one point he was expected at a wedding of an associate; either he didn't show or U.S. officials couldn't spot him.

Awlaki was an inspirational figure urging followers to take up arms against the United States; one of those who had, Major Nidal Malik Hasan, committed the Fort Hood attack that left thirteen dead in 2009. Hasan was, according to Awlaki, a "hero" and a "man of conscience."[7] More important, Awlaki was not merely a motivational speaker, whose comments, however vile or incendiary, deserved protection as free speech. He was directly connected to the assassination attempt on bin Nayef and the attempted downing of the airliner on Christmas Day 2009. The bomber in the latter attack, Abdulmutallab, had traveled to Yemen to meet Awlaki, who approved his mission and directed him to carry it out over the United States. Awlaki had also devised a plan to blow up cargo planes over the United States. He was an active terrorist conducting ongoing attacks on America.

On September 30, 2011, the Pentagon received word that U.S. operators had located Awlaki in Jawf Province, one of the more remote areas of Yemen. Awlaki was part of a small group of men eating their breakfast. Apparently hearing the drones overhead, they ran for their trucks, though not fast enough. The missiles were fired, the trucks destroyed. Awlaki and a second American, Samir Khan, were killed (Khan was not a target, and U.S. operators did not know he was there at the time).

In the aftermath, there was much debate over whether America has the legal or moral right to kill American citizens abroad. The American Civil Liberties Union filed a lawsuit naming me as its lead defendant and charging that the U.S. government was carrying out "deliberate and premeditated killings" and that those killings were "unlawful." According to the ACLU, the killing of Awlaki specifically was illegal because his actions did not pose a "concrete, specific, and imminent threat of death or serious physical injury."[8]

I'm more often allied with the ACLU than not, but in this case I didn't buy either its analysis or its assessment of Awlaki. He actively and repeatedly took action to kill Americans and instill fear. He did not just exercise his rights of speech, but rather worked directly to plant bombs on planes and in cars, specifically intending those to detonate on or above American soil. He devoted his adult life to murdering his fellow citizens, and he was continuing that work at the time of his death. His case was reviewed at the highest levels of American government, and no action was taken against him until it had been approved by the president and shared with the relevant members of Congress.

A police officer who confronts an armed suspect has the right and obligation to shoot if that suspect is about to kill someone else, irrespective of that suspect's nationality or citizenship. Surely the members of our military and intelligence forces have that same obligation. We too protect Americans, and Awlaki was an armed and dangerous suspect.

The Awlaki operation was the subject of much debate, and properly so. Unfortunately, however, much of that conversation has focused narrowly on the technology employed—what is so often and misleadingly referred to as the nation's "drone program."

When I returned to government service in 2009, the place of drones within the larger effort against Al Qaeda was a barely discussed aspect of the Bush administration's approach. In fact, I was largely unaware of it until I moved to take up my new duties. Since that time, the discussion gradually has broadened. President Obama himself, on May 23, 2013, described in considerable detail our use of drones and the care we were taking to minimize civilian casualties. He expanded on that discussion in a series of interviews and during his speech at West Point in May 2014. As the world now knows, these operations are authorized by the president, overseen by Congress, and carried out by the U.S. government. And as the president has described, the intelligence community plays an important role in finding targets and fixing their locations.

But the singular preoccupation with drones distracts from the larger context of the struggle we are waging. Yes, the United States possesses and uses drones to target senior Al Qaeda leaders who are otherwise beyond our reach to capture. And yes, I appreciate the fascination with technology. Advances in weapon design often are captivating—witness the crowds at the annual Rose Parade as they gasp when the Stealth bombers pass overhead.

But to call our campaign against Al Qaeda a "drone program" is a little like calling World War I a "machine gun program." Technology has always been an aspect of war: The North developed repeating rifles to use against the South in the Civil War; machine guns and tanks debuted in World War I; the Allies used radar, code-breaking, and nuclear weapons to defeat Nazi Germany and Imperial Japan during World War II. Those breakthroughs saved American lives and secured historic victories, though sometimes at great cost.

Today, as with those historical examples, what is most crucial is not the size of the missile or the ability to deploy it from thousands of miles away; what matters far more are the rules of law and engagement. Again, those rules reflect painstaking consideration across the government; they require presidential authorization, specific policies approved by the National Security Council, intelligence collection, and analysis by a number of agencies, legal opinions, and reviews and congressional oversight. Those legal standards in turn reflect the basic values that guide this work, and those who are involved in debating and constructing those rules work zealously to protect the values—notably the minimization of risk to American lives and those of noncombatants—that they express.

Some of my colleagues in the Obama administration argued that these operations were far too secretive and that they should be conducted with full public explanation of each operation. One official even suggested that we send out press releases with each strike. I certainly agree with President Obama that we need to be far more transparent in the way we explain our drone policy. However, I also believe that certain operational details need to remain secret. The president, as commander in chief, needs a range of tools to defend the nation, and secrecy is one of those tools.

In addition, drone strikes have been well managed within the executive branch. Changing the chain of command or creating a new interagency bureaucratic process would have sharply reduced our agility, eroded our effectiveness, and taken the pressure off the enemy. These operations fundamentally are driven by information, which can change or disappear in moments. Careful planning and then lightning speed in execution have been the keys to our success.

Moreover, just because the operations weren't announced publicly did not mean that they were kept secret within the government or that they were conducted with impunity. Congress and the White House were extensively informed. The director of national intelligence and the White House staff were briefed every morning after an operation. The key congressional committees received notifications on every operation and were even provided video when requested. Occasionally, when an especially high-value target came into view or where there were complicating circumstances, White House officials were consulted in advance of making a decision.

At one point in 2009, the president chaired a meeting to review drone operations: how they were conducted, the precise criteria for action, and how the agencies involved worked to minimize the risk of harm to noncombatants. Those with principal responsibility for this work laid it all out for the president, with maps and videos, over the course of two hours. The president was impressed, both with the success and by the care with which these missions were conducted. The operations continued and accelerated under President Obama.

I recognize that the public was not privy to those conversations, but the checks and balances of our government ensured that these operations were subjected to appropriate scrutiny while still keeping details out of the hands of our enemies.

And yet, as the president recognized that day and has since publicly acknowledged, this is an area admittedly fraught with complexity: When an American missile snuffs out an avowed enemy of this country, lives are both lost and saved.* A terrorist who is committed to blowing up an airplane or destroying a skyscraper is eliminated, and those he would have killed are spared his brutality. At the same time, a young person who loses a father or a brother, who digs out the embers of a relative from the smoking wreckage of a Hellfire missile may be radicalized, may turn his anger against those who killed his loved one. It is a hard business of agonizing choices. In the world of theory, it is easy to be certain. In the world as it is, many brave men and women risk their lives to protect others from danger, and every decision is subject to dispute.

As with enhanced interrogation, the use of drones provokes strong feelings and strenuous debate in our nation. It should. But as with the interrogation discussion, it's important to recognize that neither side has a monopoly on reason. Relying too heavily for too long on technol-

---

*President Obama directly confronted this question in his important speech on May 23, 2013: "To say that a military tactic is legal, or even effective, is not to say it is wise or moral in every instance. For the same human progress that gives us the technology to strike half a world away also demands the discipline to constrain that power—or risk abusing it."

ogy that spies down from above and can unleash deadly force from half a world away surely reinforces a worrisome image of malevolent American omniscience. Moreover, this technology is rapidly spreading across the world. Americans would undoubtedly recoil if China, for instance, were to spot a dissident in Mexico and eliminate him with a missile.

To be clear, however, there also would be consequences to not using this technology. Because it represents our only reach into certain parts of the world, refusing to take advantage of it would concede those regions to those who are actively plotting and engineering violence against our country. A training camp in Yemen can produce just as many steely fanatics as one in Afghanistan. A bomb built in Somalia is just as explosive as one built in Los Angeles. If those who are working to harm Americans have safe harbor in which to train, plot, build, and deploy, they will.

In addition, the technology of these devices is in some ways frightening but in others reassuring and even protective. They kill more precisely than bombs; they expose American soldiers to little if any danger; they allow the United States to locate and eliminate dangerous enemies with minimal risk of unintended casualties, not only to Americans but also to those who find themselves in the vicinity of terrorists who are targeted. That precision can be chilling, but surely it is more desirable to kill a single terrorist than to eliminate him by wiping out an entire village. All of which argues not only for the effectiveness of unmanned aerial vehicles but also for their morality.

As America grapples with the implications of drone warfare, the conversation should comprehend two important truths: To use drones too much, too often, or without careful consideration is to invite the world's condemnation; to use them too little or not at all is to give our enemies free rein. Our experience makes clear what they will do with that latitude.

War in the twenty-first century is no longer confined to the battlefield. The enemy we are confronting is capable of using an IED, a suicide vest, a hijacked airplane, a car bomb, or an attack on a shopping mall. We also face the potential of more traditional enemies, those who may threaten us with missiles, bombers, and ships. Faced with such diverse threats, we must be able to respond with the best-trained, best-equipped forces we can field. We are the strongest power on Earth. The key to that power is not only in the technology we have, but also in our people, and, most important, in the values that guide our action.

We must not be forced to choose between security and our values. We can and we must preserve both.

Through the fall of 2011, the main question facing the American military in Iraq was what our role would be now that combat operations had come to a conclusion. When President Obama announced the end of our combat mission in August 2010, he'd acknowledged that we would maintain troops for a while. As he put it, "Going forward, a transitional force of U.S. troops will remain in Iraq with a different mission: advising and assisting Iraq's security forces; supporting Iraqi troops in targeted counterterrorism missions; and protecting our civilians. Consistent with our agreement with the Iraqi government, all U.S. troops will leave by the end of next year."[9] Now that the deadline was upon us, however, it was clear to me—and many others— that withdrawing all our forces would endanger the fragile stability then barely holding Iraq together.

Privately, the various leadership factions in Iraq all confided that they wanted some U.S. forces to remain as a bulwark against sectarian violence. But none were willing to take that position publicly, and Prime Minister Maliki concluded that any Status of Forces Agreement, which would give legal protection to those forces, would have to be submitted to the Iraqi parliament for its approval. That made reaching agreement very difficult given the internal politics of Iraq, but representatives of the Defense and State departments, with close scrutiny from the White House, continued to try to negotiate a deal.

We had leverage. We could, for instance, have threatened to withdraw reconstruction aid to Iraq if Maliki would not support some sort of continued U.S. military presence. My fear, as I voiced to the president and others, was that if the country split apart or slid back into the pervasive violence that we'd experienced in the years immediately following the U.S. invasion, it could become a new haven for terrorists to plot attacks against the United States. Iraq's stability thus, in my view, was not only in Iraq's interest but in ours. With that in mind, I privately and publicly advocated leaving behind a residual force that could provide training and security for Iraq's military.

Michèle Flournoy did her best to press that position, which reflected not just my views but also those of the military commanders in the region and the Joint Chiefs. But the president's team at the White House pushed back, and the differences occasionally became heated. Flournoy argued our case, and those on our side of the debate viewed the White House as so eager to rid itself of Iraq that it was willing to withdraw rather than lock in arrangements that would preserve our influence and interests.

We debated with Maliki even as we debated among ourselves, with time running out. The clock wound down in December, and Ash Carter continued to argue our case, extending the deadline for the Iraqis to act, hoping that we might pull out a last-minute agreement and recognizing that once our forces left it would be essentially impossible for them to turn around and return. To my frustration, the White House coordinated the negotiations but never really led them. Officials there seemed content to endorse an agreement if State and Defense could reach one, but without the president's active advocacy, Maliki was allowed to slip away. The deal never materialized. To this day, I believe that a small, focused U.S. troop presence in Iraq could have effectively advised the Iraqi military on how to deal with Al Qaeda's resurgence and the sectarian violence that has engulfed the country.

Over the course of the following two and a half years, the situation in Iraq slowly deteriorated. Maliki was responsible, as he exacerbated the deep sectarian issues polarizing his country. Meanwhile, with the conflict in Syria raging, an Al Qaeda offshoot—ISIS, or the Islamic State in Iraq and Syria—gained strength. Using Syria as its base, it began to move into Iraq in 2014, grabbing power in towns and villages across Iraq's north, including Mosul and Tal Afar. These were strategically important cities that U.S. forces had fought and died to secure for the Iraqi people. Perhaps most distressing, Iraqi military units cut and ran, unable or unwilling to defend their own country from this new Sunni extremist element.

I watched these events from the safe distance of Monterey, but the news from Iraq bothered me to no end. In my view, the ISIS offensive in 2014 greatly increases the risk that Iraq will become Al Qaeda's next safe haven. That is exactly what they had in Afghanistan pre-9/11. They then reestablished a base in western Pakistan in the mid-2000s. After all we have done to decimate Al Qaeda's senior leadership and its core, those efforts will be for naught if we allow it to rebuild a base of operations in the Middle East.

As of this writing, each option for the United States is filled with risk. Nobody wants to see us back in a full-scale war in Iraq. That said, I do not believe America can afford to sit idly by. If we don't prevent these Sunni extremists from taking over large swaths of territory in the Middle East, it will be only a matter of time before they turn their sights on us.

Although our new defense strategy was still being crafted that fall, I shared the general themes of it with allies in Asia, where the proposed "rebalance" would have the most noticeable impact. In

October, I visited Indonesia, Japan, and South Korea, three important American partners in that region. Each stop featured reminders of America's important role in the region, and of the range and necessity of our military capacity.

In all three countries, I met with the head of state and minister of defense—sometimes together, sometimes separately—and discussed the particular issues of our bilateral relationship. Indonesia's geography, for instance, places it astride many important sea lanes, and protecting them is a major concern for both our nations. While in Indonesia, I also attended a meeting of the ASEAN defense ministers, who were trying to organize their countries to fight terrorism and create a counterweight to China's growing muscularity in the Pacific. I was there to lend my support to that effort, a gesture much appreciated by the participating countries.

In Japan, our long-standing role in that country's military defense includes bases on the Japanese islands; their future concerns both Japan and the United States. Moreover, Japan was still recovering from the earthquake and tsunami in March, an emergency that American military forces helped respond to—another example of the diverse uses of American power and presence.

And in Korea, the looming and erratic North Korean regime overshadows all other security worries. We discussed North Korea's nuclear and missile programs and reaffirmed our long-standing defense agreements, including our promise to defend South Korea from the North's aggression, and if necessary to do so with nuclear weapons.

The highlight of that stop for me was social: My South Korean counterpart, Defense Minister Kim Kwan-jin, invited me for dinner at his home. He had somehow arranged for four vocalists in the South Korean military to learn some popular Italian songs, which they performed for me after dinner. Despite being native Korean speakers, their rendition of "O Sole Mio" was spot-on; I could have closed my eyes and been in Rome.

Beyond the topics singular to each of the countries was one over-riding and unifying concern: that the efforts to cut spending at home would result in a diminished U.S. presence in the region, opening the way for China to exert greater influence at the expense of America's friends. Over and over, I assured them we were not going anywhere. President Obama and I shared the conviction that "the Pacific will remain a key priority for the United States, that we will maintain our force projection in this area, that we will maintain a presence in this area, that we will remain a Pacific power, and that we will do whatever we can to try to work with the nations of this area to develop a strong security and cooperative relationship."

To bring it home, I reminded my hosts that I grew up in a fishing town in California, looking out on the same ocean that they did. A commitment to the Pacific came naturally to me. I would not, could not lead America away from the Pacific Rim.

I was back in the United States for November—and made it with Sylvia, President Obama, and Vice President Biden to the Army-Navy game in early December. There, I joined the president on the field for the pregame ceremonies and with him switched sides from the midshipmen to the cadets at halftime. It was a moving experience to sit with them as groups were rotated to be close to me and the president. It gave us an opportunity to make small talk with the next generation of American leaders, and allowed us a glimpse of the nation's future officer corps.

After the game, I headed home and packed for one more overseas voyage in 2011, this time a trip that encapsulated many of the achievements and disappointments of my still-brief tenure as defense secretary. My first stop was Djibouti, where I'd never been before and which is the home to the largest U.S. military installation in Africa. The joint operations task force based there, at Camp Lemonnier, was a model of interservice cooperation, and was playing an integral role in the fight against Al Qaeda and Al Shabaab in nearby Somalia (we would call on them in just a few weeks to execute a dramatic rescue operation). In a town hall meeting with about two hundred service members, I complimented our troops for their fine efforts, and expected to talk with them about Al Qaeda and international terrorism. We did discuss those subjects, but another one was on many of their minds. It fell to a master sergeant to ask the question: Would budget cuts endanger military retirement pensions? I assured him they would be protected. But his question did raise the specter that the Pentagon would soon have to grapple with: how to save on the personnel costs and benefits for retirees and their families, which were eating into the funds available for readiness and training.

Djibouti represented the morphing campaign against international terrorism, and my next stop was a return to the heart of that battle: Afghanistan. There I conferred with General Allen and President Karzai and was generally pleased at the progress they described. The Afghan army was assuming a greater share of responsibility for security, the economy was gradually expanding, and education was reaching more and more children, including girls. The Taliban remained a presence, but our efforts against it—special operations forces were conducting seven or eight missions every night—were taking a toll on its leadership and dramatically degrading Al Qaeda. Noting the courage of those men and other troops fighting this long war, I was honored to present twelve Purple Hearts to soldiers who had been wounded in battle.

That's not to say the war was won or that the end was even in sight. Corruption continued to hamper the Karzai regime, and it remained unclear whether the Afghan economy could ever grow and diversify to the point that it could sustain the cost of the security apparatus we were helping to construct. But my feeling was that our presence was constructive and that as long as we were willing to remain engaged we could continue to make headway.

At the end of the trip, Karzai and I held a press conference, which was more memorable for the conditions under which it was held than for anything we said. It was late at night, in an unheated garden house on the grounds of the presidential palace. There was a small pond in the center of the house, and it was freezing. As I was taking questions, I could see members of our delegation and the press literally hopping up and down to keep warm. One of the reporters, the estimable Thom Shanker of the *New York Times*, accidentally hopped right into the shallow pool. He was soaked from his knees down, but he kept right on taking notes. He later shivered his way back to the press van.

In his dispatch from Kabul, Shanker, as well as other reporters, seemed surprised that my take on the security situation wasn't more negative. Shanker, for instance, described my assessment as "unexpectedly upbeat."[10]

The same could not be said for Iraq, where I headed next. Anytime the United States concludes a military mission, the end of the enterprise is marked by a formal ceremony in which the flag is lowered, "cased," and returned to Washington. As secretary of defense, it fell to me to perform that ceremony and to bring America's military presence in Iraq to an end.

It was no secret that I had fought to keep it from ending this way, and it was thus with profoundly mixed emotions that I arrived at Sather Air Base, an American installation at the edge of the Baghdad International Airport. I was proud of the work and sacrifices our men and women had made over the long course of the Iraq war, but I would have been lying had I tried to argue that it had ended in triumph. Instead, I spoke guardedly and heavily, praising the effort if not the result. "Your nation is deeply indebted to you," I told the soldiers who attended the ceremony. "You have done everything your nation asked you to do and more."

At the height of the Iraq war, the United States had 170,000 soldiers in that country, stationed at more than five hundred bases. By the end of 2011, we were down to about 4,000 at three bases, and those were shutting down. The premises of the war—that Iraq was a haven for Al Qaeda and that Saddam Hussein had amassed weapons of mass destruction—had turned out to be false. We had made a commitment to leave behind a country that could govern and secure itself. That was still an open question. As I spoke that day, helicopters flew overhead to provide security; other base closures had drawn insurgent fire, evidence that our attempts to leave a stable nation were at best incomplete.

At the end of my remarks to a smaller group of troops, one young serviceman asked me whether the United States was prepared to come back in force if Iraq needed help. I tried to be reassuring. "We may be ending the war," I told him, "but we are not walking away from our responsibilities." That was an expression of hope rather than fact. I cased the flag, said a silent prayer for those who had done the hard work of this war, and walked away.

After leaving Iraq, I stopped in Turkey to discuss the Arab Spring and forward deployment of radar to support NATO's missile defense system, and then traveled to Libya, becoming the first American secretary of defense ever to visit that country. Accompanied by my son Jimmy, I was confronted with the moving evidence of America's long presence in Libya.

All around we could see craters from the recent NATO bombings that had helped to topple Qaddafi. And then we were taken back in time to 1804, to a modest cemetery overlooking the Mediterranean. There, around an olive tree, were more than two dozen headstones, marking the remains of American sailors and marines who died in America's first foreign military action. (In the Marine Corps song, the line "to the shores of Tripoli" refers to those battles, waged against the

Barbary pirates.) For more than two centuries, across the tense years of Qaddafi's rule and the campaign to remove him, Libyans had cared for those American graves.

I left a wreath and one of my personal coins and headed home with a lump in my throat.

We completed our reexamination of America's defense strategy just as 2011 turned to 2012. President Obama signaled his satisfaction by making an extraordinary trip to the Pentagon to join me, Dempsey, and others as we unveiled it for the first time. It was apparently the first time any president had appeared in the Pentagon press briefing room, and it caused quite a stir among the regular Defense Department press corps.

The president opened with a brief recitation of where the nation stood in military terms. The war in Iraq was over, Qaddafi was gone, Al Qaeda was "on the path to defeat," its leader eliminated, American troops were returning from Afghanistan, which was gradually taking over responsibility for its own security. It was a remarkable and underappreciated record of achievement, having taken office amid two broken wars, a thriving Al Qaeda, and an elusive bin Laden. As the president noted, "the tide of war" was receding. [11]

But achievements cannot allow leaders to become complacent. Yes, our wars were receding, but the threats to national security were multiplying and morphing. A new military, leaner, more nimble, and more technologically advanced, was needed for a new century. That's what we tried to construct.

SIXTEEN

"In Together, Out Together"

On the night of the State of the Union address in 2012, I was in the House chamber, seated next to Hillary Clinton and across the aisle from members of the Supreme Court. As is customary, the president entered to applause and then slowly worked his way from the back of the chamber to the front, greeting members of Congress, the administration, the Joint Chiefs, and the Court. He shook my hand, swung in the direction of Justice Anthony Kennedy, then abruptly turned back and said to me, "Good job tonight. Good job tonight." He waved his finger emphatically as he said it, and I beamed. The network microphones caught the president's comment. Within minutes, the media were trying to decipher it.

On October 25, 2011, Somali kidnappers seized two humanitarian aid workers, American Jessica Buchanan and Poul Hagen Thisted, her Danish colleague. Kidnapping for ransom is a common enterprise in Somalia and the waters off its coast, and as a result, American forces in the region are sometimes called upon to respond—the dramatic 2009 raid on the pirates who took the *Maersk Alabama* and then fled in a lifeboat with its captain became the basis for the movie *Captain Phil-lips*. Bill McRaven, who operated with such calm and distinction dur-ing the bin Laden operation, oversaw that one too.

In this case, we could not dispatch a rescue team to Somalia be-cause the hostages were being moved frequently and we could not pin-point their location. Also, negotiations between the kidnappers and the hostages' employer for their release were under way, and we hoped for a peaceful resolution to the kidnapping. As the weeks dragged on, however, the negotiations grew fruitless—the kidnappers asked for $45 million—and we began to fear for Jessica's health; our intelligence indi-cated that she was suffering from an infection, and it seemed to be worsening. At about the same time, we were able to pinpoint the loca-tion of Jessica and Poul through sophisticated technology and ascertain that they were at a rough encampment under the control of a group of nine men, all armed, hundreds of miles from where they were first captured.

In the days immediately before the State of the Union, our military came up with a plan. General Dempsey and Admiral Winnefeld brought the information to me about Jessica's location and condition, and proposed the rescue. We knew this might be our only and last chance to save her. We briefed John Brennan and Tom Donilon at the White House, and then reviewed the particulars of the operation with the president. A special operations team from the United States would fly to Djibouti, to the small U.S. base in the northeast corner of Africa that I had recently visited. The plan was for our forces to parachute into the area, then hike to the camp and wrest the hostages from their captors. The intent was not to kill the kidnappers, merely to rescue Jes-sica and Poul. But our forces would not hesitate to use their weapons if they needed to.

President Obama, as he had during the bin Laden planning, lis-tened carefully, asked questions, and weighed the proposal, recognizing that it posed risks to the hostages and our forces. Ultimately he approved, clearing the raid on the morning of January 23 because that's when conditions would be ideal. The next afternoon in Washington, night in Somalia, I made my way over to the White House with Dempsey, where we monitored the mission from the Situation Room before heading to the Capitol for the State of the Union.

At the camp, the captors put up resistance, an unwise decision when confronted with an American military team. All nine were killed. Jessica and Poul were unharmed, and were whisked away within minutes of the firefight. Before leaving the scene, one American soldier recovered Jessica's shoes and a small medical bag.[1] President Obama concluded his State of the Union and then retired to a room in the Capitol with a phone. He called Jessica's father with the news that she was safe.

I n my first year, I concluded the Iraq war with reservations. I oversaw the war in Afghanistan, where we'd made progress. But much of my time and energy over that period was devoted to a third war—or, rather, to preventing a third war. For months, it teetered on the edge of exploding, held in check by a tenuous combination of personal trust and national interest.

By early 2012, Israel's leadership was becoming increasingly anxious about Iran's nuclear program. With Iran openly threatening to annihilate Israel, and Israel openly proclaiming that it would not allow Iran to develop weapons that would allow it to carry out that threat, a collision seemed unavoidable and coming on fast.

Navigating those perilous waters often fell to me and my friend and counterpart Ehud Barak, Israel's defense minister. Barak often said that once Iran began spinning centrifuges underground at Fordow, it would enter a "zone of immunity," meaning that it would be invulnerable to Israeli retaliation, a perilous position for Israel given Iran's strident insistence that it was prepared to eliminate Israel from the planet. That made Iran's threat not just serious but existential.

I had known Ehud since my years as White House chief of staff, and I liked him. We were about the same age, of similar politics. We loved our families and enjoyed politics and good food, and we both played classical piano. He had a deep laugh and a profound commitment to his country, both of which I appreciated. He had even gone to school in California—he was a graduate of Stanford. But it was clear that this matter transcended personal trust or friendship. Israel's *right* to exist was discounted by Iran's leadership, and its *ability* to exist could be threatened if that regime developed a nuclear weapon and the means of delivering it. Ehud agreed with me that the threat of an Iranian nuclear weapon still wasn't imminent, but he argued that it was necessary to act now or lose the opportunity to do so.

It was almost impossible to counsel patience under these circumstances, but I urged him to see that action had its risks as well.

"Look, Ehud," I said. "The problem is that if you attack them now, you can only set their program back by a few years. It would come back. You'll give them a black eye. We, on the other hand, can deliver the knockout punch." We had the bombs that could take out Fordow. Israel had to trust us that we would have their back if Iran began to "break out" and build a weapon.

The dilemma, then, was this: Israel could act, but not effectively; the United States could act effectively, but preferred to press diplomacy first. That meant Israel had to trust that we would act if the time came, that we would not flinch at the moment of truth even if the graver threat was not to the United States but rather to Israel. That's a lot of trust to place in an ally, even a close and historic ally.

In January, Donilon told me that President Obama's two main foreign policy goals for 2012 were to keep Iran from getting a nuclear weapon and to avoid a war in the Middle East. Both were admirable ambitions, but the president might have to choose one over the other.

I understood Ehud's reluctance to place so much in our hands. I assured him that day, as I would repeatedly through 2012, that the United States would stand with Israel, but that we did not believe Israeli military action was the best course at the current time.

"We're serious," I told him emphatically. "We won't let them have a bomb."

Making matters worse, Iran was deliberately provocative. In late December 2011, its leaders boasted that they were preparing to shut down access to the Strait of Hormuz, through which much of the world's oil flows. Appearing on CBS's *Face the Nation* on January 8, Dempsey and I laid down the gauntlet. If Iran closed the Strait of Hormuz, there would be consequences, which we purposefully declined to specify—we liked the idea that the Iranians might use their imagination.

On January 22, we sent the aircraft carrier USS *Abraham Lincoln*, accompanied by a full strike group, through the strait. Iranian vessels shadowed the carrier group. Their forces kept an eye on it but stayed within Iranian waters or airspace, and none took action against our fleet. Our implied willingness to use military force had achieved an important goal: The strait remained open.

I regarded that as an important signal of our willingness to take Iran to the brink. Israeli leaders appreciated it too, but were unconvinced that we were prepared to risk it all. Even as we were fencing with Iran over the strait, the Israelis abruptly canceled a joint U.S.-Israel military exercise, called Austere Challenge 12, slated for the spring of 2012. Although press reports speculated that Israel had canceled the exercises because it was angry at the United States for refusing to countenance an attack on Iran, in fact it took the action in part to protect Americans. If Israel launched an attack on Iran in the spring, the last thing it wanted was to trigger a war with several hundred Americans in Tel Aviv hotels, there as part of a joint operation between our countries.

I pressed Ehud to reconsider the cancellation, but he made clear why he could not: "We haven't made a decision" about whether to strike Iran, he said. "But I can't in good conscience hide the fact from our best ally that we are discussing it."

It was amid those rising tensions that I made the mistake of speaking too candidly with a reporter and not anticipating the possible impact. On a trip to Europe, the eminent national security columnist David Ignatius traveled as part of the press corps. I liked David and appreciated his experience. Maybe that's why when we sat down in my cabin I was too forthcoming about my fear that an Israeli military operation against Iran might be imminent. The terms of our interview were that Ignatius was not to quote me directly, and he honored that, but there was no mistaking that he was reflecting my views. "Panetta believes there is a strong likelihood that Israel will strike Iran in April, May or June," the column said, "before Iran enters what Israelis described as a 'zone of immunity' to commence building a nuclear bomb. Very soon, the Israelis fear, the Iranians will have stored enough enriched uranium in deep underground facilities to make a weapon—and only the United States could then stop them militarily."[2] I winced when I read it, not because it wasn't true, but because I realized I should have been more careful about sharing those views at that moment. The column made headlines around the world and led the evening news. Donilon called Jeremy and was furious. We did as much damage control as we could, but few questioned the truth of what I'd said.

Iran dominated conversations between Ehud Barak and me in the early months of the year, and also was the main point of discussion between President Obama and Prime Minister Netanyahu when the latter visited the United States in February, just a few days after the Ignatius column appeared. Israel was seriously contemplating military action; we urged them to refrain, and tried to back up our requests with public statements and gestures that would reinforce their confidence that we would not abandon them.

To that end, the president and I gave carefully crafted speeches at the annual convention of AIPAC, the powerful pro-Israel lobbying presence in Washington. President Obama went first, addressing the convention on March 4. The president's speech was shadowed by politics—Republican contenders for the presidency already were accusing him of being insufficiently protective of Israel—and he had to thread a small needle, assuring AIPAC that he was committed to Israel without appearing to veer toward war with Iran. "We all prefer to resolve this issue diplomatically," he said, but he promised emphatically that he would not allow diplomatic failure to endanger Israel. "I have said that when it comes to preventing Iran from obtaining a nuclear weapon, I will take no options off the table, and I mean what I say. That includes all elements of American power: a political effort aimed at isolating Iran, a diplomatic effort to sustain our coalition and ensure that the Iranian program is monitored, an economic effort that imposes crippling sanctions, and yes, a military effort to be prepared for any contingency."[3]

And without mentioning them by name, President Obama alluded to his Republican challengers by deploring "loose talk of war" and urging his listeners to be wary of election-year attacks on his record of support for Israel—a record he spelled out at some length. I thought the speech was forceful and balanced, and it was generally well received at the convention. Others predictably disagreed. Former Massachusetts governor Mitt Romney bluntly declared, "If Barack Obama gets re-elected, Iran will have a nuclear weapon." Newt Gingrich said that "we're being played for fools."[4]

Two days later, I was introduced at the AIPAC convention as a "strong friend" of Israel and AIPAC, and the audience gave me a warm greeting. I reviewed my long-standing support for Israel, going back to my days in Congress and time with Clinton. I mentioned that New York senator Chuck Schumer and I had once been housemates in a Capitol Hill version of *Animal House,* which was greeted with some chuckles. Coming to the point, I spelled out the extensive military support that the Obama administration was even then providing Israel. But the audience was understandably most intent on hearing what assurances the United States was prepared to make about Iran. I tried to leave no doubt.

First, I said, our policy toward Iran was not to accept some level of nuclear capacity and merely try to contain that threat. Rather, it was to thwart it. "Let me be clear," I said, echoing the president's remarks, "we do not have a policy of containment; we have a policy of preventing Iran from acquiring nuclear weapons."

I followed that with a description of the state of our efforts to put pressure on Iran, diplomacy backed by sanctions and the threat of military action. I reminded AIPAC that President Obama had proven his willingness to use force. He had sent troops into battle, forced open the Strait of Hormuz, and waged a risky and lethal campaign to destroy Al Qaeda, including his personal authorization of the bin Laden raid. "Of course we prefer the diplomatic path," I said. "As the prime minister himself has said—military action is the last alternative when all else fails. But make no mistake, when all else fails, we will act." Again the audience applauded vigorously, this time with as much relief as enthusiasm.

In March, I traveled to Kyrgyzstan, Afghanistan, and the Middle East. Just as I was preparing to depart, a shocking event threatened to overtake the trip. Late at night on March 11, 2012, Staff Sergeant Robert Bales, a thirty-nine-year-old soldier on his fourth deployment, snuck out of his base and unleashed a horrific wave of violence in the nearby villages of Alkozai and Najiban. He ransacked homes, wildly knocking over furniture and hurling dishes. In home after home, he grabbed children and shot or stabbed them. He shot one elderly woman, and when he realized she was still alive, he crushed her skull with his boot.[5]

Bales's rampage was by far the worst atrocity committed by an American soldier in Afghanistan—it was in fact the worst war crime in the post-9/11 wars—but it came on top of other disturbing breakdowns in that theater. We'd already weathered images of soldiers urinating on corpses and a misguided attempt to cut off prisoner communication by burning books, including copies of the Koran. It is true that when tens of thousands of young men and women are equipped with weapons and exposed to overwhelming stress, a certain number of bad things are bound to happen. But that's no excuse. Tell that to a family whose grandmother or baby is murdered by an American soldier. I called President Karzai as soon as I learned of Bales's actions and expressed my deep condolences.

Even before Bales's attack, public anger at the presence of foreign troops was surging in Afghanistan. In February, five days of violent unrest—apparently triggered by the videos of soldiers urinating on bodies and the burning of Korans—culminated in a shooting inside the Afghan Interior Ministry. Two American officers were killed in that shooting, and the assailant escaped. General Allen responded by pulling coalition forces out of Afghan government buildings.[6] Karzai appealed for peace, but the protests continued for a while. Finally, whether out of exhaustion or obedience, the violence slowly subsided near the end of February. And then Bales's actions inflamed the public again.

John Kelly and my travel team were nervous about my visiting the country with the security situation so unstable, and they were particularly edgy about my going into the Interior Ministry, where I was scheduled to meet with Interior Minister General Bismillah Khan Mohammadi. We considered asking for another location, but I felt we should not insult the Afghans by implying that we didn't trust their security forces. The meeting went ahead, but under extraordinarily tense arrangements. When my motorcade pulled up to the ministry, there was a security scrum as officers from both countries sought to protect their own officials, elbowing aside their foreign counterparts.

We all got jostled a bit, but finally made our way into the meeting room. My security team, largely drawn from the ranks of the army's Criminal Investigation Command, earned their danger pay at that event.

Leaving Kabul, I was happy just to be out of there, and I enjoyed the hour-long flight to Camp Bastion, headquarters of our regional command responsible for Helmand Province. My staff wasn't so relaxed, and their anxieties were ramped up when we landed. We touched down and began to taxi toward the official party that had assembled to greet me. Then the plane made an abrupt halt. The jolt caught our attention, and then, well, nothing. We just sat there. After twenty minutes or so, I asked John Kelly to find out what was up. He returned from the cockpit with an update.

"Sir, bad news," he said. "An Afghan stole a vehicle, tried to light himself on fire, and drove it in front of your plane." The car ended up in a ditch, smoke pouring from it, the driver dead.

As a terrorist attack—if that's what it was—it didn't amount to much. He'd crashed his car about a thousand yards from my plane, and hurt no one but himself. We taxied around the wreckage and went on with the day as if nothing had happened. Still, it rattled some nerves, and our handling of it angered the traveling press. When they learned what had happened, some reporters lambasted George Little for not revealing the threat against the secretary and treated it as if we had covered up the Kennedy assassination. Many of them filed grumpy stories accusing us of trying to put a good "spin" on the Afghanistan war. To this day, I don't know whether that man in the truck ever meant me any harm.

When I returned to Kabul and met with Karzai, he had just returned from the scene of the Bales crime, and he emotionally relayed stories of seeing "children soaked in their own blood." All I could do was express my profound apologies for the loss of life. Neither of us could do anything to ease that suffering. We returned to the essentials of our work, agreeing to stick to the timeline of transitioning ISAF operations from combat to support by the end of 2014.

Before leaving the country, I told reporters I thought we had made good progress in our talks, and I skirted the Bales controversy. We had, in my view, stayed focused on the goal of putting Afghan National Security Forces in the lead throughout the country. Karzai agreed, or said he did.

I left Afghanistan feeling good about the trajectory of our effort there after a rough few weeks. But progress in Afghanistan was never steady, and Karzai was always a handful. Just a few hours after we left Afghanistan, stories began to appear in which Karzai was quoted describing our talks. Among other things, he released a statement indicating that during our meeting he had insisted that "international forces should leave the villages and move to their bases,"[7] a sop to his domestic audience still enraged by the Bales rampage. That was not true; he said no such thing.

I valued my relationship with Karzai and had always offered to be available to him if he needed to discuss important matters involving our governments. I had not agreed, however, to let him roll me. "Tell the press it's bullshit," I told Jeremy and George Little. "Karzai feels he needs to kick us in the ass, but it's bullshit." Karzai was just playing politics, but I had my job to do too.

We traveled next to the United Arab Emirates, and my focus returned to Iran, whose continued belligerence was alarming its neighbors throughout the region. The UAE is a small but impressive country, blessed with abundant oil and gas. Its leaders wisely chose not to rely on those resources. Instead, they diversified their economy and built a commercial hub unrivaled in the Middle East.

My main interlocutor was Crown Prince Muhammad bin Zayed,

one of the most thoughtful leaders I have ever encountered. Soft-spoken, moderate, and proud of his country's relationship with the United States, he was prone neither to exaggeration nor to alarm. I therefore took note in our conversations that he expressed almost as much apprehension about Iran's influence and intentions as Ehud Barak did.

Bin Zayed regarded Iran's Shiite leadership as a threat not only to Western-oriented Sunni countries but to the West itself. And the prospect of such an antagonist's possessing nuclear weapons was frightening indeed. He too was eager to receive assurances that the United States would act militarily against Iran if the time came. Our conversation underscored a little-understood aspect of Middle Eastern politics as they related to Iran: Though much of the world was focused on Israel's apprehensions regarding Iran, many Arab nations were just as troubled—and just as dependent on the United States for protection.

I had been conscious of that anxiety ever since visiting Saudi king Abdullah during my first year at the CIA. In my conversation with the king, he raised similar concerns about Iran, and I responded by referring to President Obama and suggesting that our policy was to extend a hand to Iran, but that if it persisted, the other hand would be a fist. "Why don't you make that other hand a dagger?" the king suggested.

Those fears dominated not just my private meetings, but my interactions with reporters in the region as well. During an interview with Al Hurra Television, the reporter reminded me that I had laid out a fairly specific timeline for a possible attack—the Ignatius column from the previous month—but I wasn't going to make that mistake twice. I downplayed it during this interview: "President Obama has stated and I agree, we do not believe Israel has made a decision to do that. . . . The international community is unified in putting pressure on Iran and that Israel should operate with the international community in increasing that pressure on Iran. That's the better way to go right now."[8]

That night, I dined at an impressive Italian restaurant with the crown prince, his knowledgeable ambassador in Washington, Yousef al-Otaiba, and other members of his team. We talked well into the evening about Iran, and agreed that the situation was increasingly precarious. Afterward, a few of my close aides and I retired for a nightcap. I asked each of them whether they thought Israel would launch an attack before the fall of 2012. They were split right down the middle.

The Gridiron Club dinner is a stuffy springtime ritual in Washington, when journalists, government officials, and the permanent class of Washington insiders dress in white tie and tails and gather for a night of self-referential comedy. The journalists perform some skits, and a few politicians are invited to deliver humorous remarks. The 2012 dinner's Republican speaker was Texas governor Rick Perry. The Democrat was DNC chairwoman Representative Debbie Wasserman Schultz. The administration's representative was the secretary of defense, me.

I've never pretended to be a stand-up comic, but I thought I had some good material: "Speaking of advanced weaponry, DoD recently completed a sixty-five-year project to develop a cutting-edge robot. Initial testing wasn't good, but Mitt Romney's performance is improving."

I also poked fun at my Italian heritage and told a few off-color jokes. But my favorite line was one I didn't get to deliver: "Looking back on my career, I've been a Republican, a congressman, and White House chief of staff, and a defense secretary. Come to think of it, I've done everything that Dick Cheney has done. Except the guy I made sure got shot in the face was Osama bin Laden."

About ten minutes before I was to take the microphone, my speechwriter, Jacob Freedman, saw a wire story that Cheney had been hospitalized for a heart transplant. Freedman told Jeremy, who was seated across the ballroom. They quickly ran up behind the dais and whispered to me that I probably needed to pull the Cheney joke. I sort of wanted to let her rip, but Cheney was a decent man, and there was no sense in risking an ill-timed insult. Oh well. At least I got to share it now.

By 2012, the Afghan surge had run its course, and we were beginning to draw down our forces in the region. But as our hasty departure from Iraq had only recently served to remind, it's a lot easier to start wars than it is to finish them. In the case of Afghanistan, three important agreements needed to be negotiated and finalized in order for the United States to turn over responsibility for Afghan security, move from combat to support, and leave a sufficiently secure country that it would not again become a haven for terrorists. In the spring of 2012, we engaged Karzai's government and knocked off each of the agreements.

The first was the subject of long, sometimes acrimonious negotiations, and concerned the future of the Parwan Detention Center, located at Bagram Airfield. The United States had used the facility to hold prisoners taken from the battlefield and suspected of ties to insurgents or terrorist organizations. They were not charged criminally, but in the view of NATO commanders they posed a threat to our forces in the region if released. As such, we were reluctant to simply turn over the keys to the Afghan government and stand by while it released people we regarded as dangerous; instead, we negotiated a phased transfer under which we gradually yielded control of the facility to an Afghan commander while retaining some authority to review and even overrule decisions on prisoner releases. That agreement was signed on March 9.

The second area of negotiation was delicate for a different reason. It established rules and limits on nighttime raids, a particularly sore subject in Afghanistan, where villagers complained of terrifying encounters with U.S. forces in the middle of the night. Bales's recent rampage, though not a raid, had also inflamed tempers about the threat our soldiers could pose. On the other hand, relinquishing the right to fight during darkness would vastly reduce the effectiveness of our troops in the country as long as Afghanistan was not prepared to take over the lead in that area. By 2012, however, our forces had been working closely with the Afghan military, and after some deliberation we concluded that we could afford to begin giving up our lead role in those operations. On April 9, General John Allen signed the raid agreement on behalf of the U.S. government. It gave Afghan forces the lead role in future operations, and put the raids under the auspices of the Afghan criminal justice system, with requirements for warrants and the filing of charges. It also permitted Afghanistan to request American assistance at any point. And it allowed for continued, limited work by non-military representatives of the United States.

Those two agreements cleared out some of the underbrush in relations between our countries, and allowed us to turn to the largest and most complex of the negotiations: the terms of the continuing military relationship once the United States had completed its withdrawal. I was determined not to repeat what I regarded as the essential mistake of the transition in Iraq—an abrupt departure that left the United States without any presence to continue exercising influence. At the same time, the White House was eager to be able to conclude the war in Afghanistan, by then the longest in American history. And of course there was substantial pressure from Afghanistan itself, where Karzai was torn between recognizing the value of continued military assistance and growing domestic discontent with the military occupation of much of his country, discontent only exacerbated by incidents such as the Koran burnings and the murderous attack by Bales.

Around the time of these negotiations, the State Department's special representative for Afghanistan and Pakistan, Ambassador Marc Grossman, was developing plans for so-called Taliban reconciliation. The idea was to foster a political dialogue between the Karzai government and the Taliban—and plan for the eventual reintegration of the

Taliban into Afghan political life. The plan for reconciliation, which had begun under Grossman's predecessor, Dick Holbrooke, would require the Taliban to renounce violence, break ties with Al Qaeda, and embrace the Afghan constitution. Unfortunately, the Afghan government was largely kept in the dark and never fully endorsed the effort.

As Grossman began to work out the details through intermediaries with the Taliban, the Taliban came back with a proposal: to return army sergeant Bowe Bergdahl, who had been held by Taliban-linked militants since 2009, in exchange for five senior Taliban leaders whom we were holding at Guantánamo Bay.

I opposed the swap for several reasons. First, I did not believe the Taliban were sincere in their efforts to reconcile with the Afghan government; they were, after all, attacking our forces on the field of battle. Second, I did not believe it was fair to trade five for one. I might have considered one for one, but not five for one. Third, Congress had passed a law stating that no prisoner could be released from Guantánamo unless we could ensure that the country to which we were transferring the prisoner had the ability to prevent the prisoner from rejoining the fight. The Qatari government agreed to receive the prisoners, and I appreciated their efforts, but frankly I did not believe that the Qatari government's assurances were strong enough to satisfy the law.* I directed our team at the Pentagon to negotiate with the Qatari government a better deal, but at the end of the process the Taliban did not agree to many of our key demands. Secretary Clinton and I—and others—did not think we could proceed, and as much as we wanted to bring Sergeant Bergdahl home and reunite him with his family, the deal evaporated.

The controversy over his return in 2014 in some ways missed the point. Most commentators focused on his conduct and whether he "deserved" to be rescued. My view is that we should leave no man behind

---

*The law was later changed to lower the standard for transfers.

and that we should try to reunite all American prisoners of war with their families. The bigger issue is: Is this a good deal for the security interests of the United States? That depends entirely on the assurance that we received and whether in fact these five very bad men are prevented from returning to the fight.

What we hammered out in those weeks attempted to satisfy our concerns as well as those of Karzai. To Afghanistan, we offered a substantial reduction in force and new rules limiting the use of American power, some of which had already been handled in the night raid agreement. To fulfill the president's direction to draw the war to a close, we proposed bringing home the vast majority of our men and women. And to those concerned with the continued security of Afghanistan, we offered to leave a residual force with a new mission—moving from combat to support and training.

Those details were firmed up in March and April, in time for Secretary Clinton and me to bring them to the meetings of NATO defense and foreign ministers, held in Brussels. The two of us presented that group with our proposal for shifting the mission from combat to support, maintaining the bulk of our forces well into 2014 while changing the emphasis of their work. Our allies appreciated that, and expressed relief that we were resisting the urge to pull out precipitously, which they feared would tumble Afghanistan backward and leave open a path for the Taliban's return. Instead, we offered a measured plan to draw down while at the same time bolstering Afghanistan's security capacity. Our European allies were happy to join us. We were, as we said, "in together, out together."

At the conclusion of our talks, I was convinced that we had an approach that could work, and a united front in support of it. As I said then, "Allies and partners have a very clear vision and a very clear message: Our strategy is right, our strategy is working, and if we stick to it, we can achieve the mission of establishing an Afghanistan that can secure and govern itself and never again become a safe haven for terrorists."⁹ Two weeks later, President Obama slipped away from Washington and traveled to Bagram Airfield, where he joined President Karzai at a felt-covered table before the flags of both nations. They exchanged remarks, then signed the document, formally known as the "Enduring Strategic Partnership Agreement Between the United States of America and the Islamic Republic of Afghanistan."

It was in some ways a bittersweet moment, a marker in a long and often frustrating conflict, with many lives lost in pursuit of sometimes murky goals. Afghanistan was hardly a new model of democracy, nor was its long-term security assured. And yet Al Qaeda had been dislodged from its sanctuaries, and America was safer as a consequence. It was not a ringing success, but it was an achievement, albeit one won at considerable cost. In his remarks, President Obama captured that sense of ambiguity, of hope and resolve and even relief.

"Mr. President," he said, addressing Karzai, "there will be difficult days ahead. But as we move forward with our transition, I'm confident that Afghan forces will grow stronger, the Afghan people will take control of their future. With this agreement, I am confident that the Afghan people will understand that the United States will stand by them, and they will know that the United States can achieve our goal of destroying Al Qaeda and denying it a safe haven, but at the same time, we have the capacity to wind down this war and usher in a new era of peace here in Afghanistan."¹⁰

Later that month, the NATO heads of state, meeting in Chicago, ratified the agreement. With that, our longest war turned toward its conclusion.

It did leave one last question, however: At my last NATO meeting in 2013, I strongly urged the alliance to consider endorsing the maintenance of a residual force of 8,000 to 10,000 soldiers, a point I was pressing at the time with the White House as well. No decision was made at that meeting, but President Obama the following year announced that he, too, favored leaving 9,800 American troops in the country after the end of combat operations.

M emorial Day is an especially somber occasion for a secretary of defense, an opportunity to reflect on the responsibilities of peacekeeping and the price of war. In 2012, I felt those emotions acutely, as we honored those who had sacrificed in Iraq and Afghanistan, and also marked the fiftieth anniversary of the Vietnam War, during which I had served as an intelligence officer in California.*

I began the day with a visit to Arlington National Cemetery, where I joined the president and first lady in laying a wreath at the Tomb of the Unknown Soldier. Later that same day, I traveled to the Vietnam Veterans Memorial in Washington, and there was powerfully confronted with the sacrifices this nation has demanded of so many young people—in the case of that war, fifty-eight thousand soldiers, their names etched in the black marble of that stirring memorial. Some of my ROTC classmates from Santa Clara were among those whose lives were lost and whose names appear. And of course, there were many whom I'd helped to brief during their time at Fort Ord. I was moved to see those familiar names, and expressed the hope that this country could at last transcend the divisions over that war.

"The Vietnam generation, my generation, is graying now," I said to those gathered before the memorial. "But this commemoration effort gives the country an opportunity, today and in the years ahead, to try and right the wrongs of the past, to remember those who served in this war and what they did for us, their service, and their sacrifice on our behalf."

---

*There is no fixed point for identifying the beginning of the Vietnam War, but in 2012 the Defense Department began a series of events to commemorate the conflict.

I then was pleased to introduce Senator Chuck Hagel, a Vietnam veteran and friend, who was later to become my successor at the Defense Department.

The following week, I took another step toward healing the wounds of Vietnam, becoming the first American cabinet officer to return to Cam Ranh Bay, the strategically important deepwater port that served as a major American installation for the army, navy, and air force during the Vietnam War. The port was a marvel—deep and calm and protected by row after row of natural buffers. But the wonder of its topography was dwarfed by the marvel of the history that has taken place there. This ancient port had anchored trade in the region for centuries, then became an embattled outpost of American might, then a Pacific harbor for ships of the Soviet Union, and now once again, under a unified Vietnam, a welcoming port of trade and call. I visited a navy cargo ship in the harbor and spoke with sailors about that long history, then headed on to Hanoi.

The highlight of my visit was a brief exchange that helped conclude two intertwined pieces of unfinished business from that war. This particular episode began in 1966, when a young American marine named Robert Frazure led his patrol to clean up after a deadly firefight that left eleven Americans dead and fifty-five wounded in northern South Vietnam. As they were dragging the bodies of the dead from the battlefield, Frazure spotted a small red diary lying on the chest of Vu Dinh Doan, a North Vietnamese soldier killed in the same battle. Frazure shoved it in his pocket and brought it home with him as a souvenir.

Three years later, army sergeant Steven Flaherty was at work with his colleagues in the 101st Airborne in the A Shau Valley, near the Laos border. He was killed in action on March 25, 1969, and Vietnamese soldiers took four partially written letters from him. Flaherty apparently was planning to finish those notes when he returned from his mission. Instead, they were excerpted and used for propaganda purposes, as they described grisly and difficult conditions and the hard life of an American serviceman in combat. These letters had remained in Vietnam for generations.

George Little's press team—including the very able Carl Woog—heard about the diary from the PBS program *History Detectives* (Frazure had contacted the program for its help in returning the diary), and learned of the Flaherty letters from the Defense Department's POW/MIA command, which read about them in a Vietnamese newspaper. Carl put the two together and came up with the idea of an exchange. I endorsed it heartily, but as I left for my Asia trip, we still did not have the diary in hand. Carl dispatched another Pentagon aide to fetch it and jump on a commercial flight to Vietnam. He did, and arrived just in time to meet me there and hand me a FedEx envelope containing the little book.

On June 4, 2012, I presented the red diary to Vietnamese minister of defense Phung Quang Thanh (it was still inside the FedEx package), and he handed me Sergeant Flaherty's unsent letters on a small silver platter. It was the first official exchange of artifacts between our countries since the end of the war.

I brought Flaherty's letters home to the United States and, far too belatedly, had them delivered to his family in South Carolina, where he'd been raised after being adopted from a Japanese orphanage in the 1950s.[11] By the time his letters were delivered, his mother and father had passed away, but his uncle gratefully received them.

One of the notes included a line that had only grown more apt and poignant with time. Writing to a "Mrs. Wyatt" whose identity has been lost, the twenty-two-year-old sergeant said, "This is a dirty and cruel war but I'm sure people will understand the purpose of this war even though many of us might not agree." It took forty-three years for that letter to make it home, and the purpose of the war it described still remained a mystery to many. And yet our countries were now at peace.

Israel is a tough country in a tough part of the world, and Iran was hardly its only threat. In fact, at precisely the same time that we were urging Israel to hold back against Iran we were working to help it defend itself against another foe, Hamas.

The pressure from Hamas had been growing for years, and Ehud Barak had seen it coming. During one of our first meetings after I became secretary of defense, we weren't two sips into the coffee when Ehud said, rather matter-of-factly, "Leon, I need you to help me prevent the next war."

I was certainly game for that, though a little taken aback that Ehud had such a clear vision of the future. "What," I asked, "is the next war?"

"Hamas has rearmed in Gaza," he responded. "They are holding tens of thousands of short-range and medium-range rockets, artillery pieces, and mortars. If we don't stop them, they will rain hell on my people in southern Israel, and we will be forced to go back into Gaza."

That would, as Ehud recognized, trigger an international response. The Israeli government under the late Ariel Sharon had heroically picked up and left Gaza in 2005, leaving the million Palestinians who live there with the right to govern themselves. Unfortunately, the Palestinians chose Hamas in the next election, and Hamas had not allowed real elections or any progress since. Though it played a role in politics and social welfare, Hamas was still at its heart a terrorist organization bent on the destruction of Israel and the United States.

I asked Ehud how the United States could help avert that confrontation, and he calmly asked for some $700 million in American defense funding for an expansion of an Israeli antirocket system called Iron Dome. If perfected, the Iron Dome could knock Hamas's rockets out of the sky and minimize Israeli casualties. That, Barak noted, might be enough to allow Israel to absorb Hamas's aggression without having to invade to clean out the rocket infrastructure.

I appreciated Ehud's logic and already knew of the system's capacity. The Iron Dome system, which was developed with initial know-how from American defense companies and was operationalized in Israel, was truly an amazing innovation. Within seconds, it could effectively create a missile shield to protect population centers from short-range rockets and missiles. The problem was that the batteries, launchers, and interceptors were expensive, and we weren't rolling in money at that point. We had just announced that we were cutting defense spending by $487 billion in ten years. To turn around and request $700 million more for additional batteries was not going to be easy.

But the prospect of war was worse, so we went to work. Over the next several weeks, we worked with Israel to refine its request. President Obama declared his support, at least for an initial payment to get the system going. Congress wanted to help Israel as well, and soon thereafter approved full funding for the program.

In August 2012, I got my first look at the system in action. While visiting the port city of Ashkelon, I was taken to an Iron Dome battery, set in a field on the outskirts of the city. It was ringed by a series of trailers, inside of which young Israel Defense Force soldiers were riveted to computer screens, watching for any indication that a missile had been launched. In this demonstration, simulated rockets rose out of Gaza, appearing as blips on the screen. The radar immediately determined the course of the missiles—those headed for unpopulated areas were ignored while those bound for cities or towns were targeted in a flash. A barrage of interceptor missiles was launched, knocking down the incoming threats. It is an amazingly effective defense system, largely because of its sophistication in concentrating firepower on rockets whose trajectories are most threatening.

It wasn't long before it would go into action. On November 14, 2012, I was in Perth, Australia, with Chairman Dempsey and Secretary Clinton, attending the annual meeting with our Australian counterparts. Hosted by Australian defense minister Stephen Smith, we were discussing the rebalance to the Pacific and how to strengthen bilateral security ties between Australia and the United States.

During the morning's first session, Lieutenant General Tom Wald-hauser, who had replaced John Kelly as my military assistant, tapped me on the shoulder and said I had an urgent call from Ehud Barak.* I stepped out of the conference ballroom where we were meeting and took Ehud's call on a secure cell phone in the kitchen.

"Leon," he said. "The rocket firings from Gaza have become intolerable. We cannot allow our citizens to be attacked by Hamas. The prime minister has authorized a limited military operation to go into Gaza and take out the Hamas rocket infrastructure."

"Do what you have to do," I told Ehud. "Obviously, it will be important to limit civilian casualties, and you know that. But every country has to be able to defend its people and its borders. Please keep me posted." I wanted to press him on additional details, but the phone line cut out. I retook my seat in the ballroom, unable to share the news with my colleagues right away.

Ehud called back a moment later, and Jeremy spoke to him to get a few additional details about the operation, which Israel dubbed "Pillar of Defense." We consulted back at the Pentagon with Undersecretary Jim Miller, who was closely monitoring events there as well as the unfolding civil war on Israel's other border, in Syria. Finally we had a break in our discussions with the Australians, and I huddled with Marty Dempsey and Hillary Clinton on a patio overlooking the Swan River. We agreed that we would recommend to the White House that the president stand by Israel during the war, but that it was in everyone's interest not to let this erupt into a wider regional crisis. By limiting civilian casualties, Iron Dome, which knocked down more than four hundred rockets, helped make that possible.

---

*Kelly was promoted to a four-star commander of the U.S. Southern Command.

After an eight-day ground campaign, Secretary Clinton and Egypt's foreign minister successfully brokered a cease-fire, which was announced on November 21.

I have always regarded politics as personal, and the best politics as those that are the result of men and women of goodwill getting to know each other, understanding the other's point of view, and searching for solutions that can benefit both. I was reminded of that in the spring of 2012, on the very evening that I'd seen Iron Dome in action.

Ehud and I returned from the coast that afternoon and settled in for a private dinner in Tel Aviv with a few close aides. As we were wrapping up, Ehud grew serious. "Leon," he said, "tell me the story of your family in a few sentences."

"Well," I began, "my parents were immigrants from Italy who came to America with little money in their pocket, no language skills, no jobs. They made their way to California, where they opened a restaurant; I washed glasses in the back of that restaurant. They would have *never* imagined that their son would grow up to become secretary of defense of the most powerful country on earth."

"That's pretty good," Ehud said, smiling broadly.

"Now tell me yours," I countered.

"My grandparents were physically dragged out of their home to the Nazi death camp at Treblinka," he said, his voice low and grave. "They and most of my family were exterminated. They would have *never* imagined that their grandson would grow up to become defense minister of the most powerful military within a thousand miles."

As I watch events in the Middle East unfold, I often think about that "thousand miles." Since its inception, Israel has faced the hostility—and sometimes the aggression—of its immediate neighbors. Today, Israel must cope with a much broader and more complex set of threats

425

ranging from failed states on its borders to bomb-carrying terrorists to missiles to the nuclear ambitions of Iran.

The United States and Israel will not agree on everything. Neither country is obliged to shelve its judgment in order to work together. But our bond is unbreakable, and my admiration for Israel and its leadership is unsurpassed. Ehud Barak and his colleagues trusted me and mine on Iran; we helped defend Israel against Hamas, and helped negotiate the truce that brought that fighting to an end. Those were neither the first nor the last times that we will stand with each other.

Born in the aftermath of the Holocaust and under attack from its earliest days, Israel has weathered more danger than any country on earth. Those dangers remain and evolve. We face them together, as something more than allies. We face them as friends.

In the six months leading up to September 11, 2012, the National Counterterrorism Center (NCTC) identified hundreds of threats against American diplomats, embassies, and diplomatic facilities around the world. Those threats come in all shapes and sizes, from specific warnings against specific people to generalized anti-Americanism. We take them seriously, of course, but not all can be acted on equally. And because we don't have the resources to be everywhere, we have to make tough decisions about which are credible, how much and what kind of protection to deploy, and where it is needed the most.

The anniversary of 9/11 always prompts a harder than usual review of those threats, since the opportunity to strike at America on that day has the additional terror bonus of reminding the world of our losses in 2001. As I was the year before in advance of the tenth anniversary, in the weeks leading up to this September 11, I was in regular contact with officials across the intelligence community and at the White House to stay on top of the threat picture. On September 10, I hopped aboard a Marine helicopter to visit the Flight 93 National Memorial in Shanksville, Pennsylvania. Shortly before we left, I received word that the president wanted to speak with his National Security Council Principals for an update on any 9/11-related threats at home or abroad. When the door of my helicopter popped open in the Pennsylvania valley, a Chevy Suburban with tinted windows and some large satellite dishes was waiting for me.

"This is your mobile command center," my chief communications specialist told me. "We drove it here from D.C. so you could take the call with the president."

I climbed into the back of the Suburban, and the operator patched me in to the call.

General Dempsey represented the Joint Chiefs; Hillary Clinton was on for State; Director of National Intelligence Jim Clapper spoke for his agency; Matt Olsen reported for the National Counterterrorism Center; David Petraeus was there for the CIA; and John Brennan was on as the president's adviser on terrorism. The president ran the call and directed the questioning. Our assessment to the president was unanimous: Although there were persistently general threats against U.S. interests and facilities, we saw no specific intelligence or warning about an attack on or around the 9/11 anniversary.

We were already tracking an inflammatory anti-Muslim video that was circulating on the Internet and inciting anger across the Middle East against the United States—even though the U.S. government had nothing to do with it. We braced for demonstrations in Cairo and elsewhere across the region, and General Allen was especially concerned that it might lead to violence against our forces in Afghanistan. Press reports indicated that the radical anti-Muslim pastor Terry Jones—who had previously created a stir by threatening to publicly burn a Koran—was connected to the video. Several senior officials from around the government requested that Chairman Dempsey personally call Jones and ask him to disavow the video. If Dempsey's request failed, I was going to call him next. Dempsey placed the call but was only able to leave a message.

On September 11, as I was heading out of my office with General Dempsey for my weekly meeting with the president at the White House, I received the first reports of violence at our diplomatic compound in Benghazi (we later determined that the attack began at 3:42 p.m. EST, or 9:42 p.m. in Libya). Ambassador Chris Stevens, who had traveled to Benghazi from Tripoli the day before, was inside.

I arrived at the White House between 4:30 and 4:45 p.m., and Dempsey and I presented what little information we had to the president as soon as we entered the Oval Office. We told him that some kind of attack had taken place that threatened our ambassador and compound in Benghazi, but we also cautioned that these were very preliminary reports. The president directed us to do everything we could to help our embattled embassy staff. Around that time, the five diplomatic security agents at the mission were able to escape to a secret CIA facility less than a mile away, and by 5:30 p.m. Washington time there were no remaining Americans inside the compound.

As soon as I got back to the Pentagon, I asked General Kelly to get me the latest. The first reports were confusing and contradictory—one suggested that Stevens had been taken hostage—and the number of casualties was unclear. I summoned the key players to my office. They included Dempsey; members of the Joint Staff; Carter Ham, commanding general of AFRICOM, who happened to be in Washington that day; and several of our senior civilians. Admiral Winnefeld and General Kelly came in and out every few moments with additional information, and Winnefeld briefed the group on where our forces were located.

After hearing the briefing, I gave several orders. First, I directed that two Marine Fleet Anti-Terrorism Support Teams, or "FAST" teams, which were stationed in Rota, Spain, prepare to deploy to Benghazi and Tripoli. Second, I directed that a special operations team, called a "Commander's In-Extremis Force" (CIF), which was then training in the Balkans, cease the exercise and prepare for a rescue mission. Third, I directed that a hostage rescue unit from our special operations teams in the United States load up and fly to Libya in case we had an opportunity to rescue Stevens or others. Those orders went into effect immediately and were followed up that evening with written directives. Dempsey and Winnefeld advised that those were the only units that could reach Tripoli within hours to effect a rescue.

General Kelly, Jeremy, and other senior members of the DoD team spent most of the evening, into the night, tracking events from the Pentagon. At 6:30 p.m. EST, a seven-man team in Tripoli, composed of five CIA security officers and two military men, found a private plane to fly them to Benghazi, arriving an hour later. Although the seven of them worked together, they were not a military unit that had trained together for this type of mission, but acted bravely on their own initiative.

Those were all of the units that could plausibly respond. No aircraft, no aircraft carrier, no surface ship would have gotten there any faster, given the realities of moving those assets over the great distances needed to get them into position in time to make a difference.

At 11:15 p.m. EST, just before dawn in Benghazi, the CIA facility near the diplomatic compound came under fire, this time by attackers using mortars. Two CIA security officers were killed in that attack, bringing the total number of Americans killed to four. By early daylight in Libya, the first group of Americans was able to leave by plane to Tripoli. Later that morning, the remaining Americans, including the bodies of Ambassador Stevens—which had been recovered from a local hospital—Sean Smith, Tyrone Woods, and Glen Doherty, also flew from Benghazi to Tripoli.

I recount the above in such detail because the events of that night in Benghazi have unfortunately become the object of much conjecture and suspicion. The simple, sad fact of Benghazi is that we did not have intelligence that such an attack might occur, and as a result did not have forces close enough when the violence struck to be able to save our people from harm. We moved as quickly as we could, but this took place too far away for our forces to reach them in time.

Any suggestion that anyone, from the president on down, delayed or was indifferent to the ambassador and his staff in Benghazi is simply false. One conspiracy theory held that the CIA security team in Tripoli had been ordered by their own chain of command to "stand down." That was not only false but directly the opposite of the sum of everyone's efforts in response to the president's orders, which was to move as quickly as possible to help. I have had the honor of leading the brave men and women of both the Department of Defense and the CIA. One thing I know is that when Americans are in danger, you don't need to give the order to help twice. That time and distance were simply too much to overcome should never be mistaken for a lack of swift and honest effort to help our people. That conclusion was affirmed by an accountability review board, cochaired by Admiral Mullen, which said of the attempts to rescue our people that night, "The interagency response was timely and appropriate, but there simply was not enough time, given the speed of the attacks, for armed U.S. military assets to have made a difference." House Armed Services chairman Buck McKeon, a Republican stalwart, conducted his own review and arrived at the same conclusion. "I think I've pretty well been satisfied that given where the troops were, how quickly the thing all happened and how quickly it dissipated, we probably couldn't have done more than we did," he later told the press.[12]

The initial reports provided to the president and his top staff suggested that the attack in Benghazi was the work of a mob of protesters rather than an organized assault. Petraeus, working off the assessments drawn up by CIA analysts, presented the theory to the national security team at a meeting in the Situation Room the day after the attack. I questioned it from the beginning, not because I had different information but because it seemed to me that most spontaneous demonstrators don't arrive for a protest carrying rocket-propelled grenade launchers. Others agreed. Maybe the first assault was from a mob of protesters, but the second attack, hours later, certainly was not. It was not clear at the time that there were two separate incidents, separated by distance and by several hours. Petraeus defended the theory of his analysts, however, arguing that there was so much weaponry floating around Libya that it was plausible in this instance. That theory was translated into talking points prepared for the House Intelligence Committee. Although they weren't intended for use by UN ambassador Susan Rice, she used them during several interviews she gave that weekend.* The theory proved to be wrong, but Rice was not to blame, and it did not originate at the White House. To the contrary, it was the working premise of CIA analysts as of that time. Intelligence is difficult and often contradictory. That it took some time to get a handle on what happened should surprise nobody.

On Friday of that week, I was scheduled to provide closed-door testimony to the Senate Armed Services Committee. I was asked whether I thought the embassy attack was an act of terrorism, and I said it certainly looked like terrorism to me. Storming a diplomatic facility and killing a U.S. ambassador was an act of terrorism, as the president noted in the Rose Garden the day after the attack. In hindsight, we as a government could have made that point more clearly publicly following the attack, but not doing so was merely prudent reluctance to go beyond the official intelligence assessments. As was often the case, I was less cautious and could afford to be, since I was

---

*The fact that they were prepared for the Hill, not Ambassador Rice, undercuts the claim by some that the talking points were specifically written for Rice so she could "mislead" the country.

speaking in a closed-door hearing. I was asked for my opinion, and I gave it. I was proven right, but I could easily have been proven wrong. Like everyone else at that point, I was working from initial reports that could only be verified by a fuller investigation.

Before I leave this subject, let me be crystal clear: We made every effort to help the U.S. personnel in Benghazi. I wish we could have saved them, and I am heartbroken that we could not. Nothing we say or do can ever bring them back to their loved ones, and all of us charged with defending the security of our country own that responsibility. But there was no conspiracy to sacrifice them and no conspiracy to cover up our actions. We did our best. Our best is not always enough. That's been confirmed by the reports of the commission assigned to investigate the tragedy and by the Senate Intelligence Committee. The responsibility now, for both Democrats and Republicans, is to make sure it never happens again and to ensure that those responsible are brought to justice.

Tomorrow's wars will surprise us, just as history's always have. But one predictable facet of future war-fighting will be the use of cyber technology, which already commands a central place in our military calculations. That represents a profoundly new way of thinking about combat and highlights vulnerabilities that I suspect most Americans have never considered.

I first became conscious of the growing aggressiveness of cyber attacks at the CIA, where our computer system was subject to attempts to penetrate it every day. At the Defense Department, where we had nearly three million people logged on to computers, the number of attempted penetrations was almost too large to calculate.

When I became secretary, my daily briefing book included reports on attacks against American financial institutions. These efforts, known as denial-of-service attacks, were not very sophisticated (they vaguely resembled flooding a switchboard with phone calls), but they represented a new effort to hit U.S. infrastructure, and our analysts traced them to Iran. I felt it important to expose those attacks in order to make others appreciate the growing danger, so I asked Marcel Lettre, working with NSA director General Keith Alexander, to declassify as much information as possible.

On October 11, 2012, I tried to set out, within the limits imposed by security, some of the implications of the new world of warfare into which we are entering at a rapid pace. The occasion seemed right for it: I'd been invited to deliver an address to the Business Executives for National Security, a nonprofit organization dedicated to working with government to share best business practices in order to bolster national defense. The group was marking its thirtieth anniversary and gathered seven hundred of its members on the Intrepid Sea, Air, and Space Museum in New York City. I was honored at the dinner and offered the chance to make remarks.

After the introductions, I cut to the heart of the matter: "The Internet is open. It's highly accessible, as it should be. But that also presents a new terrain for warfare. It is a battlefield of the future where adversaries can seek to do harm to our country, to our economy, and to our citizens." Those threats, I explained, go way beyond the loss of personal information or identity theft. In addition to the denial-of-service attacks on American banks, hackers tied to the Iranian regime launched an even more pernicious effort against Saudi Arabia's state-run oil company. Using a virus known as "Shamoon," that attack wiped out programming files in the company's computers and replaced them with an image of a burning American flag. It destroyed thirty thousand computers.

With so many systems reliant on the Internet for communication and operation, our vulnerability is frightening to consider. Imagine, I urged that night, a hostile nation or terrorist group infecting switching systems for railroads and using that access to crash passenger trains or trains carrying toxic chemicals. Or electrical power stations? Or water treatment facilities? Should a determined enemy wage war against the United States, a combination of physical and cyber attack could reap damage unimaginable just a few years ago. It would be, as I warned that night, a "cyber Pearl Harbor" that could lay us bare.

For that reason, not only did I speak out about this issue, but we invested heavily in cyber defense, began to build up a new cadre of cyber mission forces, and launched a new initiative to work with the private sector to share information about these attacks. I pressed for legislation from Congress to strengthen cyber security and extend liability protection to companies that share data about breaches with the government. Like so much before Congress these days, that legislation got bogged down.

There is no greater challenge for future presidents, members of Congress, secretaries of defense, and business leaders than finding ways to protect computer networks—not to make it easier for the government to snoop or control commerce, but to see that the country is safe from those who will exploit our cyber vulnerability.

As much as we worked for a "rebalance to Asia," the Middle East seemed never to let us rest. In early November 2012, I was receiving my morning intelligence briefing in my office when General Dempsey interrupted to ask if he could bring in General James Mattis to see me. It was urgent, he said. I of course agreed, wondering what this was about. Mattis, who was commanding general of Central Command—responsible for the war zones and the Middle East—had a reputation for being plainspoken, whip smart, and having a spine of steel.

"Mr. Secretary," Mattis began, "we fly routine surveillance missions with a Predator unmanned airplane in international space in the Arabian Gulf to monitor activity in the Strait of Hormuz.

"Today, our plane was shot at," he continued. "An Iranian pilot flew an Su-25, an old Soviet-era 'Frogfoot' fighter, out of the Iranian airfield at Bandar Abbas along the coast. He came up alongside our drone and tried to shoot it down three times by firing his gun at it."

As Mattis and Dempsey explained, this was a clear act of hostility—an Iranian fighter trying to shoot down a U.S.-flagged military airplane operating in international airspace over international waters. And we had proof. The smart camera operator on the Predator slewed the camera over and caught the three gun runs on video. The question was: Was this a deliberate act of war by Iran or the foolish work of a rogue pilot?

Without knowing the answer to that question, we also faced a second: Should we fly the routine mission again—it occurred every few days—or call it off? If we did fly, and the drone was shot down, we'd be in an explosive situation with Iran. If we didn't, we'd effectively be acquiescing to Iran's unwarranted attack. The last thing we needed was for Iran to conclude that it could shoot at us with impunity.

Within hours, the matter was being hotly discussed inside the Pentagon and across the river at the White House. Some officials wanted us to fly again. Others said we should back off and reassess our rules of engagement. One underlying issue was the Predator itself. Should we regard it as the equivalent of an American airplane or ship, and thus defend it as we would any other military asset? Or, recognizing that it's an unmanned device, should we treat it as something less vital and less in need of defense?

I could sense that Mattis did not want to back down, and that the White House was wary of his resolve. As I knew already, the White House didn't fully trust Mattis, regarding him as too eager for a military confrontation with Iran. I disagreed, but recognized that his recommendations were going to be treated with some caution because of that impression. As for me, I felt we could not afford to back down to Iran, but I also didn't like the idea of sending the drone up just for the sake of testing our power and Iran's objections.

"Give me some options here," I told my team. "Let's get creative. The Iranians aren't smarter than us."

What came back was creative, all right. CENTCOM and Joint Staff planners, working with Jim Miller's policy shop, put together a plan that only a twenty-first-century warrior could appreciate. First, we wrote a sharply worded diplomatic rebuke—a "démarche," in diplo-speak—and sent it to the Iranian government. It said very clearly: We are going to fly this mission tomorrow. If you come near us, we are going to shoot you down.

To make good on that threat, we sent the unmanned Predator on its regular surveillance run under escort by two F-16s, pilots in the cock-pits. The escorts were there to defend American property and our right to fly in international airspace, and they were under orders to shoot down any aircraft that threatened our Predator.

Let me pause there. Yes, there's something mind-boggling about the idea that we'd send manned aircraft to defend an unmanned vehi-cle, since the whole point of unmanned aircraft is to allow us to con-duct operations without risking danger to our people. Now, instead of robots protecting people, we had two pilots defending a robot. Tech-nology and diplomacy sometimes lead us to strange places. But they also can encourage fresh thinking. And occasionally they can produce important tactical results: The Iranians let the drone and its escorts pass overhead unimpeded.

This mini-crisis was telling. Though it was only about one airplane and one flight, it also demonstrated that diplomacy is most effective when the message is clear, the determination unambiguous, and the force behind it sufficient to make it stick. That's a lesson for dealing with Iran and any number of adversaries.

SEVENTEEN

"I Cannot Imagine the Pain"

O ne hundred twenty-six million Americans cast their ballots for president of the United States on election day in 2012. The election did not have quite the energy that electrified the campaign four years earlier, but the results were fairly similar. After much handwringing about the president's decline in popularity, he ended up winning by five million votes, carrying all but two of the states he had won over John McCain in 2008 and winning nine of the ten so-called battleground states. Having secured the Republican nomination with some difficulty, Mitt Romney briefly seemed viable— President Obama turned in a strangely passive performance in the first debate between the two, and many of his supporters panicked—but Romney never capitalized on that, and his brief blip of momentum quickly sputtered out. He won just 206 electoral votes, more than a hundred fewer than Obama's 332.

For me, the final days of the campaign were a whirlwind of domestic activity, but only tangentially related to politics. Hurricane Sandy

bore down on the northeastern United States, striking first on the evening of October 29 in New Jersey. The damage was staggering. Twelve
states were hit by the hurricane; eight and a half million people lost
electrical power; more than twenty-three thousand sought emergency
shelter. New York, New Jersey, and Connecticut absorbed the brunt
of that blow, and the vast federal response included a significant contribution from the Defense Department. My offices suddenly were a
scramble. We dispatched water, blankets, and meals throughout the
Northeast. National Guardsmen were called to duty, and the Army
Corps of Engineers rushed to provide emergency power to huge areas
plunged into darkness.

It was not a typical operation for the Defense Department. There
were no enemies to combat, other than weather and fear. But in the dir-
est emergencies, the largest organization on earth can deliver a lot of
help. Our people responded with energy and a sense of common purpose, with Assistant Secretary Paul Stockton playing an important
coordinating role. And, as I noted, while this was only tangentially
related to politics, it did underscore a subtle philosophical point: To
those who think government is intrusive or irrelevant, it's worth re-
membering that when more than eight million people lose their electrical power, thousands are suddenly underwater, and hundreds of
thousands are shivering and afraid, it's not bad to have a government
that can help.

By election day I was exhausted, but the day itself was for me a day
at the office—inside the world's largest office building. I started my
morning at the Pentagon with an hour-long update on Afghanistan and
spent the afternoon discussing the budget and the military's role in
helping restore order to the communities of the northeastern United
States hit by Hurricane Sandy. I watched the election returns with Jeremy and a group of friends. I was of course delighted by the outcome
and the endorsement of the American people of the president's first
term. I did not, however, have a direct stake in the results. I had made

it clear to the president that I would only serve out his first term, and though he'd asked me to reconsider and stick around, I was committed to wrapping up my work and heading for home.

There was still plenty to do, and just three days after the election, a minor bombshell upended Obama's national security team. It began weirdly, when FBI agents in Florida opened an investigation into allegations that a Florida woman named Jill Kelley was being threatened via e-mail from an unknown account. As the agents dug into the matter, they discovered that the account belonged to Paula Broadwell, an author and protégée of General David Petraeus, then still at the CIA. And then came the coup de grâce: Broadwell, they learned, was having an affair with Petraeus.

Petraeus was hardly the first Washington official to have an affair, but I did realize this might be trouble. The announcement was a shock and an embarrassment, not only for Petraeus and his family but also for the CIA. At the CIA, officers at all levels are urged to avoid behavior that might subject them to blackmail, so it was especially awkward for the director to acknowledge conduct that would be frowned upon if committed by his colleagues and subordinates. After the FBI warned Petraeus of what it had found, he weighed his options for two weeks— at least sparing the president a scandal on the eve of the election—and then on Friday, November 9, he acknowledged the affair and resigned. It was an ugly episode for all concerned, but I thought Petraeus handled his resignation with admirable dignity—disclosing the affair, apologizing for his "unacceptable" behavior, and recognizing that it damaged both his marriage and his office. He even credited the president, who at first resisted letting him go, with "graciously" accepting his resignation.

Barely had that news settled before another shoe dropped. It was just three days later, while I was en route to Australia, that we received word that General John Allen, our commander in Afghanistan, also had exchanged e-mails with Jill Kelley, the same woman who had complained of being harassed by Broadwell. The timing was terrible: John had been picked to serve as NATO's top military officer, though the nomination had not yet formally been made; if the e-mails did reveal anything untoward, it would surely make his confirmation a difficult one.

It was late at night when the decision was made to cancel Allen's forthcoming confirmation hearing, and I knew I needed to act quickly in order to stay ahead of the news. I asked George Little to wake up the sleeping press corps and alert them to the developments. Groggy and grumbling, they snapped to attention when George told them of the e-mails and of my decision to forward the matter to the Pentagon's inspector general.

I regretted having to take that action with regard to Allen, especially when it later became clear that there was nothing improper about his communications with Jill Kelley. The tone of the messages was friendly but not unseemly, and certainly there was no evidence of any romantic relationship between the two. Still, I felt I had no choice but to order the investigation, if only to assure the public that we were not covering up a larger problem. Allen, an outstanding military officer by every measure, was cleared in early 2013. Allen was also dealing with some long-standing health issues in his family. Unfortunately, he opted to retire rather than accept the NATO nomination.

Neither David Petraeus nor John Allen broke any laws or compromised the public trust. Petraeus did expose himself to legitimate criticism, but he took responsibility for his actions and paid a steep price for them. Allen did nothing wrong at all, and, like Petraeus, had made huge contributions in Afghanistan. It was a shame to lose him.

When Congress had tried to frighten itself into behaving responsibly on the federal budget back in 2011, it had enacted the sequester—the threatened across-the-board cuts that were so universally disliked that they were supposed to brace Congress into acting responsibly. That hadn't worked, but Congress also had allowed itself one last escape from its self-inflicted wound: The cuts were only to go into effect in 2013, so if a solution could be found in the interim, there was still a way to avoid the damage.

I felt well positioned to make the case for avoiding the cliff. I had announced my intention to leave, so no one could accuse me of trying to pad my own budget. I'd balanced the budget under Clinton, so I was generally regarded as knowledgeable in this area. And I had reasonably good relations with members and leaders of both parties, so I could straddle, at least to some extent, the widening rift on Capitol Hill.

I worked it hard, trying to seize every opportunity to rail against sequestration. In June 2012, I told the Senate Subcommittee on Defense Appropriations that sequester was "designed as a disaster," and that quick, decisive action would protect the priorities of both parties. When I testified on Benghazi a few months later, I urged members to recognize that even as they were complaining about inadequate military resources in the Mediterranean to rescue our mission when it came under fire, they were standing by and allowing deep cuts to degrade those capabilities further.

"One of the . . . greatest security risks we are now facing as a nation is that this budget uncertainty could prompt the most significant military readiness crisis in more than a decade," I warned. Without congressional action, the armed services would be forced to cut $48 billion a year—after already having made cuts in 2011 and 2012. "We have a responsibility—and I take that responsibility seriously—to do everything we can to protect our citizens," I concluded. "That responsibility, however, rests with both the executive branch and Congress. If we work together, we can keep Americans safe."

I might as well have been talking to the wall. Privately, members would agree with me, would acknowledge that sequestration would damage important programs, inhibit modernization and creativity, slow economic growth, and cost the country jobs. Publicly, they dug in and hoped that whatever damage was done, the other side would get the blame. About the only people I spoke to who didn't dread the outcome were a few fringe, Tea Party types who seemed to enjoy hurling the government into disrepute, since it served their larger mission of discrediting the organization they served. Inexorably, inaction became the option of choice.

Watching it was one of the most frustrating experiences of my life. The people of this country elect representatives to help them make life better, to ease the burdens of a tough economy, to provide them with safety and security, to create opportunity and encourage prosperity. Instead, these members confronted a problem that was admittedly complex and in need of compromise, but rather than work hard and cut a deal, they gave up and deliberately made life worse for their constituents. That shameful inaction undermined the most basic rationale of representative government. Elected to help their country, they willfully and deliberately hurt it.

President Obama bore some responsibility as well, not for concocting the sequester but rather for failing to lead Congress out of it. Indeed, that episode highlighted what I regard as his most conspicuous weakness, a frustrating reticence to engage his opponents and rally support for his cause. That is not a failing of ideas or of intellect—he is, as anyone who knows him can attest, supremely intelligent, capable of absorbing and synthesizing complex information, and committed to a well-reasoned vision for the country. He does, however, sometimes lack fire. Too often, in my view, the president relies on the logic of a law professor rather than the passion of a leader.

That has given his opponents room to shape the contours of his presidency, and they have used it to the detriment of the country, sometimes in ways that seem more like parody than real life. One need only recall the dozens of theatrical votes by House Republicans to overturn the Affordable Care Act, or the countless committee hearings on Benghazi, or, even more telling, the long and shrill campaign to question Obama's birthplace. That last issue underscores a unique aspect of the attack on this president: He is the first black president of the United States. No other president's legitimacy as a person and officeholder has been challenged in the way President Obama's most extreme critics have questioned his. Those challenges have encouraged the president's caution and defensiveness, which in turn has emboldened further challenges.

It's amusing that some of President Obama's critics think he is an ideologue. I see him as a realist and a pragmatist. That's an instinct we need more of in Washington. But "playing it cool" tends to take the edge off the rhetoric needed to stir people to action. And where I've seen presidents succeed most dramatically is when they've passionately convinced people—whether the public or members of Congress or foreign leaders—that a course of action is in their best interest. I saw President Obama do that, but on occasion he avoids the battle, complains, and misses opportunities.

It's important to add, however, that those are small blots on a larger picture. President Obama overcame bitter opposition to make important progress in many areas, from fighting terrorism to righting the economy. I did not always agree with every detail of his actions, but I appreciated that they were unfailingly guided by his intelligence, his convictions, and his determination to do what was best for the country. I was proud to serve him.

I made two trips to China as a representative of the Obama administration, one as director of the CIA and the second near the end of my tenure as secretary of defense. Both were bewildering amalgams of pomp and straight talk, wariness and warmth. And both were reminders that the U.S.-China relationship will do much to shape the future of the Pacific and the world.

In the fall of 2012, on a mission that also took me to Japan and New

Zealand, I spent three days in and around Beijing and Qingdao, a port city that was home to the Chinese North Sea Fleet. The arrangements took shape slowly at first—I'd only planned to spend two days in the country, but we added a third as our increasingly excited hosts piled on more stops, clearing me to meet with Chinese cadets and to tour a submarine and a frigate as well as to meet with Vice President Xi Jinping and their nation's military leadership.

Meetings between top American and Chinese officials often play out according to a well-understood script. They chide us for our support of Taiwan, we gently inject the topic of human rights, they demand access to markets for their growing economy, we complain about violations of intellectual property and mysterious cyber activity that emanates from within China. There is a surface veneer of goodwill, and a mutual, unstated agreement not to push each other too hard.

That's pretty much what I expected as I headed for China in 2012. In fact, my visit surprised me at almost every turn. I arrived at a moment of high tension between that country and Japan, which I had just visited. The two nations have an ancient rivalry, with ample room for resentment on both sides. China still seethes over the brutal Japanese invasion and occupation beginning in 1931, and I happened to be visiting on the anniversary of that invasion. More to the point, in 2012 the two countries were battling over a pair of islands that both claimed as their own. Just before my visit, Japan angered China by purchasing the islands from their private owner as a way of strengthening its claim to them, and riots erupted in many Chinese cities, with protesters targeting Japanese businesses.

Making matters worse, as I prepared for my meeting with China's defense minister, General Liang Guanglie, I was told our intelligence had picked up reports that China was about to send a thousand fishing boats to confront Japanese vessels in the area around the islands. That was almost sure to provoke more violence, and on unpredictable seas, and it threatened to draw the United States into the conflict, since we have a defense pact with Japan pledging to provide military assistance in the event it is attacked.

I publicly urged both sides to back up and talk rather than escalating the matter, but at first it seemed they actually were eager for a confrontation—and that they'd get it. As one report concluded, "In this heady atmosphere, U.S. calls for calm are falling on deaf ears, for now."[1]

When Liang and I met privately, I tried to make use of both carrot and stick. I invited China to participate for the first time in RIMPAC, a biennial maritime exercise hosted by the United States in the Pacific (RIMPAC stands for "Rim of the Pacific"), an invitation that Liang seemed to appreciate. At the same time, referring to the reports of the boats headed for the disputed area, I was as direct as I could be. "It would be very important for you to stop this," I insisted. Liang is a stern character. His mouth is perennially stuck in a frown, and it's hard to imagine him not in a uniform. He didn't give me much in our meeting, and afterward he told reporters, standing next to me, that if there was trouble over the islands, it would be Japan's fault.[2]

And yet, curiously, the thousand fishing boats that departed for the disputed area never arrived. After our meeting, they quietly peeled off and scattered. Liang never acknowledged, at least to me, any role in dispatching the boats or calling them off. But they were gone, and the prospect of a major conflagration subsided.

The day after my conversation with Liang, I met with Vice President Xi, the charismatic, personable presumptive next-in-line for the Chinese presidency. He had been in seclusion for several weeks prior to our meeting, and much of the coverage speculated that he might be suffering from illness. Some wondered whether he would cancel our get-together, but he surprised many observers by greeting me buoyantly in the Great Hall of the People. He dispensed with any talking points, instead jumping straight to what was at the top of his mind. He wanted my explanation for what our defense "rebalance" to Asia meant for China. Was it, he asked, intended to counter China?

My answer was that it did not need to be, that America and China could coexist in the Pacific and that we could together help ensure stability in that region. We had some common challenges. We were both searching for ways to combat terrorism and piracy, and we were both called upon to provide disaster relief. Increased American presence in the Pacific could advance our mutual interests, I argued.

That said, we were rivals too, and there was no point in pretending otherwise. Rather than hammer him with accusations about cyber crime or territorial disputes with neighbors, however, I suggested that development of international forums to resolve differences in those areas might benefit both of our countries. Xi cheerfully agreed, though whether out of politeness or genuine concurrence, I couldn't tell. Finally, we briefly discussed North Korea, and I pointed out to him that its nuclear and missile programs were alarmingly destabilizing to our friends in the region and even to the United States itself. Xi almost seemed to sigh and roll his eyes. North Korea, he conceded, was an aggravation for him too. Scheduled for forty-five minutes, our meeting stretched past ninety. We parted on good terms.

High-level meetings with Chinese officials almost always conclude with a banquet, and this was no exception. After I returned from an afternoon talk at a Chinese military academy, we took our places at a gigantic table and began a long evening of toasts and expressions of mutual admiration. I'd done this before and knew that the chief enemy here was the drink—the Chinese typically serve a clear liquor known as Maotai at important functions, and it's a killer. One toast leads to another, and before you know it the room starts to wobble. I figured it was probably best not to have the American secretary of defense get sloshed in front of the leadership of the world's largest country, so I pulled John Kelly aside as we were sitting down and asked him if he could find a way for me to escape the ritual. He conferred with a waiter, who secretly substituted water for my Maotai each time my glass was filled.

Managing the U.S.-China relationship in the future will be difficult for both nations, each of which has legitimate interests in the region and the world. We come from vastly different political and cultural traditions, and we will compete for influence and some of the same markets. But we also have much in common—we both seek stability, open markets, and growth; we both need to advance environmental protection; and we both appreciate a good drink. That's something to build on.*

I have talked at length in these pages about wars—fighting them, ending them, avoiding them. Before I leave that topic, it's worth noting that there was one other deteriorating situation in 2012 that repeatedly challenged our military and national security leadership, often dividing us: Syria.

The momentum of the Arab Spring caught up with Syria in March 2011, when the first major demonstrations called for the release of political prisoners. Behind that demand was a glimpse of deeper discontent, as the protests also produced graffiti demanding that President Bashar al-Assad step down. After hesitating a bit, Assad unleashed his formidable military on the next wave of demonstrations, in April, when snipers picked off protesters and tanks rolled out to intimidate them.

With that, Assad committed himself to responding with oppression, and his use of force steadily ratcheted up through the remainder of 2011. Most of the international community was aghast, but struggled to find some way to exert leverage. The United States imposed sanctions in May, President Obama and our European allies called for

---

*My China trip also produced one of the more memorable gifts I received during my tenure as secretary of defense: I was presented with a ceremonial plate that featured a portrait of me. I was flattered, though puzzled as to how I could ever use it.

Assad to step down in August, and the Arab League suspended Syria's membership in November. None of which deterred Assad. The United Nations, meanwhile, was frozen by Russia's use of its veto power in the Security Council to block any sanctions against Assad or his regime. By the end of the year, more than five thousand Syrians were dead, and the conflict showed no sign of abating.

All of that seemed to create a strong case for intervention, and some members of Congress urged just that. Judicious use of American air power and a united NATO coalition had toppled Qaddafi in Libya, so why not Assad in Syria? At least that seemed the basic argument.

The problem with it was that Syria was not Libya. Assad was much more heavily armed, the country was far less accessible, and among the military's munitions were large storehouses of chemical weapons and modern air defense systems, the latter supplied by the Soviet Union and later Russia. Recognizing those factors, we convened a series of meetings at the Pentagon to develop options for confronting and containing Assad and for doing what we could to protect his people from their leader.

The primary concern was locating Assad's chemical weapons and preparing to seize and secure them if the situation required it. Our planners studied the matter at length and returned with an estimate of the number of troops required to enter the country and commandeer each of the known weapons repositories. Their conclusion was that it would require more than seventy-five thousand soldiers, perhaps as many as ninety thousand, roughly what we had in all of Afghanistan. I considered that impossible, and my colleagues agreed.

We presented a set of options to the National Security Council—ranging from more aggressive possibilities such as the use of limited air attacks on military targets to more modest engagement including protecting refugee camps and supporting regional allies. It was clear from those discussions that there was no strong support among the president's top advisers for direct military action.

That left us with the less aggressive measures: working with Jordan and Israel to coordinate a regional response; reaching out to the Syrian rebels to lend support and guidance; surveying Assad's air defense systems so that if a military option was called for, we could control the skies.

The Syrian rebels also posed a more difficult problem than had the forces that rose up against Qaddafi. In Syria, there was little coordination between the opposition groups, and some had unsavory ties to terrorist groups. That made us wary of overcommitting to their cause, so our initial support was nonlethal—training, for the most part, as well as supplies, but not weapons.

That did not do much to strengthen their hand against Assad, however, and the casualties inflicted by the Syrian army continued to mount. Speaking at a news conference in August, President Obama tried to warn Assad not to escalate the fighting with the weapons we knew he possessed: "We cannot have a situation in which chemical or biological weapons are falling into the hands of the wrong people. We have been very clear to the Assad regime but also to other players on the ground that a red line for us is we start seeing a whole bunch of chemical weapons moving around or being utilized." Should Assad begin to employ those weapons, the president added, "That would change my calculus. That would change my equation."

That language was subsequently much criticized. Although the president did not promise military action in response to any use of chemical weapons, merely that such use would "change my calculus," his insistence that the use of such weapons would cross a "red line" clearly implied that it would justify the use of force in response. That reflected our growing frustration with Assad's actions and our limited ability to influence events. It also hinted at the internal divisions within the national security team. The National Security Council considered a plan to step up aid to the rebels and begin sending them weapons; I supported the idea, as did David Petraeus and Hillary Clinton. All of us believed that withholding weapons was impeding our ability to develop sway with those groups and subjecting them to withering fire from the regime.

President Obama was initially hesitant, and with some justification, as the stakes were high and the situation complex. Only after Assad used chemical weapons in mid-2013 did Obama reconsider supplying those arms, a step he approved in June of that year. Assad was not deterred. On August 21, his forces unleashed a devastating attack with rockets carrying the chemical sarin; 1,429 people, including at least 426 children, were killed.[3] At that point, both the president and John Kerry, who had taken over as secretary of state on January 1, made it clear that they were leaning toward limited military action, but then President Obama vacillated, first indicating that he was prepared to order some strikes, then retreating and agreeing to submit the matter to Congress. The latter was, as he well knew, an almost certain way to scotch any action. By mid-2013, a majority of Congress could not agree on what day of the week it was, much less a resolution authorizing the use of American force in the Middle East.

The result, I felt, was a blow to American credibility. When the president as commander in chief draws a red line, it is critical that he act if the line is crossed. The power of the United States rests on its word, and clear signals are important both to deter adventurism and to reassure allies that we can be counted on. Assad's action clearly defied President Obama's warning; by failing to respond, it sent the wrong message to the world.

Perhaps still thinking it was possible we would use force, Russia pushed the Assad regime to negotiate the surrender of its chemical weapons, offering hope that a diplomatic alternative might still produce the right outcome. The removal of Syria's declared chemical weapons was finally completed in June 2014, an important accomplishment. But as of this writing, there are credible reports that the Assad regime used chlorine gas against its people in 2014, and Assad remains in power.

The threat from the Islamic State of Iraq and Syria and other terrorist groups is growing. The contested city of Homs has been decimated by Assad's bombardment and now resembles Dresden or Grozny in the aftermath of their devastations. Syria is a dangerous place, and invading it would have reaped great suffering and the loss of many American lives. It was not another Libya. Still, hesitation and half-steps have consequences as well—and those remain to be determined.

The United States military is first and foremost a fighting force. But it is also America's largest employer and an institution where cultural values are learned and transmitted. Serving as its chief sometimes requires the skills of a battlefield commander, sometimes those of a bureaucratic infighter, and sometimes those of a high school principal.

Historically, some of the military's most esteemed leaders have been reluctant to thrust the institution into the middle of the nation's social debates. As I noted earlier, a leader no less revered than George Marshall resisted calls to racially integrate the armed forces even as he led those forces into war against fascist enemies whose racism helped define their ideologies. I certainly accept that the military should not risk its capacity to fight in order to become an instrument of social progress, but I also believe it has a responsibility not only to defend American values but also to uphold them.

Those ideas made me proud of helping to eliminate "Don't Ask, Don't Tell" early in my tenure as secretary. Now, as my time wound down, I hoped to break down impediments for women in our forces as well. Those efforts took two forms.

The first was a matter of simple decency. Too many women in the services for too long had become victims of sexual assaults, many of them refusing to report the incidents for fear of being ignored, mistreated, or retaliated against. The reluctance to report such assaults exists outside the military as well but poses particular challenges in an environment where service members live and work in close quarters, where the nature of that work requires troops to trust one another, where the person adjudicating a complaint is often acquainted with both the accuser and the accused, and where movements are restricted, so victims cannot escape their assailants by leaving town or going home. Moreover, the gap between the number of crimes committed and the number reported made it extremely difficult to gauge the size of the problem and the effectiveness of efforts to combat it: If reports increased, one could argue either that we were doing a better job of encouraging victims to come forward or that the actual number of assaults was increasing.

What was clear, however, was that sexual assaults were common in the military and were vastly underreported. A survey of active-duty servicemen and -women in 2012 found that 6.1 percent of active-duty women—and 1.2 percent of active-duty men—reported having been the victim of unwanted sexual contact in the previous year. That's roughly 26,000 men and women, and yet only 2,949 victims came forward to report that illegal and destructive conduct. Of those that were reported, some were found to be groundless and some of the alleged perpetrators were not in the military, so those cases were dismissed or handled by civilian authorities. Others were adjudicated and resulted in convictions, but not many. In all, 880 servicemen and -women were convicted of sexual assault over that period. It strained credulity to think that our system was working if 26,000 people were being assaulted annually and only 880 were being found guilty.[4] It was not hard to see why victims were reluctant to come forward.

Two events brought this dismaying problem squarely to my attention in 2011. A pair of filmmakers produced a searing documentary about the problem of sexual abuse in the military and sent me a copy. I watched the film, entitled *The Invisible War,* and was moved and angered by it. At the same time, we were confronting a particularly ugly sexual abuse scandal at the Joint Base San Antonio–Lackland, an air force base in Texas where trainers used their positions of authority over air force trainees to extract sex and commit rape. More than thirty training instructors would come under investigation as part of that scandal.

I brought this matter to each of our service chiefs, and made clear to them that I demanded improvement. I was especially concerned about the air force and pressed the issue in my conversations with air force chief of staff Mark Welsh. I greatly admired Welsh, who had been part of my senior staff at the CIA, and he immediately understood my urgency.

At the end of December 2011, I implemented two measures intended to improve our handling of these cases. First, we created a new policy that allowed any person who filed a sexual assault complaint to quickly transfer out of her unit or base in order to shield that person from retaliation and distance her from the alleged perpetrator. In addition, I ordered that all records of sexual assault reports to law enforcement be retained for at least fifty years so that veterans could later access those documents in connection with later claims.

Soon after, I expanded on those policies, stepping up the certification requirements for investigators of sexual abuse claims, and also making it possible for military spouses and dependents to use our system to file abuse complaints. I ordered new training for investigators and judge advocates who specialized in sexual abuse claims, integrated our various systems for collecting and analyzing data about complaints, and ordered that we develop a new and better system for educating senior department leaders on how to prevent and respond to sexual assault. Finally, in April, I ordered that claims of serious abuse be handled by senior commanders rather than lower-level officers. That last step would, I hoped, remove some of the hesitation that victims felt about approaching their immediate supervisor, often the same person who supervised their assailant.

There is something repugnant about asking men and women to serve their country and then exposing them to assault by their colleagues. As I said at the time, it is "an affront to the basic American values we defend, and it is a stain on the good honor of the great majority of our troops and their—and our—families."

The changes I attempted to make to our system for encouraging and adjudicating those complaints will not end sexual assault in the military, but I hope and trust that they will make clear that leaders will not tolerate it, and that we fully understand how incompatible it is with the values we are sworn to uphold.

Sexual assault is a crime of violence, but in the military it also is one of culture—a culture that includes many women but that historically has regarded them as something less than equal to men. Ever since the establishment of the American armed forces, men have held the positions of preeminence. For generations, that was neither surprising nor offensive. Notions of chivalry and social position commanded that men serve as soldiers, while women, to the extent that they served at all, did so in support. But like most vestigial discrimination, the limits on women's service grew anachronistic over time, and felt more like bars to advancement than chivalric protection. By 2012, we had two hundred thousand women in the armed forces, but they were not fully equal.

It was hardly a secret that we had women in demanding positions around the world. I had greeted the caskets of women who had died in combat, had comforted their families, visited them in hospitals, seen them in the field from South Korea to South America. They were working, fighting, and dying alongside men, but they were still denied access to many positions based solely on their gender. Reflecting over the past four years, first at CIA and now at the Department of Defense, many of those who had played an instrumental role in our national security had been women: the base chief at Khost who died on December 30, 2009; the senior CIA operations officer directing our counterterrorism efforts against Al Qaeda; many members of the security detail who guarded me; a soldier I visited at Brooke Army Medical Center, to whom I awarded a Purple Heart; many of the pilots who transported me around the world; and many of the troops I visited on battlefields in Afghanistan and Iraq. All of that made clear that women were very much in the battle.

Early in my tenure, I asked the service chiefs to review the continued bars to women's service and see what impediments we could remove. They returned with a long list of areas where women were excluded that no longer seemed to serve any purpose. At my order, in early 2012 we opened fourteen thousand positions that previously excluded women. Even after opening those positions, however, the bar on women serving in direct combat roles remained.

So as I prepared to end my service as secretary of defense, I returned to the service chiefs, this time asking each what the rationale was for prohibiting women to serve because of their gender. Yes, some positions required specific physical capabilities, and I agreed with the chiefs and others who argued against making tests less rigorous merely so that women would have an easier time passing them. What I could not understand was why we would bar a woman from serving even if she could pass them. Everyone deserves a chance to succeed.

I tasked my team, including Lieutenant General Waldhauser and Monica Medina, a senior adviser to me, to work with the services on the plan to allow women into combat positions. It was not easy, requiring careful coordination by personnel specialists, lawyers, and the commanders. What made it possible was Chairman Dempsey, who did what he did best—carefully listening to the service chiefs, gathering consensus, and developing a plan for implementing the new policy. Nobody did more to bring about this historic change than Marty Dempsey.

On January 24, 2013, just days after President Obama was inaugurated to his second term in office, General Dempsey and I announced that we were rescinding the prohibition against women in combat. It was to be accompanied by a review of the military's testing and evaluation procedures—not to lower standards but only to ensure that our standards were appropriate to the jobs that candidates were aspiring to. Once those evaluations were complete, women would never again be barred from any position in the American military because of their gender—just as blacks were no longer denied any spot because of their race or gays any job because of their orientation.

President Obama, whom I had consulted throughout our deliberations, praised the announcement as a "milestone" that "reflects the courageous and patriotic service of women through more than two centuries of American history and the indispensable role of women in today's military."[5]

What I expected would be my last overseas trip as secretary of defense took me to Europe—Lisbon, Madrid, London, and Rome.* In each capital, my meetings were about winding down. Our allies were withdrawing along with us from Afghanistan, so the substance of our conversations was on concluding that war in a way that secured the future, a topic both serious and reflective.

But there was also my own winding down—these were likely my final visits as a cabinet member, and our talks concluded with wistful farewells. It put me in a pensive mood. When I spoke to students in

---

*It turned out that I would make one more trip, in early 2013. That's because President Obama named former senator Chuck Hagel to succeed me. The president had believed Hagel, a Republican, would be easily confirmed by his former colleagues, but instead he was subjected to a fairly grueling and drawn-out process. As a result, I stayed on longer than I'd intended, not leaving until February 2013.

London, I reflected back on my growing up in Monterey during World War II, with the soldiers streaming through my father's café on their way to defend their country. I was too young in those days to think of the war in political terms. It was for me a collection of images—scenes recalled from my Nono's shoulders, feelings absorbed from my parents—but those images had never left me, and seemed especially vivid on that trip.

"I can still remember the feelings of fear and uncertainty and vulnerability that pervaded those years," I said. "Blackout shades, the air raid drills, the paper drives, the soldiers and sailors who walked the streets of Monterey before they were sent off to battle. Those are all memories."

Later, I added, I would come to appreciate Churchill and Roosevelt and the great leaders of that era who refused to yield to fascism and marshaled the forces of democracy against it. Today's battles are against a different set of enemies, but democracy remains strong enough for the fight. The bonds between the United States and its European allies will be tested again, but they have withstood much. Knowing that left me with a profound feeling of security, and I turned toward my retirement with a strong sense of fulfillment.

It was in Rome, however, that I received the most personal affirmation, one that brought together strands of my life that I'd been weaving since I was a boy. It was my second visit to the Vatican in recent years—as CIA director, I'd gotten a behind-the-scenes tour of the Sistine Chapel—but this time I was invited to meet the pope himself. At the appointed hour, I entered an auditorium adjacent to Saint Peter's Basilica and was seated in the front row. Around me were groups from every imaginable country. One from Portugal was seated nearby. Behind it was a group of children from Guatemala. There was a woman in a wedding dress, kids in native garb from all over the world. Pope Benedict entered and greeted each group in its native language. He spoke to the entire assemblage, briefly discussing the reach of the church and its place in the world. And then my row was ushered up to him.

I kissed his ring, and he placed his hand on mine.

"Thank you," he said. "Thank you for your service in protecting the world."

He handed me a rosary. I gave him a military coin. For a Catholic and a son of Italy, few moments could have been more precious. As I turned to leave, I realized what the nuns had always taught me—that faith and duty go hand in hand.

I n the end, the responsibility of the secretary of defense is to protect America from harm. Doing so begins with a duty to the men and women of the armed services. If we as a country are to ask these young people to protect us from a dangerous world, we owe them the full measure of our support—they deserve to be well paid, well armed, and well led. They need to know that if they are injured, we will nurse them back to health, and that if they are killed, we will comfort and assist their families.

I visited hundreds of young men and women in military hospitals, some with injuries that would have killed them a generation ago. I regularly visited Bethesda and Walter Reed hospitals, where I met many young people with missing limbs or grave wounds. To a person, they were positive and forward-looking. Some yearned for the chance to return to service even as they learned how to operate their prosthetic devices. They were strong and resilient, even when the country was not.

That was true even among families who pay the ultimate price for our defense—the loss of a loved one. Every week that I was secretary of defense, I would spend a few quiet hours away from the phones and interruptions to read, consider, and sign letters to the families of those who had died for their country. Each time, one of my assistants would hand me a stack of folders, including a letter of condolence for my signature. Inside each were the documents that told a story—and often that story reminded me of my own. These were young women and men, often of modest backgrounds, who decided early in their lives that they would serve their country. Some came through ROTC, as I did, others through enlistment or military school. Once trained, they shipped out for posts around the world, some to carry out orders that I had specifically approved.

One day in early 2012, I was sitting at my desk and contemplating the file before me. It told the story of Benjamin Wise, a sergeant first class who had been on patrol in Balkh Province, Afghanistan, when his unit came under enemy fire. He was hit and rushed to Germany for medical treatment, only to die of his wounds. Ben left behind a wife, two sons, and a daughter. He was the son of Jean and Mary Wise, who raised him, along with two brothers and a sister, in a small town outside Little Rock, Arkansas. They were a religious family, and a patriotic one.

As I read the material before me, I was suddenly struck by a sense that I knew this family. I called in Jeremy. We leafed through the file and confirmed my worst fear: Ben Wise was the younger brother of Jeremy Wise, one of the security officers we had lost in the Khost bombing two years earlier, on one of the most awful days in the history of the CIA. This was the second letter I was writing to this same mother and father. In two years and fifteen days, Jean and Mary Wise had given their country two of their four children.

I sat alone for a few minutes imagining the depth and pain of that sacrifice. I remembered my anxiety when my son went off to war, and thought of the many Americans who care so deeply for their country that they risk everything—their families, their happiness—for its security. I thought of my own father, shoving off from Italy in search of a country that would give him an opportunity he never thought possible anywhere but here. I thought of my own attempt to return that gift by embarking on a career of public service. And I realized with a sharp pain in my heart that Jeremy and Ben had both been in harm's way because of orders I had given, issued in the interests of protecting their country, our country. The letter before me expressed the appreciation of a grateful nation, but even that seemed small compared with the magnitude of this family's contribution. After a few moments, I added a handwritten note:

"I am so very lost in my emotion of losing another son of yours to combat. As the father of three sons, I cannot imagine the pain you must be feeling. And yet, I know that like Jeremy, Ben was doing what he wanted—to fight for all of us. He is a true American hero and patriot. God bless him and you."

Ben and Jeremy Wise left behind parents and wives and children, and they will be forever missed. There is solace, I hope, in the categorical fact that their fights were worthy, and that service to this nation is service well rendered.

I finished my note, put down my pen, and called home.

Epilogue:
Leadership or Crisis

It has been almost fifty years since I put on my army uniform and flew to Washington to find myself a job, luckily landing with Senator Tom Kuchel. It won't surprise anyone to hear that a lot has changed in those years (starting with the fact that uniformed servicemen no longer get to fly at half-price). It's easy to be frustrated about that. So much seems broken. Where once government tackled big things with determination, now it often seems overwhelmed by even minor problems.

Some have given up. Many young people I meet seem resigned to a government that bickers and breaks down. They regard politicians as small-minded and self-interested, smug guardians of a system rigged to deliver benefits to special interests while ignoring real people in need. Among those young people who are eager to devote their lives to the betterment of their society, many seek a path outside of public service.

It's hard to argue with any of that. Certainly there are plenty of examples to support such cynicism. But the answer can't be to give up on government or to treat division and partisanship as inevitable and insurmountable. It can't be to accept stalemate. To reconcile ourselves to inaction is more than a loss of will. It is a failure of democratic self-rule itself.

What's called for today is what we once knew as leadership. Far-sighted, goal-oriented, sustained leadership reconstructed Europe after World War II and built the interstate highway system. Brave leaders, Kuchel included, rolled back racial and gender segregation, reduced hunger and poverty, and produced safer food and drugs. Men and women with vision and patience protected the American wilderness and put men on the moon. All of those took time, compromise, and resolve, and all were the work of the U.S. federal government. I watched some of it myself. If nothing else, my time in government has let me witness the possibilities of effective leadership and the consequences of failure.

I've often reflected on two different but related domestic debates in which I played a role—the effort to balance the federal budget under President Clinton and the imposition of sequestration under President Obama. In the first instance, the challenges were immense and the divisions deep. To shrink and then eliminate the federal budget deficit, we proposed raising taxes, which Republicans hated and opposed. President Clinton had campaigned for a middle-class tax cut, and only gave it up with great reluctance—and at political risk—when he realized how serious the deficit was and how much the tax cut would contribute to the problem. Al Gore wanted an energy tax, and didn't get it. Congressional Democrats wanted increases in social programs that we couldn't afford. No one got everything they wanted in that package, and some of those who supported it paid a price. Even with their courage, it only passed by the narrowest of margins—one vote in each house. But the deal got done. It put the country on a new financial footing, helped bring down interest rates, and laid the foundation for the economic growth of the 1990s. And it balanced the federal budget.

Contrast that with the series of events at the end of President Obama's first term that resulted in sequestration. That conversation began when House Republicans threatened to refuse raising the debt ceiling—and thus deliberately endangering the nation's credit—unless they got their way on federal spending. The Obama administration, faced with a historic meltdown, cut a deal and agreed to an enforcement mechanism that would trigger cuts no one wanted if Congress failed to do its job. Congress went right ahead and failed, and those cuts have now begun working their mischief.

In the 1993 budget debate, resolute, creative leadership crafted a package that could muster the necessary votes—granted, not by much—and the country benefited. In the 2011–12 debate, congressional leaders told me directly that they did not want what was coming, but they sat as if powerless and let it happen. The country suffered. Put another way: In 1993, President Clinton picked policy over politics—he could have insisted on his tax cut and reaped political rewards, but he dropped it when he became convinced it was the wrong time for the economy. In 2011, congressional leaders chose the opposite course—they knew that sequestration was bad policy but concluded that it was better politics than cutting popular programs or raising taxes. They took the easy way out, even though they knew it was wrong, and pretended they couldn't stop it when they could have. They gave up.

I highlight those experiences not to suggest that President Clinton was more effective than President Obama—both improved the nation's economy, protected it from foreign enemies, and devoted themselves to the national interest. President Clinton defied some of his own party's most enduring orthodoxy—from welfare to free trade to crime—and the result was a stronger economy and a new vision for politics. President Obama revamped a nearly broken economy, waged an aggressive campaign against terrorism, extricated the United States from two wars, and refocused the mission of our military; the result is a safer nation and a more prosperous one. History, in my view, will regard both as presidents who strove to create a better America.

Nor do I bring up this contrast to suggest that Democrats are good and Republicans bad. I started my life as a Republican. I grew up in Earl Warren's California. The first president I admired was Dwight Eisenhower. My first boss, Kuchel, was a Republican. I worked closely with my Republican counterparts in Congress over issues as diverse as passing the budget and protecting the California coastline, combating hunger, and expanding hospice. And during my time at the CIA and Defense, I appreciated the contributions so many Republicans made to the important work of defending this country.

Rather, my point in resurrecting those debates is to note that in the first instance, the sustaining ambition was to do something for the country, even if we disagreed about how to do it. In the second, the goal was to win. And that idea—that the purpose of governing is to secure political advantage rather than benefit the public—permeates much of our political life today.

That's a problem—a big, serious, important problem. And it needs fixing. But it's not beyond our capacity.

It's fashionable in Washington these days to say that the country has never been more divided or government more dysfunctional. The reality is that what binds us is far stronger than what divides us. We want America to be strong. We want jobs. We want good schools. We want to be safe. We want better lives for our children.

Washington is divided because it locks up on the small stuff—whether the president or Congress gets credit for a bill; whether a majority or a supermajority should be needed to approve a nominee; whether the party's base or a special interest will be offended by a vote. The country thinks differently. Americans care about the big stuff and get frustrated that Washington can't set aside the small things for long enough to address the big ones.

Moreover, the notion that we've never confronted such division is historically ludicrous. We fought a civil war. When one section of a country owns human slaves, and another is appalled by the practice, that's division, and gridlock is understandable. It was impossible for the South to peacefully give up an institution that undergirded its social and economic order, and it was impossible to persuade others that slavery could possibly be countenanced by a civilized society. It's insulting to our history to pretend that today's divisions are comparable to those.

That's important to remember, because those who maintain that these divisions are historic do so partly as an excuse. How can we be held responsible for inaction, they ask, when the country is divided as never before? The answer: The people of this country are more united than it seems on what is needed to secure their families and give their children a better life. It is the responsibility of leaders to lead America in that direction, not to score points or win reelection.

Because without leadership, there is crisis. When the members of the Super Committee walked away in 2011 without reaching an agreement that they were specifically charged with reaching, they damaged our national defense, hurt our national economy, and made a mockery of democratic government. When Congress wasted the year it gave itself to undo that damage, it compounded the committee's failure. No outside force or invading army caused that crisis. Congress caused it all by itself.

It was Lincoln, as usual, who best expressed what's at stake. As he recognized, it is the responsibility of those who govern not only to provide for the common defense and promote the general welfare, but also, in a larger sense, to prove that this system can withstand division and succeed despite it. The war Lincoln fought was in defense of a nation "conceived in liberty, and dedicated to the proposition that all men are created equal." The Civil War, as Lincoln said at Gettysburg, put to the test the question of "whether that nation, or any nation so conceived and so dedicated, can long endure." The nation suffered almost inconceivable strain to establish that principle and to protect it when it seemed most fragile. Surely we can suffer much less to keep it alive for those still to come.

As director of the CIA, I shouldered the loss of devoted officers who gave everything to pursue this nation's enemies to the far corners of the earth. They charged ahead with vigor and purpose. As secretary of defense, I ordered young men and women into harm's way. They responded without hesitation. I myself had to give orders more than once knowing that they might result in the loss of innocent life. I did so because I recognized my obligation to keep my country safe. Those are the burdens of duty. The soldiers and officers under my charge understood that passionately and carried it out bravely. If those men and women can risk their lives, the nation's leadership must be capable of risking less.

My public life is winding down, and I'm trying to pass along the lessons of my career to students. Every year, they come to the Panetta Institute, eager to contribute, hopeful to discover a Washington that still tends to the nation's needs. They inspire and invigorate and replenish hope, and they should remind us of our obligations: Those students deserve to inherit a country as bountiful as the one that welcomed my father when in 1921 he stepped from the gangplank of the *Providence* and onto the shore of Ellis Island. It is the responsibility of leadership to see that today's America is as generous as yesterday's, that enduring values—integrity, hard work, respect for others, courage—be preserved and honored. The next generation of Americans needs them just as much as mine did.

After decades of commuting across the country, I'm home with Sylvia in the house my father built. The walnut grove he planted still bears fruit, and I still care for it. My sons are grown and have families of their own. My father never went to college. Two of my sons are lawyers, and the other is a doctor.

America's gifts to me were not ideological or partisan. They were of opportunity and family and security. As Americans, we may disagree on everything from baseball to national defense, but we are united by our most basic needs and by the dreams we have in common.

Leadership can help keep us safe and let us prosper; the alternative brings instability and uncertainty, and makes life harder instead of easier.

Rediscovering our gift for leadership won't be simple. It will require sacrifice and compromise, steadiness of purpose and a willingness to listen—all of which are somewhat forgotten virtues in today's Washington. Some of our elected officials may have to make unpopular decisions, and some may lose their jobs over it. But that's no excuse for not trying.

Those who serve must learn again to subordinate their self-interest to a larger national interest. In so doing, they will preserve democracy itself. That's a worthy fight.

ACKNOWLEDGMENTS

This is my story, of course, but many people helped me tell it—my collaborator, Jim Newton, but also archivists who unearthed documents and photographs; friends, family, and colleagues who agreed to be interviewed in order to refresh my memories and add important details; readers who checked portions of the manuscript for accuracy and completeness; editors and agents who saw promise in this project and turned my reminiscences into a book.

My thanks begin and end where my life does: with my family. As in the rest of our life, work, and marriage, Sylvia was my partner in this project, recollecting details of our life together and accepting the inevitable exposure of some of our personal history. Our boys—Christopher, Carmelo, and Jimmy—were similarly supportive and helpful. They are the love of my life, and neither this book nor the story it tells would mean much without them and their wonderful families.

Among my colleagues who contributed to the project, one is without peer. As recounted in the book, I first met Jeremy Bash when I arrived at the offices of the Obama transition team in early 2009. I was immediately impressed with his efficiency and knowledge, and I came to rely on both—as well as his humor and friendship—through my years at the CIA and Department of Defense. In producing this book, his memories were invaluable, and he spent hundreds of hours helping to shape the chapters describing our work together. Jeremy is a model public servant and my dear friend; I'm grateful to him for his service to our country and for his extraordinary commitment to this project. I should add that Jeremy's colleagues Sarah Davey and Ashley Woolheater also provided important help, arranging interviews, scheduling visits, and corralling material for Jim and me to use.

Without Jeremy, this book would not exist. But it also would not have come about without another essential person: Tina Bennett. Tina spied the potential of this story at the outset, brought Jim and me together, landed it in capable hands at Penguin Press, and guided it throughout. Tina and her colleagues at William Morris Endeavor, particularly Jennifer Rudolph Walsh with her gift for strong leadership, are exquisitely professional. I consider myself lucky to be associated with them (as does Jim).

Once the project was launched, many friends and former colleagues set aside time to review our experiences. Those who generously shared their time included: Michael Morell, Stephen Kappes, Ashton Carter, Michèle Flournoy, Harold Ickes, Jodi Torkelson, John Franzén, Pat Griffin, Bill Danvers, Bruce Babbitt, Peter Edelman, Stephen Preston, Barry Munitz, Erskine Bowles, John Angell, Mickey Kantor, and George Little.

For the history of my time in Congress and with the Clinton administration, I relied on two large depositories of historical material beyond my own memories and those of my former colleagues. At the Clinton Library in Little Rock, Whitney Ross guided Jim to records that helped complete the story of our deliberations and debates in areas such as the budget and health care. And at the Panetta Institute at Cal State Monterey Bay, Ellen Wilson and Chris Haubert facilitated every phase of our research. Thanks too to Royal Calkins, recently departed editor of the *Monterey Peninsula Herald,* for making the paper's clip files available.

Once the draft was complete—or nearly complete—a number of people again generously gave time and energy to reviewing it for accuracy. Michael Morell, Ashton Carter, Tom Donilon, Michèle Flournoy, Jim Miller, General John Kelly, George Little, Marcel Lettre, Monica Medina, Jacob Freedman, Carl Woog, Craig McCormick, and Philippe Reines all sharpened the story and saved me from errors.

I would like to thank the professionals at the Department of Defense and the CIA who reviewed the manuscript to help ensure that the information was accurate and that it would not compromise future intelligence or military operations. At the Pentagon, Michael Rhodes was particularly helpful. I am also grateful for the security review and records management staffs at both DoD and the CIA who provided access to my archive and reviewed the text multiple times.

At Penguin Press, the manuscript was guided into a finished book by the skilled editing of Scott Moyers, and, of course, the experience of working with Penguin Press was overseen throughout by the inestimable Ann Godoff. She is a gift to American culture.

I am particularly pleased with the look and design of the final book, and credit for that, too, goes to a number of people. The book jacket was designed by Darren Haggar, and the photos featured in the two packets were selected by Steve Stroud, Jim's former colleague at the *Los Angeles Times,* who took on this project with gusto and an experienced eye. Mally Anderson at Penguin Press honed those selections and contributed heartily to the result.

Finally, a special thanks to Jim Newton. Over the course of this project, he became not just my collaborator but also my friend. He found my voice because he understood me, my politics, and the history and politics of California and the nation. He was always sensitive to my every thought and recollection. It is not an easy challenge to put yourself into the life of another and then to tell the story—in my case, that of a son of immigrants who had the chance to live the American dream. I will be forever grateful to Jim for his help and his friendship and for giving you, the reader, the chance to share the story of my life and worthy fights.

Leon E. Panetta
Carmel Valley, June 2014

NOTES

Chapter 1: "A Better Life"
1. For a thoughtful and evenhanded discussion of the treatment of Italian Americans during World War II, see Lawrence DiStasi, *Una Storia Segreta: The Secret History of Italian American Evacuation and Internment During World War II* (Berkeley, CA: Heyday Books, 2001).

Chapter 2: "Look at Yourself in the Mirror"
1. Quoted in Remarks of Representative Stephen Horn, "Honoring a True Public Servant: Senator Thomas Kuchel," *Congressional Record,* 107th Congress, October 10, 2002, E1856.
2. Ibid., E1857.
3. *Los Angeles Times,* obituary for Thomas Kuchel, November 23, 1994.
4. Ibid.

Chapter 3: "You Did What Was Right"
1. *Los Angeles Times,* October 11, 1995.
2. *Brown v. Board of Education of Topeka,* 347 U.S. 483 (1954).
3. Quoted in Leon Panetta and Peter Gall, *Bring Us Together: The Nixon Team and the Civil Rights Retreat* (Philadelphia: Lippincott, 1971), 77.
4. *Monterey Peninsula Herald,* May 9, 1969.
5. A clip of Goldwater's famous convention speech is available at http://www.youtube .com/watch?v=RVNoClu0h9M.
6. *New York Times,* December 21, 2000.

Chapter 4: "No More Excuses"
1. *Monterey Peninsula Herald,* April 29, 1975.
2. Ibid., March 25, 1976.
3. *Los Angeles Times,* October 12, 1976.

Chapter 5: "Working for Us"
1. *Orlando Sentinel,* September 29, 1994.
2. Ibid.
3. There are many thoughtful accounts of the Santa Barbara spill. I have relied in part on Keith C. Clarke and Jeffrey J. Hemphill, "The Santa Barbara Oil Spill: A

Retrospective," *Yearbook of the Association of Pacific Coast Geographers,* ed. Darrick Danta, University of Hawaii Press, vol. 64 (2002): 157–62. Available at http://www .geog.ucsb.edu/~kclarke/Papers/SBOilSpill1969.pdf.

4.*Los Angeles Times,* December 4, 1982.

5.*New York Times,* August 14, 1989.

6.*Monterey Peninsula Herald,* July 29, 1981; March 15, 1982.

7.New York Times News Service, November 8, 1981.

8.The full text of the statement is available at American Presidency Project, "Statement on the Federal Budget Negotiations," June 26, 1990, http://www.presidency.ucsb.edu/ ws/index.php?pid=18635&st=&st1=.

9."President's News Conference," June 29, 1990, ibid., http://www.presidency.ucsb .edu/ws/index.php?pid=18650&st=&st1=.

Chapter 6: "It's the Right Fight"

1.Historical polling data for American presidents is available through the American Presidency Project at the University of California, Santa Barbara. Presidential job approval is searchable at http://www.presidency.ucsb.edu/data/popularity .php#axzz2grexm2Dd.

2.Joe Klein, *The Natural: The Misunderstood Presidency of Bill Clinton* (New York: Doubleday, 2002), 93.

3.*New York Times,* December 6, 1992.

4.Bob Woodward, *The Agenda: Inside the Clinton White House* (New York: Simon & Schuster, 1994), Kindle edition, location 1302.

5.Bill Clinton, *My Life* (New York: Knopf, 2004), 461.

6.*Los Angeles Times,* February 17, 1993.

7.Ibid., February 21, 1993.

8.*Washington Post,* February 19, 1993.

9.*New York Times,* February 20, 1993.

10.*Washington Post,* February 19, 1993.

11.Ibid.

12.Ibid., April 27, 1993.

13.Associated Press, April 28, 1993.

14.Clinton, *My Life,* 525.

Chapter 7: "If the White House Is Falling Apart . . ."

1.Ira Magaziner records, Box 9, Scheduling, Clinton Presidential Library.

2.*Chicago Tribune,* December 19, 1993.

3.*New York Times,* September 14, 1993.

4.Ibid., November 18, 1993.

5.Stuart M. Butler, "Assuring Affordable Health Care for All Americans," the Heritage Lectures, October 2, 1989. Available at http://thf_media.s3.amazonaws.com/1989/pdf/ hl218.pdf.

6.The original Heritage Foundation proposal can be found in its entirety in ibid. The foundation's later disavowal of that analysis, once it was offered in defense of President Obama's plan, can be found at "Brief of Amicus Curiae the Heritage Foundation in Support of Plaintiffs-Appellees," United States Court of Appeals for the Eleventh Circuit, May 11, 2011, http://blog.heritage.org/wp-content/uploads/Heritage-Foundation-Amicus-Brief-05-11-11.pdf.

7.*Monterey Peninsula Herald,* September 5, 1995.

8.FBI Uniform Crime Reports, 1995, 5. Available at http://www.fbi.gov/about-us/cjis/ ucr/crime-in-the-u.s/1995/95sec2.pdf.

9.FBI Uniform Crime Reports, 2000, 5. Available at http://www.fbi.gov/about-us/cjis/ucr/crime-in-the-u.s/2000/00sec2.pdf.

10.Haiti Background, United Nations Mission in Haiti paper. UN Security Council, *Resolution 940 (1994) Adopted by the Security Council at Its 3413th Meeting, on 31 July 1994*, 31 July 1994, S/RES/940 (1994), available at http://www.refworld.org/docic/3b00f15f63.html.

11.Bill Clinton, *My Life* (New York: Knopf, 2004), 628.

12.Ibid.

13.*New York Times,* November 10, 1994.

Chapter 8: "We Thought You Would Cave"

1.McClatchy News Service, December 6, 1994.

2.Bill Clinton, *My Life* (New York: Knopf, 2004), 644.

3.*Washington Post,* February 12, 1995.

4."Letter to Congressional Leaders on the Plan to Balance the Budget," June 28, 1995. Courtesy of the American Presidency Project.

5."Remarks Prior to Meeting with Congressional Leaders and Exchange with Reporters," July 11, 1995. Courtesy of the American Presidency Project.

6."Statement on Proposed Foreign Affairs Legislation," July 26, 1995. Courtesy of the American Presidency Project.

7."Weekly Radio Address," July 29, 1995. Courtesy of the American Presidency Project.

8.Clinton, *My Life,* 679.

9.Clinton T. Bass, "Shutdown of the Federal Government: Causes, Processes and Effects," Congressional Research Service, September 25, 2013, 16–17.

10.Alec Tyson, "The Last Government Shutdown and Now: A Different Environment," Pew Research Center, September 30, 2013, http://www.pewresearch.org/fact-tank/2013/09/30/the-last-government-shutdown-and-now-a-different-environment/.

11.*Baltimore Sun,* November 16, 1995.

12.*New York Daily News,* November 16, 1995.

13.Budget Planning memo, November 30, 1995, Carolyn Curiel Records, Box 2, Budget [1] folder, Clinton Presidential Library.

14.A copy of the report is available online at http://www.climateactionproject.com/docs/POC_Exec_Summary.pdf.

15.*The Iraq Study Group Report* (New York: Vintage, 2006), "Letter from the Co-Chairs," ix. Available at http://history-world.org/061206_iraq_study_group_report .pdf.

Chapter 9: "The Combatant Commander in the War on Terrorism"

1.*Washington Post,* January 5, 2009.

2.Some of those concerns made it into the press. See, for instance, *New York Times,* December 3, 2008.

3.Bob Woodward, *Obama's Wars* (New York: Simon & Schuster, 2010), 59.

4.Hearings Before the Select Committee on Intelligence of the United States Senate, February 5 and 6, 2009, 9 (from my opening statement), http://www.intelligence .senate.gov/pdfs/111172.pdf.

5.Ibid., 19.

6.Ibid., 12 (in response to a question from Chairman Feinstein).

7.CNN.com, February 11, 2009.

Chapter 10: "Tell It Like It Is . . . Our National Security Depends on It"

1.U.S. Department of Justice, Office of Legal Counsel, Memorandum for John A. Rizzo, Senior Deputy General Counsel, Central Intelligence Agency, May 10, 2005.

2."Remarks at the Central Intelligence Agency in Langley, Virginia," April 20, 2009. Courtesy of the American Presidency Project.

3.Rodriguez makes this case in his *Hard Measures: How Aggressive CIA Actions After 9/11 Saved American Lives* (New York: Simon & Schuster, 2012).

Chapter 11: "Disrupt, Dismantle, Defeat"

1.Central Intelligence Agency, "The Work of a Nation," https://www.cia.gov/library/publications/additional-publications/the-work-of-a-nation/cia-director-and-principles/centers-in-the-cia.html.

2.Raffaelo Pantucci, "A Biography of Rashid Rauf: Al-Qa'ida's British Operative," Combating Terrorism Center at West Point. Rauf also helped plan the July 7, 2005, attacks on London's public transportation system in which fifty-two people died.

3.*Saudi Gazette*, undated article, "Fourth Assassination Attempt Against Prince Foiled." Other details from BBC, "Profile: Al Qaeda Bomb Maker Ibrahim al-Asiri," May 9, 2012.

4.Final Report of the William H. Webster Commission on the Federal Bureau of Investigation, Counterterrorism Intelligence and the Events at Fort Hood, Texas, on November 5, 2009, 35.

5.Rob Wise, "Al Shabaab," Center for Strategic International Studies, July 2011.

6.U.S. Department of Justice, Office of Public Affairs, Press Release, September 24, 2009. Available at http://www.justice.gov/opa/pr/2009/September/09-ag-1017.html.

7.This debate is well captured by Bob Woodward in *Obama's Wars*.

8.Ibid., 194. Also *Los Angeles Times,* October 6, 2009.

9."Remarks at the United States Military Academy at West Point, New York," December 1, 2009. Courtesy of the American Presidency Project.

10.Daniel Klaidman, *Kill or Capture: The War on Terror and the Soul of the Obama Presidency* (New York: Houghton Mifflin Harcourt, 2012), 173.

11.*New York Times,* December 30, 2009.

12.Mike Allen, "Dick Cheney: Barack Obama 'Trying to Pretend,'" *Politico,* December 30, 2009.

13."Remarks at a Memorial Service for Central Intelligence Agency Officers in Langley, Virginia," February 5, 2010. Courtesy of the American Presidency Project.

14.Al Baker and William K. Rashbaum, "Police Find Car Bomb in Times Square," *New York Times,* May 1, 2010.

15.Press release, United States Attorney, Southern District of New York, "Faisal Shahzad Sentenced in Manhattan Federal Court to Life in Prison for Attempted Car Bombing in Times Square," October 5, 2010.

Chapter 12: "Everywhere in the World"

1.*Washington Post,* December 22, 1963.

2.Nicholas Cullather, "Operation PBSUCCESS: The United States and Guatemala, 1952–1954," History staff, Center for the Study of Intelligence, Central Intelligence Agency, 1994.

Chapter 13: "Go In and Get Bin Laden"

1."Bush Tells Barnes Capturing Bin Laden Is 'Not a Top Priority Use of American Resources,'" Fox News, September 14, 2006.

2.The debate transcript is available at http://elections.nytimes.com/2008/president/debates/transcripts/second-presidential-debate.html.

3."Remarks on the Death of Al Qaeda Terrorist Organization Leader Osama bin Laden," May 1, 2011. Courtesy of the American Presidency Project.

Chapter 14: "To Be Free, We Must Also Be Secure"
1.*Congressional Record,* Senate, June 21, 2011, S3960.
2.Ibid.
3.Congressional Research Service, "A Guide to U.S. Military Casualty Statistics: Operation New Dawn, Operation Iraqi Freedom and Operation Enduring Freedom," February 19, 2014. See also http://icasualties.org/, which continues to track casualties in Afghanistan.
4.*Washington Post,* April 16, 2012.
5.*New York Times,* July 12, 2011.
6.Ibid., August 6, 2011.

Chapter 15: "A New Defense Strategy for the Twenty-first Century"
1.Bill Clinton, *My Life* (New York: Knopf, 2004), 483.
2.Ibid.
3.Department of Defense, *Report of the Comprehensive Review of the Issues Associated with a Repeal of "Don't Ask, Don't Tell,"* November 30, 2012, 82.
4.Ibid.
5.*Washington Post,* January 7, 2013.
6.BBC, "Pakistan 'Backed Haqqani Attack on Kabul'—Mike Mullen," September 22, 2011.
7.*New York Times,* March 9, 2013.
8.See *Al-Aulaqi v. Panetta,* filed July 18, 2012, in U.S. District Court for the District of Columbia.
9."Address to the Nation on the End of Combat Operations in Iraq," August 31, 2010. Courtesy of the American Presidency Project.
10.*New York Times,* December 14, 2011.
11.Barack Obama, "Remarks at the Pentagon in Arlington, Virginia," January 5, 2012. Courtesy of the American Presidency Project.

Chapter 16: "In Together, Out Together"
1.Jessica Buchanan and Erik Landemalm, *Impossible Odds: The Kidnapping of Jessica Buchanan and Her Dramatic Rescue by SEAL Team Six* (New York: Atria Books, 2013), 261–68.
2.*Washington Post,* February 2, 2012.
3."Remarks at the American Israel Public Affairs Committee Policy Conference," March 4, 2012. Courtesy of the American Presidency Project.
4.*New York Times,* March 4, 2012.
5.Ibid., August 20, 2013.
6.Ibid., February 25, 2012.
7.Ibid., March 15, 2012.
8.Interview with Al Hurra Television, March 16, 2012. Courtesy of the Department of Defense, Press Operations, News Transcript.
9.American Forces Press Service, April 18, 2012.
10."Barack Obama, Remarks with President Hamid Karzai," May 2, 2012. Courtesy of the American Presidency Project.
11.*Stars and Stripes,* June 4, 2012.
12.Associated Press, cited on Fox News Web site, April 10, 2014, http://www.foxnews.com/us/2014/04/10/gop-chairman-satisfied-with-military-response-to-benghazi-attack/.

Chapter 17: "I Cannot Imagine the Pain"
1.National Public Radio, September 18, 2012.
2.CBS News, September 18, 2012.
3."United Nations Mission to Investigate Allegations of the Use of Chemical Weapons in the Syrian Arab Republic," transmitted September 13, 2013. The full report can be found at http://www.un.org/disarmament/content/slideshow/Secretary_General_Report_of_CW_Investigation.pdf. See also "Government Assessment of the Syrian Government's Use of Chemical Weapons on August 21, 2013," released by the White House on August 30, 2013.
4.Department of Defense, *Annual Report on Sexual Assault in the Military, Fiscal Year 2012*, 4.
5.*USA Today,* January 24, 2013.

INDEX

PHOTOGRAPH CREDITS

Page 1, above and below: Courtesy of the Panetta family.
Page 2, above and below: Courtesy of the Panetta family.
Page 3, above and below: Courtesy of the Panetta family.
Page 4: Courtesy of the Panetta family.
Page 5, above and below: Courtesy of the Panetta Institute.
Page 6: © George Rose/Getty Images.
Page 7, above and below: Courtesy, William J. Clinton Presidential Library.
Page 8, above: AP Photo/Ron Edmonds. Below: AP Photo/Charles Tasnadi, File.
Page 9: David Hume Kennerly/Getty Images.
Page 10, above: Courtesy, William J. Clinton Presidential Library. Below: Andrew A. Nelles, Sun-Times Media.
Page 11: Courtesy of the Panetta Institute.
Page 12: © Molly Riley/Reuters/Corbis.
Page 13, above: AP Photo/J. Scott Applewhite. Below: Ron Sachs/Pool/Getty Images News.
Page 14: Courtesy of the Panetta Institute.
Page 15, above and below: Courtesy of the Panetta Institute.
Page 16: Ali Al-Saadi/Getty Images.
Page 17, above: AP Photo/Manuel Balce Ceneta. Below: © Jim Young/Reuters/Corbis.
Page 18: Rex Features via AP Images.
Page 19, above: Department of Defense. Below: Scott Olson/Getty Images.
Page 20: © Jason Reed/Reuters/Corbis.
Page 21, above: AP Photo/Susan Walsh, Pool. Below: © Philip Cheung/Corbis.
Page 22, above: AP Photo/Evan Vucci. Below: © POOL/Reuters/Corbis.
Page 23: © Xinhua Press/DOD/Glenn Fawcett/Corbis.
Page 24: © Flash90/Guy Assayag/EPA/Corbis.
Page 25, above: © KHAM/Reuters/Corbis. Below: © Erin A. Kirk-Cuomo/Department of Defense, courtesy of the Panetta Institute.
Page 26: © Larry Downing/Pool/Getty Images.

Page 27, above: AP Photo/L'Osservatore Romano, ho. Below: AP Photo/ Jacquelyn Martin.

Page 28, above: © Erin A. Kirk-Cuomo/Department of Defense, courtesy of the Panetta Institute. Below: AP Photo/Jacquelyn Martin.

Page 29: Saul Loeb/AFP/Getty Images.

Page 30: Saul Loeb/AFP/Getty Images.

Page 31, above and below: Saul Loeb/AFP/Getty Images.

Page 32, above: courtesy of the Panetta Institute. Below: courtesy of the Panetta family.